PAUL IN CHAINS

PAUL IN CHAINS

*Roman Imprisonment and
the Letters of St. Paul*

by
RICHARD J. CASSIDY

A Herder and Herder Book
The Crossroad Publishing Company
New York

The Crossroad Publishing Company
481 Eighth Avenue, New York, NY 10001

Printed in the United States of America

Library of Congress Cataloging-in-Publication Data

Cassidy, Richard J.
    Paul in chains : Roman imprisonment and the letters of St. Paul /
Richard J. Cassidy.
        p.   cm.
    Includes bibliographical references and indexes.
    ISBN 0-8245-1920-5 (hardcover) — ISBN 0-8245-1921-3 (pbk.)
    1. Bible. N.T. Epistles of Paul—Criticism, interpretation, etc. 2.
Paul, the Apostle, Saint. 3. Imprisonment (Roman law) 4. Rome in the
Bible. 5. Persecution—History—Early church, ca. 30–600.   I. Title.
BS2650.2 .C35 2001
227'.067—dc21

                                                    2001002048

1   2   3   4   5   6   7   8   9   10   05   04   03   02   01

Dedication

To Bernice Cassidy, Cardinal Avery Dulles, and Bishop Bernard Harrington who encouraged this work at every stage.

To Victor Clore, Peter Drilling, Barbara Green, Susan Mathews, Stephen Scharper, Charles Talbert, and Joan Wagner. These seven, with the three just named, are truly "Friends of Paul."

And to Paul himself. Paul a recipient of Christ's extraordinary grace as an apostle and servant and, ultimately, as a Roman prisoner. Paul who testified to Christ Jesus his Lord with unsurpassed eloquence and faithfulness, audaciously asking those whom he loved to "remember his chains."

Contents

Preface

PAUL'S RADICAL FAITHFULNESS to Jesus his sovereign Lord! My initial estimations of Paul's faithfulness only deepened as this study progressed and I attempted to come to terms with Paul's trajectory from Romans to Philippians. I wish now to express my gratitude to all who played a role in enabling me to undertake this analysis and to bring it to publication seven years later.

In inviting me to the faculty of Christ the King Seminary, Msgr. Frederick Leising expressed his personal support for this proposed book and put in place several institutional arrangements that greatly facilitated the writing. Principal among these arrangements was his assignment of Mrs. Rose Marie Beale to oversee the word processing of the manuscript. I am especially grateful to Msgr. Leising for his solicitude and to Mrs. Beale for her faithfulness to me and to Paul over many months and years. Sometimes, during the various revisions, Rose Marie would ask me if I were writing "a perpetual book." And when she indicated to me that she wanted to come in weekends after her retirement, she stated that she wanted to see this "perpetual book" through to its completion. This expression of appreciation to Rose Marie Beale leads me to express my gratitude to all of the staff members who have served in the CKS Administration Building during these past years; from these individuals I have received a flowing stream of services kindly rendered.

As the manuscript progressed I received valuable feedback as a result of my Pauline courses with the seminarians, graduate students, and certificate students who constitute the student body at CKS. The fine holdings of the CKS Library, ably administered by Fr. Bonaventure Hayes,

OFM, and the CKS library staff, have also been invaluable resources for me. In particular my thanks go to Sr. Tiburtia Gorecki, FSSJ, for her diligent help in processing my many interlibrary loan requests. At a somewhat later stage, when Mr. Michael Murphy arrived at CKS as Director of Facilities, I felt that new energy had been given to me for my efforts to bring the manuscript as a whole to completion. Michael escorted me into the world of word processing and presciently arranged for the phrase *Paul in Chains* to scroll as a default screensaver . Subsequently, under Michael's auspices, I received *lukejohnpaul* as my first e-address and other specific considerations as well.

At several meetings of the Catholic Biblical Association of America in the late 1990s, drafts of chapters were presented at sessions of the Biblical Perspectives on Social and Political Suffering task force. I wish to acknowledge the helpful oral and written responses that were given to these papers by various task force members. I am greatly indebted to Professor Susan Mathews and to Professor Charles Talbert for their time and care in reviewing the entire first draft of the manuscript. Professor Barbara Green, OP, also reviewed the entire first draft and presented me with numerous suggestions designed to enhance the precision of the exposition and its readability. For her challenging comments underscoring the prevailing scholarly estimations of the authenticity of Colossians, Ephesians, and 2 Timothy, I am also indebted to Professor Wendy Cotter, CSJ. It goes almost without saying that any deficiencies in the final positions and the final wording that I adopted are not due to the contributions made by these friends and colleagues.

When one is engaged in research and writing for a period of seven years, it is important to be able to draw sustenance from the community where one is located and from other communities with whom one is connected. I thus begin by expressing my appreciation to the leadership of Christ the King Seminary. As noted, Msgr. Frederick Leising invited me to CKS under propitious circumstances, and Fr. Richard Siepka, his successor as rector, has continued to promote this Seminary as a congenial setting for the life of faith, the life of scholarship, and the life of formation for pastoral ministry. I also herewith express my thanks to Bishop Henry Mansell (the ordinary of the Diocese of Buffalo and Chair of the Board of Directors of Christ the King Seminary) and to Cardinal Adam Maida (the ordinary of my home diocese, the Archdiocese of Detroit). Bishop Mansell and Cardinal Maida have both repeatedly expressed their general support for research and writing and their particular support for the present effort to delve more deeply into these dimensions of Paul's heritage.

Let the members of the CKS kitchen staff, maintenance staff, and housekeeping staff also be heralded for their own contributions to Paul's cause! Their dedicated daily work kept these surroundings highly functional and supplied a healthful, sustaining diet. The steadfast, generous service provided by Fr. Gregory Faulhaber and Fr. Walter Szczesny as directors of the CKS Formation Program represents service in another area that is critical to the life of the Seminary. Indeed, without this solid foundation for priestly formation, the very mission of Christ the King Seminary would be jeopardized. Still another form of assistance, often behind the scenes, is that rendered by Mrs. June Dombrowski, who has served with dedication as the secretary for both CKS rectors named above. Here I mention particularly her assistance to the CKS seminarians from Colombia. The substantive contribution made by Patrick Hulsman, CKS Director of Institutional Advancement, and by his committed staff, in the promotion of this book is also gratefully recognized. In expressing gratitude for the generosity of the Seminary's faculty and staff, I also wish to signal my appreciation for the enrichment and support that I received during this period from the staff members of the St. Joseph Center for Spirituality, directed by Sr. Joan Wagner, SSJ.

Turning beyond the immediate setting of the Seminary, I want to express my appreciation for two accomplished scholars who serve as pastors "in the Pauline fashion." These two priests, their pastoral associates, and the parish communities they serve have extended significant hospitality and encouragement to me during these last seven years: Fr. Victor Clore and Christ the King parish in Detroit, Michigan; Fr. Peter Drilling and St. Anthony Parish in Lackawanna, New York. I also wish to express particular thanks to two families whose friendships lent energy to my writing as it progressed through its various stages: Christine and David Doby and their children, Michael and Margaret; Dennis and Kathleen Castillo and their children, Paul, John, and Teresa. In a similar vein I mention Donald and Theresa Hayes. Theresa is a CKS Curé of Ars recipient in my heart. The friendship that I have enjoyed with Msgr. William Sherzer over many years is also a beneficent influence that I would mention here.

In previous works, I had striven to interpret Luke's Gospel, the Acts of the Apostles, and John's Gospel focusing on Roman rule as the general context for Jesus, the first Christian communities, and the evangelists Luke and John. From that platform I resolved to attempt a comparable interpretation of Paul's letters. Fr. Avery Dulles, SJ, perhaps the first to learn of this proposed new venture, unhesitatingly offered his encouragement for the idea of focusing on Paul's Roman chains. At approximately the same time, I shared my preliminary ideas with Msgr. Bernard Harrington who quickly responded with characteristic enthusiasm. Both of these friends remained unstinting supporters of the book as it progressed from stage to stage. (I here specifically recall my discussions with Fr. Dulles about the book's title and I also recall Bishop Harrington's diligence in searching through the Vatican Gardens to determine whether a sculpture in the wooded area of the gardens represented Paul in Chains. Since this sculpture actually proved to be a (another) fine rendering of St. Peter in Chains, I thus direct an appeal to contemporary artists for depictions of St. Paul in Chains!) Initially, the memorable admonition of Colossians 4:18, "Remember My Chains," served as the working title for the book.

Years later, as publication drew nearer, my dialogues with the editorial and marketing staff of Crossroad/Herder and Herder regarding the scope and intended audience of the book resulted in the agreement that *Paul in Chains* would be the title under which the book would actually be sent forth. Ms. Alison Donohue, Dr. Gwendolin Herder, and Dr. John Jones are indeed "Friends of Paul." And in this decision, as well as in many other careful decisions, I felt that Paul himself was somehow guiding us forward. At this same time, the stellar efforts of Professor Stephen Scharper of the Toronto School of Theology on behalf of the book again came to the fore as he strove to arrange for Canadian co-publication.

The work of Dr. Paul Kobelski and Dr. Maurya Horgan (co-directors of The Scriptorium) in copy-editing the manuscript, in presenting the maps, and in evolving the attractive format of the book is also a contribution that I wish to acknowledge. Another enhancement for the presentation of this book resulted from an afternoon visit that Professor Charles Talbert and I made to the Mamertine Prison in Rome. (This visit occurred during the pleasing days of the ceremonies honoring Cardinal Dulles.) Within the lower prison, Charles and I encountered a sculpture depicting St. Paul and St. Peter baptizing other prisoners/guards while in their Roman chains. Permission to use a photograph of this sculpture has now been given by Fr. Etore Fedrizzi, rector of the Oblates of the Blessed Virgin, the community entrusted with the care of the shrine church at the Mamertine. I am grateful to Fr. Fedrizzi and I additionally thank Cardinal Edmund Szoka (President of the Pontifical Commission for Vatican City State) and Fr. Todd Laginess, Secretary to Cardinal Szoka, for their assistance and care in transmitting my request to Fr. Fedrizzi.

The initiatives described in the last paragraphs all occurred in the Spring of 2001 under the general auspices of Gwendolin Herder and Alison Donohue. During these intense days, it has indeed been a pleasing and satisfying experience to work with these two loyal friends of Paul, friends who are not in any manner ashamed of Paul's chains! May the faithfulness of Paul himself, a faithfulness manifested in and through his bonds, be celebrated by all who read this work. And may an intensified allegiance to the one who is Paul's Lord, and our own, be the unending consequence.

CHAPTER ONE

Orientation to Paul's Perspectives Regarding Roman Rule

"REMEMBER MY CHAINS!" By adhering to this imperative from the letter to the Colossians, the present study seeks to investigate the momentous change in Paul's perspective that occurred between Romans 13:1-7 and the letter to the Philippians. Within Pauline studies, Romans 13 has all too often been taken as the apex of Paul's teaching regarding Christians and the Roman order. Such an assessment neglects Paul's intervening years in chains and the ultimate importance of Philippians, a letter that Paul wrote from Rome while awaiting trial as a chained prisoner.

The intent of the present study is to focus upon the Roman context for his life and ministry and to analyze Romans 13:1-7 and Paul's prison letters with explicit attention to the Roman factors to which Paul was responding. Philemon and especially Philippians are the letters that ground this study's principal conclusions. These two letters will be interpreted in the light of Roman penal and judicial procedures and with reference to various ways in which Roman practices challenged Christian discipleship.

1. Initial Reflections Regarding the Roman Context of Paul's Apostleship

Clearly there are many facets to the figure of Paul, aspects of his identity and background that can only be noted briefly given the principal interests of the present work.[1] From the outset, a particular objective of the present study is to use the lens of Roman rule for viewing Paul and his surroundings. And, with respect to Paul's chronology, the present study is principally focused on Paul's life between the time of Romans and the time of his imprisonment in Rome.

Nevertheless, even though Paul's early years are not here an area of analysis, it is still useful to pose several questions regarding this period of his life in order to utilize the lens of Roman rule from the very outset. The following questions serve to broaden horizons regarding Paul and "things Roman" even if very little can be offered in answer to them. Through his early life experience, how familiar was Paul with the various facts of Roman rule? In his early education, was Paul exposed to any writings pertaining to Roman history and culture? How well did Paul understand Roman institutions, including Roman law? When did Paul become conscious of the fact that, from the Roman perspective, his life was being lived within the context of provinces whose obligations and privileges were decreed from Rome?

The extent and the pervasiveness of Rome's power in the era of Paul's youth! This aspect, at once so simple and so obvious, is all too frequently undervalued in the desire to investigate two other factors that undoubtedly influenced Paul.

On the one hand, it is common for studies to situate Paul and interpret his endeavors against the context of Judaism, whether Palestinian or Hellenistic Judaism.[2] And justly so. For Paul's Jewish identity consistently came to expression in both his thought and his conduct. It could not be otherwise. Paul was Jewish! Yet Paul was Jewish within the social and political context of Roman rule.

On the other hand, it is common for Paul to be interpreted against the background of Hellenistic culture.[3] And certainly Paul's familiarity with Hellenistic culture and Hellenistic rhetoric must be emphasized in any overall assessment of his thought and his sensibilities. Paul could speak Greek, and he wrote in Greek, and, patently, he derived significant benefit from his contact with the traditions of Greek learning. Nevertheless, Paul's Hellenistic heritage exercised its influence within the context of Roman imperial rule.

Consider further the course of Paul's mature years as an apostle of Jesus his Lord. Where else did he go, proclaiming the name of Jesus and establishing Christian communities, than to the cities and regions of Rome's eastern provinces? Were not the signs of Roman power about him everywhere that he went? The roads upon which he traveled, the harbors from which and to which he sailed, the soldiers he encountered everywhere. Were not all of these administered by, and subject to, the authorities in Rome?

Until section four of chapter two, these brief references must suffice as indications for the way in which Paul encountered his Roman surroundings. At this stage of the discussion it is simply a matter of providing an initial orientation regarding this important dimension. His Jewish identity and belonging and the influences of Hellenistic culture on him are now explicitly emphasized as important factors for understanding and interpreting Paul. In the chapters that follow, the focus will be on the various Roman factors that influenced him, especially his Roman chains.

2. Methodological Considerations

Given the competing theories that have been advanced concerning the authorship and chronology of the letters that constitute the Pauline corpus within the New Testament writings, several methodological issues need to be addressed at the outset of this study. Initially it is important to emphasize that Romans, Philemon, and Philippians are the letters of the Pauline corpus that are of critical importance within the analysis that follows. Further, it is the existing text, that is, the canonical text, of each one of these letters that is the object of interpretation.

A practical consequence of this last consideration is that Romans 13:1-7 is here considered to be an authentic, integral part of the larger letter that Paul sent to the Christians of that city.[4] Similarly, even though some scholars have claimed to see elements of two or more letters present within canonical Philippians, this study will analyze Philippians as a single, integrated letter.[5] In contrast, because Philemon is such a brief, compact, and single-purpose letter, theories regarding earlier stages of composition have not arisen in connection with it.

Regarding Colossians, Ephesians, and 2 Timothy, three other letters that have traditionally been designated "prison letters," the matter is more complicated owing to the fact that significant numbers of New Testament scholars have concluded that one, two, or all three of these letters were written by another person or persons in Paul's name.[6] Significantly, all of these letters present Paul in Roman chains

and all of them portray him commenting on these chains in vivid,
memorable ways.

Essentially, Colossians, Ephesians, and 2 Timothy function within
the framework of the present study to contextualize the conclusions
that will be reached from the analysis of Philemon and Philippians.
If it is assumed that one or more of these letters was written by someone other than Paul, the author(s) in question still referred to Paul's
chains in memorable terms. By highlighting Paul's chains and portraying his response to them, such writers testify to the importance
of Paul's imprisonment and help to interpret its meaning.

Alternatively, if these letters are from the apostle's own hand, the
poetry and the rhetoric with which Paul refers to his chains underscore their impact upon him. Without adding any crucial insights
over and beyond those already present in Philemon and Philippians,
Paul's references in Colossians and Ephesians amplify the perspectives presented in Philemon and Philippians. Expressly claiming to be
written from Rome, 2 Timothy similarly functions to amplify several
of Paul's leading concerns in writing to the Philippian Christians. To
be sure, Paul's perspective in Philippians can be adequately apprehended apart from 2 Timothy. Nevertheless, 2 Timothy provides several significant reports relative to Paul's experience in Rome.

In summary, this study's principal thesis unfolds independently of
the material present in chapters seven and eight, i.e., it unfolds apart
from the analysis of Colossians, Ephesians, and 2 Timothy. Nevertheless, the treatment of these letters that is provided in those chapters helps to fulfill a second important objective of the present study:
the analysis of all major New Testament passages pertaining to the
subject of Paul's Roman imprisonment.

For this same reason an appendix analyzing Paul's circumstances
as a Roman prisoner according to the Acts of the Apostles is also
included below. Properly interpreted, Luke's accounts in Acts can
indeed provide a wealth of valuable information concerning Paul's
arrest and chaining and his experiences as a Roman prisoner. Nevertheless, in deference to the reservations expressed by many scholars
regarding the use of material from Acts in works analyzing Paul's letters, the present study will base its analysis fundamentally in terms of
Paul's undisputed writings.[7]

Within the present study, it is clear that Philippians and Philemon
possess central importance. But where are these two letters to be situated in relationship to Romans? The evidence underpinning the

conclusion that both prison letters were written *after* Romans will be presented in chapters six and nine below. The arguments supporting the interpretation that Philippians was written after Philemon are also presented in chapter nine.

In summary, this study's reconstruction of Paul's chronology and letters is as follows. Romans was written by Paul after he had completed much of his ministry in the empire's eastern provinces. At the time of Romans, however, Paul had not been subject to sustained imprisonment. It was only later that he was imprisoned and chained for an extended period of time. During this interval of custody Paul wrote his letter to Philemon, reflecting on his chains yet of the mind that he would soon be released from them. Philippians was written after Philemon. By that time, Paul was no longer so focused on his prospects for release. Indeed, in Philippians, he distinctly envisions the possibility of his execution by the Roman authorities.

3. The Structure of the Present Study

Because several strands of analysis are interwoven with the present study, its overall structure is somewhat complex. With reference to Paul's undisputed letters, the analysis begins with Romans 13, continues with Philemon, and ends with Philippians. These letters are studied respectively in chapters three, six, and eleven with the first section of chapter twelve providing further reflections on Philippians.

How then does the material presented in the remaining chapters pertain to the structure and the objectives of this study? Chapters four, five, and ten provide analyses of Roman phenomena that are important for the respective contexts in which Paul's prison letters were written. Chapters seven and eight provide an interpretation of Colossians, Ephesians, and 2 Timothy, letters that need to be assessed with methodological care.

With reference to this study's fundamental argument, the framework established by chapter two's description of three contrasting approaches to Roman rule should be noted. These three approaches serve to locate Paul's perspective regarding Roman rule at the time of Romans, and they serve to locate his perspective at the time of Philippians. The fundamental argument of this study is that a dramatic shift occurs in Paul's outlook between Romans and Philippians. In effect, Philippians contains a critical perspective regarding the Roman authorities that Romans simply does not possess.

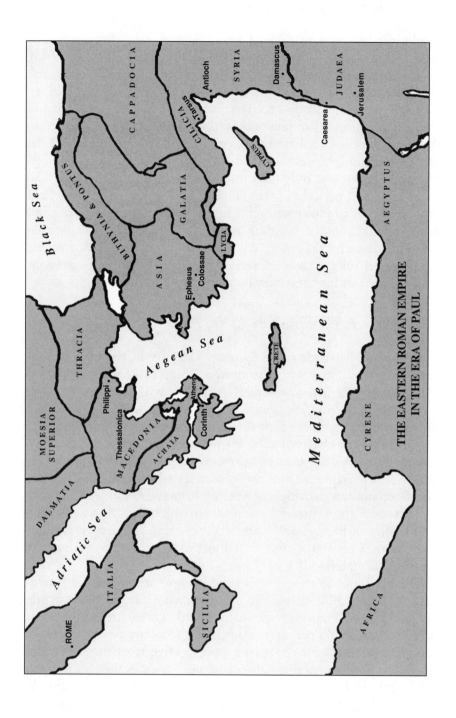

THE EASTERN ROMAN EMPIRE
IN THE ERA OF PAUL

CHAPTER TWO

Contrasting Approaches
to Roman Rule

THE PRIMARY PURPOSE of the present chapter is to provide a context for the perspective on the Roman social order that Paul presented in his letter to the Christians at Rome and the perspective that he subsequently reflected in his letter to the Christians of Philippi. In the sections that follow, three approaches to Roman rule will be briefly considered: the approach of Cerialis according to Tacitus, that of Judas the Gaulanite according to Josephus, and that of Jesus according to Luke.

In chapter twelve, at the end of this study, these three approaches will be revisited. At that point it will be possible to look backward and to appreciate that Paul's own approach changed dramatically between the time when he wrote Romans and the time when he composed Philippians.

Clearly, in undertaking such an analysis, methodological caution must be observed. In what follows, a basic methodological strategy will be to utilize the approaches of Cerialis, Judas, and Jesus primarily as three *types* of approaches that first-century persons or groups might follow vis-à-vis the Roman empire.

In terms of such a methodology it is not necessary to establish that Tacitus represented a Roman general's position with exactitude, that Josephus portrayed the position of a Jewish revolutionary in all of its complexity, or that Luke has distilled the essential stance of Jesus of Nazareth. In effect, it will be sufficient to indicate that such types of approaches were available for consideration at the time when Paul was formulating his own approach.

Further, Paul presumably had a distinct familiarity with at least two of these approaches. The fourth section of this chapter will focus upon this consideration. In that section it will be observed that Paul was experientially familiar with the workings of Roman rule, and it will be argued that he was aware of the views of the apologists for this rule as well as the sentiments of those who adamantly opposed it.

1. An Apology for Roman Rule

Before proceeding to consider conditions in the Roman empire during Paul's adult years, it must be cautioned that the dates of Paul's birth and death cannot be securely established. The first six decades of the first century A.D. may well supply the time frame for Paul's life.[1] Yet just how old Paul was when he first encountered his risen Lord, as well as the exact place and time of his death, cannot be determined from the New Testament writings.

Still, given the success that Augustus had already achieved by the beginning of the first century, it can be safely assumed that, whatever Paul's precise birth year, he was born at a time when Roman imperial rule was ascendant. Indeed, for numerous decades before Paul's birth, the Romans had been in the process of extending their way southward, eastward, and westward from the earliest Roman territories on the Italian peninsula. The general lines of this expansion are well known and do not need to be detailed here.

Nevertheless it should be observed that only in rare instances was Roman rule extended to new territories without armed struggle or the threat of armed struggle. There were undeniable advantages associated with Roman rule. Yet, the benefits of Roman "peace" and Roman public works seemingly did not commend themselves to unconquered peoples without the "benefit" of Roman military power.

What is of particular significance for the present section is the fact that leading Roman officials and Roman rhetoricians developed a skillful and effective apology for the empire they served and profited from. In this book's later chapters the exaggerated claims and the personal depravities of the emperor Nero will be considered. Yet presumably in the minds of most apologists for the empire, Nero was an aberration, an emperor whose rule was a real but temporary disgrace.

When Cornelius Tacitus published his work *The Histories* circa

A.D. 109–110,[2] virtually forty years had elapsed since the subjugation of the Gallic tribes by the Roman general Cerialis in A.D. 70.
Nevertheless, the speech that Tacitus reports Cerialis making on that
occasion stands as an expression of the Romans' message to their
conquered subjects in virtually every age of the empire. Cerialis'
words were particularly apposite in the interval just after Nero's suicide and damnation by the senate. Yet his words regarding cruel
emperors were not restricted to Nero. Further, his reference to the
benefits for Roman rule and his emphasis upon the role of Roman
taxes were pertinent to the objectives of emperors from Augustus to
Trajan and beyond.

Consider, then, Cerialis' full speech as a brilliant apology on
behalf of Rome's traditional objectives. Once again, the sentiments
expressed are not restricted to such figures as Tacitus and Cerialis.
Rather, they are easily upon the lips of convinced proponents of
Roman rule who lived before, during, and after the decades that
Paul's life encompassed:

> There were always kings and wars throughout Gaul until you submit-
> ted to our laws. Although often provoked by you, the only use we
> have made of our rights as victors has been to impose on you the
> necessary costs of maintaining the peace; for you cannot secure tran-
> quility among nations without armies, nor maintain armies without
> pay, nor provide pay without taxes: everything else we have in com-
> mon. You often command our legions; you rule these and other
> provinces; we claim no privileges, you suffer no exclusion. You enjoy
> the advantage of good emperors equally with us, although you dwell
> far from the capital: the cruel emperors assail those nearest them. . . .
> (*The Histories* 4.74)[3]

2. A Call to Revolt Against Roman Taxation

Just as Tacitus' Cerialis may be taken as a model or a type for all of
those who would argue in favor of Roman rule and Roman taxation,
so may Judas the Gaulanite in the writings of Flavius Josephus serve
as a model for those who opposed the imposition of Roman taxes and
subjugation under the Roman empire. As portrayed by Josephus,
Judas the Gaulanite is, in fact, the antitype for Tacitus' Cerialis.
Cerialis is convinced of the benefits of Roman order and urges taxes

to finance the military forces that are required to establish this order. Judas, in contrast, sees prosperity apart from Roman domination and urges that the rejection of Roman taxes be accompanied, as inevitably it must be accompanied, by a full-scale revolt against Roman rule.

As a leader in the Jewish uprising against Roman rule in A.D. 66, Josephus was well familiar with the history of Judea prior to this uprising and with the arguments made to encourage the revolt.[4] Captured by the Roman forces, Josephus then cast his lot with the Romans, writing two works that argued the foolhardiness of this attempt to revolt against Roman rule. The first work, *The Jewish War*, was published between 75 and 79, during Vespasian's reign as emperor. His later work, *Jewish Antiquities*, was probably published in the early 90s. Both works portray the speech and the activity of Judas the Gaulanite in and around the year 6 as key elements in the historical process that eventually resulted in full-scale revolt in the year 66. Significantly, one of the key leaders in the actual uprising was a *son* of this Judas.

In the selection from *The Jewish War* that follows, Josephus briefly characterizes Judas' response to the Roman tax announced under Coponius. His account in *Jewish Antiquities* presents the underpinnings of Judas' position in greater detail. Both of these passages are now presented:[5]

Under his [Coponius'] administration, a Galilean, named Judas, incited his countrymen to revolt, upbraiding them as cowards for consenting to pay tribute to the Romans and tolerating mortal masters, after having God for their lord. (*The Jewish War* 2.8.1)

But a certain Judas, a Gaulanite from a city named Gamala, who had enlisted the aid of Saddok, a Pharisee, threw himself into the cause of rebellion. They said that the assessment carried with it a status amounting to downright slavery, no less, and appealed to the nation to make a bid for independence. They urged that in case of success the Jews would have laid the foundation of prosperity, while if they failed to obtain any such boon, they would win honor and renown for their lofty aim; and that Heaven would be their zealous helper to no lesser end than the furthering of their enterprise until it succeeded—all the more if with high devotion in their hearts they stood firm and did not shrink from the bloodshed that might be necessary. (*Jewish Antiquities* 18.1.1)

3. Jesus and the Roman Order According to Luke

With the analysis previously made in R. Cassidy, *Jesus, Politics, and Society: A Study of Luke's Gospel,* as a frame of reference, several points regarding Luke's Jesus can be presented briefly here. These points pertain to Jesus' affirmation of God's ultimate sovereignty, his emphasis on service and humility, his attitude toward the ruling authorities, and his teaching on the specific issue of Roman taxation.

Within Luke's Gospel it is clear that Jesus regards God as sovereign over all of creation. Numerous passages attest to this perspective, perhaps none more memorably than 12:22-31, where God's care of the birds of the air and the flowers of the field is focused on, and 6:35-36, where God's graciousness to the ungrateful and the selfish is referenced as an encouragement for the disciples to love their enemies.

Fundamentally interwoven with this conviction regarding God's sovereignty is Jesus' teaching regarding service, humility, and concern for the lowly. These teachings, numerous within Luke's Gospel, reflect and concretize the sovereignty and compassion of God. Because it utilizes a radical commitment to service as a grounds for critiquing those who would dominate over others, the passage now to be cited is particularly significant. There is in this passage a clear contrast between the approach of service espoused by Jesus and the approach of domination practiced by the rulers of the Gentiles:

> A dispute also arose among them, which of them was to be regarded as the greatest. And he said to them, "The kings of the Gentiles exercise lordship over them; and those in authority over them are called benefactors. But not so with you; rather let the greatest among you become as the youngest, and the leader as one who serves. For which is the greater, one who sits at table, or one who serves? Is it not the one who sits at table? But I am among you as one who serves." (Luke 22:24-27)

Who are "the kings of the Gentiles" that Jesus references here? And why are they desirous of being called "benefactors"? In these words is an indication of Jesus' implicit critique of the Roman emperors and those associated with them in their efforts to dominate. In another passage in the same vein, Luke portrays Jesus responding to Herod Antipas' threat by derisively referring to him as "that fox" (13:32). Further indirect critiques of the Roman authorities occur when Jesus encourages his disciples to be forthright in testifying before hostile "kings and governors" (21:12) and before "rulers and the authorities" (22:11).

Recognizing that the social stance of Jesus is significantly at variance with the values and patterns adhered to by the Roman authorities, and recognizing that Jesus did not refrain from critical references to these same authorities, is it to be thought that Luke's Jesus is somehow of the persuasion of the Zealots? For Luke does make it clear that Simon, a member of the Zealots, was numbered among the twelve (Luke 6:15; Acts 2:13).

For two reasons the answer to this question is simply and directly in the negative. First, nothing in Luke's Gospel suggests that Jesus explicitly envisioned the overthrow of Roman rule. Implicitly Jesus makes serious critiques of the foundation of that rule, yet there is nothing to indicate that he advocated political independence for Judea let along self-determination for all of the Mediterranean and European territories conquered by the Roman military forces.

The second, even more fundamental, reason for distinguishing Jesus from the Zealots is Jesus' explicit rejection of violence against persons as a means for accomplishing one's personal or social goals. This conviction, expressed in various ways within the Gospel, especially in 22:51, decisively separates Jesus from the Zealot revolutionaries just as it decisively separates him from the imperial violence of Rome. Although Pilate used the pretext that Jesus was a Zealot to execute him, he himself presumably knew the true reality: while Jesus had challenged the corruption of the chief priests authoritatively and aggressively, he could not be grouped with the Zealots.

Jesus' distance from Roman domination and the Zealots' revolutionary stance is concretely evident in the question of the chief priests' spies put to him regarding the payment of Roman tribute. The words at the center of his response are as follows (Luke 20:25): "Then render to Caesar the things that are Caesar's and to God the things that are God's." Such a reply satisfied neither the Zealots, who urged a total refusal of all tax payments, nor the Romans, who demanded compliance with their taxes without deliberation or hesitation.

Properly interpreted, Jesus' reply called for the "evaluation" of Roman taxes against the standard of "the things of God." For what things does Caesar really have or possess? Ultimately, the entire created world and all human life are authored by God with Caesar having only a secondary stewardship. Caesar's practices are thus to be evaluated against the concerns and standards of God and only then will it be possible to know whether taxes are to be paid or not. Does Caesar's rule foster the concerns of God or contravene them? The task of formulating a response to this prior question requires entry into a process of reflection and dialogue. This process is a precondition for a responsible reply regarding the payment of Roman taxes.

4. In Romans, Paul and the Contrasting Approaches to Roman Rule

It was noted above that Paul was born and raised within the boundaries of the Roman empire. It is now appropriate to reflect upon the adult Paul's familiarity with the various aspects of Roman rule.

Recall that Paul traveled extensively as an apostle of Jesus in such Roman provinces as Judea, Syria, Cilicia, Galatia, Asia, Macedonia, and Achaia. As a person of intelligence and acumen, Paul would have recognized and assessed the unmistakable signs of Roman dominion and Roman order in these eastern territories.

Consider, for example, the reality of peace and public order. Who had achieved the degree of peace that existed in Paul's day?[6] Clearly, Roman rule had brought with it the degree of peace that existed. Who had the ultimate responsibility for maintaining public order in each of the provinces Paul visited? Certainly it was the Roman governor or legate, who governed in terms of existing Roman law, supported by whatever number of Roman troops was deemed necessary.

Consider, for example, the accomplishment of public works. Stretching throughout the provincial territories, the vaunted system of Roman roads testified unmistakably to the successful working of the Roman order. And similar Roman accomplishments in terms of harbors, aqueducts, amphitheaters, gymnasia, and other public construction would also have been evident to Paul.

Two final illustrations of Roman presence concern the areas of coinage and taxation. Roman taxes came in a wide variety of forms, shapes, and frequencies and were not merely a matter of annual poll taxes.[7] Indeed, depending on the individual's profession and areas of activity, certain Roman taxes might be paid daily. To take but two examples, perhaps situations that pertained particularly to Paul, consider first the various tolls that were required for travel upon the principal Roman roads. These tolls were in addition to the fee paid for the official pass that all authorized travelers must possess. Second, a wide variety of customs fees was also in effect. If Paul carried any tools or supplies with him as he traveled by land and by sea, these items may well have been taxed at every new stage of his journey.

Widely circulating Roman coins also testified to the pervasiveness of Roman rule. Paul presumably used at least some of these coins in his various commercial transactions. Indeed, it is warranted to imagine Paul paying his Roman tolls and taxes with Roman-authorized and even Roman-minted coins.

If Paul can thus be judged to have had a close familiarity with the workings of the Roman system, including Roman taxes, was he also familiar with the three types of responses to Roman rule briefly described above? That is, can Paul be presumed to be familiar with the approach of Tacitus' Cerialis, the approach of Josephus' Judas, and that of Luke's Jesus? With respect to the pro-Roman approach represented by Cerialis and the revolutionary approach represented by Judas, there is ample basis for an affirmative reply. As will be seen, however, it is difficult to determine whether Paul was familiar with the "evaluation" approach proposed by Jesus in Luke's Gospel.

Traveling as extensively as he did throughout the eastern provinces of the empire, Paul would have exposure to the ideas and convictions of those who endorsed the benefits of Roman rule and affirmed the taxation that inevitably accompanied and supported such rule. First, the Roman authorities themselves sought to win acceptance for their rule by a great variety of communications measures, including the inscriptions attached to public buildings and the propagandistic symbols and extolments imprinted on most coins. Second, there were not lacking writers, orators, and political and religious officials in Rome and throughout the provinces who aggressively articulated Roman achievements and goals.

As regards his contact with revolutionary sentiments, Paul was enthusiastically committed to his Jewish heritage, and it was especially in Judea that a systemic, powerful resistance to Roman rule blossomed. Certainly, resistance to Roman rule and revolutionary uprisings occurred elsewhere in the areas covered by the empire, especially during times of Roman expansion. In Judea during the time of the Zealots, however, the premise for revolution was explicitly theological. In this perspective God desired the liberation of the Jewish people, and God would provide divine support for those who entered upon this cause.

Was Paul, as someone vitally engaged with first-century Judaism, brought into contact with such an articulation of Jewish faith? It is hard to imagine that such a perspective was not known to him. Was Paul familiar with other provincials, apart from Jews, who sought to be free of Roman domination? In his travels did he encounter vigorous reaction against Roman taxation or against specific taxes? Paul's commitment to Judaism, coupled with the existence of a revolutionary movement in Judea, seemingly provides sufficient grounds for positing his awareness of the proposal for revolution against Roman rule fully apart from any encounters with such perspectives that might have occurred during his extensive travels.

What did Paul know of the perspective concerning the Roman order that Luke attributes to Jesus? To express this query more pointedly, did Paul know of the teachings of Jesus promoting a service ethic as a challenge to the prevailing imperial patterns of domination? And did he know the substance of Jesus' challenging reply to the question regarding Roman tribute?[8]

Clearly, uncertainties abound in all efforts to analyze the initial stages of Paul's formation as a disciple of Jesus. How much teaching pertaining to ministry did the risen Jesus impart to Paul? How much information regarding Jesus' perspectives did Paul receive from other disciples who had been associated with Jesus during the time of public ministry? Even Paul's famous statement to the Corinthian Christians, "Be imitators of me, as I am of Christ" (1 Cor 11:1), does not resolve this question. The many dimensions in which Paul presumably felt that he represented the approach of Christ Jesus are not explicitly identified within Paul's encouraging invitation.

In this discussion of Paul's familiarity with the approach of Jesus presented by Luke, one further consideration should also be mentioned. It is conceivable that Paul came to new insights regarding the mind of Jesus his Lord as his own journey of discipleship unfolded. Indeed, the change in Paul's perspective on the Roman order that this study seeks to establish is actually predicated on Paul's deepening appreciation for the true implications of Jesus' call.

In summary, as an apostle in the service of Christ Jesus, Paul possessed a considerable first-hand familiarity with the workings of the
Roman empire. Presumably he was familiar with the perspective of
those who articulately acclaimed the benefits of Roman rule. He was
also arguably familiar with the perspective of the Zealots of Judea in
rejecting the Roman regimen and seeking to overthrow it. Nevertheless, it is not certain whether Paul himself, especially at the time of
Romans, was familiar with the nuanced approach recommended by
Jesus in response to the question regarding Roman taxation.

   Given his own personal experience and his familiarity with competing viewpoints, what approach did Paul adopt in writing to the
Christians at Rome when he took up the topic of Roman taxes and
the role of the Roman authorities themselves? A preliminary answer
can be given here, an answer that will be considerably amplified in
the next chapter. In writing to the Christians at Rome, urging them
to comply with all Roman taxes, Paul adopted an approach that
would have been warmly affirmed by Cerialis, Tacitus' articulate
Roman general. That is, Paul advocated an approach of full compliance with the demands of the Roman rulers.

CHAPTER THREE

Paul's Perspective in Romans 13:1-7

PAUL'S LETTER to the Christian community at Rome is his most theologically rich letter and also his longest. As a consequence it has been intensively and exhaustively analyzed within New Testament studies. In addition to the hundreds of commentaries that have been written on the letter as a whole, a surpassing number of studies and articles have been written on Rom 13:1-7, the passage that is of specific concern here. Indeed, Rom 13:1-7 may well be the most commented-on passage in all of Paul's writings.

Although the interpretation of Rom 13:1-7 will be the principal task of the present chapter, it should be noted that Paul's words in chapter fifteen about his collection for the Jerusalem church and about his plans for traveling to Spain possess major significance for the thesis of this study that Romans predates Paul's letters to Philemon and to the Christians at Philippi.

The issue of Paul's relationship with the Christian community at Rome, a subject to be considered more fully in section one below, also has implications for the analysis that will be undertaken at later stages of this study. It will be argued in chapter nine that Philippians was written from Rome and that Philippians portrays Paul in sharp tension with some members of the Roman Christian community. Thus it is useful to observe here that at the time when Paul wrote to the Romans he was clearly concerned to establish cordial bonds with the Christians located in the imperial capital. This concern is evident in a variety of places but especially in 15:14 where Paul states, "I myself am satisfied about you, my brethren, that you yourselves are full of goodness, filled with all knowledge and able to instruct one another."

The members of the Roman Christian community thus were in contact with Paul's ministry at two distinct stages. Paul was not the founder of this community. He did, however, address his most comprehensive letter to them, a letter in which he boldly counseled them to be subject to the imperial authorities. Later on Paul came in contact with the members of this community as a prisoner in Roman chains. It was during this second stage of contact that Paul authored his highly personal letter to the Philippians.

Before commencing with the body of this chapter it is well to indicate once again that, when the full analysis of Rom 13:1-7 has been completed, it will be seen that Paul's position in those verses is one of virtually unqualified support for the authorities of the Roman empire. Various factors will be cited as having possibly influenced him. In the end, the reasons that motivated him are far from clear. What is crystal clear is the startling level of affirmation and support that Paul affords to the existing authorities.

Nevertheless, it still must be kept in mind that Paul's perspective in Rom 13:1-7 represents only his *initial* perspective on the Roman authorities. His ultimate, defining perspective, a perspective explicitly grounded in Paul's allegiance to Jesus, is expressed in Philippians.

1. Paul's Various Purposes in Writing Romans.

Within a letter fully sixteen chapters in length,[1] the present study is primarily concerned with a passage comprising only seven verses. These seven verses occur within a larger section providing ethical teaching, but the letter as a whole provides extended doctrinal teaching and also incorporates pastoral elements such as Paul's announcement of his proposed travel plans and his personal greetings to individual members of the Roman community.

Within Pauline studies a discussion has long been underway regarding Paul's degree of familiarity with the situation of the Roman Christians at the time when he wrote to them.[2] Paul may well have been knowledgeable about the pastoral circumstances of the Christian community at Rome even though he had not founded that community nor even yet visited it.[3] If this is indeed the case, then the doctrinal and ethical sections of Paul's letter can be regarded as teaching that especially responds to the Roman Christians' circumstances. Nevertheless, the door should not be closed to the possibility that Paul may have purposely formulated his teaching in such a way that it could also address and serve Christians living in other communities throughout the empire.[4]

These general observations also hold with respect to 13:1-7. It is certainly possible that Paul's very pointed teachings on subjection and tax compliance were given in the light of Paul's knowledge of conditions affecting the Christians living in Rome. Still, there is such an unqualified character to Paul's teaching in this passage that he may well have envisioned its applicability for Christians living outside of Rome in other parts of the empire.

Keeping in mind these considerations regarding Paul's knowledge of the Christians to whom he wrote, it is well to identify purposes that seem to motivate him in the doctrinal, ethical, and personal itinerary sections of Romans. With reference to the doctrinal section of the letter, a section extending from Paul's initial greeting to 11:36, at least three major subjects areas are touched on by Paul.[5] First, in the estimation of many scholars, Paul's exposition and defense of the gospel he has preached is the principal or at least one of the major subjects motivating him to write. Second, related to this, of course, is the subject of the relationships between Jewish Christians and Gentile Christians, relationships that may well have been fundamental to the life of the Christian community in Rome. And third, probably as a consequence of his teaching regarding justification through faith, Paul seems especially concerned to address the situation of those in Israel who have not responded with faith; he does this in chapters 9, 10, and 11.

In addition to having purposes that were more doctrinal in character, Paul was also concerned to specify forms of conduct that would be upbuilding for the community life of the Roman Christians.[6] Indeed, from 12:1 to 15:13, Paul treats a number of Christian lifestyle issues in a way that resembles the approach he followed in treating a comparable series of pastoral issues in 1 Corinthians.[7] In some of these passages Paul's counsel is couched in more general terms and, as mentioned, could be regarded as relevant for Christian readers in other communities throughout the empire.

Along with his other doctrinal and ethical purposes Paul very definitely was also concerned to direct his readers to right conduct vis-à-vis the Roman authorities and their taxes. In some respects the transition from 12:21 to 13:1-7 is somewhat abrupt, and, as a consequence, it has been suggested that 13:1-7 is a later insertion expressing a perspective that is not Paul's own.[8] Standing against this view, however, is the incontrovertible datum that all of the earliest manuscripts of Romans contain these verses. In addition, a close analysis reveals that the transition to this topic of rulers and taxes is not as abrupt as it initially seems to be. There is, in fact, a certain thematic appropriateness for this passage's appearance at this point in the letter.[9] Thus, to provide his readers with counsel regarding behavior toward the Roman authorities and Roman taxes certainly seems to have been one of Paul's purposes in writing.

Allowing, then, for the likelihood that Paul had a number of doctrinal and ethical concerns motivating him to write Romans, let attention now be given to Paul's personal travel plans as a factor motivating him to write. Where was Paul in terms of his personal journey for Christ when he wrote? And where was he headed? These questions deserve to be explored at some length because many scholars consider Paul's desire to gain a travel base in Rome as a major factor occasioning Romans.[10] From the perspective of this study, the confident spirit that Paul exhibits, his confident outlook as he announces his plans for Spain—this itself is also a factor of considerable importance.

Paul states in his opening chapter that he has long hoped to visit the Roman Christians. On the one hand he unhesitatingly asserts that he has an obligation to preach to them. On the other hand, however, he speaks in terms of mutuality, the mutual encouragement that will result from his visit:

> I mention you always in my prayers, asking that somehow by God's will I may now at last succeed in coming to you. For I long to see you, that I may impart to you some spiritual gift to strengthen you, that, is, that we may be mutually encouraged by each other's faith, both yours and mine. I want you to know, brethren, that I have often intended to come to you (but thus far have been prevented) in order that I may reap some harvest among you as well as among the rest of the Gentiles. I am under obligation both to Greeks and to barbarians, both to the wise and to the foolish: so I am eager to preach the gospel to you also who are in Rome. (Rom 1:9b-15)

It is not until chapter 15 that Paul explains the circumstances that now make it possible for him to envision visiting the Christians at Rome. In this passage he first broaches the subject of his projected travel to Spain. Notice also the extremely broad vista against which Paul situates himself and his missionary travels on behalf of Christ. There are four significantly separated geographic locations mentioned in these verses:

> But now, since I no longer have any room for work in these regions, and since I have longed for many years to come to you, I hope to see you in passing as I go to Spain, and to be sped on my journey there by you, once I have enjoyed your company for a little. At present, however, I am going to Jerusalem with aid for the saints. For Macedonia and Achaia have been pleased to make some contribution for the poor among the saints at Jerusalem; they were pleased to do it, and indeed they are in debt to them, for if the Gentiles have come to share in their spiritual blessings, they ought also to be of service to them in material blessings. When therefore I have completed this, and have delivered to them what has been raised, I shall go on by way of you to Spain. (Rom 15:23-28)

From Macedonia and Achaia to Jerusalem. From Jerusalem to Rome. Then from Rome to Spain. Paul is surely projecting vast travels and undertakings for himself in the months and the years that are ahead. And yet to any who might question him about the magnitude of such endeavors, Paul's response is already present within the words he had expressed in Rom 15:18-19 only a few verses earlier. For, to any who might marvel regarding such bold travel plans, Paul was ready to testify that the Holy Spirit had *already* enabled him to preach the gospel of Christ the full distance from Jerusalem to Illyricum:

> For I will not venture to speak of anything except what Christ has wrought through me to win obedience from the Gentiles, by word and deed, by the power of signs and wonders, by the power of the Holy Spirit, so that *from Jerusalem and as far round as Illyricum* I have fully preached the Gospel of Christ. . . . (Rom 15:18-19; emphasis supplied)

Where was Paul when he wrote these words? Almost certainly he was somewhere in the eastern provinces of the empire, with several factors favoring Corinth in the province of Achaia as his *geographi-cal* location.[11] Yet, as mentioned above, it is Paul's *biographical* loca-tion within his journey for Christ that possesses particular importance within this study. At this juncture, where is Paul within the trajectory of his service as Christ's apostle? From the perspective of this study, there are four closely related features of Paul's location to be noted, two of them explicitly mentioned within chapter 15.

Although they are separated by a few intervening verses in chap-ter 15, Paul's two statements regarding what he has achieved by the power of the Holy Spirit are truly remarkable. In 15:19b he boldly asserts, "from Jerusalem and as far round as Illyricum, I have fully preached the Gospel of Christ. . . ." Then in 15:23a he auda-ciously states, "since I no longer have any room for work in these regions. . . ." From these two statements in Romans as well as from the sense of Paul's ministry that can be gained from considering the texts of such letters as 1 Thessalonians and 1 and 2 Corinthians, it is clear that Paul is well advanced on his journey as a faithful witness and apostle of Jesus his Lord.[12]

Grave suffering has also been a part of Paul's fruitful ministry on behalf of Jesus. Paul does not emphasize this aspect of his ministry in writing to the Christians at Rome. In his previous letters to the Corinthian Christians, however, Paul provided ample descriptions of the various hardships and sufferings he had endured: for example, 1 Cor 4:9-13; 15:30-32; and 2 Cor 1:8-11; 11:23-27.

Nevertheless, while these sufferings did include imprisonment (2 Cor 11:23), Paul does not mention *sustained* imprisonment, and the general sense of his words regarding beatings and imprisonments was that these measures were ad hoc and temporary. Severe punish-ments though they were, they were not of such a character as to occa-sion for Paul the self-designation of "prisoner" or "prisoner for Christ Jesus."[13]

In summary, it can be said that, in writing to the Roman Chris-tians, Paul was at the stage of having completed a fruitful ministry in the eastern provinces. He had suffered extensively in the course of his ministry but had not yet experienced a sustained imprisonment at the hands of the Roman authorities. These three features of Paul's situa-tion are complemented by a fourth feature: Paul audaciously looks forward to a continuing ministry on behalf of Jesus that will bring him to Rome itself and then westward to Spain. With an exuberance that almost prescinds from the suffering he has already endured and the tremendous energy he has already expended, Paul projects the future of his ministry: to Jerusalem, to Rome, and then onward to Spain!

And the thought that he would come to Rome not as a free traveler boldly proclaiming Christ but rather as a prisoner in chains— that thought could not been conceivable to Paul as he took pen in hand to write Romans. Indeed, it is this thought's inconceivability that must be kept in mind in assessing Paul's words regarding the Roman authorities in this letter.

Paul is filled with remarkable confidence and energy as he now addresses the Christians of the empire's capital. He will be coming to visit them at the center of the empire and then he will travel beyond them to Spain. Paul knows well how to travel within the empire! There are no constraints on him! He has traveled extensively and effectively in the eastern provinces as Christ's apostle. And he now projects unabashedly regarding the major journeys that he will yet undertake on Christ's behalf.

2. Expulsions from Rome and Tax Protests: Context for Romans?

A verse-by-verse interpretation of Rom 13:1-7 will be provided in the following section. It is the objective of the present section to present preliminary conjectures about Paul's awareness of certain factors pertaining to Jews, Christians, and the Roman authorities.

Presumably *something* must have been on Paul's mind or else he would not have included such a precise and forceful teaching about compliance with the Roman authorities and their taxes. After all, nowhere else in any of Paul's surviving letters is the subject of taxes even mentioned. What then might Paul have known that would have influenced him to offer such firm directions to the Christians at Rome on these matters?

Again, it must not be ruled out that Paul's view may have encompassed more than the conditions of Christians at Rome even though it was them to whom he was writing primarily. While respecting this possibility, there are still two considerations pertaining to the pastoral situation of the Christians at Rome that may have influenced

Paul to include within his letter this very precise paragraph on the Roman rulers and their taxes.

If Paul was especially concerned that the Christian community at Rome live peaceably and without controversy at the heart of the empire, he may have had at the back of his mind the two previous occasions on which the Jewish community had been expelled from Rome. Also, if Paul had not already completed his letter by that time, he may have received reports of the protests against indirect taxes that were occurring in Rome late in the 50s and felt compelled to dissuade the Roman Christians from participating in these protests in any way.

With respect to the expulsion of Jews, the Jewish historian Josephus writes that the emperor Tiberius ordered the expulsion of the entire Jewish community from Rome in A.D. 19.[14] And writing in the second century, the Roman historian Suetonius indicates that the emperor Claudius enacted a comparable expulsion during his own reign (A.D. 41-54).[15]

Given the limitations of the available resources, the full consequences of each of these imperial orders cannot be determined. Nevertheless, inasmuch as the Roman authorities had twice acted decisively again the Jewish community when disturbances of one sort or another had occurred, Paul may have been concerned to stipulate that the Christians of Rome should respectfully cooperate with the Roman officials and thereby avoid any risk of expulsion. The earlier expulsions had been *from Rome*, after all. And thus Paul, in writing to the Christians *at Rome* may have judged it appropriate to urge them to act is such a way as to win the approval of the Roman authorities.

In the same vein, it is conceivable that Paul may have been knowledgeable about and influenced by the protests over indirect taxes that, according to the Roman historian Tacitus, occurred in Rome in A.D. 58.[16] Certainly it is a matter of some significance that Paul distinguishes in Rom 13:7 between direct taxes (*phoros*) and indirect taxes (*telos*).[17] Paul's counsel is that *both* kinds of taxes are to be paid, the indirect as well as the direct. And, once again, his intention may have been to ensure that the Christians of Rome would live peaceably under the imperial authorities.

The full discussion of Paul's possible reasons in setting forth such an accommodative response is a discussion proper to section four below. The reason which has just emerged in the preceding paragraphs, however, should receive a preliminary comment here. For, in effect, it has been suggested that Rom 13:1-7 evidences Paul's concern to have the Roman Christians go about their lives without engendering repressive reactions from the authorities. Because they would give evidence of respect for these authorities and because they would cooperate fully in the matter of tax payments, these Roman Christians would be free to build up their common life and give witness to Christ their Lord without risk of disruption or expulsion.

At the same time that this first "explanation" for Paul's position is mentioned, it needs to be emphasized that Paul was not compelled by this or by any other reason to adopt the stance that he adopted. Even if Paul was well aware of the previous troubled relations between the Jewish community and the authorities at Rome and even if he knew of the controversy over indirect taxes, it does not follow that this knowledge somehow *constrained* him to give the counsel of cooperation that he provided in Rom 13:1-7.

On what basis is Paul's freedom to challenge Roman authority hereby asserted? It is asserted on the grounds that Paul was first and foremost a disciple of the *crucified* Jesus! It was thus not unthinkable for Paul to have reminded the Roman Christians of Jesus' Roman crucifixion and to bid them to be faithful to Jesus in all things. Indeed, it is not inconceivable that Paul could have instructed these Christians that every form of political allegiance on earth had to be viewed from the perspective of Christ's sovereignty and their own full citizenship in heaven.

In Rom 13:1-7, now to be analyzed in detail, Paul did not speak in terms of Christ's sovereignty, nor did he allude to any other factor that might have conditioned or nuanced his counsel that Christians should be subject to the Roman authorities. However, in chapter eleven below, it will be demonstrated that, writing to the Philippians as a Roman prisoner, Paul did emphasize the sovereignty of Jesus, did emphasize the power of Jesus' name, and did emphasize the worth of the citizenship in heaven.

3. The Interpretation of Romans 13:1-7

At the beginning of this interpretation of Rom 13:1-7, it is important to emphasize that "the governing authorities" to whom Paul refers in this passage are not a group of rulers unknown to Paul's readers. Further, the imposition of taxes and the use of the sword, activities to which Paul refers, are not somehow abstract activities that are removed from a particular time and place. No, the governing authorities in question are the rulers of the Roman empire and their personal identities are well known to Paul's readers just as their specific policies and activities are known.

Which Roman rulers did Paul have in view when he composed this passage? To answer this question, the prior question of when Paul wrote Romans must first be addressed.

While the difficulties involved in setting exact dates for Paul's letters are well known, scholarly opinions regarding the date for Romans converge on the interval from A.D. 54 to 59.[18] This means that Nero was the emperor in power at the time when Romans was written. Since Nero ruled from 54 to 68, Romans was sent to the Christians at Rome sometime during the first five years of Nero's reign.[19] Later referred to as his *quinquennium*,[20] the young emperor's rule during these initial years apparently attracted a favorable response from many within the empire.

From the perspective of the present study, the fact that Romans was authored during the reign of Nero is highly significant.[21] For, in effect, Nero is thus the central figure among "the governing authorities" referred to in Rom 13:1. Along with Nero, Paul seemingly refers to the senators, prefects, and other officials who ruled in Rome and by extension to the proconsuls, governors, and other magistrates who ruled in the provinces.[22]

To reiterate, Paul's readers, living in the empire's capital, certainly knew the identities of these "governing authorities." Paul's readers also knew well the kinds of taxes these rulers levied. Until Paul's letter arrived, however, the Christians at Rome did not know of Paul's general support for the imperial authorities. Neither did they know of his specific support for the various taxes enacted by these rulers.

Nevertheless, once these Roman Christians reached chapter 13 in Paul's letter, there was no mistaking the nature of the approach that this noted apostle was advocating. In the very first sentence of this section, Paul decisively instructed his audience to "be subject" to the Roman authorities. In the next verses he then set forth two lines of argument to explain why such subjection was fully appropriate.

Continuing in v. 6, he referred to the fact that the Roman Christians had already been paying their taxes and admonished them to continue to do so. In his last clause he then returned to the thematic content of his opening statement: Christians are obliged to give the governing authorities the respect and honor due them. Bearing in mind that Paul's overall argumentation is carefully constructed and tightly woven,[23] it is now appropriate to consider his counsels and his arguments verse by verse.

In focusing first on v. 1, the exceptionless character and the forcefulness of Paul's opening counsel are both to be noted. With the use of the phrase *pasa psychē*, Paul indicates that *every* Christian at Rome is now being counseled.[24] And by choosing the verb *hypotassō* instead of the milder verb *hypakouō*, he indicates that the decisive response of "being subject" is the response that should be given.[25] Here then is the text of Paul's extremely resolute opening injunction.

Let every person be subject to the governing authorities. (Rom 13:1)

As mentioned, Paul's next sentences indicate the rationale for such subjection. Paul's perspective here is twofold. First, anyone resisting the authorities incurs God's judgment. And second, resistance will call forth a justified punishment or "wrath" from the authorities themselves.

Perhaps the most startling feature of Paul's assertion that to resist the Roman authorities is to incur God's judgment is the underlying premise that these authorities have been designated by God to hold and exercise power.[26] In Paul's words, they have been *hypo theou tetagmenai eisin*, "instituted by God." Paul expresses his entire argument in the following way:

For there is no authority except from God, and those that exist have been instituted by God. Therefore he who resists the authorities resists what God has appointed, and those who resist will incur judgment. (Rom 13:1a-2)

Paul's second argument regarding the Roman officials' role in punishing those who resist them also relies on the premise that these authorities have their role entrusted to them by God. Paul here straightforwardly assumes that these authorities will operate for the good even if it means using the sword to punish anyone who is a "wrongdoer" (*tō kakon prassonti*). Looking ahead to Paul's own imprisonment, is there not a considerable irony in Paul's words here?

> For rulers are not a terror to good conduct, but to bad. Would you have no fear of him who is in authority? Then do what is good, and you will receive his approval, for he is God's servant for your good. But if you do wrong, be afraid, for he does not bear the sword in vain; he is the servant of God to execute his wrath on the wrongdoer. (Rom 13:3-4)

Having thus elaborated two arguments in support of his initial admonition to be subject to the governing authorities, Paul, in v.5, then repeats this admonition and refers again to the two arguments he has just adduced. In terms of the structure of Paul's argument, v.5 thus functions to synthesize and summarize the fundamental message regarding subjection to the Roman authorities that Paul is setting forward in the first five verses of this passage. It should also be noted that "conscience" (*syneidēsin*) probably refers to the fact that Paul's readers are motivated to be subject out of moral conviction as well as from the desire to avoid punishment:[27]

> Therefore one must be subject, not only to avoid God's wrath but also for the sake of conscience. (Rom 13:5)

If subjection to the Roman authorities is thus the concern of the first five verses of this passage, v. 6 and the first part of v. 7 reflect Paul's concern with the specific topic of Roman taxes. Indeed this movement from the general topic of subjection to the specific topic of taxes might suggest that, from the outset, Paul was primarily concerned with tax payments. Did Paul emphasize subjection so strongly in the first five verses because he wanted to lay a firm foundation for his subsequent admonitions regarding taxes? Possibly. However, the fact that Paul returns to the theme of being subject to the authorities in v. 7b probably indicates that his overriding concern was to encourage subjection to the Roman authorities. His admonition to pay all taxes would then be an example of what such "subjection" would mean in practice.

Let the character of Paul's instructions about taxes and his instructions about giving respect and honor to the authorities now be considered. In the translation that follows, "Give to each one what is due . . . ," is substituted for the RSV's "Pay all of them their dues. . . ." Paul's closing recommendations regarding taxes and rulers are as follows:

> For the same reason you also pay taxes, for the authorities are ministers of God attending to this very thing. Give to each one what is due, taxes to whom taxes are due, revenue to whom revenue is due, respect to whom respect is due, honor to whom honor is due. (Rom 13:6-7)

In the Greek underlying these verses, there are several nuances that should be noted. The first is the manner by which Paul subtly shifts from the indicative mode (*teleite*) in v. 6 to the imperative mood (*apodote*) at the beginning of v. 7 Paul seemingly knows (or assumes) that the Roman Christians have been paying their taxes all along: "For this same reason you also pay taxes. . . ." Now he emphasizes that they are to continue to do so and, what is more, they are to comply with both categories of Rome's taxes: "Give to each one what is due, taxes (*phoron*) to whom taxes are due, revenue (*telos*)to whom revenue is due."

A certain penchant for inclusiveness is also reflected as Paul identifies the types of deference to be given to Roman officials distinguishing between "respect" (*phobon*) and "honor" (*timēn*). These two different terms may well have reflected the differing ranks and roles of various Roman officials. Just as with taxes, Paul insists that both categories of deference are obligatory.

In effect, these last words mark a return to the foundational premise that Paul expressed at the outset and thus give further testimony to the careful way in which this passage is constructed. In 13:1 Paul urged, "Let every person be subject to the governing authorities. . . ." In 13:5a he summarized, "Therefore one must be subject. . . ." Now in 13:7 he insists, "Give . . . respect to whom respect is due and honor to whom honor is due." Again, it is Nero and the officials of the Roman empire who are the recipients of the subjection he counsels.

4. Underscoring and Explaining
Paul's Accommodation

As used within this study, the terms "accommodative" and "resistant" refer to the two alternative stances that can be adopted in the face of the formidable political realities represented by the Roman empire. Generally speaking, someone adopting an accommodative approach would acquiesce in, cooperate with, afford support for the endeavors of those holding imperial power. Generally speaking, someone adopting a resistant stance would criticize, dissent from, and oppose those engaged in establishing and administering such an empire.

If Paul, at the time of Romans, is to be positioned on an accommodative-resistant spectrum, then he must surely be regarded as proposing an extremely accommodative approach. Indeed, as has already been adumbrated in chapter one, the primary thesis of this study asserts that Paul gave highly accommodatory counsel regarding the Roman rulers at the time of Rom 13:1-7 but was much changed in his perspective by the time of Philippians. Nevertheless, before proceeding to the latter part of this study with its analysis of Philippians and Paul's other prison letters, it is appropriate to underscore Paul's accommodation in Rom 13:1-7 and to provide a general overview of four factors that can be regarded as possible explanations for this approach.

As a means of illuminating and underscoring the fundamentally accommodative character of Rom 13:1-7, let it be imagined that this section of Paul's letter to the Roman Christians has just been introduced into legal proceedings in which Paul is a defendant. Paul's trial is being conducted by the emperor himself, that is, by Nero.

A similar approach will be followed in chapter eleven below when an imperial trial scene will be imagined as a setting for several passages from Paul's letter to the Philippians. At issue in both cases is what Nero would be able to deduce about Paul from reading certain key passages from the apostle's letters.

Any emperor concerned with the security of his own position and with the consolidation of imperial power could only have responded approvingly to the directives expressed in Rom 13:1-7. Indeed, it is plausible to conjecture that Nero or any emperor of the period would have been more than pleased to have this counsel disseminated widely throughout the empire.

Let it be emphasized that Rom 13:1-7 repeatedly advises subjection to the governing authorities, including full compliance with the taxes levied by these authorities. Further, within the framework of this consistent exhortation regarding subjection, Paul makes the following assertions regarding *a divine sanction* for the authorities' powers:

> For there is no authority except from God, and those that exist have been instituted by God. (Rom 13:1b).

> Therefore he who resists the authorities resists what God has appointed, and those who resist will incur judgment. (Rom 13:2)

> Would you have no fear of him who is in authority? Then do what is good, and you will receive his approval, for he is God's servant for your good. (Rom 13:3b-4a)

Because they legitimize and endorse the Roman authorities in such a fashion, such declarations are highly accommodatory in the sense discussed above. Do not such sentiments even surpass those of Tacitus' Cerialis in the degree of support that they provide for the general perpetuation of Roman rule and the specific continuance of the reigning emperor? Surely Paul's link between the purposes of God and the continuance of the existing authorities in their offices would have been viewed with extreme favor in the highest echelons of the empire.

What is more, in Romans 13:4b, Paul included an admonition about the authorities' use of the sword that could plausibly have elicited from Nero (or any emperor of Paul's era), an expression akin to astonished approval as he read it or heard it for the first time. Imagine Nero's satisfaction in learning that an influential leader among the Christians (regardless of how numerous Christians were at the time) was instructing the members of this group to regard the emperor's sword in the following way:

> But if you do wrong, be afraid, for he does not bear the sword in vain; he is the servant of God to execute his wrath on the wrongdoer. (Rom 13:4b)

Now that Paul's startling compliance in Rom 13:1-7 has been underscored, *explaining* this approach becomes the objective for the remaining pages of this chapter. Yet here a cautioning word is immediately appropriate. For, even when four possible explanations have been considered, it will not be certain whether any one of them, alone or in combination with others, suffices to provide a definitive explanation for Paul's highly acquiescent position.

One factor pertaining to Paul's motivation for writing Rom 13:1-7 has already been mentioned. In section two of this chapter, when Paul's level of familiarity with the pastoral situation at Rome was discussed, it was noted that Paul's knowledge of tax protests and previous expulsions of Jews might have influenced his admonitions. It is now appropriate to consider this and other possible factors in a systematic fashion, noting that there can indeed be complementarity and even a certain overlapping between particular factors.

Let Paul's concern with the continuance and the upbuilding of the Christian community at Rome be the first factor to be considered. Even if Paul was not aware of the prior expulsions of the Jewish community from Rome and even if he was not informed regarding the contemporary or near contemporary tax protests against indirect taxes, Paul still may have given the instructions of Rom 13:1-7 out of a general intuitive concern for the well-being of the Roman Christian community. If he was informed concerning these specific facets of the Christians' situation, then his concern would obviously have been intensified.

It is evident from even the most general reading of such letters as 1 Thessalonians, 1 and 2 Corinthians, and Galatians that Paul viewed the building up of Christian communities as a very high priority. And certainly within Romans itself Paul is obviously concerned with other issues pertaining to community life, especially the mutual appreciation of Jewish Christians and Gentile Christians.

Given these factors it is plausible to argue that Paul's directives regarding the Roman authorities and their taxes arise from his basic concern to have the members of the Christian community live in peace with these authorities. After all, *this* Christian community is located at the center of the empire, immediately under the purview of the emperor and the ranking members of his administration. It is thus fitting to instruct the Roman Christians, so Paul may have reasoned, about the importance of staying on the best possible terms with Nero and the other imperial authorities.

A second possible factor for explaining Paul's accommodation is the factor of eschatology. The basic argument with respect to eschatology can be briefly stated as follows: At the time of Romans, Paul was convinced that the interval until Jesus' return in glory was short, and this conviction led him to adopt a compliant approach regarding cooperation with the Roman system. Why should energy, concern, and time be given to a situation that was soon to be fundamentally transformed by Christ's return? Regardless of how vexatious the imperial authorities' policies might be, the Roman Christians should comply with the authorities' directives. It was useless to become embroiled in controversy because of the short time remaining. Rather, all emphasis should be given to prayer and to all endeavors appropriate to the strengthening of the internal life of the Christian community.

Significantly, although Romans does not evidence the intense eschatological expectation of 1 Thessalonians—this comparative lack of urgency is noted by those who deny eschatology as a motivation for Paul's compliance—there is one passage within Romans that tends to show Paul thinking in such terms.[28] That passage is separated from Rom 13:1-7 by only a few verses; it reads as follows: "For salvation is nearer to us now than when we first believed; the night is far gone, the day is at hand" (Rom 13:11b-12a).

Paul's familiarity with Jewish wisdom sayings can be regarded as a third possible factor explaining his approach at Rom 13:1-7. From whence did Paul derive his assertion that the authority of the existing Roman rulers was linked with the authority of God and his assertion that the authorities wielded the sword to execute God's punishment? Conceivably Paul could have derived this perspective from the traditions of Jewish wisdom sayings as expressed, for example, in the following verses from the book of Proverbs:

> My son, fear the Lord and the king, and do not disobey either of them; for disaster from them will rise suddenly, and who knows the ruin that will come from them both? (Prov 24:21-22)

While the correspondence between this text and the views expressed in Rom 13:1-7 is not exact, the general thrust of these wisdom verses could have been taken over by Paul. Yet, if Paul did choose to draw on this aspect of his Jewish heritage, it should be observed that he was thereby *not* drawing on the more revolutionary currents within Jewish tradition, for example, the earlier rebellion of the Maccabees against the Seleucid dynasty and the contemporary insurgency against Roman rule launched by Judas the Gaulanite and his allies.

A fourth possible factor concerns Paul's own personal valuation of the Roman empire. Precisely what perspective did Paul have regarding the empire that included and surrounded him? The first two factors that have just been considered, Paul's concern for the upbuilding of the Roman Christian community and his concern with eschatology, do not necessarily imply that Paul valued the Roman empire and its rulers. In fact, Paul could have written Rom 13:1-7 exactly as he did despite the fact that he did *not* esteem the Roman authorities.

But what if Paul's own personal judgment was that the empire and its rulers were actually playing a positive role in bringing about peace and order within the world? What if Paul actually considered the Roman emperors to be competent leaders? As a fourth possible factor explaining Paul's accommodation in Rom 13:1-7, it is now appropriate to consider whether Paul might not have been influenced by his own personal, positive assessment of the empire and its leaders.

If Paul did value the Roman empire highly when he wrote to the Christians at Rome, two elements, one positive and one privative, may have contributed to his favorable outlook. Both of these elements, Paul's positive experiences as a Roman traveler and his lack of any sustained experience as a chained Roman prisoner, have previously been mentioned. It is now appropriate to reflect that the combination of these two elements may have given Paul a rose-colored view of Roman rule.

Well-maintained roads for travel; many safely navigable ports and rivers; significant protection on land from bandits; significant protection on sea from pirates; everywhere the presence of Roman soldiers and the Roman network of communication. The foregoing benefits were certainly features that commended the Roman system to the wide-traveling apostle. Indeed, when Paul proclaims in Romans 15:19 that he had already preached the gospel faithfully "from Jerusalem and as far round as Illyricum," is it not to be recognized that the Roman system, in all of its material facets, was a considerable benefit to him in conducting this ministry?

On the other hand, 2 Cor 11:23-33 does clearly indicate that Paul experienced incredible hardships during the time of these early apostolic travels. Nevertheless, the sufferings that Paul details occurred, in great measure, apart from the Roman system. To be sure, his decrying of "far more imprisonments, with countless beatings" in verse 11:23 could indicate that Paul had experienced severe punishments by local Roman authorities. Even if Rome-approved authorities are to be understood as the perpetrators of these punishments, however, these ad hoc measures are to be clearly distinguished from an officially mandated custody, enduring for an extended period of time.

Paul may not yet have experienced the Roman *system* operating in a deleterious way when he authored Romans. If he had suffered mistreatment under the aegis of Roman authority, this mistreatment had not been of such a character or such duration as to goad him to any fundamental reservations regarding Roman rule.

Paul's generally positive experiences of Roman rule as a traveler in the eastern province combined with the lack of any egregiously disillusioning encounters with the Roman judicial system may thus represent an additional factor influencing the sunny estimation of the Roman authorities that he expressed at the time of Romans. Yet, as mentioned previously, neither this factor nor any of the other three factors discussed above can be taken as a *certain* influence on Paul.

In summary, Paul's accommodation in Rom 13:1-7 is readily apparent. The factor or factors explaining his accommodation cannot be established with any compelling degree of certainty.

CHAPTER FOUR

Images of Imprisonment

THE PURPOSE OF THE present chapter is to establish a context for the references that Paul makes to his identity as a prisoner in Philemon and Philippians. What can be known of the material and social conditions that characterized imprisonment in various parts of the empire and in Rome itself? How did other particular prisoners of the time experience their own forms of imprisonment? Topics suggested by such questions as these will be treated in the sections below.

It should be stressed at the outset that the thrust of the present chapter is primarily descriptive. The sections that follow do not seek to present a complete sociology of Roman custody, an objective that is scarcely attainable given the character of the existing sources. Rather these sections treat selected aspects of Roman imprisonment with the objective of engendering a basic appreciation for what Roman imprisonment *could* involve. Once a general sensitivity for the various dimensions of first-century imprisonment has been gained, the process of interpreting what Paul actually indicates about his own situation will proceed with much greater facility.

In the Pauline prison writings, there is scant reference to the material conditions of Paul's imprisonment and no explicit reference to the juridical category of his custody. Nevertheless, Paul certainly was detained under particular conditions and his case certainly was covered by established legal categories. Thus it is appropriate to begin this chapter with two sections treating the legal categories and the material conditions under which various Roman prisoners could be held. These initial sections will be followed by sections considering the roles of other prisoners and informers and the roles of outside friends. A final section will consider the types of endeavor that prisoners might pursue.

Several of the ancient authors cited below were contemporaries of Paul or nearly contemporary with him. Yet others lived earlier, and others, such as Philostratus, considerably later. In light of these significant variations, care must be observed lest prison references that were made over a span of several centuries be accorded the same weight. The prison practices that prevailed in Paul's day may have differed considerably from the practices that prevailed much earlier or much later in Roman history.

Further, no ancient historian or commentator provides a systematic description of the practices that the various Roman authorities adopted with respect to imprisonment, or at least no such comprehensive description has survived. Rather the surviving reports are characteristically focused on the treatment that a particular Roman ruler decreed for a *specific* enemy, law-breaker, or rival. The anecdotal character of these reports must thus be underscored.

Nevertheless, inasmuch as the primary objective of this chapter is to engender an appreciation for the references to his custody that Paul makes in Philemon and Philippians, not every feature of the prevailing Roman practices needs to be determined and analyzed. It is sufficient that the existing pieces of information be presented in such a way as to engage the reader's imagination regarding the range of prison situations that Roman prisoners during Paul's era may have faced.

1. Categories and Grades of Imprisonment

In the codification of Roman law made at a much later date by the emperor Justinian,[1] three principal categories of Roman custody are distinguished according to their severity.[2] The first and most harsh category is that of "prison" (*carcer*).[3] The less severe "military custody" (*custodia militaris*) is next in order followed by the comparatively mild "free custody" (*custodia libera*). These three categories can be utilized as one means of organizing and presenting important literary passages attesting to various kinds and degrees of imprisonment.

A. *Carcer*

To foster sensitivity for the horrendous conditions that Roman imprisonment might have involved, it is useful to consider the report by Diodorus Siculus concerning the fate of the captured Macedonian king Perseus in the Roman prison at Alba Fucens in central Italy. Diodorus' *Library of History* was written during the years from 56 to 30 B.C.[4] Perseus' defeat and imprisonment occurred over one hundred years earlier, circa 167 B.C.[5] Whether this particular prison was still being maintained at the time of Paul is not ascertainable. Certainly these were not the prison conditions that Paul himself experienced:

> The misfortunes that Perseus encountered were so great that his sufferings seem like the inventions of fiction, yet even so he was not willing to be quit of life. For before the senate had decided on the penalty he should suffer, one of the urban praetors had him cast with his children into the prison at Alba. This prison is a deep underground dungeon, no larger than a nine-couch room, dark, and noisome from the large numbers committed to the place, who were men under condemnation on capital charges, for most of this category were incarcerated there at that period. With so many shut up in such close quarters, the poor wretches were reduced to the physical appearance of brutes, and since their food and everything pertaining to their other needs was all foully commingled, a stench so terrible assailed anyone who drew near that it could scarcely be endured. There for seven days Perseus remained, in such sorry plight that he begged succour even from men of the meanest stamp, whose food was the prison ration. They, indeed, affected by the magnitude of his misfortune, in which they shared, wept and generously gave him a portion of whatever they received. A sword with which to kill himself was thrown down to him, and a noose for hanging, with full freedom to use them as he might wish. (*The Library of History* 31.9.1-4)

A significant distinction can be made between being consigned to a prison *and* bound with chains as opposed to being confined in a prison where chains are not employed. Clearly, the prison at Alba Fucens was a horrific experience even absent the use of chains. However, in his *Life of Apollonius*, published approximately in A.D. 217,[6] Philostratus memorably presents the distinction between a prison in which chains are used and one in which they are not.

From the perspective of the present study, it is noteworthy that Philostratus recounts that the philosopher Apollonius was initially persecuted under Nero (54-68) but lived to experience imprisonment and jeopardy at the hands of Domitian (81-96). It is in detailing Apollonius' encounter with Domitian that Philostratus portrays the distinction between a prison in which prisoners are chained and a prison in which they are able to move about within their place of confinement. Philostratus seemingly implicitly portrays Rome as the location for these two prisons, and research has tentatively identified four prison sites within ancient Rome.[7] Nevertheless, the correspondence between Philostratus' reports and historical reality is far from certain.

According to Philostratus' narration of the events after Apollonius' arrest, a noteworthy sequence occurred involving transfers between the two types of prisons. Initially Aelian, Domitian's staff officer, ordered Apollonius to the prison where "the captives were not bound" (to eleutherion oikein desmoterion),[8] a prison where about fifty other prisoners were being held.[9] After sending a spy into the prison,[10] Domitian then summoned Apollonius to a private meeting that was not a part of his formal hearing.[11] As a result of Apollonius' comments during this meeting, Domitian became enraged and ordered that Apollonius again be placed in chains and that his confinement now be "among the vilest felons."[12]

Other events then ensued, including Domitian's use of a second spy.[13] As indicated within the passage now to be cited, however, Domitian then decided to restore Apollonius to the prison without chains:

> After Apollonius had thus revealed himself to Damis, and held some further conversation, about mid-day some one presented himself to them and made the following intimation verbally: "The Emperor, Apollonius, releases you from these fetters by the advice of Aelian; and he permits you to take up your quarters in the prison where criminals are not bound, until the time comes for you to make your defence, but you will probably be called upon to plead your cause five days from now." "Who then," said Apollonius, "is to get me out of this place?" "I," said the messenger, "so follow me." And when the prisoners in the free prison saw him again, they all flocked round him, as around one restored to them against all expectations. . . . (Life of Apollonius 7.40)

B. Military Custody

As an illustration for the category of Roman custody known as "military custody," the report supplied by the Jewish historian Josephus regarding the custody to which Tiberius (14-37) subjected Herod Agrippa I is extremely valuable. As with the historians previously cited, Josephus' reports frequently reflect embellishment and other distortions. Nevertheless, keeping these considerations in mind, it is still possible to accept Josephus' narrative concerning Herod Agrippa as suggestive of some forms of military custody.

The key event preparing for the passage now to be considered was Herod Agrippa's treasonous comment to Tiberius' heir, the future emperor Gaius. Agrippa had been raised with him and was a close friend of Gaius from an early age.[14] As a result of this comment, Tiberius ordered that Agrippa should be bound with chains and guarded closely. The severity of this decision was lessened, however, due to the influence of Antonia, Tiberius' sister-in-law and a friend of Herod Agrippa's mother, who worked through Macro, the praetorian prefect.

The following excerpts from the *Jewish Antiquities* describe the essentials of Herod Agrippa's situation. He is very definitely chained and guarded by soldiers under the direction of a centurion. But his friends and his servants move freely about the premises providing for his needs. As the narrative unfolds, Agrippa's guards are portrayed as highly susceptible to the prevailing political winds. Josephus' narrative also provides a view of the types of rapport that might come to exist between a noteworthy prisoner and those guarding him.

Here then are the relevant passages from Josephus' narrative. It is to be noted that the words used by Josephus in reference to Agrippa's chains are related to the terms that Paul uses in reference to his own chains when he writes to Philemon.[15]

Antonia, though distressed at the misfortune of Agrippa, saw that it would be too much of an undertaking to discuss his case with Tiberius and would besides be useless. She gained from Macro the following concessions for him, that the soldiers who were to guard him and that the centurion who would be in charge of them and would also be handcuffed to him should be of humane character, that he should be permitted to bathe every day and receive visits from his freedmen and friends, and that he should have other bodily comforts too. His friend

Silas and two of his freedmen, Marysyas and Stoecheus, visited him bringing him his favorite viands and doing whatever service they could. They brought him garments that they pretended to sell, but, when night came, they made him a bed with the connivance of the soldiers, who had Macro's orders to do so. These things went on for six months. . . .

But Marysyas, the freeman of Agrippa, having learned of the death of Tiberius, forced his way at top speed to announce the good news to Agrippa. Finding him on his way out to the bath, he beckoned to him and said in Hebrew, "The lion is dead." Agrippa grasped his meaning and, giddy with joy at this announcement said, "My unbounded thanks to you for your whole service and for this happy news. I only hope it is true."

Now the centurion, who commanded Agrippa's guards, seeing in what a hurry Marysyas had come and how pleased Agrippa was as soon as he heard the message, surmised that something novel had been said and asked them about the message in question. For a time they put him off, but, when he insisted, Agrippa, being now on friendly terms with him, told him the truth without reserve. He joined in the rejoicing at the news because it was to Agrippa's advantage and treated him to a dinner.

While they were feasting and the drinking was under way, someone came in and said that Tiberius was alive and would return to the city within a few days. The centurion was so shockingly perturbed at this report, since the penalty set for such things as he had done was death, that is, both to have dined together with a prisoner and to have rejoiced at the news of the emperor's death, that he pushed Agrippa off the couch and said: "So you thought you would fool me with a false report of the emperor's death, and would not pay for it with your own head?" With these words he ordered the manacles to be put on Agrippa, though he had previously taken them off, and a stricter guard to be kept than before.

Such was the wretched condition of Agrippa through the night. On the following day, however, the reports of Tiberius' death were more numerous and assured in the city. (*Jewish Antiquities* 18.6.7 and 18.6.10)

C. Free Custody

The chief feature distinguishing *custodia libera* from *custodia militaris* was the use of other agents, apart from military personnel, for the supervision of the prisoner. Prisoners subject to this form of custody were frequently detained under the supervision of magistrates. In certain instances a prisoner's confinement might even be supervised by a family member. A further consideration is that chains were not employed for prisoners in free custody while, as disclosed in the preceding section, they might be utilized for prisoners under military custody.[16]

The three examples of *custodia libera* now to be considered date from the reign of Tiberius. The first concerns one Junius Gallio, a Roman senator. In the year A.D. 32, according to the report of Tacitus, Gallio earned Tiberius' wrath by advocating a policy change that would have brought additional benefits to the Roman soldiers who served as members of the Praetorian guards. Suspecting that sinister motives lay beneath Gallio's proposal, Tiberius first ordered that he be exiled but then decided on a course of action that was more severe. Gallio would not be placed in chains but he would be detained indefinitely in quarters provided by the city magistrates at Rome:

> Such was the reward of Gallio's studied adulation: he was ejected at once from the senate; later from Italy; and, as the charge was made that he would carry his exile lightly, since he had chosen the famous and pleasant island of Lesbos, he was dragged back to the capital and detained under the roof of various magistrates. (*The Annals* 6.3)

Suetonius, writing at the beginning of the second century, identifies another example of *custodia libera*, a case in which confinement was supervised by a relative, when he describes the events that befell Publius Vitellius. Formerly a praetor, Publius was implicated in the conspiracy of Sejanus and was remanded to custody in A.D. 35:

> Arrested among the accomplices of Sejanus, after holding the praetorship, and handed over to his own brother to be kept in confinement, he opened his veins with a penknife, but allowed himself to be bandaged and restored, not so much from unwillingness to die, as because of the entreaties of his friends; and he met a natural death while still in confinement. (*The Lives of the Caesars: Vitellius* 7.3)

At the outset of this section it was observed that significant gradations could be present within each of the three categories of custody. Normally those confined under *custodia libera* conditions would experience more humane circumstances than prisoners confined under *custodia militaris*. But a third example, this provided by Dio Cassius, indicates that the absence of chains was no guarantee that a prisoner's circumstances would be more tolerable.

In this instance Tiberius formulated a decidedly macabre approach in dealing with the threat represented by Asinius Gallus. On the very day that he arranged for the Roman senate to condemn him, Tiberius invited Gallus to a banquet in Tiberius' own house and pledged the cup of friendship with him!

Normally, execution would have occurred on official condemnation by the senate. Yet, according to Dio Cassius' report, Tiberius decided that Gallus' immediate death would be too inconsequential an outcome:

> Instead, in order to make his lot as cruel as possible, he bade Gallus be of good cheer and instructed the senate that he should be guarded without bonds until he himself should reach the city; his object, as I said, was to make the prisoner suffer as long as possible both from the loss of his civic rights and from terror. And so it came to pass; for he was kept under the eyes of the consuls of each year, except when Tiberius held the office, in which case he was guarded by praetors; and this was done, not to prevent his escape, but to prevent his death. He had no companion or servant with him, spoke to no one, and saw no one, except when he was compelled to take food. And the food was of such quality and amount as neither to afford him any satisfaction or strength nor yet to allow him to die. This was, in fact, the most terrible part of his punishment. (*Roman History* 58.3.5)

2. Factors Affecting the Health and Survival of Prisoners

Adequate food and adequate hygiene are obviously factors of critical significance for the survival of any prisoner. It was noted in the preceding section that Tiberius regulated the food available to Asinius Gallus so as to deny him satisfaction or strength while keeping him just barely alive. Since Gallus was not chained and was kept under the supervision of consuls, it was presumably this lack of adequate food that imposed the greatest hardship on him.

In the state prison in which King Perseus was cast, also considered above, the prison food, eaten in stench-filled surroundings, was but one factor undermining his health. He was confined with other prisoners in a deep underground dungeon that was so crowded and so unhygienic that those confined there assumed the physical appearance of brutes. While no mention is made of contamination from disease or vermin, these factors too would presumably be hazards in such a prison setting.

Another arduous prison setting is referrred to by Philostratus when he relates, in connection with Apollonius' first visit to Rome, that Nero had already cast the philosopher Musonius into prison for practicing philosophy. Philostratus does not describe this prison in detail or give its precise location. He does emphasize, however, that Musonius "would have died for all his gaoler cared, if it had not been for the strength of his constitution" (*Life of Apollonius* 4.35).

A *carcer* such as the one Perseus experienced and perhaps the prison experienced by Musonius represented the most extreme form of Roman custody. What can be said with respect to the types of food and hygiene available to prisoners under military custody? In essence, very little. Presumably a great deal depended on the military personnel or other authorities into whose custody a prisoner was remanded. As the previously cited case of Herod Agrippa indicates, the official immediately in charge of guarding a prisoner had considerable discretion regarding the arrangements for the prisoner's food, hygiene, and sleeping.

In the continuation of his narrative regarding Perseus, Diodorus indicates that it was ultimately the ill rapport between Perseus and those guarding him that cost the king his life. Even after the Roman senate decreed his release from the central prison lest he die as a result of the severe conditions there, death still befell him in the following way:

> As a result, Perseus was placed in more suitable custody, and, because of the senate's kindness, sustained himself by vain hopes, only to meet at last an end that matched his earlier misfortunes. For after clinging to life for two years, he offended the barbarians who were his guards, and was prevented from sleeping until he died of it. (*The Library of History* 31.9.5)

Was Perseus physically chained to guards on rotating shifts? If so, then their reported plan to keep him from sleeping until death occurred can have been easily achieved.

Seneca, the philosopher who was mentor to Nero, implies in one of his *Epistulae Morales*[17] that the practice of having prisoners chained to their guards was a common one during the era of Nero and the lifetime of Paul. The subject of the epistle now to be considered is not custody and punishment. Seneca rather makes reference to a prisoner's chains in order to illustrate the relationship between hope and fear. According to Seneca, hope and fear are closely connected just as a prisoner is closely connected to the guard to whom he is chained:

> *Just as the same chain fastens the prisoner and the soldier who guards him,* so hope and fear, dissimilar as they are, keep step together. (*Epistle* 5.7; emphasis added)

One further illustration that the guard(s) to whom a prisoner was chained exercised considerable influence over that prisoner's welfare can be given. The events narrated by Ignatius of Antioch occurred perhaps sixty years after Paul's own imprisonment. During the reign of the emperor Trajan (98-117), Ignatius was being brought from Antioch to Rome as a heavily guarded prisoner. During the course of this journey, Ignatius wrote seven letters to Christians in various locations in Asia Minor and Greece, adverting in several of them to his approaching martyrdom.

A noteworthy aspect of his custody was the fact that Ignatius was actually allowed to compose and send these letters. This latitude was significant given the fact that Ignatius was normally chained to one or more of the ten soldiers charged with bringing him safely to Rome.

Ignatius does not comment on the conditions he experienced relative to food, hygiene, and sleep deprivation. He does, however, mention one aspect of his custody as particularly distressing. Expressing his resentment regarding the soldiers to whom he was chained, Ignatius refers to them as "ten leopards," and he states significantly that these soldiers "grow more brutal the better they are treated," with the result that "the wrongs they do me (Ignatius) make me a better disciple."[18]

What kinds of activity were open to prisoners who were physically chained to their guards? As noted, Ignatius was able to author seven letters. Was he released from his chains for certain periods and able to use such times for writing? Or were his letters dictated?

If an affirmative answer is given to this last question, then what were the conditions under which Ignatius could converse and even dictate? Was every conversation monitored by guards who remained close at hand? And once letters were completed, what were the next steps in the process? Were these writings censored by his guards or by officers who were literate? Who then carried these letters to the Christian communities for whom they were intended?

A startling contrast for Ignatius' relative liberty to compose and send letters is provided by a report from Suetonius regarding the severe conditions of imprisonment that Tiberius sometimes mandated. And as will be seen, this report not only describes the practice of solitary confinement; it also emphasizes that many Romans preferred suicide to this form of imprisonment:

> Some of those who were consigned to prison were denied not only the consolation of reading, but even the privilege of conversing and talking together. Of those who were cited to plead their causes some opened their veins at home, feeling sure of being condemned and wishing to avoid annoyance and humiliation, while others drank poison in full view of the senate; yet the wounds of the former were bandaged and they were hurried half-dead, but still quivering, to the prison. (*The Lives of the Caesars: Tiberius* 41.4)

The final factor to be considered relative to the health and survival of prisoners is the very physicality of the chains employed to bind them. Not all prisoners were kept in chains; but for those who were, the types of chains used and their weight were both significant features.[19]

Chains might be employed for the prisoners' arms and hands (manacles) or for their legs and feet (pedicles). An iron collar might also be used. While the chains utilized for the daylight hours might allow a relative freedom of movement, security would usually be increased during the hours of darkness. Stocks designed to immobilize the prisoners almost completely were a practice in at least some situations.

To assist in imaging the potential impact of chains on a prisoner, reference can be made to Lucian's work *Toxaris or Friendship*. This work was written circa A.D. 163 and presents the remarkable story

of the friendship between Demetrius and Antiphilus. Just how accu-
rately Lucian's account reflects conditions in the prisons of his day is
impossible to say. In addition to its descriptions of their chains, this
passage also presents a picture of prisoners enduring unhygienic conditions and sleeplessness:

> Consequently, he sickened at length and was ill, as might be expected
> in view of the fact that he slept on the ground and at night could not
> even stretch out his legs, which were confined in the stocks. By day, to
> be sure, the collar was sufficient, together with manacles upon one
> hand; but for the night he had to be fully secured by his bonds. More-
> over, the stench of the room and its stifling air (since many were con-
> fined in the same place, cramped for room, and scarcely able to draw
> breath), the clash of iron, the scanty sleep—all these conditions were
> difficult and intolerable for such a man, unwonted to them and
> unschooled to a life so rigorous. (*Toxaris or Friendship* 29)[20]

3. Other Prisoners and Informers

For any prisoner ordered to confinement in an institutional prison,
the presence of other prisoners within the same confines was a factor
to be reckoned with. The noise, disease, and stench present in over-
crowded prisons have already been noted. A previously cited passage
has also depicted prisoners under capital sentence as "the vilest
felons." Confinement in close quarters with persons prone to hostile
behavior would thus be an additional negative factor facing any
prisoner.

The presence of other prisoners, however, could also be beneficial.
Much obviously depends on the particular features of the prison in
question. In section five below, it will be seen that Philostratus
images a prison scene in which prisoners awaiting trial are able to
give time to the preparation of their defenses. Philostratus' description of this scene also suggests that these prisoners could offer support and counsel to one another in this situation.

For prisoners awaiting trial, confinement with other prisoners
might involve an additional feature that should not be overlooked:
the possible presence of spies and informers within the prison population. As previously mentioned, Philostratus indicates that, during
the time that Domitian kept Apollonius in custody, the emperor sent

a spy into the prison. But as the passage now to be cited makes apparent, Apollonius quickly saw through this ruse:

> On the next day he was haranguing them in a discourse of the same tenor, when a man was sent into the prison privately by Domitian to listen to what he said. In his deportment this person had a downcast air, and, as he himself admitted, looked as if he ran a great risk. He had great volubility of speech, as is usually the case with sycophants who have been chosen to draw up eight or ten informations. Apollonius saw through the trick and talked about themes which could in no way serve his purpose; for he told his audience about rivers and mountains, and he described wild animals and trees to them, so that they were amused, while the informer gained nothing to his purpose. And when he tried to draw him away from these subjects and get him to abuse the tyrant, "My good friend," said Apollonius, "you say what you like, for I am the last man in the world to inform against you; but if I find anything to blame in the Emperor, I'll say it to his face." (*Life of Apollonius* 7.27)

4. *The Assistance of Friends*

For the person consigned to Roman custody and especially for those experiencing its most severe forms, the assistance of friends was vital. Just as Roman imprisonment and Roman chains were a test for the prisoner, however, so too did they constitute a test for the prisoner's friends. If Roman chains brought suffering and humiliation to the prisoner, they could also engender embarrassment and despair for that individual's friends. Indeed, friends needed to possess substantive character if they were to continue to manifest the qualities of friendship toward the one accused.

In one of his *Epistles*, Seneca employs the memorable image of friends who will desert "at the first rattle of the chain." This phrase appears within a passage on the desertion of unreliable friends that is worth considering in its entirety:

> The end will be like the beginning: he has made friends with one who might assist him out of bondage; at the first rattle of the chain such a friend will desert him. These are the so-called "fair-weather" friendships; one who is chosen for the sake of utility will be satisfactory only so long as he is useful. Hence prosperous men are blockaded by troops

of friends; but those who have failed stand amid vast loneliness, their friends fleeing from the very crisis which is to test their worth. Hence, also, we notice those many shameful cases of persons who, through fear, desert or betray. (*Epistle 9.9*)

This phenomenon of friends deserting one who is imprisoned, or one soon to be in prison, is also focused on by Philostratus when he describes the developments that occurred as Apollonius and a band of younger philosophers drew near to Rome and a warning of Nero's hostility toward philosophy was communicated to them by Philolaus, a philosopher who was fleeing the city.

Apollonius' most trusted disciple, Damis, voiced apprehension that the warnings given by Philolaus would weaken the commitment of many in the group. But to Damis' surprise, Apollonius welcomed this development since it meant that the young philosophers now could not avoid facing the reality that suffering might result from their commitment to philosophy. As Philostratus then indicates, twenty-six out of the thirty-four young philosophers did indeed depart:

> But Apollonius said: "Well, of all the blessings which have been vouchsafed to me by the gods, often without my praying for them at all, this present one, I may say, is the greatest that I have ever enjoyed; for chance has thrown in my way a touchstone to test these young men, of a kind to prove most thoroughly which of them are philosophers, and which of them prefer some other line of conduct than that of the philosopher." And in fact the knock-kneed among them were detected in no time, for under the influence of what Philolaus said, some of them declared that they were ill, others that they had no provisions for the journey, others that they were homesick, others that they had been deterred by dreams; and in the result the thirty-four companions of Apollonius who were willing to accompany him to Rome were reduced to eight. And all the rest ran away from Nero and philosophy, both at once, and took to their heels. (*Life of Apollonius* 4.37)

In section two of this chapter, Lucian's description of the harsh prison conditions experienced by Antiphilus was cited. This description occurred in the context of Lucian's narrative regarding the extraordinary friendship that Demetrius displayed toward Antiphilus while the latter experienced the degradation of prison. It is now appropriate to focus on the extraordinary measures by which Demetrius brought himself into solidarity with his unjustly imprisoned friend. After finding his now unkempt friend, Demetrius initially took the following steps:

> Then he bade him have no fear, and tearing his short cloak in two, put on one of the halves himself and gave the remainder to Antiphilus, after stripping from him the filthy, worn-out rags that he was wearing. From that time forth, too, he shared his life in every way, attending and cherishing him; for by hiring himself out to the shipmen in the harbour from early morning until noon, he earned a good deal of money as a stevedore. Then, on returning from his work, he would give part of his pay to the keeper, thus rendering him tractable and peaceful, and the rest sufficed well enough for the maintenance of his friend. Each afternoon he remained with Antiphilus, keeping him in heart; and when night overtook him, he slept just in front of the prison door, where he had made a place to lie and had put down some leaves. (*Toxaris or Friendship* 30-31)

That friends could sometimes enter a prison and provide a prisoner with clothing and other necessities and that a bribe might sometimes be paid to the jailer to secure better treatment for the imprisoned are two of the possibilities suggested by the passage just cited. Inasmuch as Lucian's narrative concerning friendship seems minimally related to the lives of historical persons, caution needs to be exercised in assessing the various elements and developments that he includes in his narrative.

This caution is especially relevant with respect to the next passage from *Toxaris* that will now be cited. Lucian narrates that, after security at the prison was tightened and it was no longer possible for him to minister to Antiphilus in the manner just described, Demetrius contrived to be cast into the same prison so as to be able to remain at Antiphilus' side! In the end, both Demetrius and Antiphilus gained their release from this unjust imprisonment. Before that outcome occurred, however, Demetrius manifested his friendship in the following way:

> Perplexed and distressed over this situation, as he had no other way to be with his comrade, he went to the governor and incriminated himself, alleging that he had been an accomplice in the attempt upon

Anubis. When he had made that statement, he was haled straight to prison, and on being brought in with Antiphilus, he managed with difficulty, by dint of urgent entreaties addressed to the warden, to obtain from him one concession, at least—that of being confined near Antiphilus and in the same set of irons (*Toxaris or Friendship* 32)

One other work by Lucian also sheds light on the situation of prisoners when they were assisted by one or more loyal friends. *The Passing of Peregrinus,* written shortly after A.D. 165, represents a more historical mode of writing. In it Lucian is very definitely concerned to describe an individual's passage through life.

Significantly, Lucian considers Proteus to be a charlatan. Previously a philosopher, Proteus used the name *Peregrinus* during the period in which he adopted Christianity. As a Christian, Peregrinus received extensive support from a network of Christian friends during the time of his imprisonment by the Roman governor of Syria.[21] He subsequently abandoned Christianity, however, and resumed life as an expositor of the Cynic philosophy. The excerpt now to be considered describes the high degree of support that Peregrinus/Proteus received from his Christian associates while he was imprisoned:

Then at length Proteus was apprehended for this and thrown into prison, which itself gave him no little reputation as an asset for his future career and the charlatanism and notoriety-seeking that he was enamored of. Well, when he had been imprisoned, the Christians, regarding the incident as a calamity, left nothing undone in the effort to rescue him. Then, as this was impossible, every other form of attention was shown him, not in any casual way but with assiduity; and from the very break of day aged widows and orphan children could be seen waiting near the prison, while their officials even slept inside with him after bribing the guards. Then elaborate meals were brought in, and sacred books of theirs were read aloud, and excellent Peregrinus—for he still went by that name—was called by them "the new Socrates" (*The Passing of Peregrinus* 12-13)

5. The Endeavors of Prisoners

Regarding the activities of prisoners, it is well to begin with reflections regarding the natural impulse to maintain communication. Certainly there would be an incentive for all prisoners whose family members were still living and for all prisoners who possessed property to strive for contact with the outside world. Depending on the specific circumstances of the prisoner's custody, this contact could be maintained by means of visitors coming to the prison and through letters and messages carried by such intermediaries as guards and discharged prisoners. Clearly the attitude of the jailers and those with general jurisdiction over the prisoners would be a crucial factor influencing the type and degree of communication that might be achieved.

For those prisoners being kept in custody prior to a trial, the time of confinement could afford them, again, depending upon the circumstances, an opportunity for preparing a legal defense. When Apollonius traveled to Rome during Nero's regime, the philosopher Musonius lay confined in the imperial dungeon awaiting trial. Musonius refused Apollonius' offer to visit him lest both of their lives be endangered. This response led Apollonius to write that Musonius might be following a course similar to Socrates in eschewing the attention of friends. In his reply, however, Musonius insisted on his own commitment to preparing a defense for the coming trial: "Socrates was put to death, because he would not take the trouble to defend himself; but I shall defend myself" (*Life of Apollonius* 4.46).

Later, when Apollonius himself was imprisoned by Domitian, two passages by Philostratus indicate the possibility of using one's time in custody to prepare a trial defense. In the first example from *The Life of Apollonius* 7.10, Damis reproaches Apollonius for *not* using his prison time to prepare a formal defense: "Then you are going to defend your life *extempore*?" In reply Apollonius clearly explains why he will not do so: "Yes, by Heaven, for it is an *extempore* life that I have always led."

Nevertheless, many of those imprisoned with Apollonius were taking advantage of the interval before their trials in order to prepare their defenses. So concentrated were they in this endeavor that Damis hesitates to interrupt them when Apollonius proposes to initiate conversation:

> "Let us talk, Damis, with the people here. For what else is there for us to do until the time comes when the despot will give me such audience as he desires?" "Will they not think us babblers," said Damis, "and bores, if we interrupt them in the preparation of their defense; and

moreover, it is a mistake to talk philosophy with men so broken in spirit as they." (*Life of Apollonius* 7.22)

The last clause in the preceding excerpt serves as a bridge to a consideration of the most fundamental endeavor for those prisoners experiencing the most severe forms of Roman custody: the effort to survive. As observed in the preceding sections, the more severe gradations of Roman custody were so opprobrious that survival itself was questionable. Would prisoners maintain the hope that they could eventually emerge from custody with a capacity for resuming their former lives? Or would their experience of confinement wear upon them so as to diminish their will to survive? The latter was the situation of the prisoners that Philostratus portrays in another scene from within Domitian's prison:

Some of them were sick, some of them had given way to dejection, some of them expected death with certainty and with resignation, some of them bewailed and called upon their children and their parents and their wives. (*Life of Apollonius* 7.26)

Presumably suicide was an alternative contemplated by many prisoners whose situation was one of grave suffering and scant hope. As observed above, the praetor Publius became so dispirited in his confinement (even though his custody was being supervised by his brother and was not severe) that he opened his veins with a penknife in an attempt at suicide.[22]

Prisoners held under adverse circumstances also presumably contemplated the possibility for escape, an endeavor for which the diligence and competence of the jailers and soldiers, or the lack thereof, was critical. Regarding the situation of guards and prison personnel in relation to escape, the *Digest* of Justinian reflects the practice of holding soldiers at risk for the prisoners in their custody. Sentences up to death could be imposed upon soldiers who cooperated unlawfully in the release of any prisoner.[23] Sentences up to death could also be sanctioned for soldiers who allowed a prisoner to escape due to negligence.[24]

As a concluding note to this chapter's presentation regarding the conditions of custody that obtained within the Roman empire of Paul's day, as well as conditions prior to and subsequent to Paul, it should be observed that Paul's own custody, as depicted in his letter to Philemon and in his letter to the Philippians, had a particular character not fully encompassed under the categories that have just been employed. Nevertheless, the material that has just been presented will prove to have considerable value in facilitating an appreciation for the specific situation(s) that Paul experienced as a prisoner.

CHAPTER FIVE

Images of Maiestas

INASMUCH AS THE MATERIAL now to be presented pertains to the imperial trial that is in the offing at the time of Philippians, this chapter could conceivably be positioned later in the book. Indeed, some readers may wish to defer consideration of this material until they have completed chapter ten below.

Nevertheless, since as the sources of this chapter are entirely extrabiblical, and since the excerpts included here are designed to suggest *images* for the fundamental issue underpinning Paul's trial, there is a logical basis for locating this chapter adjacent to chapter four. The present chapter is also similar to chapter four in that it adopts a suggestive and anecdotal approach to its topic.

For reasons that will become evident as this study proceeds, *maiestas* was almost certainly the principal charge that Paul faced in Nero's Rome. Accordingly, the objective of the present chapter is to familiarize the reader with various ancient writings that relate episodes involving *maiestas* during Nero's reign as well as during the reigns of emperors who preceded and succeeded him.

It should also be noted at this juncture that Apollonius, who is used to illustrate *maiestas* under both Nero and Domitian, is a figure whose historical journey is wrapped in obscurity. When Apollonius magically disappears from Domitian's courtroom at the end of this chapter, the reader may well wonder whether anything at all in Philostratus' presentation regarding Apollonius is grounded in historical reality.[1] To different degrees, similar reservations can also be expressed regarding the passages from Dio Cassius and Suetonius that are included below. Nevertheless, these various selections from ancient authors, especially when they are read thematically, serve to delineate the range of responses that an emperor, keenly sensitive regarding his *maiestas*, could have had to Paul.

1. The Development of Maiestas

"Treason" is the preferred English word for expressing the meaning of *maiestas*.[2] Both the republican and imperial statutes pertaining to *maiestas* had as their ultimate objective the prevention of treasonous conduct.

While originally restricted to certain specific forms of subversive activity, such as military revolt or collaboration with the enemy, *maiestas* eventually came to be interpreted as any type of conduct that diminished the "majesty" of the Roman people.

Very significantly, once the imperial era commenced, the majesty that could be violated or threatened by various forms of conduct was preeminently the majesty of the reigning emperor. But who determined that an activity represented such a violation of the emperor's majesty that its perpetrator should be liable to death or exile? From the onset of the imperial era, cases involving *maiestas* could be brought by the emperor to the senate for judgment or else be brought to the emperor himself by other magistrates. It is clear that real conspiracies and actual assassinations rendered those who held the imperial office highly sensitive to potential threats.[3] As illustrated below, however, it soon became commonplace for the slightest of remarks and gestures to be reckoned a diminution of imperial majesty.

2. Maiestas in the Era of Tiberius

Tacitus credits Tiberius with reviving the *lex maiestatis*, "the law of treason," and extending its applicability.[4] Tacitus also indicates, however, that Tiberius was reluctant to have the law applied in the cases of Falonius and Rubrius, the first two cases brought forward.

In their own assessments of how Tiberius wielded this law, Dio Cassius and Suetonius present reports that are far more damaging to the emperor. Conceivably the reports of these two authors may themselves be embellished. Yet, even allowing for possible exaggeration, it seems clear that Tiberius became so convinced of his own vulnerability that he considered it prudent to be aggressively vigilant regarding any development that could be construed as undermining his position.

In the first passage to be considered, Dio Cassius begins by recognizing the achievements that Tiberius has made in other areas of endeavor. He then reports that Tiberius vigorously pursued anyone who apparently diminished Tiberius' own reputation or that of his predecessor, Augustus:

> Up to this time, as we have seen, Tiberius had done a great many excellent things and had made but few errors; but now, when he no longer had a rival biding his chance, he changed to precisely the reverse of his previous conduct, which had included much that was good. Among other ways in which his rule became cruel, he pushed to the bitter end the trials for *maiestas,* in cases where complaint was made against anyone for committing any improper act, or uttering any improper speech, not only against Augustus but also against Tiberius himself and against his mother. (*Roman History* 57.19)

Suetonius' presentation of Tiberius' outlook in cases involving *maiestas* is similar in many respects to Dio Cassius'. Suetonius here moves beyond the general statements of Dio Cassius in the passage just cited by listing several of the acts that Tiberius caused to be reckoned as capital crimes, that is, offenses punishable by death or exile. In Suetonius' view, by attempting to safeguard the memory of Augustus, Tiberius was indirectly seeking to enhance his own imperial stature:

> It was at about this time that a praetor asked him whether he should have the courts convened to consider cases of lese-majesty; to which he replied that the laws must be enforced, and he did enforce them most rigorously. One man had removed the head from a statue of Augustus, to substitute that of another; the case was tried in the senate, and since the evidence was conflicting, the witnesses were examined by torture. After the defendant had been condemned, this kind of accusation gradually went so far that even such acts as these were regarded as capital crimes: to beat a slave near a statue of Augustus, or to change one's clothes there; to carry a ring or coin stamped with his image into a privy or a brothel, or to criticize any word or act of his. Finally, a man was put to death merely for allowing an honour to be voted him in his native town on the same day that honours had previously been voted to Augustus. (*The Lives of the Caesars: Tiberius* 3.58)

Finally, a later passage from Dio Cassius indicates that Tiberius'
behavior in this area became increasingly bizarre as his reign progressed. According to this report, Tiberius had numerous persons put
to death if their remarks or actions could be interpreted as in any way
lessening regard for himself. In time, Tiberius became increasingly
disoriented by the webs of treasonous behavior that he detected
around him. He ultimately began to allege treasonous comments pertaining to certain of his personal defects that were known to him
alone:

> Suffice it, then, to state, briefly, that many were put to death by him
> for such offences, and furthermore that while investigating carefully,
> case by case, all the slighting remarks that any persons were accused
> of having uttered about him, he was really calling himself all the evil
> names that men had invented. For even if a man made some remark
> secretly to a single companion, he would publish this, too, by having
> it entered in the public records; and often he falsely added, from his
> own consciousness of his defects, what no one had ever said, as if it
> had really been uttered, in order that he might appear to have every
> justification for his anger. Consequently it came to pass that he heaped
> upon himself all the abuse for which he was wont to punish others on
> the charge of *maiestas,* and incurred ridicule besides. For, when per-
> sons denied having uttered certain remarks, he, by insisting and
> swearing that they had been uttered, was more truly wronging him-
> self. On this very account some suspected that he was bereft of his
> senses. Yet he was not believed to be really insane because of this
> behaviour, since he handled all other matters in a thoroughly compe-
> tent manner. (*Roman History* 59.6)

3. Maiestas during the Reign of Gaius

Perhaps because he came to the imperial throne in circumstances of
vulnerability, as a young successor lacking in familiarity in the exercise of power, Gaius initially proceeded in a somewhat moderate
manner in the area of *maiestas*. Or rather, according to the report
given by Dio Cassius, Gaius appeared to behave moderately:

> He did away with the complaints for *maiestas,* which he saw were the
> commonest cause of the prisoners' present plight, and he heaped up
> and burned (or so he pretended) the papers pertaining to their cases

that Tiberius had left, declaring: "I have done this in order that, no matter how strongly I may some day desire to harbour malice against any one for my mother's and my brothers' sake, I shall nevertheless be unable to punish him." For this he was commended, as it was expected that he would be truthful above all else; for by reason of his youth it was not thought possible that he could be guilty of duplicity in thought or speech. (*Roman History* 59.6)

Gaius' true character was not long in manifesting itself, however. His cruelty and viciousness soon became apparent as did his arrogance and callousness. No longer was there any reluctance as regards *maiestas*. Trifling occurrences were judged to be violations of Gaius' majesty, and Romans of various walks of life were now readily consigned to death on these grounds.

The passage now to be cited from Dio Cassius indicates the large number put to death and also indicates Gaius' delusions about his divinity. Apparently Gaius still gave lip service to the idea that he would not condemn anyone to death in an arbitrary manner:

Though he put an end to the charges of *maiestas,* he nevertheless made these the cause of a great many persons' downfall. Again, though, according to his own account, he had given up his anger against those who had conspired against his father and mother and brothers, and even burned their letters, he yet put to death great numbers of them on the strength of those letters. He did, it is true, actually destroy some letters, but they were not the originals containing the absolute proof, but rather copies that he had made. Furthermore, though he at first forbade any one to set up images of him, he even went on to manufacture statues himself; and though he once requested the annulment of a decree ordering sacrifices to be offered to his Fortune, and even caused this action of his to be inscribed on a tablet, he afterwards ordered temples to be erected and sacrifices to be offered to himself as to a god. (*Roman History* 59.4)

Dio Cassius provides one further report concerning this issue. This report pertains to the selling of hot water as a treasonous activity! To give the most favorable interpretation to Gaius' decree, prohibiting the sale of hot water may have been intended as a measure to reduce public drunkenness.[5] Apparently, it was a custom in Rome at this time for hot water flavored with spices or herbs to be served along with wine. Yet regardless of any ameliorating factors that may have been present, it is evident that Dio Cassius considered it an incredible travesty that anyone be condemned to death for selling hot water:

> One single incident will give the key to all that happened at that time; the emperor charged with *maiestas* and put to death a man who had sold hot water. (*Roman History* 59.12)

4. Claudius' Initial Intention Regarding Maiestas

In an effort to make a radical break with the patterns of Tiberius and Gaius, Claudius initially abolished the charge of *maiestas* and ordered release for those who had been imprisoned on this charge by his predecessors. Dio Cassius describes Claudius' initial approach in this matter in the following terms:

> He abolished the charge of *maiestas* not only in the case of writings but in the case of overt acts as well, and punished no one on this ground for offenses committed either before this time or later. . . .
>
> Of the persons in prison—and a very large number were thus confined—he liberated those who had been put there for *maiestas* and similar charges, but punished those who were guilty of actual wrongdoing. For he investigated all the cases very carefully, in order that those who had committed crimes should not be released along with those who had been falsely accused, nor the latter, on the other hand, perish along with the former. (*Roman History* 60.3-4)

Within the context just indicated, the circumstances of Lucius Vitellius' case should now be considered. From the reports of Tacitus especially and also Suetonius, it emerges that, near the end of his life, this former consul was denounced for having aspirations regarding empery. Tacitus indicates that, at this point in time, Claudius was inclined to take this charge of *maiestas* seriously and proceed against Vitellius. In this instance, however, Claudius' new wife, Agrippina, intervened and persuaded him to reject the accusation against Vitellius and to interdict Junius Lupus for having brought this accusation in the first place.[6]

Suetonius' passage concerning Lucius Vitellius does not explicitly indicate that this consul was denounced for *maiestas*. In describing the actions taken by the senate after Vitellius' death, however, Suetonius' report can be interpreted as indicating that *maiestas* had been at issue at some point in Vitellius' career. Suetonius relates that the senate honored Vitellius with a public funeral and accorded him a statue on the rostra bearing the following inscription: *Pietatis Immobilis erga Principem*, "Of Unwavering Loyalty to His Emperor."[7] Clearly the wording of this inscription emphasizes the steadfast loyalty that is the antithesis of treasonous conduct.

Whatever his initial concerns for ending denunciations for *maiestas*, Claudius departed from these convictions as his reign progressed. Like his predecessors, Claudius had reason to fear conspiracies against his own life. And, as time progressed, various individuals thought to be disloyal were put to death as a result of Claudius' decisions. In the end, Claudius' own death came about not at the hands of rivals outside of his palace but seemingly from within, possibly from poisoning instigated by Agrippina, the niece who had become his wife.[8] Significantly, Agrippina was also Nero's mother and zealous for her son's ascendancy and for her own.

5. *Maiestas under Nero*

It will be explicated in chapter ten that Nero's obsession with his status and his prerogatives expressed itself in a multiplicity of forms. In the present section the focus is narrower. Here the object of the presentation is only to indicate that, during Nero's reign, *maiestas* continued as a legal mechanism for protecting the emperor's position and prerogatives.

In *The Annals* Tacitus makes reference to two cases in which Nero invoked *maiestas*.[9] In addition, two selections from the writings of Philostratus will now be considered. Both of these excerpts portray "impiety" toward Nero, that is, behavior that was taken to diminish his status as the sovereign. Both selections indicate how the safeguarding of Nero's majesty could indeed be carried to fantastic extremes.

Given that Philostratus wrote these passages approximately 150 years after Nero's death and given that *The Life of Apollonius* is characterized by many fanciful reconstructions, can any degree of credibility be attached to either of these selections in terms of historical reliability? Is anything regarding Nero's historical practice regarding *maiestas* reflected in these accounts? Given the negative responses offered by many specialists in the writings of Philostratus, any affirmative response to these questions must be given guardedly and tentatively.[10] Certainly Philostratus' penchant for inventing scenes and constructing dialogues must be recognized. Nevertheless, on the grounds that Philostratus, as a member of the Severan court, presumably had access to documents and received traditions regarding Nero's reign,[11] and on the grounds that his portrayal of Nero's fanatical concern with *maiestas* is consistent with the portrayal of this emperor given by other ancient authors,[12] these two passages may be taken as circumscribed testimony that denunciations for *maiestas* were a feature of Nero's reign just as they had been a feature of the regimes of his predecessors. In other words, Nero's ardent concern with his own *maiestas* is alleged within these passages even if Apollonius himself is portrayed in a highly exaggerated way.

In the first passage, Apollonius and those of his associates who have not been intimidated by the warnings given them approach Rome and encounter a drunken minstrel. This troubadour, a comic figure, had been hired to perform songs that were composed by Nero. But there is a potentially ominous dimension to the minstrel's drunken warbling. For anyone who did not respect the Neronian compositions performed by this minstrel could be denounced for *maiestas*:

> And they put up at an inn close to the gate, and were taking their supper, for it was already eventide, when a drunken fellow with a far from harsh voice turned up as it were for a revel; and he was one it seems who was in the habit of going round about Rome singing Nero's songs and hired for the purpose, and anyone who neglected to listen to him or refused to pay him for his music, he had the right to arrest for violating Nero's *majesty*. . . . As they listened with some indifference, he proceeded to accuse them of violating Nero's *majesty* and of being enemies of his divine voice; but they paid no attention to him. Then Menippus asked Apollonius how he appreciated these remarks, whereupon he said: "How do I appreciate them? Why, just as I did his songs. Let us, however, O Menippus, not take too much offence at his remarks, but let us give him something for his performance and dismiss him to sacrifice to the Muses of Nero." (*Life of Apollonius* 4.39; emphasis added)

In the second passage Philostratus portrays Apollonius as having been denounced on a different charge of *maiestas* to Tigellinus, the

prefect of the praetorian guard and Nero's chief lieutenant. Apollonius' offense in this instance has been to rebuke the folly of those
who flocked to the pagan temples anxious over Nero's swollen
throat and harsh voice. He has thus been guilty of "impiety" or
maiestas:

> Just then a distemper broke out in Rome, called by the physicians
> influenza; and it was attended, it seems, by coughings, and the voice
> of speakers was affected by it. Now the temples were full of people
> supplicating the gods, because Nero had a swollen throat, and his
> voice was hoarse. But Apollonius vehemently denounced the folly of
> the crowd, though without rebuking anyone in particular; nay, he
> even restrained Menippus, who was irritated by such goings on, and
> persuaded him to moderate his indignation, urging him to pardon the
> gods if they did show pleasure in the mimes of buffoons. This utter-
> ance was reported to Tigellinus, who immediately sent police to take
> him to prison, and summoned him to defend himself from the charge
> of *impiety* against Nero. And an accuser was retained against him who
> had already undone a great many people, and won a number of such
> Olympic victories. This accuser too held in his hands a scroll of paper
> on which the charge was written out, and he brandished it like a
> sword against the sage, and declared that it was so sharp that it would
> slay and ruin him. (*Life of Apollonius* 4.44)

6. *Apollonius and Maiestas under Domitian*

During Nero's reign, Apollonius adroitly outmaneuvered his
accusers and Tigellinus and departed from Rome unharmed. According to Philostratus' narrative, the sage engaged in a variety of endeavors and pursuits relating to philosophy over the next three decades.
His journeys brought him to various parts of the empire, but not
until the reign of Domitian did he return to Rome. Within Philostratus' dramatic narrative, it was an auspicious return.

It should again be noted that Philostratus' embellishments are
present to such a degree that virtually every scene he portrays should
be carefully scrutinized. Certainly two descriptions pertaining to
Domitian's era, that is, the account of Apollonius miraculously
removing his leg from the leg chains and then reinserting it and, even
more memorably, the report that, in the midst of the formal trial,

Apollonius simply vanished from Domitian's courtroom, both indicate that Philostratus can freely insert fantastic occurrences within his narrative.

Nevertheless, given his own location at the imperial court, it is likely that Philostratus was well informed about Domitian's character and his practices. And thus it is admissible to hold that he plausibly portrays Domitian's attitude toward *maiestas* and that he also provides a plausible description of Domitian's initiatives against those imprisoned on this charge.[13]

That Apollonius has been charged with *maiestas* is a fundamental feature of the situation that Philostratus portrays. The charges against him arose from the allegation that he offered support for a conspiracy against Domitian that would bring Nerva to the imperial throne.[14] In the context of this denunciation, Apollonius was explicitly accused of having "uttered certain sentiments to the detriment of the sovereign, some of them openly, some of them obscurely and privately, and some of them in the pretense that you learned them from heaven." Additionally, the philosopher was assailed for his "style of dress" and for his "way of living in general."[15]

Philostratus provides an extended account of Apollonius' interactions with varying persons in Domitian's employ as well as with Domitian himself. Elements of his narrative that are of particular interest to the present study will be investigated under the following headings: (a) arrest and initial imprisonment; (b) the preliminary hearing before Domitian; (c) subsequent imprisonment; (d) the formal trial. It should be recalled that an analysis of Philostratus' description of the two prisons into which Apollonius was consigned, the severe prison with chains and the less severe prison without chains, has been made in chapter four of this study. That analysis should be kept in mind here along with the previous mention of those prisoners who utilized their time in prison in order to prepare their defenses.

With respect to Apollonius' arrest, a significant feature is that Aelian, the person portrayed functioning as chief lieutenant for Domitian, had previously been on friendly terms with Apollonius in Egypt. Aelian had first attempted to deflect Domitian's hostility from Apollonius and, subsequent to the philosopher's arrest, Aelian spoke secretly with Apollonius, indicating what limited assistance he, Aelian, might be able to provide. The following excerpt gives

Aelian's summary of Domitian's outlook concerning Apollonius as well as that of Nerva and others with whom Apollonius was allegedly linked:

> Now what his verdict will be in your case I do not know; but his temper is that of people who are anxious to condemn a person, but are ashamed to do so except upon some real evidence, and he wishes to make you an excuse for destroying these men of consular rank. So his wishes you see are criminal, but he observes a certain formality in his actions in order to preserve a semblance of justice. (*Life of Apollonius* 7.28)

Once Apollonius was remanded to prison he received not one but two anonymous visitors. The first was an informer whom Domitian himself had sent with a view to entrapping the philosopher through his own words. This ruse was quickly detected by Apollonius. The second was an emissary from Aelian who provided information regarding the preliminary hearing with Domitian to which Apollonius would be summoned. This emissary counseled Apollonius not to be taken aback or frightened by the emperor's physical appearance, which was disagreeable and ominous, or by the deepness of Domitian's speaking voice.

Not long after the departure of the second emissary, an imperial notary arrived at the prison summoning Apollonius for his interview. This notary emphasized that the interview was preliminary to the formal trial and told Apollonius pointedly that Domitian desired "to see you and find out who you are. . . ."[16]

This intimation that Apollonius' full being would be under Domitian's scrutiny is confirmed in the conversation that Apollonius subsequently held with his trusted friend Damis. Damis worried whether Apollonius should, without a prepared text, defend "the course of his life" (*hyper tou biou*).[17] As has been previously indicated, Apollonius replied that he would do so.

When this preliminary hearing took place, Domitian did indeed delve into various aspects of Apollonius' life as a philosopher.[18] But he soon directly referred to the accusation concerning Nerva's conspiracy and Apollonius' complicity in it. Apollonius denied the validity of these charges and boldly suggested that Domitian would be conducting the trial with prejudice if he already believed such slander. At this point Domitian became angry and insulting, ordering that Apollonius' hair and beard be cut off and that he be reimprisoned "among the vilest felons" pending his trial.[19]

After Apollonius had been confined for two days, Domitian sent a second spy into the prison in another effort to secure evidence for use at the trial. This spy, a man from Syracuse, attempted to bait Apollonius with mocking questions such as: "And how can your legs endure the weight of the fetters?"[20] Apollonius, however, again circumvented the entrapment, responding in the following fashion:

> Now Apollonius understood that the Syracusan was trying to drive him into some such admission as the Emperor had tried to get out of him, and that he imagined that out of sheer weariness of his imprisonment he would tell some falsehood to the detriment of his friends, and accordingly he answered: "My excellent friend, if I have been cast into prison for telling Domitian the truth, what would happen to me if I refrained from telling it? For he apparently regards truth as something to be punished with imprisonment, just as I regard falsehood." (*Life of Apollonius* 7.36)

Following the departure of the spy, Apollonius discoursed to Damis on the nature of freedom.[21] It was at this juncture in the narrative that Apollonius removed his leg from the chains and then reinserted it in order to demonstrate his complete freedom. After this, an official messenger arrived announcing that Apollonius was to be transferred to the prison without chains for the time remaining before his trial. Apollonius then dismissed Damis, bidding that he travel to the town of Dicaearchia and wait for him there. This step was, in retrospect, a preparation for Apollonius' plan to vanish from Domitian's courtroom and reappear in Dicaearchia.

Several features from Philostratus' account of the actual trial deserve attention. In the first passage to be cited, it is significant that the legal arrangements call for Apollonius to face a prosecutor with Domitian himself taking the role of judge over the proceedings. It is also to be noted that Apollonius bridles at these arrangements, contending that the emperor himself should be subject to philosophy's judgment! In the following excerpt Apollonius is conversing with the secretary who is conducting him into the courtroom:

> "Whom am I going to plead against?" "Why," said the other, "against your accuser, of course, and the Emperor will be judge." "And," said

Apollonius, "who is going to be judge between myself and the Emperor?" For I shall prove that he is wronging philosophy." "And what concern," said the other, "has the Emperor for philosophy, even if he does happen to do her wrong?" "Nay, but philosophy," said Apollonius, "is much concerned about the Emperor, that he should govern as he should." (*Life of Apollonius* 8.2)

According to Philostratus' account of the proceedings, Apollonius' trial was held with full protocol. Given the focus of the present study, not all of what transpired before Apollonius vanished from the tribunal needs to be presented. One element, however, from within the following excerpt does deserve emphasis. It is the conflict that arose from the prosecutor's homage to Domitian as "the god of all mankind" (*ton apantōn anthrōpōn theon*), certainly a deifying reference. Apollonius would not concur with the premise that Domitian possessed such status and refused to accord him such acclaim:

Such were the preliminary skirmishes which preceded the trial, but the conduct of the trial itself was as follows: The court was fitted up as if for an audience listening to a panegyrical discourse; and all the illustrious men of the city were present at the trial, because the Emperor was intent upon proving before as many people as possible that Apollonius was an accomplice of Nerva and his friends. Apollonius, however, ignored the Emperor's presence so completely as not even to glance at him; and when his accuser upbraided him for want of respect, and bade him turn his eyes upon the god of all mankind, Apollonius raised his eyes to the ceiling, by way of giving a hint that he was looking up to Zeus, and that he regarded the recipient of such profane flattery as worse than he who administered it. (*Life of Apollonius* 8.4)

The preceding paragraphs analyzing the encounter between Apollonius and Domitian conclude the present chapter's examination of the imperial charge of *maiestas*. It is again to be emphasized that the objective of the present chapter has been to provide a suggestive, rather than comprehensive, treatment of this subject. The images of *maiestas* that have been presented function to promote a sensitivity for the personal encounter that probably occurred between Paul and Nero. Indeed, the task of chapters nine, ten, and eleven of this study will be to focus attention on various aspects of Paul's situation as he awaited imperial trial in Nero's Rome.

CHAPTER SIX

Roman Imprisonment and Paul's Letter to Philemon

THE TASK OF THE present chapter is to undertake an analysis of Paul's shortest composition, his letter to Philemon. Comprising only twenty-five verses, it manifestly differs from the letter to the Romans in terms of length. Philemon is also to be distinguished fundamentally from Romans because of the circumstances in which it was composed. For, as its very first words make evident, Philemon was composed while Paul was a chained Roman prisoner!

Once it is recognized that a situation of Roman imprisonment is the venue for this letter, the rationale for the presentation made in chapter four becomes apparent. Indeed, the categories used for analyzing Roman custody in chapter four will now be used in analyzing Paul's own custody as it is reflected in this brief communication. It must be cautioned at the outset that Paul's letter is silent regarding many aspects of his situation; nevertheless the letter still does provide significant information that takes on added meaning in the light of chapter four's analysis.

The plan of the present chapter is as follows. In the initial section a careful study will be made of the two instances within the letter in which Paul refers to his chains *per se* and to the three instances in which he refers to his status as a prisoner. It will emerge from this analysis that Paul's self-description as a prisoner in chains is central to the appeal that he is addressing to Philemon. The next two sections of this chapter will then provide a fuller description of Paul's context by utilizing the categories of chapter four. In these sections an analysis will be made regarding the technical form of custody that

Paul was experiencing and regarding the various factors that pertained to his health and survival. Particular attention will be given to the role of Paul's friends in support of him and also to Paul's own endeavors while he remained a prisoner.

In the fourth section of this chapter it will be argued that Paul's letter to Philemon was written significantly *after* his letter to the Romans. While the arguments of this section are still to be made, it is appropriate to signal here that a Romans-then-Philemon sequence possesses great significance within the present study. For, as this work progresses, focused attention will be given to the impact that Paul's imprisonment had on his ministry and outlook. Paul's chains came on him in a way fully unanticipated at the time of Romans, and these chains profoundly altered his consciousness of the witness and service to which he was being called.

1. Paul's Self-Image as a Chained Prisoner

Before considering the striking manner in which Paul portrays himself to Philemon, it is useful to reflect on the Roman world in which Paul was imprisoned and Philemon was located. It is also useful to conjecture, in a preliminary way, whether Philemon was informed about Paul's imprisonment prior to receiving his letter.

At the time of the letter it is virtually certain that Philemon and Paul were both located within the boundaries of the Roman empire. This insight, so evident on a moment's reflection, has frequently been neglected by scholars who have commented on this letter and the other Pauline prison letters.[1] Yet where else did Paul establish faith communities and where else did he travel, save within the confines of the Roman empire?

Once it is grasped that Roman rule is the pervasive context for Paul's personal situation at the time of this letter, the way is prepared for two additional specific insights regarding the circumstances of his confinement. When his letter to Philemon is read with a due regard for the surrounding Roman atmosphere, it emerges (a) that Paul's confinement must have been ordered by those with Roman authority and (b) that the arrangements under which Paul is being held are not extralegal but actually in conformity with the procedures authorized under the Roman system.

Paul's statement in v. 10 of the letter that he has "begotten"

Onesimus as his spiritual son is an indication that his confinement
has endured over an extended interval of time.[2] In its turn, this
insight allows for the inference that Roman officials themselves were
the ones who decreed his imprisonment. For, within the confines of
the empire ruled by Rome, what authorities other than the Romans
possessed the capability for imposing *extended* imprisonment?

It is well to underscore this point by noting that neither the
Jerusalem temple authorities nor officials at any of the synagogues
scattered throughout the empire would have possessed the authority
for imprisoning someone in such a fashion. Similarly, any client ruler
keeping prisoners in chains for an extended period of time necessarily would have possessed at least tacit Roman authorization.

Further, when Philemon is read from beginning to end, is it not the
sense of the letter as a whole that Paul is being kept in custody under
arrangements and procedures that are in accord with the prevailing
norms? Careful phrasings and subtle nuances characterize this letter.
Yet, there is not so much as a single allusion to suggest that Paul considers himself *procedurally* mistreated. Paul's fascination that he has
become a *prisoner* is well attested in the letter. But as to *who* is keeping him in custody and *how* they are detaining him, there is no sense
of astonishment.

Did Philemon learn of Paul's imprisonment only when Paul's letter reached him?[3] Since Paul had already been in chains for a significant interval of time prior to writing,[4] it is possible that Philemon
could have already received information about Paul's situation by
means of oral reports or even other letters. Conceivably specific
reports from Timothy or from one of the co-workers named by Paul
in v. 24 may have reached Philemon and his household in advance of
Paul's letter.

If Philemon and his community did not know that Paul was being
held prisoner by the Roman authorities, what was their reaction to
the first words of Paul's letter? On the one hand, they held Paul in
high esteem, and they knew that he was not a criminal. On the other
hand, it could be startling, even disconcerting, to learn that Paul was
now under Roman guard, bound with chains. Such news even had
the potential to make the most loyal of Paul's associates ashamed
of him.[5]

Even if Philemon already knew of Paul's imprisonment, the challenge facing Paul was still a considerable one. His principal purpose

was to appeal to Philemon on behalf of Onesimus, but Philemon would surely be expecting Paul to say something about his own circumstances. What to say about his imprisonment? What to say about his chains? For how long a time did Paul ponder and pray over the tack he should take?

In the actual writing, Paul pursued a course of utter directness! That is, he boldly identified himself as a prisoner in the first words that he wrote. In this unflinching opening, Paul simultaneously emphasized his continuing commitment to Christ. He was now *a prisoner*, but it was *for Christ Jesus* that he was in chains! With just four momentous words did Paul thus begin: *Paulos desmios Christou Iēsou* ("Paul, a prisoner for Christ Jesus"). With these opening words, he succeeded in conveying, in a breathtaking fashion, the profoundly new identity that he had come to possess.

The term that Paul uses to describe himself here, *desmios* ("prisoner"), is also the term that he uses in referring to himself in v. 9. It is important to note that the *desm-* root for this word possesses the fundamental meaning of "binding." Thus, when Paul refers to himself as a *prisoner* in these two instances, the foundational meaning is that he is now someone bound against his will.[6]

The contrast that this self-designation makes with Paul's opening self-descriptions in such letters as 1 and 2 Corinthians and Galatians should not escape notice. In these other letters, Paul is extremely conscious of his standing as an *apostle*. He emphasizes his apostolic calling and status at the outset of each letter, and then, as each letter unfolds, he invokes this credential in persuading and exhorting those to whom he writes. The same pattern holds true for his letter to Philemon, except for the fact that Paul's status is now that of a chained prisoner. This is the "credential" that he will now invoke in seeking to persuade and exhort Philemon. Paul's literal chains thus become a crucial frame of reference for the argument he advances within the body of the letter. The essence of his appeal is that Paul does not want Onesimus to be literally or figuratively placed in the chains that Paul himself now wears!

As mentioned, the second time that Paul identifies himself as a prisoner is in v. 9. This second reference is couched in such a way as to once again confront Paul's readers with the unexpected change of status that Paul has experienced as he has perdured in faithful service to Christ. In v. 9 Paul first indicates that he has become a *presbytēs* ("an old man") in his service of Christ.[7] He then imparts that he is also a prisoner, utilizing an adverb-conjunction combination, "and now" (*nuni de*), to connect "prisoner" strikingly with "old man." The intensity generated by this juxtaposition of memorable images may have been equally significant for Paul and Philemon.[8] Paul's exact wording is as follows: "I, Paul, an old man, and now a prisoner also. . . ."

To grasp just how central Paul's status as a prisoner is for the request he addresses to Philemon, vv. 9 and 10 of the letter need to be translated with attention focused on the manner in which Paul twice employs the Greek word *parakalō* ("I appeal"). Coupled with the first use of this verb is Paul's explanation concerning the person making the appeal. It is precisely here that Paul designates himself as "an old man and now a prisoner also."

Coupled with his second use of *parakalō* is Paul's explanation regarding the person *for whom* Paul appeals. Philemon's own slave, Onesimus, is now at Paul's side. Further, a striking, wonderful development has occurred regarding Onesimus: he has become a Christian with Paul as his spiritual father.[9] Remarkably, this development has occurred during the interval in which Paul has been kept in chains!

The following translation seeks to convey the rhetorical force of Paul's Greek in vv. 9b and 10. The four features of Paul's phrasing deserving particular attention are placed in italics in the translation:

> *I appeal* as Paul, an old man, and now *a prisoner* for Christ Jesus. *I appeal* concerning my child Onesimus, whom I have fathered *in chains*. (Phlm 9b-10)

In the translation just given, *en tois desmois* has been rendered "in chains" and in the comments above regarding Paul's situation it has been emphasized that he was literally bound with chains. Far too often translators have opted to translate *desmos* with its *secondary* meaning of "imprisonment."[10] Such a translation lamentably obscures a crucial element in Paul's actual circumstances, that is, that he is physically bound with metal chains.

Indeed, the decisive role that Paul's chains play in defining his circumstances must be emphasized. Paul is undergoing "imprisonment" not because he is being kept in a prison per se but rather because he is being kept *in chains*. The Roman authorities have not consigned Paul to a *carcer* or a quarry but rather have ordered that he be kept in chained custody at an undetermined place. Paul's chains (and his guards) are what fundamentally establish his confinement. He is "imprisoned" because of his chains. And thus does he speak of having fathered Onesimus while *in chains*.

Just as Paul's references to himself as a prisoner in v. 1 and in v. 9 and his references to his chains in v. 10 all provide encouragement for Philemon to act generously toward Onesimus, so too does Paul's reference to his chains in v. 13. In this latter occurrence Paul presents from a slightly different angle his case for Onesimus' release, reflecting on the fact that Onesimus has been rendering valuable service to Paul *while Paul has endured his chains*. Now, however, Paul is again acting with generosity *toward Philemon*! Paul, *remaining in chains*, now freely sends Onesimus, whom he regards with significant affection, back to Philemon.[11]

Paul's phrasing in v. 13 and elsewhere in the letter indicates the extremely positive rapport that exists between himself and Philemon. Philemon's personal indebtedness to Paul is well established within the letter and Philemon's gratitude could seemingly have constituted a sufficient basis for Paul's appeal. Nevertheless, within this verse Paul once again references his chains, implicitly making them a basis for his appeal.[12] Paul could have continued to benefit from Onesimus' service and could even have interpreted it as a service contributed by *Philemon*. Yet he has now made the decision to continue witnessing to the gospel *in chains* without Onesimus' assistance.[13] In such a nuanced fashion does Paul thus indicate his own willingness to be deprived of Onesimus' service:

> I would have liked to keep him with me in order that he might serve me, *in chains for the gospel,* on your behalf. (Phlm 13; author's translation)

Paul has now referred to his confinement and his chains four times within thirteen verses. Nevertheless, when he pens the conclusion of the letter a few verses later, Paul does not refrain from making one final reference to his controversial status. Before expressing his own closing benediction, Paul conveys Epaphras' greetings to Philemon. Such a sharing of greetings from other Christians is Paul's common practice at the end of his letters. In this instance, however, he desig-

74

PAUL IN CHAINS

nates Epaphras with the unusual term of esteem, *synaichmalōtos* ("fellow prisoner"). Paul's exact wording is as follows: "Epaphras, *my fellow prisoner* in Christ Jesus, sends greeting to you" (Phlm 23; emphasis added).

It is important to consider Paul's intended meaning in employing this term. In what sense is Epaphras Paul's "fellow prisoner"? Could Epaphras also have been in Roman custody, confined in the same location where Paul was confined? Such a situation of two associates, both under chains, cannot be ruled out; but two considerations argue against such an understanding of Paul's situation.

First, if Paul were signaling that Epaphras was a prisoner in chains and physically proximate to Paul, then the Greek word *syndesmos* (literally, "someone sharing chains") would have been the more apt Greek word for him to employ. Second, the nuances of the letter as a whole seem to indicate that Paul now finds himself in an unprecedented, solitary witness on Christ's behalf. Would Paul have written of his chains and his imprisonment in such a personal, dramatic fashion if Epaphras and he had *both* been bound with chains?

A more probable interpretation is that *synaichmalōtos* is used here to affirm that Epaphras shared in the experience of Paul's imprisonment in a way that the other members of Paul's support circle did not. Without being chained in the manner that Paul was chained, Epaphras may have shared voluntarily in some of the other material conditions of Paul's imprisonment.[14]

Under this interpretation, Epaphras, moved by the desire to support his chained mentor, tried to share in Paul's circumstances to the degree that it was possible and appropriate for him to do so. Conceivably, he may have received permission to remain near to Paul, assisting with many facets of the prisoner's daily regimen. Possibly, he may have undertaken to prepare or bring meals for Paul. It is not to be ruled out that Epaphras even served as Paul's scribe, for the service of such an assistant is seemingly indicated by v. 19.[15]

Whatever Epaphras' precise relationship with Paul at this juncture, at least two things are clear. First, Paul expresses a definite appreciation for Epaphras in speaking of him as *synaichmalōtos*.[16] Second, by using this precise term, Paul again reminds Philemon of Paul's own status. At the end of his letter, by highlighting Epaphras' role as an esteemed fellow prisoner, Paul underscores that he himself remains *the prisoner*.

2. Known and Unknown Aspects
of Paul's Circumstances

When the letter to Philemon is surveyed for signs of Roman custody arrangements, certain features are immediately evident. At the same time, other aspects remain in obscurity with the result that a full reconstruction of Paul's situation cannot be achieved.

A. Roman Custody

In the preceding section it was mentioned that Paul was not consigned to a *carcer* or a quarry, the structures commonly used by the Romans as places of severe confinement. Such severe circumstances would not have allowed Paul the freedom for instructing Onesimus, for actually writing to Philemon, or for keeping in good contact with Timothy, Epaphras, and four other co-workers. Also Paul's confinement in the letter to Philemon does not seem to be physically burdening to him, something that would not have been the case if he had been confined in a *carcer* or quarry. Given these considerations it seems secure to assume that Paul was actually being held in *custodia militaris* ("military custody"), a less severe confinement.

To be sure, Paul is chained! This feature of his situation is what renders military custody more likely than the third category, *custodia liberis* ("free custody").

Some mechanism of supervision is essential for an individual remanded to chains. What procedures will be followed to house and feed such a prisoner, to oversee the comings and goings of visitors, to monitor the prisoner during the night? In writing to Philemon, Paul does not comment regarding those who are supervising his custody. Nevertheless, the presence of guards must be presumed. In effect, Roman soldiers were responsible for keeping Paul securely confined and for monitoring all aspects of his situation.

B. Factors Affecting Paul's Health and Survival

While Paul makes multiple references to his chains, he makes virtually no other references to his material circumstances as a Roman prisoner. Such a presentation is probably due to the fact that Paul

presumed Philemon's general familiarity with the phenomenon of
Roman imprisonment. Nevertheless, the result is that contemporary
readers who desire to appreciate the specific material conditions of
Paul's imprisonment find themselves exploring a *via negativa* in their
efforts to gain an appreciation for the circumstances affecting Paul's
health and his prospects for survival.

What constituted Paul's diet during the interval in which Philemon
was written? Who prepared the meals that he ate? And under what
conditions did he eat them? Such questions can be posed regarding
the conditions faced by any Roman prisoner. Paul himself sheds no
direct light on these issues concerning diet and sustenance.

With respect to the sanitary and hygienic conditions that Paul experienced, the letter to Philemon is also silent. Was the place where Paul
was confined free from filth and vermin? Were fresh air and sunlight
a part of his surroundings? Was he sufficiently free from cold and
dampness and from debilitating heat? Did he have access to a latrine
and to fresh water for bathing? What were his conditions for sleeping? Such factors, normally important considerations with respect to
a prisoner's well-being, are not touched on within Philemon.

Finally, precisely how was Paul chained and guarded? As just
argued, Paul's confinement was supervised by Roman soldiers. On
the one hand, he might have been physically chained to one or more
soldiers during the day and or during the night. On the other hand,
Paul's chains may have fastened him to a wall or have been of such a
weight and encumbrance that their very physicality restricted his
movements. If either of these latter situations pertained, then the
Roman soldiers who guarded him may not have been immediately
proximate to him at all times. Rather, their assigned position may
have been at the entrance to Paul's place of confinement.

While Paul's chains are extremely significant for the appeal that he
addresses to Philemon, he never remarks whether he was bound in
hand chains, leg chains, body chains or, as just mentioned, secured to
a Roman soldier. He never indicates whether his chains are heavy,
whether they chafe him, or that they cause him physical pain. Again,
Paul may have assumed that Philemon and his circle would be familiar with the type of chains employed by the Roman authorities in
such circumstances.[17] At any event, it is the very *fact* that he is
bound, and not any specific attribute of his chains, that is fundamental to his letter.

C. Informers, Other Prisoners, and Censorship

As indicated above, Paul uses the term *synaichmalōtos* ("fellow prisoner") in acclaiming Epaphras in v. 23. However, for the reasons mentioned, it is improbable that Epaphras was actually imprisoned with Paul. Was Paul possibly confined with other prisoners who were not Christians? This subject is not touched on in Paul's letter. The related topic of informers and spies present among a group of prisoners is also not accessible given the contents of this letter.

What can be said regarding the possibility that Paul's letter was itself subject to censorship? This issue is akin to the topic of informers and spies inasmuch as such forms of surveillance were certainly open to the Roman authorities. Did Paul need to have permission in advance to write a letter of this type? Once it was complete, did such a letter have to pass review before it could be sent? It should be noted in passing that the careful nuances of Philemon are all the more significant if it was the case that this letter had to be reviewed by the authorities supervising Paul's case! Once Paul finalized the text, what were the next steps in the process of transmitting this letter to Philemon?

D. The Assistance of Friends

The question of possible censorship of the letter becomes even more complex when it is observed that Timothy is named as a co-sender of this letter. As previously discussed, Paul forthrightly describes himself as a prisoner in v. 1a. In v. 1b Timothy is referred to as "our brother," but there is no indication that he is a prisoner. Still, Paul's words seem to imply that Timothy is at Paul's side or is at least in close proximity to him at the time of the letter.[18]

Presumably, this opening reference to Timothy serves to assure Philemon and his circle that Paul has not been isolated from his network of friends and co-ministers despite his new circumstances as a prisoner in chains. In addition to Timothy, the closing of the letter indicates that Paul is in contact with five other Christians.

In v. 23 Epaphras, Paul's "fellow prisoner," sends greetings to Philemon and in v. 24 so also do Mark, Aristarchus, Demas, and Luke. These latter four persons are designated "my fellow workers" (*hoi synergoi mou*), but Paul does not explicate his use of this term.

It seems that Paul must be in ongoing contact with these disciples at the time of the letter. Probably these four co-workers were physically proximate to the place of Paul's confinement.[19]

No definite conclusion can be drawn about the exact situation that Paul was experiencing or regarding the degree of support that he was receiving from these four associates. If Mark, Aristarchus, Demas and Luke were themselves present at the site where Paul was kept in chains, however, then Paul was actually receiving support from at least seven persons at the time when he wrote to Philemon! In addition to Timothy and Epaphras, Onesimus, the very person on whom the letter focuses, must be counted at this point. For, regarding Onesimus, Paul states in v. 13, "I would have been glad to keep him with me, *in order that he might serve me on your behalf....*"[20]

These conjectures and surmises regarding a sizeable group of associates present at Paul's side give rise to an additional set of questions. Where were the various members of such a support group living? How often could they visit Paul? What concrete forms of assistance and support were they able to give to him? The implication of v. 13 (just cited) is that Onesimus in particular has rendered definite service to Paul. Also, as previously mentioned, v. 19 implies that Paul was assisted with the actual writing of the letter by an unnamed person serving as his secretary.

3. Paul's Endeavors as a Prisoner

That Paul was able to conduct at least some forms of Christian ministry during the period of his custody is evident from what he has already been able to accomplish on Onesimus' behalf and from what he is striving now to accomplish. Paul has been instrumental in forming Onesimus as a Christian. As observed previously, v. 10 of the letter reads, "I appeal to you for my child Onesimus whom I have begotten in chains." This "begetting" of Onesimus as a fledgling Christian represents a significant exercise of a pastoral ministry that certainly involved instruction in the various facets of Christ Jesus. The time shared for instruction and formation was also a time conducive to the growth of personal affection. As various phrases within the letter make apparent, for example, vv. 12, 13, 16, Paul's own relationship with Onesimus came to be so significant that Paul was reluctant to see this "son" depart.

What was the setting in which Paul met with Onesimus and how frequently were they able to meet? During their visits, was Paul temporarily released from his chains so as to be able to converse in a relaxed manner? Was there the possibility of private conversation or were the soldiers guarding Paul immediately at hand? Once again, the possibility that Paul may have been chained to one or more soldiers should be kept in mind. Was Paul able to introduce Onesimus to Timothy and Epaphras and any other co-workers who were immediately in the vicinity?

A second form of Paul's ministry as a prisoner is represented by the very writing of this letter. Paul's intention is at least to secure Philemon's rehabilitation of Onesimus and very probably he intended to secure Onesimus' full emancipation.[21] Here the question of whether Onesimus consciously fled to Paul's side deserves to be seriously considered. If Onesimus knew that Paul was a close friend of his master and fled to Paul for assistance, then Paul, Onesimus, and Philemon may have been interacting in the context of Roman procedures regarding *amicus domini* ("friend of the lord") as well as within the context of discipleship in Christ.[22]

Whatever the exact dimensions of Onesimus' instruction and conversion, what is indisputable is that, in writing this letter, Paul undertakes a second form of ministry relative to Onesimus. Paul has already "begotten" Onesimus in Christ. Now, by means of this letter, he is attempting to secure Onesimus' liberation.

Two aspects of Paul's ministry as a prisoner are thus reflected in the letter. Despite being a prisoner, Paul has continued his ministry of imparting the gospel and forming disciples. Despite being a prisoner, Paul has also, as this letter itself testifies, continued his ministry of pastoral care through writing. Onesimus was clearly a beneficiary of both forms of Paul's ministry.

Were there unnamed others, besides Onesimus, who were brought to Christ by Paul at this time? If co-workers such as Timothy and Epaphras were also interacting with Onesimus and other potential Christians, it would not be unwarranted to suggest the image of a small community of co-ministers and catechumens gathered around the central figure of Paul—Paul now a prisoner for Christ Jesus.

It was emphasized at the beginning of this chapter that Paul's custody and his chains were Roman. This initial insight should be recalled now in considering Paul's undertakings while in custody.

Somewhat surprisingly, there is nothing within the text of Philemon to indicate that Paul was engaged in preparing to defend himself before the Roman authorities. One possible explanation for this silence is the fact that Philemon is an extremely brief letter with only one principal objective: generous treatment for Onesimus.

A second explanation for Paul's silence about his legal circumstances may be his expectation of being released in the relatively near future. Certainly, after being released from custody, Paul would be in a far better position to remark about his judicial proceedings and the nature of his confinement. Once released, he would be able to communicate with Philemon at his leisure and with far greater confidentiality.

What signs indicate Paul's expectation of being released from custody in the relatively near future? In two passages within the letter, Paul implies a reunion with Philemon in the not distant future and release from custody is an obvious prerequisite for any such reunion. Paul does not advert to what the judicial mechanism for his release might be. Nevertheless, the commitment to Philemon that Paul makes in v. 19a and the request to Philemon that he addresses in v. 22a are both expressed in such a way as to indicate release within the foreseeable future.

In v. 19a Paul dramatically expresses his own commitment to repay anything that is owed to Philemon in the wake of Onesimus' departure. In the following translation the first person pronoun is italicized to highlight Paul's personal commitment: "*I*, Paul, write this with my own hand, *I* will repay it. . . ." If Paul did not expect to visit Philemon in the foreseeable future, the force of this promise would be considerably diminished. He sends Onesimus back to Philemon *as of this writing*. Is it not the implied meaning that Paul himself will soon journey to Philemon's location, fully prepared to address any unresolved aspects of Onesimus' case?

This meaning is confirmed and nuanced by Paul's exigent request in v. 22a. of the letter. "At the same time, prepare a guest room for me. . . ." How long should Philemon be prepared to keep this room in readiness for Paul? It should be emphasized that no specific dates are given. And, significantly, it becomes clear as Paul continues with this sentence that his release is not yet fully secure even if he does consider it near at hand.[23]

In effect, v. 22b softens the direct request that Paul has just made:

"For I am hoping through your prayers to be granted to you." Once again a close mutual bond is attested. Paul has expressed his own prayers for Philemon previously in the letter. Now he expresses his desire to receive Philemon's prayers. Indeed, these prayers have a role in securing Paul's release. Paul very definitely desires to be reunited with Philemon, to be "granted" to him. He trusts that, aided by Philemon's prayers, their reunion will take place in the future that is not far off.

4. Dating Philemon after Romans

Keeping in mind the analysis of the preceding sections relative to Paul's circumstances as a Roman prisoner, it is now appropriate to examine the temporal relationship between Philemon and Romans. The basic thesis to be argued in the paragraphs that follow is that Paul first wrote to the Roman Christians and then, after an interval that cannot be determined precisely, he wrote to Philemon. Essentially, there are three sets of considerations about these two letters that argue in favor of a Romans-then-Philemon sequence.

The first set of considerations focuses on the image of himself that Paul presents in each letter, self-images that include his plans for the future. Fundamentally, a great vigorousness pervades Romans. Paul is filled with energy for his service as Christ's apostle, and he enthusiastically projects a bold scenario for his future travel and endeavors on Christ's behalf. The following words from Romans 15, previously cited, testify to Paul's energy for the wide-ranging journey that is yet before him:

> But now, since I no longer have any room for work in these regions, and since I have longed for many years to come to you, I hope to see you in passing as I go to Spain, and to be sped on my journey there by you, once I have enjoyed your company for a little. At present, however, I am going to Jerusalem with aid for the saints. For Macedonia and Achaia have been pleased to make some contribution for the poor among the saints at Jerusalem; they were pleased to do it, and indeed they are in debt to them, for if the Gentiles have come to share in their spiritual blessings, they ought also to be of service to them in material blessings. When therefore I have completed this, and have delivered to them what has been raised, I shall go by way of you to Spain. (Rom 15:23-28)

With respect to the image Paul presents to his Christian readers in Rome it should also be noted that nowhere in that letter does he make mention of having been a chained prisoner of the Roman authorities. And Romans itself is not a letter written from prison! Rather, within Romans, Paul's self-understanding is that of an apostle with a continuing ministry among both Gentiles and Jews, including a projected mission to Spain.

In contrast Paul's self-image within Philemon is that of a prisoner who is in chains for Christ Jesus. What is more, the travel plans he articulates are extremely modest in comparison with those in Romans. There is no mention of travel to Spain. Now his stated intention is to travel to Philemon's residence, a journey over terrain that is already familiar to him.

It can also be argued that Paul's depiction of himself as "an old man" in Phlm 9 carries the implication that a significant interval of time intervened between Romans and Philemon. Actually, there are two time segments to be considered. The first is the interval between the writing of Romans and Paul's entry into Roman chains. The second interval is from the beginning of Roman chains to the writing of Philemon. Paul's "begetting" of Onesimus as a Christian occurred during this second time interval.

The second set of considerations favoring a Romans–Philemon sequence has to do with Paul's effort to collect and to transport funds in support of the Jerusalem church. In the verses just cited from Romans 15, Paul implies that this project is now nearing completion. Indeed, once the collection has been delivered, his intention is to begin his journey to Rome and to Spain.

Paul says nothing at all about this collection in writing to Philemon. What are plausible explanations for his complete silence about an undertaking that was obviously so important to him at the times of his correspondence with the Christians residing at Corinth and at Rome?

If Paul had written Philemon prior to Romans, would he have failed to include at least a passing reference to his collection?[24] In Paul's letter, Philemon is revealed to be an extremely close co-worker of Paul. And, as the head of a house church and the owner of at least one slave, he also emerges as a Gentile Christian of some means. As such, Philemon presumably would have been an excellent prospect relative to Paul's collection. *If* the collection was proceeding forward during the time of Paul's imprisonment, would Paul have refrained from reminding Philemon about it?

Caution must be observed regarding conjecture of this sort. For Paul's silence about his collection could be due to the very brevity of this letter and its singular focus. Still, *if* the collection were underway at that time when Paul wrote and Philemon was involved or was to be involved with the collection in any way, a single additional phrase would have been sufficient for affirming or inviting Philemon's participation.

In contrast, once a Romans–Philemon sequence replaces a Philemon–Romans sequence, the way is open for a more plausible explanation regarding Paul's silence about the collection in writing to Philemon. In effect, Paul is silent regarding the collection because it was an endeavor *completed* at an earlier stage of his ministry.

At the time of Romans, the collection was one of Paul's major commitments. After writing Romans Paul completed this commitment. Subsequently, in a fully unexpected development, he found himself in Roman custody. Nevertheless, despite his chains, Paul undertook to "beget" Onesimus. These two aspects—his concern for Onesimus and his preoccupation with his own chains—were principally in view when he wrote to Philemon, and he did not turn from these subjects for any comment regarding the now-completed collection.

The third set of considerations arguing for a Romans-Philemon sequence focuses on Paul's explicit endorsement of the Roman authorities in Rom 13:1-7 and the absence of any endorsement for these authorities in Philemon.

Certainly, Paul is not going to provide an endorsement for those who have cast him into chains! Assuredly, he is not going to commend those responsible for consigning him to custody! Readers and interpreters of Philemon can be expected to voice such sentiments in their initial response to the thesis that Paul's failure to commend the Roman authorities is a significant datum. Nevertheless, the easily overlooked absence of any commendation for the Roman authorities within Paul's letter to Philemon merits further consideration.

It should be emphasized again at this point that officials who have their legitimacy and their coercive power within the Roman imperial system are responsible for Paul's custody and his chains. As previously observed, Paul was kept in custody for an extended period of time somewhere within the boundaries of the empire. Yet, within the imperial system, only officials and military personnel designated by Rome had the capacity for decreeing and effecting extended imprisonment.

In writing to Philemon, should Paul have commended these authorities for their diligence in keeping him in custody? Clearly a negative reply must be given to this question. Yet this negative response has an applicability extending beyond one letter. If any endorsement for Roman personnel is out of place for Paul in writing to Philemon, is it not out of place for Paul, having experienced Roman chains, to write to the Christians in Rome urging unqualified compliance with the Roman authorities?

The full thrust of the present argument now appears. If Paul had experienced a period of Roman imprisonment, complete with chains, prior to the time when he wrote to the Roman Christians, would he have counseled them with the directives of Rom 13:1-7, particularly those in vv. 3-4?

> Let every person be subject to the governing authorities. For there is no authority except from God, and those that exist have been instituted by God. Therefore he who resists the authorities resists what God has appointed, and those who resist will incur judgment. *For rulers are not a terror to good conduct, but to bad. Would you have no fear of him who is in authority? Then do what is good, and you will receive his approval, for he is God's servant for your good. But if you do wrong, be afraid, for he does not bear the sword in vain; he is the servant of God to execute his wrath on the wrongdoer.* Therefore one must be subject, not only to avoid God's wrath but also for the sake of conscience. For the same reason you also pay taxes, for the authorities are ministers of God, attending to this very thing. Pay all of them their dues, taxes to whom taxes are due, revenue to whom revenue is due, respect to whom respect is due, honor to whom honor is due. (Rom 13:1-7; emphasis added)

If Paul could not have written such words after being confined in Roman chains, if they would be fully incongruous sentiments from one who had unjustly experienced Roman imprisonment, the implications are then clear for the temporal sequence of Romans and Philemon. Paul wrote his letter to the Roman Christians, including Rom 13:1-7, before he was ever subjected to the experience of Roman chains that is reflected in Philemon. After writing Romans, Paul then had Roman chains placed upon him. He endured this custody at least long enough for him to become the spiritual father of Onesimus. And it was in this context that he wrote to Philemon.

CHAPTER SEVEN

The Testimony of Colossians and Ephesians

IT IS TO BE RECALLED at the outset of this chapter that a majority of New Testament scholars presently dispute the status of Colossians and especially the status of Ephesians as authentic letters of Paul.[1] Nevertheless, even if not from Paul, these canonical letters are significant for this study because they vividly and substantively image Paul as a prisoner in chains. It is Colossians that provides the compelling view of Paul appealing to his readers: "Remember my chains." And it is Ephesians that depicts Paul boldly proclaiming that he now served Christ as "an ambassador in a chain."

There are noteworthy correspondences to be observed between Colossians and Ephesians. At this juncture two features can be observed to stimulate reflection regarding the possible connections between these two letters. One very remarkable feature is the verbal identity between phrases in the closing of Colossians (4:7-9) and phrases in the closing of Ephesians (6:21-22). A second noteworthy feature is that both letters are to be brought to their respective destinations by the same person, Tychicus (Col 4:7; Eph 6:21-22).

There are, however, significant differences between the two letters with respect both to content and literary character. Colossians is very much in the category of a letter, responding to the pastoral situation of the Christian community to which it is addressed. In contrast, Ephesians has more the character of an epistle. Essentially, this means that Ephesians makes a generalized, systematic presentation of Christian theology and provides little by way of counsel for a particular local church.

1. Possible Dates and Locations

As just mentioned (and as observed in chapter one), the contents of Colossians and Ephesians possess considerable value for the present study even if it is judged that these letters were written by one or more other Christians and not by Paul himself. The implications of authorship by a person or persons other than Paul will be considered more fully below.

It is to be noted that both Colossians and Ephesians are like Philemon in portraying Paul in a situation of *sustained* Roman imprisonment.[2] This factor is significant with respect to the *conceptual* dates of these two letters. For it means that Colossians and Ephesians, like Philemon, are to be viewed as pertaining to Paul's journey after Romans.[3] *Conceptually*, both of these letters are also to be located prior to Philippians. In Philippians, Paul envisions that his imprisonment may well end in death. Such a perspective is not to be found in either Colossians or Ephesians.

Given the prevailing uncertainty regarding Paul's authorship of Colossians and Ephesians, any discussion of the dates and sequence of Philemon, Colossians, and Ephesians is inevitably complex. Even if it is assumed that Paul himself authored all three letters, there is still no firm basis for determining the sequence in which he wrote them. Moreover, there is no indication regarding the interval(s) of time separating these three letters.[4]

Comparable uncertainties abound with respect to the place of authorship. As was the case with Philemon, nothing in the text of either Colossians or Ephesians enables Paul's prison location(s) to be pinpointed. Nevertheless, all three letters do agree in projecting one extremely noteworthy feature of Paul's circumstances. Whatever the precise location(s) of his confinement, Paul is bound with chains.

The prominence of Paul's chains within both Colossians and Ephesians is also a feature that pertains to the question of the authorship of these two letters. This feature has been generally overlooked in most of the critical debate over authenticity. Scholars who argue that Paul himself authored Colossians and Ephesians usually have not based their conclusions on the various references to chains made within these letters.[5] Similarly, scholars who argue that Colossians and Ephesians are deutero-Pauline have not generally given attention to the presence and function of Paul's chains.[6] What is the contribution of the present study on the question of authorship? As observed in the section on methodology in chapter one, the conclusions of the present study do not presume Paul's authorship of Colossians or Ephesians nor is the principal thesis of this study based on data from Colossians, Ephesians, or 2 Timothy. Nevertheless, it can be stated here that considerations relative to the chains Paul wears in these letters speak on the side of authorship by Paul.

It will be seen below that Colossians and Ephesians both portray Paul reflecting intensely on his chains and almost literally raising them for his readers to contemplate. In both letters, bold and summoning statements are made regarding these chains. Accordingly it must be emphasized that, for individuals to write in Paul's name and bind themselves, figuratively, with Paul's chains, a considerable audacity would be required.

Would a co-worker or a disciple of Paul have ventured to assume the persona of Paul in chains during Paul's lifetime? Such a direct question serves to place the issue of pseudepigraphy, the issue of writing under another's name, in sharp focus. Almost immediately, questions arise about the objectives of such an author. What objectives would motivate another Christian to assume Paul's chains in a literary fashion even as Paul himself literally suffered under these chains?

The more common reconstruction by scholars who argue for deutero-Pauline authorship is that these letters were by disciples of Paul in the decades after Paul's death, perhaps even as late as the turn of the first century. Nevertheless, what brazenness for anyone who would not merely adopt Paul's identity as an apostle, but also purport to assume Paul's identity as a Roman prisoner!

It may be argued that the purposes of Colossians and Ephesians are to promote the doctrinal and ethical positions taken in each letter. But could not such objectives be authoritatively advanced simply by a writer's claim to be *the apostle*? In other words, as Christianity made its way into the Roman empire in the 70s, 80s, and 90s, *under the Flavian dynasty*, would later disciples of Paul have considered it politically advantageous to keep emphasizing that the premier exponent of the Christian movement had been a chained Roman prisoner?[7]

If Colossians and Ephesians were indeed written by later Christians, then these authors themselves clearly attached a surpassing importance to Paul's chains! These later Christian writers considered

Paul's prisoner status to be such an integral aspect of his identity that it was to be insisted upon whatever the resulting political repercussions. Again, it must not be forgotten that such authors and the communities for whom they wrote would certainly be within the boundaries of the empire.

To summarize, it is the perspective of the present study that, whether authored by Paul himself or by another Christian assuming Paul's persona, the prisoner passages of both Colossians and Ephesians possess great significance and repay careful attention. Either Paul himself or someone writing in his name sought to indicate that Paul's chains were a highly momentous development. These chains emerge as a significant element in the image of Paul that each letter presents, and they also emerge as a significant element for the exposition made within each letter.

2. Paul as a Prisoner in Colossians

With respect to the topic of Paul's imprisonment and his chains, the powerful character of Colossians' presentation only becomes apparent in the last chapter of the letter. In Colossians 1, Paul (or an author assuming Paul's name)[8] makes a general reference to his sufferings, but it is not until the beginning of chapter 4 that he explicitly refers to his condition as a chained prisoner. Then, at the very close of the letter, he makes a further reference to his chains that is so stunning as to cast the entire letter in a significantly enhanced perspective. Because of the highly significant image of Paul that it presents, the letter's final verse will be analyzed in a separate section below.

Colossians opens with a greeting comparable to that employed by Paul in a number of letters: "Paul, an apostle of Christ Jesus by the will of God, and Timothy our brother." Paul thus initially refers to himself as an apostle and alerts his readers to the fact that Timothy joins him in the sending of this letter. The next twenty-three verses of the letter, especially the hymnic words of 1:15-18, are highly positive in tone. Paul has been in communication with this community through Epaphras (1:7), and he desires to begin by encouraging them strongly in their mutual faith.

It was noted above that the first reference to Paul's suffering is phrased in such general terms that the nature of his adversity is not immediately apparent. This reference is as follows:

> Now I rejoice in my sufferings for your sake, and in my flesh I com-
> plete what is lacking in Christ's afflictions for the sake of his body, that
> is, the church. (Col 1:24)

The interpretation that Paul's imprisonment is a chief source of
these sufferings had traditionally *not* been put forward. Given the
character of the reference to chains and confinement that occur at the
end of the letter, however, the probability that Paul's imprisonment is
referred to in this verse is high. In support of this interpretation, it is
to be noted that Paul explicitly claims to "complete in my own flesh
what is lacking in Christ's afflictions. . . ." Is there not present here
some identification between Paul suffering as a prisoner and Christ
suffering as one bound and "handed over"?[9]

Whatever the degree to which Paul's prison sufferings are referenced in 1:24, it is unmistakable that his situation as a prisoner is
central to the meaning expressed in 4:2-4, at the end of the letter. Did
the Christians at Colossae know of Paul's imprisonment before they
received this letter?[10] If they did not, then these verses conveyed this
startling information to them. Significantly, Paul takes care to assure
his readers that his chains are for a noble purpose. The translation of
these verses is now given as it appears in the RSV, except for one
modification:

> Continue steadfastly in prayer, being watchful in it with thanksgiving;
> and pray for us also, that God may open a door for the word, to
> declare the mystery of Christ, on account of which I am *in chains,* that
> I may make it clear as I ought to speak. (Col 4:2-4, emphasis added)

As discussed above in chapter four, the primary meaning of the
Greek verb *dedemai* is "bound with chains." This wording could
itself be used in the passage just cited, but the simpler substitution of
"in chains" for the RSV's "in prison" suffices to convey the fundamental reality of Paul's situation. Paul is portrayed in Colossians in
the same way that he is imaged in Philemon. Not merely kept in confinement, he is literally bound with chains.[11]

Further, it must be underscored that Paul is again portrayed in
Roman chains. Paul has now apparently worn his chains long
enough for him to grow reflective about them. And nothing in the
letter suggests that this confinement is soon to end. This feature of
sustained imprisonment, for the reasons previously discussed in

chapter four, is a clear indication that Paul's chains and his confinement are by order of the Roman authorities.

Like Philemon, Colossians makes no mention of the legal grounds
on which Paul suffers his chains. What Colossians does explain,
however, is that Paul's status as a chained prisoner has resulted from
his faithfulness on Christ's behalf. The Christians at Colossae are not
to think that Paul has been involved in any form of wrongdoing.
Rather, it is because of his efforts "to declare the mystery of Christ"
that Paul now finds himself in Roman custody. There is a note of
nobility and idealism proclaimed here. Paul has been zealous as
regards God's saving purpose in Christ for Jews and Gentiles alike.
And it is because of his unswerving commitment to this high mission
that he presently suffers confinement and constraint.

Precisely, it is restriction from his normal apostolic activity that
seems to weigh heavily upon Paul. The verses from 4:7 to 4:14 make
it clear that, along with Timothy, Paul does have a number of co-ministers present to him. Further, the implication of 4:18a, where Paul
takes the writing instrument in his own hand, is that the apostle also
has the services of an amanuensis. Indeed his possibility for writing
and sending this letter demonstrates that Paul's chains do not completely prevent him from communicating with those to whom he has
ministered. Nevertheless, Paul does rue the loss of his normal freedom of mobility for apostolic ministry.

The hope that Paul expresses within these verses is that God will
"open a door for the word." The image of a door being open for
fruitful ministry has been used by Paul twice previously in writing to
the Christians of Corinth (1 Cor 16:9 and 2 Cor 2:12). The thrust of
this reference here in Colossians is that Paul desires to resume his
normal apostolic ministry—something his chains prevent.[12] He thus
desires to receive the Colossians' prayers for the sake of his ministry
"to declare the mystery of Christ."

It should be noted that, in requesting prayers for the sake of his
ministry, Paul is implicitly requesting prayers that will lead to release
from his chains. In effect, then, this petition for prayers signals Paul's
frustration with his confinement. He resents his chains and desires
release from them in order to resume the ministry in which he has
heretofore been vigorously engaged.

In order to appreciate that the Colossian "portrait" of Paul contrasts with the image of him conveyed by Philemon, it should be observed that, in Colossians, Paul's chains seemingly wear heavily upon him. Clearly, Philemon has its own particular character owing to its primary concern with Onesimus' release. Nevertheless, bearing that consideration in mind, it may still be said that, in writing to Philemon, Paul manifests a tendency to look *beyond* his chains. Indeed, in that letter he clearly envisioned this possibility that he would soon be staying in Philemon's guest room.

In Colossians the perspective is slightly different. Paul wants to be released from his chains in order to resume his normal active ministry—that much is clear. Yet there is no suggestion that Paul's release is imminent. It is as though Paul foresees no immediate way out of his chains, except for what he hopes can be opened to him through prayer.

As noted previously, a fuller perspective on the nuances of Paul's outlook in these verses will emerge after the words that close the letter are analyzed in the next section of this chapter. But before proceeding to that analysis, it is well to note that one additional reference to Paul's prisoner status is given in 4:10, a verse in which greetings are transmitted from Aristarchus "my fellow prisoner" (*synaichmalōtos*).

Paul used this same term of Epaphras in Philemon 23. In chapter six above, it was suggested that Epaphras, not formally charged and chained as was Paul, nevertheless voluntarily shared in some of the conditions of Paul's confinement.[13] These same considerations would now apply for Aristarchus' role in the context of Colossians. Does Colossians suggest that Aristarchus lived voluntarily at Paul's side and assisted him in various ways, perhaps even serving as the scribe for the letter? While certainty is not possible about Aristarchus' exact role, what is certain is that Paul recognizes and appreciates Aristarchus' service on his behalf.

Finally, it should be noted that Col 4:7-14 also portrays Paul having a significant number of supporters beyond the aforementioned Timothy, Epaphras, and Aristarchus. Four others who appear to be in Paul's immediate circle are Mark, Jesus called Justus, Luke, and Demas. Further, Paul's letter is apparently to be delivered to the Colossians by Tychicus and Onesimus. Again, the location of Paul's confinement cannot be projected from the text of the letter. But wherever he is located, whatever his exact prison circumstances, Paul does enjoy contact with, and presumably support from, a number of others who serve with him in Christ's name.

3. Paul's Entreaty: "Remember My Chains"

After Paul expresses greetings from those with him and extends his own greetings along with instructions as to how this letter shall be read, he takes the writing instrument in hand to write three concluding sentences in his own script. From the standpoint of the present study, one of these three sentences communicates with extraordinary vividness and brings the letter as a whole to an astonishing conclusion. This startling, summoning sentence consists of only four Greek words (Col 4:18b): *mnēmoneuete mou tōn desmōn*. Respecting the concrete meaning of *desmōn*, "chains," Paul's Greek is appropriately rendered: "Remember my chains."

To begin to grasp the impact of this startling entreaty, let Paul's concluding verse be considered without this exhortation. The final verse of Colossians would then read: "I, Paul, write this greeting with my own hand. Grace be with you." Such sentences would well close the letter and would be well within the range of closings utilized in the other New Testament letters generally regarded as authentically from Paul. But Paul himself, or someone writing in his name, was not content with such a closing and instead closed the letter with the following sequence of sentences:

> I, Paul, write this greeting with my own hand. *Remember my chains.* Grace be with you. (Col 4:18; emphasis added)

It should be stressed that two aspects serve to place these words regarding Paul's chains in extraordinarily high relief. The first aspect pertains to placement. This entreaty is positioned at the very end of the letter, a positioning that makes Paul in chains the closing image imparted to the Colossians. The second aspect pertains to the rendering of this appeal in Paul's own script. In writing Philemon, Paul inscribed in his own hand a commitment of great importance, namely, that he personally would provide surety for Onesimus (v. 19). Similarly, here in Colossians Paul's concern to have his chains remembered is so exigent that he expresses it personally and emphatically in his own hand.

One further consideration should be suggested. It is the possibility that the image articulated by the sentence—"I, Paul, write this greeting with my own hand"—is to be understood as contributing visually to the image conveyed by the sentence "Remember my chains." If Paul's two sentences are to be understood in this way, the full image communicated is that of Paul actually writing these sentences, perhaps roughly and somewhat clumsily, *with manacled hands*.[14]

Clearly then, the prominent placement of this appeal and the fact that Paul writes it in his own script both attest to the importance that Paul attached to his chains. Paul's chains do indeed matter! They matter to him personally. And in addition, Paul's chains are central to his overall communication with the community at Colossae.

Upon a moment's reflection, it is not difficult to see that appreciation for, and adherence to, what Paul has taught in the other sections of the letter can only be strengthened as a result of his reminder in closing that he remains faithful to Christ in his chains.[15] In 2:8–3:4, Paul has exhorted his Colossian readers to turn away from false perspectives and idolatrous practices while striving for deeper grounding in their new Christian lives. And in 3:5–4:5, the letter makes an extended admonition regarding specific forms of conduct that are to be rejected and the virtuous qualities that are to be embraced. In essence, Paul's powerful closing image of himself in chains urges and inspires his readers to a more full-hearted acceptance of his teaching regarding a faith perspective free from distortions and his exposition regarding right conduct.

As well as functioning as a credential for the teaching he imparts to the Colossians, Paul's reference to his chains also functions to intensify his request for the Colossians' prayers. As previously discussed, 4:3 indicates that Paul desired to be released from his chains and restored to the more active ministry to which he was accustomed. He specifically sought the Colossians' assistance to this end, stating, "And pray for us also that God may open to us a door for the word. . . ." When Paul now adds at the end of the letter, "Remember my chains," who among the Colossians would not be moved to pray steadfastly for Paul's release?[16]

From the standpoint of rhetoric, Paul's dramatic depiction of himself in chains in the last verse of Colossians can thus be regarded as an extremely effective device for furthering two of his principal objectives in writing to the Colossians. Yet over and beyond assisting him in securing respect for his teaching and securing his readers' prayers, Paul's words regarding his chains also express sentiments that are emotional and visceral. In effect, Paul's words have about them the quality of an ad hoc outburst railing against the metal links of chain that bind him. Here Paul seemingly lets rise to the surface his frustration regarding his confinement. His chains constrain him and restrict him. He should not be encumbered by them. He would be rid of them.

Finally, do these four Greek words not also manifest Paul's concern to display for his readers the new insignia, the new credentials that he now finds himself possessing as a consequence of his faithful service to Christ? The sense of Colossians is that Paul has had the opportunity to ponder his chains, to meditate upon them, even to become preoccupied with them. In holding them up for his readers' consideration, Paul may even derive a certain satisfaction from presenting his chains as the insignia of the apostolic service he has faithfully rendered.

Paul's imprisonment in Colossians is "open ended." He has been engaged in coming to terms with the meaning of his chains as his time in custody has worn on. He desires to be released from these fetters. Yet he is faithful to Christ in bearing them. Paul's chains have all of these dimensions of meaning and more. Let Paul's chains be remembered!

4. Paul as a Prisoner in Ephesians

As previously mentioned, Ephesians contrasts noticeably with Colossians because of its more sustained, systematic reflections regarding the mystery of God's plan and purposes.[17] And, unlike Colossians, Ephesians does not address the issues or even the members of a local church. Indeed, in marked contrast to Colossians, no disciple, except for Tychicus, is mentioned in Ephesians.[18]

Within Ephesians there are three references to Paul's imprisonment. Significantly, all of these references evidence a care to situate Paul's new circumstances as a prisoner within the larger framework of Paul's ministerial purposes and Christ's continuing grace to him. The judgment by a preponderance of Pauline scholars that one or more persons, other than Paul, wrote Ephesians should again be recalled. Nevertheless, if Ephesians is to be regarded as deutero-Pauline, it must again be observed that the writer adroitly adopted the chains of Paul and expressed perspectives regarding these chains that fit extremely well with the stance adopted by Paul himself in Philemon and Philippians.[19]

In contrast with Philemon, Paul does not refer to himself as a prisoner at the outset of Ephesians. Rather, the letter is sent by "Paul, an apostle of Christ Jesus by the will of God" (1:1a). The first two references to his status as prisoner occur in 3:1 and 4:1, within the body of the letter; the third reference then occurs in 6:20 as a part of the letter's closing.[20] Paul's first reference, in which any verb form is lacking, is as follows: "For this reason, I, Paul, a prisoner for Christ Jesus on behalf of you Gentiles . . ." (Eph 3:1).

In interpreting the meaning of this verse, it is to be recalled that the first chapters of Ephesians describe and emphasize the mystery of God's saving grace extended to the Gentiles through Christ.[21] It is thus in the context of Christ's work in reconciling Jew and Gentile that Paul initially mentions his imprisonment. Without explaining the lines of causality involved, Paul asserts in 3:1 that it is "on behalf of you Gentiles" that he is now a prisoner. Further, far from being due to any scandalous reason, Paul is actually being confined "for Christ Jesus."

It is well to reexpress the powerful rhetorical meaning conveyed by these words. Paul is a Roman prisoner not for any criminal matter, not for any fall from grace. His confinement is actually for the one whom he has unceasingly proclaimed up until this time. It is for Christ Jesus. Further his custody is on behalf of "you" (hymōn) Gentiles.[22] It is somehow a consequence of Paul's dedication and concern for the very persons to whom he is writing!

When is it viewed in such a way, this sentence fragment can be regarded as an extremely effective piece of rhetoric. Paul, or a disciple writing in his name, here sets forth two compelling explications of his circumstances. The fundamental power of these explications derives from the fact that both are grounded in Paul's core convictions. Paul is indeed viscerally convinced that he is imprisoned for Christ and on behalf of the Gentiles.

Paul's characterization of himself as ho desmios at the beginning of this verse is also highly significant. First, it is to be recalled that the fundamental meaning of words in the *desm-* word group is that of "binding." When *desmios* is translated as "prisoner," the root meaning is thus that of "one who is bound."[23]

A second nuance of meaning resides in the fact that the Greek article *ho* is used here. (It is used in Eph 4:1 but not in Phlmn 1 or 9.) If the article is rendered literally, the resulting translation would be "the prisoner."[24] Such wording gives rise to at least two possible meanings. Conceivably, the article might have been used in this way to differentiate Paul from other prisoners that the Romans have in custody. They are prisoners for various offenses; Paul is *the* prisoner for Christ. It is also possible that the article underscores the great shift in Paul's own circumstances. He is now Paul, *the* prisoner. The use of the first person pronoun further intensifies the meaning. The author thus pens *four* emphatic words: "I, Paul, the prisoner."[25]

When these various aspects of Paul's self-presentation in 3:1 are all reflected on, is there not the implication that Paul has spent a considerable amount of time in custody? He is able to present himself to his readers in terms that are well thought out. He has a facility in speaking about his status that seemingly reflects an extended experience of imprisonment.

This impression of an extended confinement will be confirmed in the two passages still to be considered, 4:1 and 6:18-20. It is for this reason that, in the preceding paragraphs, *Roman* imprisonment has been assumed. Paul's imprisonment in Ephesians is not merely a brief interruption in his ministry. And for the reasons previously given, a sustained imprisonment implies Roman imprisonment.

Reference to 3:13, the verse that completes Paul's thought about his confinement, also confirms that the imprisonment he is experiencing is indeed onerous. It is possible for the Greek of this verse to be translated in two distinct ways. Yet in either translation there is still the sense that the confinement is vexatious and perduring. It is well at this juncture to cite the RSV's principal translation and then the alternate translation given at the margin:

> So I ask you not to lose heart over what I am suffering for you, which is your glory. (Eph 3:13)

> So I ask that I may not lose heart over what I am suffering for you, which is your glory. (Eph 3:13; RSV marginal translation)

Either it is the case that Paul's readers should not be disheartened or else it is the case that Paul prays that *he* not be disheartened. But clearly, there are grounds for being discouraged or disheartened over what Paul is suffering. And this is the reason for arguing that 3:13 itself provides evidence that Paul's imprisonment is onerous and sustained. What Paul is experiencing is indeed "suffering" (*thlipsis*). And his release from this suffering does not seem to be envisioned at the time when the letter is written.

Note that this mention of suffering functions to incline Paul's readers sympathetically toward him. According to the RSV's preferred translation Paul asks his readers not "to lose heart" over what he is suffering. This translation conveys the meaning that Paul is explicitly asking his readers to be steadfast in their support. In the RSV's alternate translation, Paul is not making a direct appeal to his readers. Nevertheless, because his suffering is for them and because he is praying for perseverance in his witness, the net result of his words is to incline his readers to his cause.

Paul's facility in repeating the truth that his suffering is for his readers' benefit deserves to be highlighted. In 3:1 he averred that his imprisonment was "on behalf of you Gentiles." Now in 3:13 he states that his suffering is "for you." Further, Paul implies that his suffering advances his readers' progress to "glory" (*doxa*). According to the mystery of God's plan in Christ, Paul's own sufferings help his readers on their way to the heavenly glory to which they are called.[26]

As mentioned, Ephesians' second reference to Paul's imprisonment occurs at the beginning of chapter four. Before proceeding to analyze the clause emphasizing Paul's prisoner status, it is well to note that, with 4:1, a transition is being effected from the doctrinal teaching of the first chapters of the letter to the ethical exhortations characteristic of the latter chapters.[27] The use of the conjunction *oun*, "therefore," is crucial to this transition. This small word functions with axial force. Around it, the letter pivots from one topic area to the other, explicating that God's grace in Christ provide the letter's readers with ample incentive for a more noble manner of life. For the sake of completeness, the three verses that express Paul's thought at this juncture are now cited in their entirety:

I, therefore, a prisoner for the Lord, beg you to lead a life worthy of
the calling to which you have been called, with all lowliness and meek-
ness, with patience, forbearing one another in love, eager to maintain
the unity of the Spirit in the bond of peace. (Eph 4:1-3)

It should be noted that Paul's reference to his prisoner status is not
essential to the appeal that he is now launching regarding exemplary
moral conduct. If this clause were omitted, the sentence would still
achieve an effective transition: "I, therefore, beg you to lead a life
worthy of the calling. . . ."[28] And, as mentioned, Paul would still be
basing his appeal upon the rich doctrinal insights presented in the
first chapters of the letter. In point of fact, however, Paul did allude
to his imprisonment at this juncture. And he seemingly did so for two
reasons: to provide an additional rationale for his appeal to exemplary conduct and to reemphasize his own status as a prisoner for
Christ.

The Greek words used in this crucial clause are *egō ho desmios en
kyriō*. Paul is again "the prisoner" for the sake of Christ.[29] Since the
first person singular pronoun is already given in the ending of the
verb, *parakalō*, "I beg," the use of the separate pronoun *egō* was not
required. Yet Paul did write this personal pronoun. Indeed, in order
to respect Paul's conscious use of both means for expressing the first
person, the opening words of this sentence could be translated as follows: "Therefore I beg you, *I, the prisoner* for the Lord. . . ."

To be noted in the above translation is the way in which "prisoner" and "I" are in apposition. This reflects the manner in which
ho desmios is conjoined to *egō* in the Greek. In 3:1 Paul wrote forcefully: "I, Paul, the prisoner." Here the impact is comparable: "I, the
prisoner, I beg you. . . ."[30] Paul is, in effect, holding high "prisoner-
ship" as a startling dimension of his Christian identity.

This second reference to his standing as a prisoner who is utterly
faithful to Christ reinforces Paul's preceding doctrinal reflections on
the riches of grace that have been given in Christ. At this juncture,
the readers of Ephesians are encouraged to adopt high ethical standards out of appreciation for the treasures they have received in
Christ. They are additionally encouraged to embrace Paul's pastoral
and ethical instructions out of regard for him as one who renders
faithful and self-sacrificing service to Christ as a prisoner.[31]

5. An Ambassador in a Chain

Following after "apostle" and "prisoner" the third significant self-description for Paul in Ephesians is that of "an ambassador in a chain."[32] In a way comparable to Colossians, this striking image of Paul is positioned only a few verses before the end of the letter. Indeed, the closing of Ephesians is such as to engender vivid reflections regarding Paul's chained condition and the juridical and political procedures of Rome. Before proceeding to a thorough examination of Paul's ambassadorial image and its relation to prayer and to boldness, the passage itself is appropriately cited in full:

> Pray at all times in the Spirit, with all prayers and supplication. To that end keep alert with all perseverance, making supplication for all the saints, and also for me, that utterance may be given me in opening my mouth boldly to proclaim the mystery of the gospel, for which I am an ambassador in chains; that I may declare it boldly, as I ought to speak. (Eph 6:18-20)

The RSV translators here render *presbeuō,* a verb indicating service as an ambassador, with a noun construction, "I am an ambassador." The meanings associated with this term are fundamentally political and juridical,[33] and there is ample reason for holding that the author of Ephesians knew the political meaning of *presbeuō* and the corresponding Latin noun, *legatus.*

A priori, someone of Paul's broad learning and travel experience would certainly have been familiar with the responsibilities and prerogatives of ambassadors. Further, reference to 2 Cor 5:20 confirms that Paul had already imaged his service to Christ with reference to the service rendered by an ambassador.

With a view to a still deeper appreciation for the various facets of meaning conveyed by Eph 6:20, it is well to consider briefly several aspects of an ambassador's role and status within a world in which Rome's power was dominant. Indeed, because of the increasing power of Rome, the sending forth of legates *from* Rome (and the sending of embassies or ambassadors[34] *to* Rome) was of considerable significance in the world of those reading Ephesians.

What missions might an emperor entrust to his ambassador? Certainly there was wide variation.[35] In some cases the ambassador was to deliver an authoritative message on behalf of the emperor. In other circumstances the ambassador might be vested with specific admin-istrative authority for adjudicating a dispute, negotiating a treaty, or levying taxes. For example, the emperor Trajan conferred an extremely broad range of powers upon Pliny when he appointed Pliny as his legate for the province of Bithynia-Pontus.[36]

What qualities would an emperor seek in candidates prior to appointing them as ambassadors? Above all else, unqualified loyalty was the prerequisite for ambassadorial service. Other elements such as intelligence, diplomatic skills, robust health were also valued. Nevertheless the ambassador's unswerving loyalty to the person or entity conferring the embassy was, in the end, a compelling rationale for such an appointment.

Once appointed to office, the prerogatives afforded to Roman ambassadors were considerable. Above all else, the personal safety of the *legatus* was guaranteed. Depending upon the circumstances, Roman troops might be assigned directly to legates or else be made available to them as needed. Those selected for this office could also expect to receive a number of other protections and amenities. Plainly, Roman ambassadors were never to be subjected to humilia-tion or dishonor during the conduct of their embassies. They were, in fact, to be accorded the deference befitting them as authorized rep-resentatives possessing *imperium*, full Roman power.

Frequently already persons of wealth, those selected as legates could still expect to benefit materially as a result of their appoint-ments. As a result of rendering this service to the empire, those appointed almost always secured the direct or indirect compensation that was available to them. One additional element to be kept in mind is that appointment as a legate could well serve to advance the recipient's progress along the *cursus honorum*, the official Roman career path.

Somewhat similarly to nominations to the senate, appointments to the office of *legatus* were highly valued and esteemed. A small piece of anecdotal evidence illustrates the comparable desirability of these two offices. Circa A.D. 3-4, a petitioner presented the following two questions to an Egyptian oracle for deliberation: "Shall I become an ambassador? Am I to become a senator?"[37]

Drawing on these considerations pertaining to the role and the prerogatives of a Roman ambassador, it is now appropriate to inter-pret Ephesians' reference to Paul as a chained ambassador. As a first step toward a comprehensive analysis, it is useful to consider why Paul, or someone writing in his name, would have appropriated the image of an ambassador to describing his service to Christ. There are actually a number of reasons why such an image might have suggested itself. One cluster of reasons has to do with the specific character of Paul's ministry, the other set of reasons pertaining to the circumstances of the readers of Ephesians themselves.

With respect to the character of Paul's ministry, does Paul not resemble an ambassador in the authoritative way that he proclaims the saving purposes of God in Christ? Related to this consideration is the fact of Paul's unqualified loyalty to Christ Jesus his Lord. Consider that no matter how loyal any ambassador was to a given Roman emperor, that loyalty could not approach the quality of Paul's loyalty to Jesus.

Because there can be a certain nobility involved in the missions of a dedicated and faithful ambassador, "ambassador" is an appropriate and fitting title for Paul. For does not Paul characteristically communicate that he is involved in an undertaking of great nobility and great consequence? This feature is easily to be seen in the passages in which Ephesians is so eloquent about the grandeur of all that God is accomplishing in Christ. Thus, as Christ's ambassador, Paul claims for himself some sharing in an undertaking of grace and truth that reflects the most exalted levels of Christian vocation.[38]

In addition to his own personal appreciation for the meanings present in "ambassador," the author of Ephesians may also have decided to employ it because he knew it was a concept that was well established within the experience of his readers. Asia was an important Roman province and also a territory through which various ambassadors passed in traveling from and to Rome. Readers living outside of Asia would also be easily able to grasp the rich meaning of Paul as Christ's ambassador.[39]

It should be recalled that Paul presented himself as Christ's apostle in 1:1. Given that "apostle" conveys a meaning somewhat comparable to the meaning of "ambassador," what influenced the employment of "ambassador" instead of "apostle" now at the conclusion of Ephesians? The answer to this question may reside in the juridical and political overtones that "ambassador" communicates.

As analyzed above, Paul has twice referred to his prisoner status in the body of the letter, references that have political meaning, given that his imprisonment was by decree of the Roman authorities. Paul may thus have elected a term with dimensions of political meaning in order to achieve the powerful paradoxical thrust that is afforded in the image of a chained ambassador. Conceivably Paul might have used "an apostle in a chain." Yet this latter formulation does not have the politically incandescent meaning of "an ambassador in a chain."

As just mentioned, Paul earlier in this letter has previously referred to himself as the prisoner, using *ho desmios*, a term imaging him as confined and chained. Paul's use of *en halysei* is a still more vivid way for referencing his chained condition. *Halysis* literally means "a (metal) chain" and conveys the image of such a chain around Paul's arms, legs, waist in some fashion.[40] This reference to a chain is memorable in its own right. Once the image of a chain is joined with the image of an ambassador, however, the resultant combination, "an ambassador in a chain," is synergistically powerful.

Let it be recalled that, within the framework of Roman power, the fundamental prerogative of all ambassadors was for their own persons to be protected. Far from enjoying this normal and expected personal security, Paul himself was now subject to chaining. A Roman ambassador could also expect respect and, depending upon the circumstances, even acclaim from those receiving the embassy. In contrast with other ambassadors, Paul now had to contend with the scandal that his chain might engender among those to whom Christ had sent him.

Finally, for a Roman ambassador, the consequence of a faithfully executed embassy might well be significant advancement through the "course of honors." In contrast, what was the outcome for Paul, more faithful as Christ's ambassador than any Roman legate ever was to a commissioning Roman emperor? In the present, *according to Roman valuation*, the outcome for Paul was not advancement in secular honor, but rather a descent into civil shame.

In the future, of course, Paul aspired to achieve the true and lasting glory of Christ, his Lord. Nevertheless, what a powerful paradox did Paul now articulate (and live!): a paradox of status and mistreatment, a paradox of faithfulness and humiliation, a paradox of grace and dishonor. All of these aspects, and others as well, did Paul successfully encompass by memorably identifying himself to his readers as "an ambassador in a chain."

It was stated at the outset of this section that, when Paul (or another writing in Paul's name) projected the unforgettable image of himself as a chained ambassador, he was concerned to gain his readers' prayers for his own *boldness*. It is now appropriate to consider the particular emphasis that Paul places upon this quality. It should be noted that he refers to the attribute of boldness twice, using a noun form as well as a verb form, within the principal sentence comprising Eph 6:18-20.

Significantly, "boldness" (*parrēsia*) can have the specific meaning of giving forthright or unintimidated testimony in the face of persecution or pressure[41] from those with political power. *Parrēsia* probably has such meaning in the present passage given the fact that Paul is using a political term, *ambassador*, and referencing a political reality, his chained status. As considered above, the fundamental responsibility of an ambassador was to represent authentically and authoritatively the wishes of the person commissioning the embassy. For an ambassador to do this with boldness, despite the pressures or intimidations of another power, would surely be estimable.

Paul asks prayers that he may open his mouth "in boldness" (*en parrēsia*) to proclaim the mystery of the gospel. These prayers will assist him "that I may declare it boldly, as I ought to speak." Clearly Paul is here cognizant of his responsibilities as Christ's ambassador, and he is seeking prayerful support for the faithful discharge of his mission.

Do Paul's words indicate that, in some way, he considers himself in danger of failing in his embassy? Posing such a question can promote a still deeper appreciation for the portrayal of Paul and his circumstances that is given at the close of Ephesians. Are there any suggestions in the text as to why Paul twice expresses a concern that his testimony on behalf of Jesus be given "boldly"?

There are perhaps two aspects of Paul's situation that need to be considered in this connection. The first, expressly mentioned in the text, is Paul's own conviction that boldness is not *optional* but rather a quality or attribute that is expected of him. This sense is communicated by the clause "as I ought to speak."[42] As Paul understands his ambassadorial role, it is not merely a matter of describing the mystery of the gospel. More than that is required of him: Christ has asked him to declare the gospel *boldly*.

A second aspect pertaining to Paul's request of prayers for boldness can only be appreciated by reflecting upon subject areas in which the text is silent. Upon a moment's reflection, it is evident that none of the three "prisoner passages" from Ephesians shows Paul adverting to (a) how much time he has already spent in prison or (b) his possibility for being released from his chains. In effect, Paul's imprisonment within Ephesians is open ended.

Taking these various aspects into consideration it can be concluded that the Paul of Ephesians solicits prayers for boldness in order to present uncompromised testimony on behalf of Christ for howsoever long his imprisonment endures. In Ephesians Paul anticipates bearing his chains for the foreseeable future. And he asks prayers that the boldness of his witness will not diminish over whatever time Christ decrees for this important ambassadorial representation.

CHAPTER EIGHT

The Circumstances of Paul in 2 Timothy

IN ORDER TO BRING into clear focus several features pertaining to the authorship and character of 2 Timothy, the present chapter will begin with a brief note discussing pseudepigraphy followed by a brief section locating 2 Timothy in terms of Paul's trajectory as a prisoner. Section three will then analyze the text of the letter to consider the multiple purposes intended by the author. Finally, sections four, five, and six will treat the circumstances of Paul's imprisonment and his undiminished faithfulness to Jesus within these circumstances.

1. An Additional Note Regarding Pseudepigraphy

In the estimation of a majority of New Testament scholars, Colossians, and especially Ephesians and 2 Timothy, are pseudepigraphical letters. Within the perspective of the present study, Colossians, Ephesians, and 2 Timothy are remarkably comparable in the way in which each initially affirms Paul's calling as Christ's apostle and then proceeds to emphasize his standing as a chained prisoner. They are also comparable as regards the manner in which each effectively utilizes Paul's situation as a prisoner as a leading theme within the overall message of the letter.

The impact of these latter considerations for the question of pseudepigraphy resides in the insight that, if associates or later disciples of Paul wrote in his name, they did not hesitate to adopt the most politically controversial aspect of Paul's identity. For, within these letters, Paul's persona as a Roman prisoner is indeed presented in high relief.

In Colossians and 2 Timothy the positioning of the figure of Timothy also has relevance for the question of pseudepigraphy. In Colossians Timothy is a co-sender of the letter, located at the side of Paul as Paul reflects on his sufferings and his chains.[1] In 2 Timothy, Paul apprises Timothy of developments in his judicial and personal situation, even as he summons Timothy to his side.[2]

As previously articulated, the central theses of this study are being argued independently of the material contained in Colossians, Ephesians, and 2 Timothy. In other words, a conclusion that Paul himself authored one, two, or all three of these letters is not a necessary condition for sustaining the principal arguments of this study.[3] If one or more of these letters is authored by Paul, the impact that Paul's chains had upon him is delineated with greater amplitude. Yet, even if all three letters are deutero-Pauline, these texts still indicate that the chains worn by Paul were deemed by his disciples and associates to have been a highly significant phenomenon.

2. 2 Timothy and Paul's Trajectory as a Prisoner

In chapter seven it was observed that the portrayal of Paul's prison situation in Colossians and Ephesians is roughly approximate to the prison situation indicated by Paul's various references in Philemon. In the present section it is now suggested that 2 Timothy appears to depict a later stage in Paul's "journey" as a prisoner. There are several aspects of 2 Timothy that support such a conclusion.

First, it should be noted that 2 Timothy portrays Paul facing condemnation and death, outcomes that were never alluded to in Philemon. According to 2 Timothy, Paul has already experienced one judicial proceeding in which he narrowly escaped a negative outcome (4:16-17). At the time of writing, he faces an interval in chains (2:9b). Nevertheless, his condemnation is on the horizon. That Paul considers himself perilously close to the end of his journey and anticipates that his imprisonment may end in death is signaled in memorable terms by the following passage in chapter four:[4]

For I am already at the point of being sacrificed; the time of my departure has come. I have fought the good fight, I have finished the race; I
have kept the faith. (2 Tim 4:6-7)

Second, it is also possible to argue the *conceptual* temporal priority of Philemon on the grounds that 2 Tim 4:6-7 and 4:16-17 can
plausibly be interpreted as following Phlm 22 while the reverse
sequence is much less plausible. In this interpretation, Paul's expectation for using Philemon's guest room was dissolved as his case took
a turn for the worse, leaving Paul in grave jeopardy.[5]

Finally, the references made in both letters to Demas (reliable in
Philemon, unreliable in 2 Timothy), to Luke, and to Timothy also
support the interpretation that Paul is imaged at a later stage of
imprisonment in 2 Timothy. According to 2 Timothy, Paul has the
steadfast support of Luke and Timothy just as he did at the time of
Philemon. Demas, faithful to Paul at the time of Philemon, (Phlm
24), has subsequently proved unreliable (2 Tim 4:10).[6]

3. The Purposes of 2 Timothy

For the most part, this letter contains instructions and counsel that
pertain to Timothy personally. Since other Christians, including
those named at the end of the letter (4:19-20), will undoubtedly read
the letter or become apprised of its contents, the directives communicated regarding false teaching were undoubtedly intended for
others beyond Timothy. Nevertheless, the letter on the whole concentrates upon Timothy and the steps that this young associate of
Paul is now called to take in support of his mentor, who is in chains.

First and foremost, Paul intensely desires that Timothy come to his
side. Paul makes this request three times within the letter. Initially, in
1:4, he states poignantly: "As I remember your tears, I long night and
day to see you, that I may be filled with joy." In 4:9, near the letter's
conclusion, Paul explicitly requests that Timothy hasten on his way:
"Do your best to come soon (*tacheos*)." At 4:21a this summons is
made even more specific: "Do your best to come *before winter.*"

Paul's second purpose is to emphasize that his own chains are not
a cause for shame before God. Accordingly, Timothy should not be

influenced to turn away from the imprisoned Paul; rather he should strive to be associated with Paul in his suffering.[7]

It is worth considering in some detail the words that Paul pens in 2 Tim 1:1-17, a passage in which the concepts of shamefulness and faithfulness are clearly of central importance. In 1:8a Timothy is urged, "Do not be ashamed then (*mē oun epaischynthēs*) of testifying to our Lord, nor of me his prisoner (*ton desmion autou*) but share in suffering for the gospel in the power of God."[8] 2 Tim 1:9-10 then reflect on the sovereignty of God and the way in which God's plan has reached its culmination in the decisive "appearing" (*epiphaneias*) of Christ Jesus who is "our Savior" (*tou sōtēros hēmōn*).[9] Paul then expressly affirms that it is this Jesus "who abolished death and brought life and immortality to light through the gospel" (1:10b).

After emphasizing Jesus' ultimate sovereignty, Paul then refers to his own suffering for Jesus' gospel. In 1:11 he notes that he has been "a preacher and apostle and teacher" for this gospel, thereby indicating that he has been called to serve the gospel in a prominent and significant way. Now his call to serve the gospel has brought him into Roman custody. Despite being in circumstances that might well be considered shameful, however, Paul states resolutely and emphatically (1:12b), "But, I am not ashamed" (*all' ouk epaischynomai*).[10]

Two distinct yet related considerations are fundamental to any understanding of why Paul is not ashamed. Both of these points are touched upon as Paul continues in v. 12. The first consideration is embedded in the admonition with which he began this series of reflections at v. 8. Paul is a prisoner for the Lord's sake. He is in chains not for any other reason save for the testimony he has given regarding Christ Jesus.

Second, Paul is not ashamed because he is convinced of Jesus' capacity to vindicate faithfulness on the day of his triumph. In his heart Paul is fully convinced that Jesus will ultimately uphold his faithfulness and give him vindication. This second aspect will be taken up again in section six below.

As his reflections on shamefulness and faithfulness proceed, Paul cites two examples for Timothy to consider, one negative and one positive. The exact nature of the negative development that is referred to in 1:15 is difficult to determine: "You are aware that all who are in Asia turned away from me and among them Phygelus and Hermogenes" (2 Tim 1:15).

Probably the meaning here is that an extraordinary number of Christians (this number is so proportionately high that Paul writes "all" [*pantes*][11]) in the province of Asia have refused to support Paul, in effect turning their backs on him.

Paul explicitly states that Timothy is aware of this discouraging development. The sense of Paul's wording is that Timothy has met Phygelus and Hermogenes, members of the group that has turned away from Paul. If 2 Timothy presumes that Timothy is somewhere in Asia,[12] then he may indeed be well informed about the entire situation.

Why this group of Christians has proved disloyal to Paul is an intriguing question. Paul's circumstances as a Roman prisoner may well be the grounds on which this group has deserted him. In other words, this group may have turned away from Paul because they have become *ashamed* of his *chains*.

This hypothesis emerges from a consideration of the next verses, in which attention is directed to someone who is highly faithful to Paul, despite Paul's humiliating circumstances. In order to appreciate the full scope of Onesiphorus' fidelity, it is desirable to cite verses 1:16-18 in their entirety. Clearly, Onesiphorus' refusal to be ashamed of Paul in chains contrasts with the response of the group who turned from Paul. As will be explicated in the following section, these verses are also significant for the light that they shed on Paul's exact circumstances as a prisoner:

> May the Lord grant mercy to the household of Onesiphorus, for he often refreshed me; he was not ashamed of my chains, but when he arrived in Rome he searched for me eagerly and found me—may the Lord grant him to find mercy from the Lord on that Day—and you well know all the service that he rendered at Ephesus. (2 Tim 1:16-18)

In writing that Onesiphorus sought him out diligently and "refreshed" him,[13] Paul is seemingly providing new information to Timothy. Do his words also convey the meaning that Onesiphorus has since died? Paul's petition that the Lord grant mercy to the household of Onesiphorus could imply this meaning. So also could Paul's prayer that Onesiphorus himself receive mercy from the Lord on the Day of Christ's appearing?[14] If Onesiphorus were no longer providing support to Paul because he had recently died, there would be a further rationale for the urgency in Paul's request that Timothy join him in Rome.

Whether Onesiphorus had died in the meantime, is on his way to another destination, or remains in Rome, what is clear is that Timothy should take encouragement from Onesiphorus' refusal to be ashamed of Paul's chains. Onesiphorus has previously served Paul well at Ephesus. Now, in marked contrast with many other who were previously associated with Paul's ministry, he has explicitly gazed on Paul bound with chains and far from turning away, often refreshed him.

Besides having the objectives that Timothy not be ashamed of Paul's chains and that he proceed directly to Paul's side, the letter also has the purpose of providing admonitions regarding false teachers and pagan surroundings.[15] Further, Timothy himself is given extensive instructions concerning his own progress toward mature discipleship.[16] Because it dwells on these and related themes, the letter has sometimes been assessed as having the character of a final testament.[17] Several passages in which Paul himself retrospectively reflects on his journey in Christ's service also give the letter this character. These last mentioned passages will be considered in section five below.

4. Paul's Faithfulness as a Prisoner in Rome

2 Timothy provides a memorable portrait of Paul as a Roman prisoner suffering abandonment. If authored by another Christian in Paul's name, that author was not merely concerned to portray Paul's chains but also the apostle's experience of isolation and abandonment. In the paragraphs that follow it will emerge that Paul's prison circumstances and his response to them are indeed central to the meaning of 2 Timothy.

As regards Paul's circumstances, it bears emphasizing first that Rome is unmistakably the site of his imprisonment. Presumably aware that Paul was being held in Rome, Onesiphorus traveled to the imperial capital and it was there that he searched diligently for Paul and found him (1:17).[18] Second, Paul is very definitely in chains. To Onesiphorus' credit (1:16), he was not ashamed of Paul's chains (*tēn halysin mou*). It will be elaborated below that Paul's chains affront him because they are the chains that befit a criminal (2:9).

The fact that he is in chains does not signify that Paul is being held in an official public prison. Rather his confinement is at a less prominent location. This conclusion is first suggested by Paul's mention that Onesiphorus searched for him eagerly before finally finding him. If Paul were situated in an official *carcer*, Onesiphorus presumably would not have needed to search for him so diligently. A second factor, already mentioned, is that Onesiphorus was able to "refresh" Paul on an ongoing basis once he found him. This would not be easily accomplished if Paul were under severe custody. Third, the very fact that this letter could be written at all argues for conditions of confinement more relaxed than those normally associated with confinement in a *carcer*.

If 2 Timothy portrays Paul as far from being "ashamed" of his chains, the letter does not portray him as acquiescing in them either. Indeed, the modifiers "resentful" and "resistant" can be utilized in describing Paul's attitudinal response toward his bonds. In 2 Timothy, Paul is not *ashamed* of his chains, but he does *resent* them.

What is the basis for Paul's resentment? The fundamental fact that he is not a criminal is what engenders his resentment. Since he is innocent of wrongdoing, Paul's sharp comment in 2:9a is that he should not be "wearing chains like a criminal" (*mechri desmōn hōs kakourgos*).

In effect, what Paul has been doing is proclaiming the word of God in Christ. That is why he has been put into chains, wrongfully so. In the next part of this verse Paul's words suggest an attitude of resistance and defiance regarding the injustice of his chains: "But the word of God is not chained" (2 Tim 2:9b).

On one level these words can be regarded as a kind of resistance slogan imparted to Timothy. Yet on another level they express Paul's defiance toward those who have chained him: it is impossible for them to imprison and circumscribe the message that Paul has been commissioned to deliver.

Upon a moment's reflection it can be recognized that the Roman authorities themselves are the only possible referents for Paul's words of reproach. Who else is treating Paul like a criminal, chaining him in a demeaning fashion? It is the Roman authorities and no one else. And who is implicitly operating on the premise that they will contain Paul's message if they chain and execute Paul? Only the Roman authorities.

That Paul anticipates his death at the hands of these authorities is also a key feature of the circumstances which 2 Timothy portrays. This aspect has already received attention in section two above. There is still time for Timothy to undertake the journey and still time for him to be of service to Paul once he arrives. Nevertheless, Paul's time is limited; he is convinced that the end of his life is at hand.

Because it also emphasizes his faithfulness, the passage in which Paul indicates his sense of impending death deserves to be cited again in its entirety. In 2 Tim 4:5 Paul counseled Timothy to fulfill his ministry with great steadfastness, regardless of the suffering that might come. Within this context, he then reflects that the end of his own service is at hand:

> For I am already on the point of being sacrificed; the time of my departure has come. I have fought the good fight, I have finished the race, I have kept the faith. (2 Tim 4:6-7)

Two nuances of temporal meaning contribute to the definiteness with which Paul speaks about his death here. He is "already" (*hēdē*) at the point of being sacrificed.[19] The "time" (*kairos*), the decisive time, of his "departure"(*analyseōs*) is at hand. Paul will soon be leaving this life.[20] It is in this context that he evidences a certain satisfaction as regards his own steadfastness in Christ's service.

It must be emphasized that, according to 2 Timothy, these memorable words are enunciated while Paul continues as a Roman prisoner. These circumstances add a particular poignancy to Paul's words. "I have fought the good fight." Paul has conducted himself well in various situations of hardship and has continued to do so despite his sense of being abandoned by many. "I have finished the race." For many, it is a cause for shame that Paul's "race" (*ton dromon*) has brought him first to Roman chains and now to the verge of Roman execution. Yet for Paul himself, his death represents the sealing of his course of discipleship, the achievement of his goal.

"I have kept the faith." As Paul looks backward, he knows unalterably that he has been faithful to Christ. Now he will not shrink from a faithfulness unto death. The same faithfulness manifested in all that has transpired previously will be manifested anew when the verdict of his Roman judges propels him toward a martyr's death.

5. Reliable and Unreliable Christians

If 2 Timothy highlights Paul's faithfulness during the period before his condemnation, it also presents a wide spectrum of responses by other Christians to Paul in chains. Timothy himself is portrayed as steadfastly loyal, and Paul presumes Timothy's reliability throughout the letter. Others such as Luke are also faithful and reliable. To a noteworthy degree, however, 2 Timothy portrays the responses of a goodly number of Christians to Paul, Christ's prisoner, in severe terms.

In analyzing the distressful situation that Paul was facing, it is useful to begin with Hymanaeus and Philetus and the larger group to which they belong. From the character of Paul's instructions in 2:14-19, it can be deduced that Timothy knows these individuals, possibly they are located together in the same region. In this passage nothing is mentioned explicitly regarding Hymenaeus' and Philetus' response to Paul's chains. Rather, it is their false teaching and their generally ignoble conduct that is critiqued. For they "have swerved from the truth by holding that the resurrection is already past. They are upsetting the faith of some" (2:18).

Alexander the coppersmith, mentioned in 2 Tim 4:14, is another figure with whom Timothy has contact at his present location or with whom he may well have contact as he journeys to Paul's side in Rome. Again nothing in the text explicitly indicates that Alexander was ashamed of Paul's chains. But if the "harm" to which Paul refers is the harm of Paul's abandonment, then Alexander may somehow have had a role in contributing to this abandonment. Whatever the nature of Alexander's offense, even if it has nothing to do with Paul's imprisonment, it is evidently a grievous one since Paul adverts to the divine retribution that will come upon his opponent. His forceful words against Alexander are the following:

> Alexander the coppersmith did me great harm (*polla . . . kaka*); the Lord will requite him for his deeds. Beware of him yourself, for he strongly opposed our message. (2 Tim 4:14-15)

In addition to the three parties just mentioned (Hymenaeus, Philetus, and Alexander) Phygelus and Hermogenes and the group to which they themselves belong should also be mentioned in this context. As discussed in section three above, the explanation for this group's "turning away" probably should be attributed to their perception that Paul's chains and imprisonment discredited him. While there is a tone of lament in Paul's comment regarding this group (1:15), he does not criticize them severely or suggest that they will have a harsh reckoning at the day of the Lord's judgment.

To complete this overview of unreliable Christians in 2 Timothy, the responses given to Paul at the time of his formal judicial proceedings must be considered. On this topic, one verse of the letter is as significant as it is problematic: "At my first defense no one took my part; all deserted me. May it not be charged against them!" (2 Tim 4:16).

This verse poses two fundamental challenges for interpretation. Paul's reference, "at my first defense," represents the first challenge. These words hold the key for understanding Paul's legal and juridical situation in 2 Timothy. The second challenge arises from Paul's repeated assertions, "No one took my part; all deserted me." The task of the following paragraphs is to comment on both of these enigmatic references, proceeding sequentially.

Regarding Paul's first statement, the principal issue is whether the Greek term *apologia* ("defense") here refers to a full Roman trial or only to the preliminary investigation used to establish the basis for a full trial. Since *apologia* can have either meaning, it is useful to consider the implications for Paul's situation if this term denotes a preliminary hearing or if it denotes a full trial.

If *apologia* does mean a full trial and if Paul was "rescued" at the end of it, as 4:17 states, then Paul conceivably may have been free for a time only to be re-arrested and cast back into chains. On this interpretation he is now facing a *second* trial and fully expects that he will be condemned at the end of it.

The principal consideration arguing against this interpretation is the fact that had such events —official acquittal, release from chains, and new arrest—actually transpired, Timothy could be expected to know something about these developments already.[21] Yet, the contents and tone of 2 Timothy do not support the view that Timothy is aware of Paul's situation. In fact, Paul seemingly writes to familiarize Timothy with what has occurred since the time that Timothy was last with him.

On the other hand, if *apologia* refers to a preliminary hearing, then Paul has remained continuously in chains.[22] At the first court session Paul had no one to take his part. Nevertheless he was "rescued" from a totally negative outcome. His prospects are not favorable, however. He has a measure of time until his full trial commences. Convinced that this trial will end in his condemnation, Paul is at peace with the martyr's death that is on the horizon.

It should be emphasized that, in either of the two scenarios just described, Paul remains in chains awaiting a verdict that will condemn him. According to either scenario, there is still an interval of time before the final verdict will be pronounced. It is for this reason that Paul urges Timothy to join him. He desires to make good use of the time interval that he has until the Roman legal processes resume.

The present discussion now turns to consider the identity of those who were associated with Paul yet failed to take his part at his *apologia*. This issue is the second challenge for interpretation presented in 4:16. Precisely to whom is Paul referring? And what was it that Paul expected from these Christians? What should they have done to assist him?

What complicates the interpretation of this part of 4:16 is the fact that Paul elsewhere in the letter speaks of Luke as still with him ("Luke alone is with me" [Luke 4:11]). Paul also sends Timothy greetings from Eubulus, Pudens, Linus, Claudia, and "all the brethren" (4:21), other Christians who are presumably present. The statement that Luke *alone* is with him seems to imply that Paul (and Timothy) considers Luke to be in a ministerial category that is distinct from the category of the four persons mentioned at the end of the letter. Paul thus appears to have a degree of support from one esteemed associate, from four other named individuals, and from others besides them. How then can he speak so sweepingly in 4:16 when he states that *no one* took his part and that *all* deserted him?

At least three possibilities should be mentioned here.[23] The first is that Paul may mean that, apart from those few whom he mentions favorably, no one *else* took his part. In other words, except for the small handful of Christians referred to in the letter, everyone else deserted him. The second, less likely, possibility is that those mentioned favorably in the letter may have temporarily abandoned Paul at the time of his defense.[24]

The third interpretation is that Paul is referring to those Christians at Rome who have legal expertise and/or political influence and is indicating that all of *these* Christians abandoned him. According to this interpretation, Luke and the others referred to favorably were loyal to Paul at the time of his defense. Their skills and competence, however, were not such as to enable them to enter into the judicial proceedings in any way. Other Christians at Rome did possess the requisite skills and influence. But none of these Christians afforded help to Paul. Shocked by the manifest absence of support from this group, Paul emphasized this point in writing to Timothy.

Precisely what kind of support had Paul expected to receive at the time of his *apologia*? It is possible that Paul was expecting some type of legal counsel or legal intervention. The Greek *parageneto*, translated here as "take my part," has the root meaning of "be present."[25] It may indicate, however, service as a legal advocate, and it can also have the meaning of testifying as a witness at a trial.[26] If either of these latter meanings is present in Paul's use of this verb, then his expectation was for some of the Christians around him to have participated actively in his trial. But *none* of them did so.

Instead, Paul experienced abandonment and a certain isolation when he was before his judges. All of those he had been relying on for juridical assistance chose to be elsewhere. To use Paul's word, they *deserted* him.[27]

On the other hand, if Paul's use of *parageneto* does not have technical, legal meaning here but rather its fundamental meaning, "be present," then, what he is lamenting is the failure of certain Christians to be present to him, to stand with him, to minister to him. Instead of identifying themselves with Paul's cause, they have acted in the manner of Demas (4:10). They have put distance between themselves and Paul. They have all, every one of this group, deserted him.

Whatever their exact nuances of meaning, Paul's words within this passage indicate that he was still smarting over what had occurred. In the specific situation that Paul had faced, the conduct of these Christians was clearly less than what Paul had expected from them. This sharp disappointment is what he laments to Timothy.

If Paul's first words reflect an edge of bitterness as well as hurt, it is significant that his next words reflect concern for those who turned from him. "May it not be charged against them."[28] These words indicate Paul's conviction that an offense has been committed. Perhaps he does so haltingly. Paul nevertheless expresses forgiveness. The benign character of these last words is still more apparent when they are compared with the malediction regarding Alexander the coppersmith in 4:14. In the present passage nothing suggests that these Christians have turned away from Christ Jesus. But they have turned away from Paul, Christ's prisoner.

In section two of this chapter, the striking departure of Demas from Paul's side was considered as a datum that shed light on Paul's trajectory as a Roman prisoner. This event can now be regarded as one more reason why Paul is desirous of having Timothy hurry to his side before the winter season.

Within 2 Timothy, Paul does not utilize any designation such as "co-worker" in referring to Demas. It has been noted above that the same is true as regards Luke. The same absence of any ministerial designation is also a characteristic of Paul's references to Crescens and Titus in 4:10 and Tychicus in 4:12. Yet presumably Demas, Luke, Crescens, Titus, and Tychicus are to be located in a ministerial category that is distinct from the more general standing of Eubulus, Pudens, Linus, Claudia, and "all the brethren" who send greetings to Timothy at the very end of the letter.

In 4:11b Paul urges Timothy, "Get Mark and bring him with you; for he is very useful in serving me." And regarding Tychicus, Paul states in 4:12: "Tychicus I have sent to Ephesus." The inference may thus be drawn that Paul holds some form of moral influence with Mark, Tychicus, and the others he mentions at this point. Perhaps the implication is that those mentioned have ministered or served with Paul or under his auspices.

If, as seems likely, Demas has been ministering with Paul or ministering to him, then how significant is his decision to leave Paul's side *for no worthy reason*.[29] Paul has himself sent Tychicus to Ephesus. Crescens and Titus have departed, respectively, for Galatia and Dalmatia. They have seemingly done so with Paul's acquiescence— he voices no criticism regarding their departures. In contrast, Demas has left in a manner that Paul considers unwise and irresponsible. The sharpness in Paul's words describing Demas' motivation is to be emphasized (4:10): "For Demas, *in love with the present world*, has deserted me and gone to Thessalonica."

What is the core meaning of "in love with the present world" (*agapēsas ton nun aiōna*)? Seemingly disdain, and perhaps even scorn, is expressed through these words. Why does Paul deem it so reprehensible that Demas has deserted him out of love for the present world?

Two related reasons suggest themselves. The first explanation emerges from Paul's conviction that, at the second "appearing" of Jesus,[30] all of humankind will be judged by the standards of Jesus. Thus, it is manifestly foolish for Demas to follow any course of action that is not in conformity with the standards of Jesus.

The second explanation relates to the validity of Paul's witness to Jesus through his chains. Paul himself is fully convinced that his chains are not grounds for shame but rather the concrete symbols of his faithfulness. It may thus be that Paul considers Demas to be guided by the code of honor and shame followed by the secular Roman world instead of being oriented to the truly unimpeachable status that Paul possesses as Christ's prisoner.

With Demas' desertion and the departure of Tychicus, Crescens, and Titus, Paul is now cut off from everyone with whom he has previously ministered, save for Luke. It is this new situation that motivates him to appeal directly and authoritatively to Timothy.[31] Paul even appends detailed assignments to his fundamental request. As previously noted, Timothy is to get Mark and bring him along with him (4:11b). Timothy is also to bring the cloak that Paul left with Carpus at Troas and Paul's books, especially his parchments (4:13).[32]

Timothy, in contrast with Demas, will be Paul's unfailingly reliable co-minister. Far from distancing himself from Paul, Timothy will continue to revere Christ's chained prisoner and will speed to Paul's side bringing all the resources Paul has requested.

6. God's Salvation and Paul's Vindication

Although 2 Timothy images Paul experiencing abandonment and isolation, he also holds two convictions regarding salvation and personal vindication that encourage him to be resolutely faithful as Christ's prisoner. There are two passages in which 2 Timothy portrays Paul's belief that God is using his imprisonment for the purposes of salvation. In four highly significant passages Paul also expresses the conviction that he himself will *ultimately* be vindicated by Christ. These various aspects of Paul's perspective will now be considered.

What good purpose is being served through Paul's imprisonment? As previously observed, 2:9a indicates that Paul resented being kept in chains as though he were a criminal. Continuing in 2:9b Paul added the defiant reflection that the word of God cannot be chained. In the verse now cited, he then reflects on God's saving purpose in this imprisonment. Paul describes the good that is being accomplished in the following way:

> Therefore I endure everything for the sake of the elect, that they also may obtain salvation in Christ Jesus with its eternal glory. (2 Tim 2:10)

Paul's fundamental meaning here is that his faithfulness in his imprisonment is somehow a part of God's plan to bring Paul and others ("the elect") to *salvation* in Christ.[33] By means of a causality that is affirmed but not explained, God will effect a salvation that is characterized by "eternal glory." Because Paul's steadfastness in his chains somehow serves God's salvific purposes, it is important that Paul endure his imprisonment with faithfulness; Paul is indeed doing this.

If the insight that is given by Paul's words later in the letter can be integrated validly at this point, God's achievement of salvation through Paul's imprisonment also involves Paul's own proclamation of the gospel as a chained prisoner. In 4:17, when he reflects on what occurred after others deserted him at his defense, Paul states, "But the Lord stood by me and gave me strength to proclaim the message fully, that all the Gentiles might hear it" (2 Tim 4:17a).

Note that what Paul receives strength for is "to proclaim the message fully" (*to kērygma plērophorēthē*). This full proclamation is seemingly crucial in that, without it, the Gentiles of Paul's audience will not become familiar with the central truths about Christ. The reference to "all the Gentiles" seemingly has immediate reference to the Roman officials who were present at Paul's first defense, that is, the judge(s), court personnel, and soldiers who were there.[34]

Presumably God's sovereign purposes called for this immediate group to come in contact with, and be challenged by, the crucial truths concerning Jesus previously crucified but now risen. It was for this particular mission, this particular proclaiming of Jesus to these Roman officials, and to others through them, that Paul received new strength from his Lord.

In addition to holding the conviction that his imprisonment

advanced the saving purposes of God and Christ, Paul is also fully convinced that he himself will be completely vindicated when Christ returns to enact judgment and confer glory. That Christ will indeed carry him far beyond the limitations of a Roman judgment can be regarded as one of the fundamental perspectives of the letter.

Paul's conviction regarding Christ's sovereign power is expressed at the outset of 2 Timothy; however, before considering his words in chapter one it is first useful to consider the continuation of the passage that has just been analyzed. After indicating that the Lord strengthened him to proclaim the message for the sake of the Gentiles, Paul then reflects concerning Christ's power to rescue him:

> So I was rescued from the lion's mouth. The Lord will rescue me from every evil and save me for his heavenly kingdom. To him be the glory for ever and ever. Amen. (2 Tim 4:17b-18a)

The first time that "rescue" appears within this passage, it refers to a past event. The second time it is used, the reference is to a rescue that will occur in the future. Significantly, Paul's experience of the first rescue is what engenders his trust regarding the rescue he anticipates in the future.

The phrase "from the lion's mouth" can refer to Paul's deliverance from Satan, from the power of the Roman empire, from the hands of the emperor, or from death itself.[35] Paul may, however, be referring to deliverance from a *combination* of these evils.

Building upon this experience of deliverance in the present, Paul looks to the future. In the future he will be rescued, not from one specific evil or even from a specific combination of evils. Rather, he will be rescued "from every evil."[36]

It should also be emphasized that the Lord will *save* Paul for his *heavenly kingdom*. This concept of Jesus effecting Paul's salvation (here *sōsei*) is particularly significant in a Roman context in which "savior" has become a title for acclaiming the Roman emperor. The concept of Jesus bringing Paul into a heavenly kingdom (*tēn basileian autou tēn epouranion*) also has the potential for engendering tensions in a Roman world that acknowledges only one empire and one universal ruler.

Paul's words in these verses indicate that his entry into Jesus' kingdom will take place sometime in the future. Nevertheless, the kingdom of which Jesus is the supreme ruler is in existence even as Paul writes. Manifestly, Paul has not yet entered this kingdom. But Jesus does have the sovereign power to save him and bring him there.

Paul's confidence in Jesus' capacity to rescue him is grounded in his belief that God has already used Jesus' initial appearing (*epiphaneias*) to abolish death and confer unending life. This concept of the earthly arrival of Jesus as an "appearing" that effectuates salvation is well articulated at 2 Tim 1:10, a passage whose full analysis was deferred until now. Note that the appearing of Jesus is here explicitly the appearing of a *savior*. "Savior" is, in fact, Jesus' explicit title. Paul writes that God's purpose and grace has now been manifested "through the *appearing* of our Savior Christ Jesus, who abolished death and brought life and immortality to light through the gospel."

Just as "saving" and "kingdom," two concepts with implications for the Roman world, were combined in a remarkable way at 2 Tim 4:17-18, a comparable combination can be observed in this verse. As noted, "savior" has particular meaning with reference to the cult of the emperors. So also does the term "appearing."

Five decades before Jesus' birth, Julius Caesar was acclaimed at Ephesus as "the god who has *appeared* . . . the common *savior* of human life."[37] By way of comparison, Paul's claims for Jesus in this passage (and elsewhere in the letter) are far more sweeping than the claims of grandeur that the Ephesians advanced for Julius Caesar. According to 2 Timothy, Jesus has the decisive power to abolish death and confer life and immortality. Jesus' power is thus of a magnitude incomparably greater than that of any emperor.[38]

Another common feature of the two passages in 2 Timothy that refer to Jesus' second coming is that both passages mention Jesus' role as a supremely sovereign judge. Such an emphasis on the definitive judgment of Jesus his Lord is of particular significance from the standpoint of Paul's situation as a prisoner who faces the verdict of a Roman judge.

In the passage now to be considered, Paul solemnly urges Timothy to be steadfast in his preaching and in all aspects of his ministry, regardless of the circumstances:

I charge you in the presence of God and of Christ Jesus who is to judge the living and the dead, and by his appearing and his kingdom: preach the word, be urgent in season and out of season, convince, rebuke, and exhort, be unfailing in patience and in teaching. (2 Tim 4:1-2)

Three motivating factors are cited by Paul as he adjures Timothy. The "appearing" (*epiphaneian*) and the "kingdom" (*basileian*) of Christ are cited as factors to inspire perseverance. Paul's appeal is also given in the presence of God and in the presence of Jesus, who will exercise a definitive judgment.

This image of Jesus as sovereign judge of the living and of the dead is integrally related to his final appearing and is an integral aspect of the larger plan of God in Christ Jesus.[39] In Paul's perspective, no one is excluded from Christ's sovereign assize. *All* of the living and *all* of the dead will be subject to Christ's scrutiny.

Such a perspective regarding Christ's universal judgment inevitably relativizes the meaning of any verdict that the Roman authorities might pronounce against Paul. The verdict of Paul's Roman judges fades to nothingness in comparison with the judgment about Paul that Jesus will pronounce at his final appearing.

The verdict of these authorities and *these authorities themselves* will ultimately be subjected to Christ's judgment. Like Paul himself and like all of the living and all of the dead, these Roman authorities will ultimately stand before Christ and be assessed according to Christ's own standards.

Regarding Paul's vindication, one further reference remains to be considered. In 4:8 Jesus is again imaged as a sovereign judge. That which was implicit at 4:1 is now made explicit. The judgment that Jesus will render on the day of his appearing will explicitly affirm and reward Paul's faithfulness:

> Henceforth there is laid up for me the crown of righteousness, which the Lord, the righteous judge, will award to me on that Day, and not only to me but also to all who have loved his appearing. (2 Tim 4:8)

With reference to the christological images present in 2 Timothy, it should be observed that a new attribute of Jesus is presented here, the attribute of righteous judging. Jesus is *the righteous* judge. He will ultimately judge Paul with a righteousness that will relativize any verdict against Paul given by his Roman judges.[40] It must be underscored that Paul makes this avowal as a chained Roman prisoner.

In this passage Jesus is also *the Lord*.[41] Jesus, Paul's Lord, will decisively vindicate Paul and every other faithful disciple. He will do so in his capacity as the sovereign judge over all who are living and all who are dead.

What specifically does Paul expect to receive from Christ? On the great day of Christ's appearing, Paul expects to receive an insignia that will splendidly confirm the faithful service that he has rendered. This emblem will be "the crown of righteousness."[42] Christ will award it to him on that Day. And Christ will award it not only to Paul but to all who have *loved* his appearing.[43]

CHAPTER NINE

Rome and the Era of Nero as the Setting for Philippians

IN CHAPTER ELEVEN the lustrous teaching that Paul imparts in writing to the Christians at Philippi will be considered in detail. In several respects the analysis of Philippians that will be made in that chapter represents the summit of the present study. In order to prepare properly for his powerful, arresting statements in Philippians, however, the context from which Paul wrote will be analyzed in this chapter and in chapter ten.

The principal conclusions of the present chapter are that Paul wrote Philippians from Rome and that it was written at a comparatively late date in his ministry.[1] Once the analysis supporting these two positions has been presented, an additional conclusion can be established with relative ease: that Paul was almost certainly a prisoner during the reign of Nero, A.D. 54-68.

1. Rome as the Location for Philippians

Various references within the text of Philippians will constitute the prime grounding for the argument that this letter was written from Rome. But before proceeding to consider those references, it is well to examine briefly the reports from other New Testament writings and other early Christian documents that situate Paul in Rome first as a prisoner and then as a martyr. While these reports do not establish that Paul wrote Philippians from Rome, it is significant that they place him in the imperial capital. For, if Paul was in Rome as a prisoner, then he could have conceivably written Philippians from there and his letter should be scrutinized for evidence of a Roman venue.

As previously noted, methodological caution is being observed with respect to the utilization of reports from the Acts of the Apostles and from 2 Timothy within this study. Here it suffices to note briefly that each of these documents conveys that Paul became a prisoner of the Roman authorities and that he experienced Roman custody, with chains, in Rome.

It will be explained more fully below in the appendix on the Acts of the Apostles that Luke portrays Paul in Roman chains for a substantial period of time and that, as Acts closes, Paul is in Rome itself ministering with full boldness as a bound prisoner under a kind of house arrest (28:16-31). As discussed in the preceding chapter, 2 Timothy depicts Paul in chains (1:16; 2:9) and implies that a negative verdict is in the offing (4:6). Further, Rome is unmistakably the site where he is being held prisoner (1:17).

Neither Acts nor 2 Timothy provides information regarding the circumstances of Paul's death, and the New Testament as a whole does not offer any information about the end of Paul's life. Notice regarding Paul's martyrdom implied to take place in Rome, however, does come from the *Epistle of Clement to the Corinthians*, a letter written from Rome at the end of the first century or the beginning of the second.[2] Without entering into an extended analysis of this letter or the other forms of Christian tradition pertaining to the circumstances of Paul's martyrdom, it can be stated that virtually all of the early Christian sources that touch on this question assume that Paul died as a martyr and that his death took place at Rome.[3]

But did Paul write Philippians from Rome? This question must now be treated with reference to data that pertain explicitly to Philippians. It is of some significance that slim external evidence associates Philippians with the time of Paul's imprisonment in Rome. More substantively, there are at least five references internal to Philippians that point to a Roman venue.

The exact process by which letters attributed to Paul came to be included within the canon of the New Testament is far from certain. There is also uncertainty concerning the processes by which the Greek texts were first translated into Latin and concerning the role of various editors and Christian communities in sponsoring such translations. Further, the role played within this process by Marcion, a Christian writer and leader later judged heretical, is also difficult to determine.[4]

Nevertheless, some of the earliest surviving *Latin* manuscripts contain brief prefaces for the letters attributed to Paul and some scholars have concluded that these prefaces originated with Marcion. For the purposes of the present study, what is significant is that testimony regarding the location for Philippians is given in one of these prefaces. In the preface to Philippians, Marcion or some other early Christian writer began by explaining that the Philippians were Macedonians who accepted and persevered in the faith. The author then states that Paul "praises them, writing to them *from Rome*, out of prison by Epaphroditus" (emphasis added).[5]

Clearly, this declaration provides support for the thesis presently being argued regarding Paul's location in Rome. Nevertheless only minimal weight can be given to this prologue because of the obscurity that surrounds its origins. Was it written by Marcion? If so, at what date and for what exact purpose? And what is the author's own evidence for making such a statement about Paul's situation in Rome?

It is now appropriate to consider the five references within Philippians that argue on behalf of authorship from Rome. Two of these references concern the praetorian guard and Caesar's household, groups that were well established in Rome. In addition, Paul mentions three other aspects of his situation that reflect a setting in Rome and, indeed, are fully intelligible only within that setting.

It should be emphasized at the outset that it is the cumulative weight of these five references that is decisive. While some of these references could be interpreted as pertaining to another site such as Caesarea or Ephesus (the two alternative sites most frequently mentioned), it is hardly conceivable that *all five* of these references can be imaged for any location other than the imperial capital itself.

It is well to begin the analysis of these five references with a consideration of the reference to "the whole praetorian guard" that occurs at the beginning of the letter. In effect this allusion represents one part of the "defense" that Paul intends to present to his friends at Philippi. Phil 1:12-13 are thus now cited in their entirety:[6]

> I want you to know, brethren, that what has happened to me has really
> served to advance the gospel, so that it has become known through-

out the whole praetorian guard and to all the rest that these chains of mine are for Christ. (Phil 1:12-13)

It should be noted at the outset that the Greek phrase *en holō tō praitōriō* can refer to an imperial place. It is difficult to pinpoint the precise meaning of the underlying Latin word, *praetorium*, but originally it may have designated the command headquarters of a praetor.[7] Certainly, this locational meaning is present in the other New Testament occurrences of this term where it refers to the headquarters of Herod the Great in Caesarea or the headquarters of the Roman governors who ruled Judea as an *imperial* province.[8]

Nevertheless, in this instance Paul's next phrase serves to clarify that he is actually referring to the corps of praetorian guards and not to a headquarters or a camp. The accompanying phrase, "and to all the rest" (*kai tois loipois pasin*), clearly indicates that Paul is speaking about persons, about the various people who are becoming aware that his chains are for Christ.[9] In effect, he is explaining that throughout the corps of the praetorian guards,[10] and among other individuals who are involved in the administration of his case, the word has circulated that Paul's dedication to Christ is the ultimate reason for his imprisonment.

Paul is indeed evidently satisfied to be able to communicate this development. The Philippians already know that he is in Rome.[11] Paul now informs them, if they did not know, that he is under the custody of the emperor's fabled personal guards.[12] He does not want his friends to be disheartened by this news, for he himself is not discouraged or despirited by these difficult circumstances. On the contrary, he rejoices in the fact that he has been able to witness effectively to Christ among the members of this formidable and dreaded group.[13]

Parenthetically it should be noted that this just-mentioned element of satisfaction argues against the possibility that Paul could have been located at Herod's praetorium in Caesarea. As mentioned previously, the headquarters built by Herod the Great in that small coastal city was regarded as a *praetorium*. But it is difficult to imagine that Paul would have expressed such marked satisfaction if it were only in the circumscribed setting of Caesarea (with its relatively small number of Roman soldiers and other personnel) that his testimony to Christ was becoming known.[14]

Paul's reference to "Caesar's household" also contributes to the argument that Philippians was written from Rome. This reference occurs as a part of the closing greetings that Paul imparts on his own behalf and on behalf of others:

> Greet every saint in Christ Jesus. The brethren who are with me greet you. All the saints greet you, *especially those of Caesar's household.* (Phil 4:21-22; emphasis added)

It should be noted that the meaning of *Kaisaros oikias* ("Caesar's household") was not restricted to the immediate family and relatives of the emperor but encompassed also the extensive number of freed slaves who functioned in various capacities as support staff for the emperor.[15] The operation of the imperial household required a large variety of service personnel. The staffing needs of the various administrative departments of the empire were, if anything, even greater. The gradations in rank that attached to the various levels of service in each of these distinct spheres were carefully established, and a perceptible status accrued to those who served even in the most menial way.

There are two features to consider in reference to the argument that Paul's reference to "Caesar's household" indicates a location in Rome. The first feature relates to the high concentration of members of Caesar's staff in Rome. This contrasts with the lesser numbers of imperial staff members assigned to any provincial city. Presumably Paul's Christian associates (are any of them his converts?) among the members of Caesar's household are numerous enough to justify his mention of their greetings at the end of his letter. At a location where large numbers of the imperial household are concentrated, it is not difficult to imagine that there would be a significant number of Christians within their midst.[16]

The second aspect affording support for a Roman venue is related to Paul's use of the qualifier *malista* ("especially") in conveying greetings from the Christians of the imperial household. This term is particularly significant given the judicial situation that Paul is now facing. As is to be explained below, Paul's judicial surroundings themselves constitute an argument for a Roman venue. Here the point to be adverted to is that Paul is in a setting where he faces a verdict by the highest imperial tribunal. The person of the emperor now looms large in Paul's situation. Because this is so, Paul finds it useful to convey to his readers greetings *especially* from those of Caesar's immediate household.

In effect, then, this greeting from the members of Caesar's household functions as a part of Paul's encouragement to his friends at Philippi. It is true (again, Paul's readers know this) that Paul is in jeopardy from Nero and from other high Roman officials. Nevertheless, some of those who are affiliated with the emperor can be numbered among those who are actually committed to the Lord Jesus Christ. This is indeed a significant datum. It is a factor in Paul's circumstances that affords him particular consolation and he is pleased to share this encouraging piece of information with the saints at Philippi.[17]

As mentioned, what Philippians indicates with respect to Paul's judicial situation also serves to establish that this letter was written from a Roman venue. It must now be demonstrated that Philippians reflects an extended period of imprisonment and that it also intimates a death verdict as a distinct possible outcome.

How long was Paul in Rome before he had occasion to write to the Christian community at Philippi? In order for several of the developments that Paul mentions in the letter to have occurred, it seems evident that a significant period of time would have had to pass, even though it is not possible to identify this interval precisely in terms of elapsed calendar time.

The first development has already been mentioned. There has been time for the *explanation* regarding Paul's imprisonment to become known throughout the *entire* praetorian guard. It is not simply that a routine report concerning a new prisoner has spread among the Roman soldiers. Rather, there has been time for Paul's "apology" to be disseminated. Paul's chains are "for Christ." And according to his statement in 1:13, it is this explanation, this testimony, that has had time to permeate throughout the membership of the praetorian guard "and to all the rest."

The second development signaling the passage of time has not previously been mentioned. This development concerns the divisions regarding Paul that have emerged within the Christian community in the location where he is now a prisoner. These startling events are described in Phil 1:14-18, a passage that will be analyzed more fully later in this section. Here the point to be grasped is that the development of such a breach was surely not an overnight phenomenon. Presumably two groups of Christians have both had time to form an impression of Paul and the ministry he has undertaken as a prisoner. Seemingly the members of each of these groups have altered their approaches to preaching the gospel as a consequence of their respective responses to Paul. These developments are obviously known to Paul and he speaks of them as though they have been underway for some time.

Finally the situation that Paul describes in commending Timothy to the Philippians in 2:19-23 also presupposes that he has been in his chains for an extended period of time. What Paul reports is startling because he indicates a lack of reliable support at his location. Paul writes of Timothy (2:20-21): "I have no one like him, who will be genuinely anxious for your welfare. They all look after their own interests, not those of Jesus Christ." Paul's circumstances will be analyzed more carefully below. Here it is emphasized that a significant period of time must have passed, with various events and contacts intervening, before Paul would have reached the point of stating such an acute truth.

In addition to the fact that Paul has been a prisoner in Rome for an extended period of time, it is significant that Paul envisions a death sentence as a possible outcome of his judicial proceedings. Paul's first allusion to such an outcome occurs in 1:20-23 where he expresses his willingness to accept either death or continued life in this world for the sake of Christ. In this regard verse 1:20 is especially significant: "it is my eager expectation and hope that I shall not be at all ashamed, but that with full courage now as always Christ will be honored in my body, *whether by life or by death*" (emphasis added).[18]

Paul's second allusion to the possibility of a death sentence comes at 2:17 where his language is liturgical and sacrificial in character.[19] Unmistakably, the "pouring out" he refers to here is that of his own life: "Even if I am to be poured as a libation upon the sacrificial offering of your faith, I am glad and rejoice with you all."

Paul's third allusion to death comes just a few verses later. Reflecting the fact that he is being held on charges that could result in a death verdict, he refers again to his uncertain prospects when he states, "I hope therefore to send him [Timothy] just as soon as I see *how it will go with me* . . ." (2:23; emphasis added).

It is clear, then, that at the time of Philippians Paul considers his judicial situation to be grave. He has been kept in chains for a significant period of time and he has come to the point of envisioning that a negative verdict may be the result when his case is eventually adjudicated. But what are the precise charges that Paul is being held on? What is the nature of the alleged crimes that are keeping him in chains?

Clearly the charges against Paul are *capital*. Presumably, if Paul is found guilty of them, no punishment less than death will result. Yet what precise violation of Roman law is he charged with? It is worth pausing for a moment to reflect concerning the various dimensions of this question. When Paul's teaching and conduct, as reflected in his undisputed letters, is evaluated against the traditional categories utilized by Roman law to designate criminal activity, what is Paul's transgression? It will be elaborated in chapter eleven that *maiestas* had almost certainly emerged as the principal issue in Paul's case. And indeed, a negative verdict on this charge could result in a sentence of death.

It is now appropriate to gather together these various insights regarding Paul's judicial circumstances. As Philippians is being composed, Paul's case is on its way to an authoritative resolution because of the *ultimate* authority of the tribunals at Rome. In Philippians, Paul also envisions that the judicial outcome of his current imprisonment could be death. If the emperor[20] exonerates him, then Paul will immediately be freed to travel to his beloved friends at Philippi. If Paul is found guilty by the authorities at Rome, however, then his death will follow with equal immediacy. (Again, Paul actually contemplates this possibility.) Because he is imprisoned in Rome, Paul knows well that the decision of those who judge him will be decisive to the point of death or life.

This chapter's final argument on behalf of a location in Rome is related to a successful interpretation of the perplexing words at Phil 1:14-18. Once it is grasped that Rome is Paul's location, a remarkably satisfying interpretation can be provided for these verses. Clearly, there is a degree of circularity involved in making such an argument. (Paul is in Rome. The events described in this passage are highly plausible events within the life of the Christian community at Rome. Therefore Paul is in Rome). Nevertheless, when locations other than Rome are conjectured as the setting for this passage, it is not possible to explain in as convincing a way the meaning of Paul's words.

Here then is Paul's report describing the contrasting reactions and the respective undertakings by a majority and a minority of the Christian community in the place where he is being kept in chains:

> And most of the brethren have been made confident in the Lord because of my chains, and are much more bold to speak the word of God without fear. Some indeed preach Christ from envy and rivalry, but others from good will. The latter do it out of love, knowing that I am put here for the defense of the gospel; the former proclaim Christ out of partisanship, not sincerely but thinking to afflict me in my chains. What then? Only that in every way, whether in pretense or in truth, Christ is proclaimed; and in that I rejoice. (Phil 1:14-18; *author's translation*)

A sampling from among the major commentaries on Philippians reveals a great disparity of opinions regarding the groups that Paul is referring to here. In particular, there are significant disagreements regarding the motivation of the group that is hostile to Paul. According to one approach the members of this group are acting out of personal rivalry with him. According to another perspective, the members of this group are striving to advance different points of doctrine in opposition to Paul's teaching.[21]

In contrast with the interpretations that have traditionally been proposed for this passage, the decipherment now set forth focuses on Paul's chains and asserts that Paul's status as a chained prisoner has been decisive for both of the groups identified in this passage. The majority group has been inspired to a fearless proclamation of Christ *in solidarity with Paul.* But the view of the minority is that Paul should not be accepted as the authoritative spokesperson for the Christian community. These minority members have thus become motivated to proclaim Christ more vigorously. They have been doing so, however, *fully apart from Paul.*

The fundamental sense that a minority group is behaving hurtfully toward Paul is clearly communicated within the foregoing passage. Paul is evidently experiencing distress as a result of the conduct of this group. Yet he does not charge them with preaching a distorted gospel or with failing to preach the gospel. Indeed, because he considers them to be preaching Christ in an effective way, he can even bring himself to rejoice in what they are accomplishing.[22]

But if this minority group cannot be faulted for what they proclaim about Christ, why does Paul charge them with acting "from envy and rivalry" and with acting "out of partisanship, not sincerely but thinking to afflict me in my chains"?[23] Clearly these are severe criticisms for Paul to make and clearly his words express deep personal hurt over the way in which the members of this group of Christians have proceeded.

It has been emphasized above that a location in Rome corresponds extremely well with the developments that Paul describes in these verses. How is this so? How can the present situation be reconciled with the prior contact that Paul has had with the Christians of Rome through his letter to the Romans? In the sequence of developments that is now being delineated, Paul's personal experience with *some* members of the Christian community at Rome turned out to be vastly different from the kind of support he envisioned when he wrote magisterially to them in Romans.

It should be recalled in this context that Paul was not the founder of, or an influential figure in the development of, the Christian community at Rome. As discussed in chapter three above, however, Paul did address this community magisterially when he wrote to them prior to his departure for Jerusalem. In Romans, Paul reflected on his own calling and the expansiveness of his endeavors on behalf of Christ. He would come to Rome and then travel to Spain as someone unsurpassed in Christ's service.

Nevertheless, in the actual sequence of events, Christ's plan for Paul turned out to be far different from what Paul had anticipated. He did indeed come to Rome, but he did not come as a free apostle well able to testify to the gospel of Christ without restriction. Rather he came as a prisoner of the Roman authorities, bound with chains and guarded on capital charges.

To have subsequently encountered Paul in such shocking circumstances may well have been disorienting for many of those who had been the recipients of his earlier magnificent letter. For who among Paul's original audience would have been prepared for the sight of such a gifted expositor of Christ's gospel now in their midst but bound with imperial chains?

Yet Paul himself was not intimidated or daunted by his chains or by his other humiliations as a prisoner. That he was not intimidated is in fact central to the meaning of Philippians. Despite being in chains, indeed now *because of his chains*, Paul still considered himself to be an authoritative representative of Christ. And he proceeded to conduct himself as someone with the highest credentials for continuing service in Christ's name. Far from being humbled by his chains, he proceeded to take full advantage of any opportunities available to him to testify boldly on behalf of Christ "throughout the whole praetorian guard," to the members of the Caesar's household, and to "all the rest."

Presumably, in the eyes of a minority of Roman Christians, Paul's status as a prisoner and the chains he wore were a profound embarrassment. Indeed, for this minority, it was not tolerable that the prisoner Paul be taken as *the* authoritative exponent of Christ *in Rome*. These Christians had antedated Paul in Rome by many years, and they had built up their community life, working out their own *modus vivendi* regarding the imperial authorities.

To them, Paul's chains were a cause for scandal, especially in light of the teachings given in Rom 13:1-7. And if Paul were allowed to emerge as the chief proclaimer of Christ in the capital, his proclamations could pose dangers for the entire conclave of Christians now present in Rome. Nevertheless, Paul refused to be chastened by his chains and was instead witnessing boldly and powerfully. Unless his testimony could be marginalized, other Christians, voluntarily or involuntarily, could be brought to such chains!

Such a line of interpretation, with Rome presumed as the location where Paul was a prisoner, opens the way to a plausible interpretation of Paul's startling words at 1:14-18 and in other parts of the letter. Acting to counter the growing influence of Paul, a Christian minority intensified its own efforts to preach Christ. And, according to Paul's grudging acknowledgment, their proclamation of Christ was authentic.

Nevertheless, Paul perceives the baseness that alloys their preaching. He recognizes that the objective of this group was to proclaim Christ in such a way that Paul's own proclamation of Christ, *in his chains*, would be devalued. Thus does Paul strike out against the members of this group. He knows, in effect, that they are seeking to isolate him and to diminish his authoritative proclamation, as though his chains were not worn in utter faithfulness to the crucified Christ!

Paul thus experiences anguish and betrayal as a consequence of this group's activities. He uses the phrase "sorrow upon sorrow" later in the letter (2:27), speaking of Epaphroditus' brush with death as something that would have been added to Paul's other feelings of isolation. Paul knows well that other *Christians* were seeking to marginalize him, and he shares with his Philippian supporters that this experience has added greatly to the burden that he already carries in his chains!

The majority of the Christians at Rome, though, have responded favorably to Paul's witness and have been encouraged and emboldened by Paul's faithfulness. For as indicated in 1:14, the greater number of the Roman Christians "have been made confident in the Lord because of my chains and are much more bold to speak the word of God without fear." The response of this group is indeed heartening for Paul. In contrast with the negative motives he attributes to the minority, Paul commends the majority, stating that they preach Christ "from good will" and "out of love, knowing that I am put here for the defense of the gospel" (1:16).

This last clause is especially telling because it indicates the fundamental difference in perspective that separates the majority from the minority. The majority of the Roman Christians look upon Paul's chains and conclude, with Paul himself, that his chains are a part of Christ's plan for the "defense" of the gospel. The minority of Christians at Rome look upon Paul's chains, view them as scandalous and dangerous, and seek to diminish the importance of Paul's proclamation of Christ at least while he remains a chained prisoner.

It is thus the case that once these key features of Paul's circumstances are grasped, the interpretation of 1:14-18, until now a *crux interpretum*, can be accomplished with lucidity and comprehensiveness. Absent the recognition that Paul is writing to the Philippians from stressful circumstances in Rome, this passage remains a conundrum. But with the recognition that Paul now writes powerfully from the capital of the empire, what formerly was obscure now stands forth in startling light.

2. The Romans, Philemon, Philippians Sequence

In the preceding pages of this study, it has been asserted several times that the three letters possessing critical importance for this study were written in the sequence (1) Romans, (2) Philemon, (3) Philippians. The evidence for this assertion can now be marshaled. Since warrant for the thesis that Philemon was authored after Romans was presented in chapter four, two additional sets of evidence remain to be presented.

First, at a general level, support must be provided for the view that Philippians was written after Romans. Second, evidence for the thesis that Philippians was written later than Philemon must also be presented. Arguments in support of this second thesis will in fact constitute a significant part of the material for this section.

In general terms, the view that Philippians was written after Romans is easily established once it has been concluded that Philippians was written from Rome. Indeed, a Romans–Philippians sequence is virtually beyond dispute once Philippians' Roman venue has been established. The fundamental point to be stressed here is that Paul did not have personal experience with the Roman Christians and their situation in the capital when he wrote Romans. Yet, by the time of Philippians, Paul has first-hand familiarity with the evangelizing efforts by a majority group and by a minority group of these Christians at Rome. In addition, he is now obviously familiar with many other aspects of the situation in Rome.

As regards the thesis that Paul wrote Philippians after Philemon, the character of the supporting evidence is somewhat more complex. One principal argument regards the different judicial circumstances that are reflected in each letter. The other principal argument regards ministerial associates who are present with Paul at the time of each letter.

Two points from the previous analysis of Philemon in chapter six are particularly relevant for the argument regarding judicial circumstances. First, Paul closed Philemon with words expressing hope for a timely release from his chains. Second, nowhere in Philemon is there any indication that Paul envisioned a death sentence as a result of the judicial proceedings against him.

In contrast, Philippians contains references to a much different judicial situation. In Philippians Paul is uncertain as to whether the outcome of his case will be exoneration followed by release. He can indeed envision an outcome that will free him to visit Philippi. But he also reflects about a capital sentence that would allow him to depart and be with Christ.

Further, in Philippians, Paul implies that a decisive verdict is imminent. This point is evident from the fact that he wants Timothy to remain at his side for the time being. Focusing in 2:23 on a verdict that may exonerate him, Paul writes that he will send Timothy "just as soon as I see how it will go with me."

Given these significant differences regarding the judicial circumstances reflected in each letter, it must now be asked whether a

Philemon-then-Philippians sequence or a Philippians-then-Philemon sequence better accords with this data. While it is difficult to envision a plausible scenario based on Philippians preceding Philemon, such a scenario can easily be developed on the premise that Philemon is the prior letter.

Such a scenario is the following: Paul experienced Roman chains and Roman imprisonment for a certain period of time before writing to Philemon. At the time when he wrote, however, there was nothing on the judicial horizon to suggest to him that his imprisonment might end in death. Indeed, he actually contemplated exoneration and a release from his chains that would enable him to partake of Philemon's hospitality in the near future.

By the time of Philippians, however, Paul's judicial circumstances are much more ominous. Condemnation and death are now distinct possibilities. Further, the verdict, whether death or life, was not far off. Thus, while Paul hoped to visit the Philippians once again, he also recognized the distinct possibility that this visit would never occur.

The scenario just sketched is fully consistent with respect to the data contained in both letters. In contrast, efforts to reverse the sequence of the two letters and describe plausible scenarios almost immediately encounter serious difficulties. For example, is it conceivable that Paul would have refrained from mentioning that he had been saved from a negative verdict (an outcome contemplated in Philippians) when he subsequently wrote to Philemon?

An analysis of Paul's respective situations regarding ministerial associates supports the conclusion that Philemon was written prior to Philippians. In Philemon, Timothy is a co-sender of the letter, and in vv. 23-24 Epaphras, Mark, Aristarchus, Demas, and Luke are his co-ministers. At the time of Philippians, apart from Epaphroditus, who has been sent to Paul by the Philippians, Paul seemingly has only Timothy to rely on. Indeed in Phil 2:20a he poignantly writes: "I have no one like him. . . ."

Is it likely that, after writing these words to the Philippians, Paul would then have written the following words to Philemon: "Epaphras, my fellow prisoner in Christ Jesus, sends greetings to you, and so do Mark, Aristarchus, Demas, and Luke my fellow workers"? Looking toward death in Philippians, with Timothy alone to rely on, did Paul's situation shift so radically that four trusted co-ministers were now at his side?

When a negative reply is given to those questions, it then remains to ask whether the statements regarding co-workers are plausible when Phlm 23-24 precedes Phil 2:20a. This second question can be answered affirmatively. For unspecified reasons (see the following section for further comments on this development), the many associates present with Paul at the time of Philemon are no longer present with him at the time of Philippians.

3. The Elapsed Time Between Romans and Philippians

It is thus the case that analyses of Paul's judicial circumstances and his ministerial associates in Philemon and Philippians coalesce in the same conclusion, that is, that Philippians was written after Philemon. But how long was the interval between the two letters? This important question is integrally related to the larger question concerning the elapse of time between Romans and Philippians.

At this stage there are a number of developments to be analyzed that do not readily lend themselves to a precise quantification. These developments pertain to the interval between Romans and Philemon as well as to the interval between Philemon and Philippians. While the fundamental focus of this study is on the broad interval between Romans and Philippians, it is useful to assess the two subintervals separately.

For three reasons it can be concluded that a significant period of time elapsed between the writing of Romans and the writing of Philemon. The first reason regards the time necessary for the completion of the Jerusalem collection. Paul's plan to oversee this collection, announced in Romans, was apparently carried out by the time that he wrote to Philemon. Admittedly caution must be exercised in making the argument that silence about the collection in the letter to Philemon means that the collection was an accomplished fact. Yet Philemon and the church around him presumably had involvement or at least interest in this collection and seemingly, if the collection were not *fait accompli*, Paul would have mentioned it at least in passing.

Second, Paul states in Phlm 10 that he became Onesimus' spiritual father during his imprisonment. The length of time required for such a development to take place is an open question involving considerations about the conditions under which Paul could receive visitors, Onesimus' disposition, and other factors. Yet presumably a substantive amount of time would be required for Onesimus to become a well-grounded and dedicated Christian and a valued support person for Paul.

Third, is there not a fundamental sense emanating from the whole text of the letter that Paul has been in prison for a significant interval before he has had the occasion, or the inclination, to write to Philemon?[24] From the manner in which he refers to them, Paul's chains seem not to have been newly in place. Rather Paul has had time to become acclimated to imprisonment. Indeed he has come to terms with his chains to such a degree that he is able to make reference to them artfully and creatively in urging Onesimus' release.

In considering the second interval, the interval that elapsed between Philemon and Philippians, it is well to consider once again the reduction in the number of associates who are present with Paul at the time of Philippians. Presumably if Paul still enjoyed the proximate support afforded by these Christians, he would have mentioned his appreciation for them when he informed the Philippians regarding the salient features of his situation.

Are there plausible explanations that can be given for the absence of these five associates? At least two explanations can be elaborated. One possibility is that each of the five found it necessary to depart from Paul's side as a result of other priorities. Under this hypothesis, Paul remained a prisoner at the location from which he wrote Philemon. For various reasons, however, those who were initially with him subsequently departed.

A second possibility is that the location of Paul's imprisonment changed.[25] Paul's five associates thus remained at the site where Paul was originally imprisoned or else traveled elsewhere, but not to Paul's new destination. In this interpretation, Philemon was written while Paul was in chains. It was not written from Rome, though, and Paul's supporters at the time of Philemon, for undetermined reasons, did not travel to the capital.

Significantly, a requirement for either of these scenarios is an elapse of time—the very fact that holds primary importance in the present discussion. If Paul's friends left because of their own priorities, presumably they did not do so collectively and suddenly, but rather individually and over a period of time.

Yet, if Paul became separated from his supporters due to a change in the site of his imprisonment, the elapse of a certain amount of travel time is still to be reckoned with. How much time? Neither proposed scenario provides a basis for calculating a definite period of months and weeks. In terms of the circumstances that have just been considered, a sizable interval of time would seemingly have been involved.

Indications regarding the passage of time can also be gleaned from references that Paul makes within this letter to Epaphroditus. At some stage in Paul's imprisonment, the Philippian Christians sent Epaphroditus to Paul's side as a "messenger and minister" (2:25b; 4:18). During the time of his travel to Paul's side or during the time he ministered to Paul, however, Epaphroditus took ill and came close to death (2:26-27, 30).

This troubling news was then communicated to the Philippians in some unspecified way. In turn, the Philippian Christians communicated their concern back to Paul in Rome (2:26). Nevertheless, Epaphroditus did recover, and Paul thereupon resolved to send him back to Philippi carrying this letter.

The interval of time in which Epaphras journeyed, fell ill, and recovered could have occurred within the interval of time in which Paul's five associates took leave of him. (This observation presumes a scenario in which Paul remained in the same place of imprisonment, that is, in Rome.) The time required for news of the reason for Paul's imprisonment to spread throughout the praetorian guard and among all the rest, another time interval indicated within the text, could also have occurred within the same time interval in which the departure of Paul's five associates occurred. Still, whatever the precise sequence of events and the degree of overlapping, it seems clear that a substantial interval of time is required to allow for the various developments indicated or implied by the contents of Philippians.

When these considerations about the elapse of time between Philemon and Philippians are placed alongside the previous considerations about the elapse of time between Romans and Philemon, it emerges that a significant interval of time passed between the occasion of sending Romans *to* Rome and the occasion of sending Philippians *from* Rome. Allowing for the possibility that some developments could have occurred simultaneously, the total elapsed time would seem not to be less than the sum of the following intervals:

(1) the interval of time for Paul to complete his collection for the Jerusalem church

(2) the interval of time for the events resulting in Paul's imprisonment and chaining to have transpired

(3) the interval of time required for Paul, in prison, to have become Onesimus' spiritual father

(4) the interval of time required for Paul to have suffered the loss of the five co-workers who were present to him when he authored Philemon

Again, it would be helpful to be able to specify in terms of years, months, and weeks, the time that elapsed between the writing of Romans and the composition of Philippians. But the available data do not permit such exactness. Still, the two principal conclusions that have been reached should not be neglected.

As delineated above, it is a significant conclusion, first, that Romans, followed by Philemon, followed by Philippians was the sequence of these three undisputed letters of Paul. Second, it is a significant conclusion that a substantial period of time elapsed between the writing of Romans and the composition of Philippians. Apart from the time required for Paul to oversee the completion of the Jerusalem collection, the remainder of this interval was time that Paul spent in Roman chains.

4. Paul Held Prisoner During Nero's Reign

As noted in chapter three, the dates for Tiberius Claudius Nero Caesar, commonly known as Nero, are A.D. 54 to 68. The sudden death of Claudius (perhaps arranged by Agrippina) enabled his mother, Agrippina, to maneuver Nero to the imperial throne when he was only seventeen. Thirteen years later, when he committed suicide to avert a worse death at the hands of Roman soldiers in revolt, he was only thirty. Yet what an extraordinarily brutal and disgusting period of rule did Nero's reign represent. As will be described, the nature of Nero's conduct was so reprehensible that, on his death, the Roman senate took the unprecedented step of officially damning his memory.

Was Paul a prisoner under Nero? In section one of this chapter mention was made of reports from the Acts of the Apostles, 2 Timothy, and *1 Clement* relating to Paul's imprisonment and death in Rome. It should now be noted that none of these works explicitly states that Nero was involved in Paul's case. Further, neither Philippians itself nor any of Paul's other letters mentions Nero by name. Nevertheless, given the fundamental chronology of Paul's life, it is virtually certain that Nero was the reigning emperor during the time of Paul's imprisonment in Rome. Further, as mentioned above, given what is known regarding the emperor's participation in capital cases, it is probable that Nero was the ultimate judge over Paul's own case.

To be sure, there are uncertainties regarding Paul's date of birth and doubts regarding the exact date of his conversion and commission by the risen Jesus. In addition there are uncertainties regarding key events in his ministry and regarding the precise time of his imprisonment. Nevertheless, in terms of datable events referenced in Paul's own letters and in the Acts of the Apostles, Pauline scholars have been able to identify intervals or bands of time, within which given events in Paul's life can be located with assurance.

And thus, while there is still speculation about the exact dates of Paul's time in Rome, virtually all scholars who treat this question[26] locate Paul's imprisonment within the years of Nero's rule.[27] In effect, wherever a scholar locates Paul's Roman imprisonment within the interval of time that runs from the late 50s to the middle 60s, Paul was still a prisoner within the era of Nero.

In chapter ten, additional reflections about Paul's presence in Rome will be presented in reference to two key events within Nero's relatively long reign: Nero's murder of his mother Agrippina in the year 59 and his barbaric persecutions of Christians presumably in the year 64. In reference to these and other Neronian events, it would be gratifying to know the exact duration of Paul's imprisonment. But the fact that Nero exercised supreme power while Paul was a prisoner in chains is a datum of extraordinary consequence in and of itself.

In effect, the stage has now been set for the three chapters that remain in this study. It has been established that Philippians is chronologically the last of Paul's undisputed letters and that Philippians was written from Rome. Further, Philippians was written during the years when Nero reigned. In the next chapter it will be seen that Paul and Nero diverged significantly in regard to Nero's claims of sovereignty and Jesus' ultimate sovereign power. The final two chapters will explicate that Philippians itself reflects Paul's conscious effort to emphasize Jesus' sovereignty in the face of every competing claim and at the possible cost of Paul's own life.

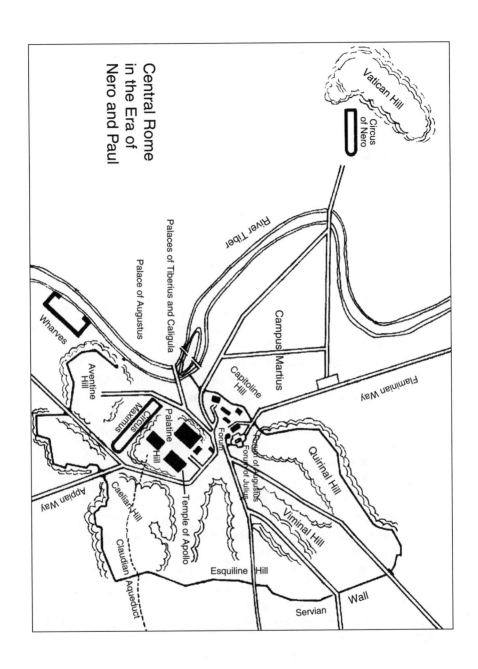

Central Rome
in the Era of
Nero and Paul

Vatican Hill

Circus
of Nero

River Tiber

Campus Martius

Flaminian Way

Palaces of Tiberius and Caligula

Palace of Augustus

Wharves

Aventine
Hill

Capitoline
Hill

Forum

Quirinal Hill

Forum of Augustus

Forum of Julius

Circus Maximus

Palatine
Hill

Viminal Hill

Appian Way

Caelian Hill

Temple of Apollo

Esquiline Hill

Claudian Aqueduct

Servian   Wall

CHAPTER TEN

Nero and Paul:
Key Areas of Divergence

HAVING DETERMINED THAT PAUL was held prisoner in Rome during Nero's reign, it is now relevant to focus attention on various areas in which attitudes and practices that are reliably attributed to Nero dramatically diverge from attitudes and practices favored by Paul. Within this analysis, a passage from Paul's letter to the Christians at Rome that previously received brief mention will now receive extended consideration. This passage, Rom 1:18-32, assumes particular importance when its application is extended to encompass Nero and his circle.

Rom 13:1-7, the noteworthy passage in which Paul recommended subjection to Nero and the other authorities of the empire, is also in the background at this point. Indeed, it is extremely significant that both Rom 13:1-7 and Rom 1:18-32 are contained in the magisterial letter that Paul previously sent to the Christians in the very city where he now finds himself in chains!

The developing multifaceted relationship between Paul and the Christian community at Rome needs to be kept in mind as the present chapter unfolds. How extensively had Paul's letter circulated among the members of this community? What assessment of his teachings had been made by the time that Paul arrived as a prisoner? Did the Christians at Rome view his teaching in 1:18-32 as applicable to Nero? And what was their reaction when they reached Paul's teaching in 13:1-7?

Did Paul have any direct contact with Nero when he first arrived

in Rome as a prisoner? Absent any personal contact, Paul still presumably received reports about aspects of the emperor's practice that
conflicted with the standards of the gospel. The purpose of the present chapter is to document the profound contrast between Nero's
outlook on the world and Paul's. The way will then be open for the
argument of chapters eleven and twelve that Paul intended Philippians to stand as a response to Nero's practices and claims.

1. Nero's Depravity and Murderousness

There are three principal ancient authors who delineate the depravity and the murderousness of Nero: Tacitus, Suetonius, and Dio
Cassius. Cornelius Tacitus was born around the year 55 and published *The Annals* in A.D. 116. Gaius Suetonius was born approximately fifteen years after Tacitus but published his *Lives of the
Caesars* in the year 120, shortly after the appearance of *The Annals*.
Dio Cassius flourished approximately one hundred years after his
two more acclaimed predecessors. Born between 155 and 164, he
composed his *Roman History* in the interval between 200 to 222. In
addition to the treatments of Nero given by these three authors, the
passing references to Nero's reign that are made by the Mestrius
Plutarchus (Plutarch) within his work *Parallel Lives* also repay attention. Plutarch was born in Greece c. A.D. 50 and died c. 120. *Parallel Lives* was finalized near the end of his own life.

For the purposes of the present investigation, it is not necessary to
conduct an extended discussion of the hermeneutical issues involved
in utilizing the writings of Tacitus, Suetonius, and Dio Cassius. Each
of these writers presents a highly negative picture of Nero and his
reign. Though only Tacitus can claim to have had a first-hand experience of Nero's Rome, all three had access to various official documents, archival materials, and testimonies.

Clearly, once Nero had been pursued to his death and his memory
had been formally damned by the Roman senate, these events exercised a significant impact on the various assessments of Nero's years,
particularly those written from a senatorial perspective. While some
modern historians have written more favorably of Nero, emphasizing various achievements made during his reign, it remains incontrovertible that Tacitus, Suetonius, and Dio Cassius, those whose
accounts are closest to Nero's circumstances, all depict Nero's

depraved and murderous behavior overshadowing any positive accomplishments.

Indeed, the portraits of Nero that are presented by these major works are remarkable for the consistency with which they attribute morally repugnant behavior to him. Even allowing for negative predispositions by Tacitus and Suetonius and the comparative lateness of Dio Cassius' work, it still seems unassailable that Nero himself provided a basis for the disgusting reports about him that are to be found in these surviving accounts.

In what follows, passages from Tacitus and from Dio Cassius will be cited, each testifying to Nero's sexual depravity. These excerpts will be followed by representative passages from Suetonius, Plutarch, and Tacitus describing episodes involving Nero's murderousness.

After these examples of Nero's behavior have been considered, passages expressly repudiating such conduct from Paul's own writings will then be considered. This first phase of dialectic will prepare the way for a second phase that is yet more significant within the framework of this study. This second phase will juxtapose Paul's fundamental perspective regarding "gods and lords" with Nero's obsession regarding popular acclaim and his desire to have all possible honors accorded to him.

In the following passage from Tacitus describing Nero's licentiousness, an aspect that Tacitus mentions in his first sentence deserves particular emphasis within the context of the present study. It is Tacitus' methodological statement that he intends this single report detailing Nero's aberrant behavior to represent effectively all of the comparable degrading episodes that will not be reported. Tacitus himself was convinced that Nero frequently indulged in such debauchery. He did not wish, however, to narrate the same basic story over and over again.

> In point of extravagance and notoriety, the most celebrated of the feasts was that arranged by Tigellinus; which I shall describe as a type, instead of narrating time and again the monotonous tale of prodigality. He constructed, then, a raft on the Pool of Agrippa, and superimposed a banquet, to be set in motion by other craft acting as tugs. The vessels were gay with gold and ivory, and the oarsmen were catamites marshalled according to their ages and their libidinous attainments. He had collected birds and wild beasts from the ends of the earth, and marine animals from the ocean itself. On the quays of the lake stood

brothels, filled with women of high rank; and opposite, naked harlots met the view. First came obscene gestures and dances; then, as darkness advanced, the whole of the neighbouring grove together with the dwelling-houses around, began to echo with song and glitter with lights. Nero himself, defiled by every natural and unnatural lust had left no abomination in reserve with which to crown his vicious existence; except that, a few days later, he became, with the full rites of legitimate marriage, the wife of one of that herd of degenerates who bore the name of Pythagoras. The veil was drawn over the imperial head, witnesses were despatched to the scene; the dowry, the couch of wedded love, the nuptial torches, were there: everything, in fine, which night enshrouds even if a woman is the bride, was left open to the view. (*The Annals* 15.37)

Dio Cassius, in the excerpt from his *Roman History* that is now cited, describes Nero's personal licentiousness and his sponsorship of debauchery in terms comparable to those of Tacitus.[1] The distinctive note added by Dio Cassius is that such orgies could spawn conflict and murder. It is to be noted also that, although this particular report pertains to the year A.D. 64, such profligate behavior is attributed to Nero not only at that time, but also at earlier and later stages of his rule:

Tigellinus had been appointed director of the banquet and everything had been provided on a lavish scale. The arrangements made were as follows. In the centre of the lake there had first been lowered the great wooden casks used for holding wine, and on top of these, planks had been fastened, while round about this platform taverns and booths had been erected. Thus Nero and Tigellinus and their fellow-banqueters occupied the centre, where they held their feast on purple rugs and soft cushions, while all the rest made merry in the taverns. They would also enter the brothels and without let or hindrance have intercourse with any of the women who were seated there, among whom were the most beautiful and distinguished in the city, both slaves and free, courtesans and virgins and married women; and these were not merely of the common people but also of the very noblest families, both girls and grown women. Every man had the privilege of enjoying whichever one he wishes, as the women were not allowed to refuse anyone. Consequently, indiscriminate rabble as the throng was, they not only drank greedily but also wantoned riotously; and now a slave would debauch his mistress in the presence of his master, and now a gladiator would debauch a girl of noble family before the eyes of her father. The pushing and fighting and general uproar that took place, both on the part of those who were actually going in and on the part of those who were standing round outside, were disgraceful. Many men met their death in these encounters, and many women, too, some of the latter being suffocated and some being seized and carried off. (*Roman History, Epitome of Book* 62.15.1-6)

Since it describes still another aspect of Nero's unbridled behavior, Suetonius' report regarding the ease with which Nero undertook murder is now appropriately considered. The previous excerpt from Dio Cassius testified that at Nero's orgies, riotous behavior sometimes eventuated in murder. Here Suetonius reports that Nero consciously and steadily eliminated those who appeared to rival him. According to this report, Nero's murders and forced suicides were not restricted to imagined rivals for the imperial throne. Individuals who simply displeased Nero or fell from his favor were also among those who forfeited their lives:

Indeed there is no kind of relationship that he did not violate in his career of crime. He put to death Antonia, daughter of Claudius, for refusing to marry him after Poppaea's death, charging her with an attempt at revolution; and he treated in the same way all others who were in any way connected with him by blood or by marriage. Among these was the young Aulus Plautius, whom he forcibly defiled before his death, saying, "Let my mother come now and kiss my successor," openly charging that Agrippina had loved Plautius and that this had roused him to hopes of the throne. Rufrius Crispinus, a mere boy, his stepson and the child of Poppaea, he ordered to be drowned by the child's own slaves while he was fishing, because it was said that he used to play at being a general and an emperor. He banished his nurse's son Tuscus, because when procurator in Egypt, he had bathed in some baths which were built for a visit of Nero's. He drove his tutor Seneca to suicide, although when the old man often pleaded to be allowed to retire and offered to give up his estates, he had sworn most solemnly that he did wrong to suspect him and that he would rather die than harm him. He sent poison to Burrus, prefect of the Guard, in place of a throat medicine which he had promised him. The old and wealthy freedmen who had helped him first to his adoption and later to the throne, and aided him by their advice, he killed by poison, administered partly in their food and partly in their drink. (*The Lives of the Caesars: Nero* 35.4-5)

The defining moment for Nero's brutal murderousness occurred with the murder of Agrippina, his own mother, in A.D. 59.[2] Agrippina seems to have exemplified a libidinousness and murderousness not unlike Nero's own. As noted above, she was widely credited with having arranged the poisoning of her uncle and subsequent husband, Claudius, in order to open the way to the emperorship for Nero, her son by a previous marriage. At the outset of his rule Nero was highly influenced and gravely constrained by this formidable woman, his mother. After five years, however, Nero elected to take the reins of imperial power fully unto himself by ordering and overseeing his mother's death. With this deed the aberrant, amoral character of the now twenty-two year old emperor became publicly defined.

Nero's machinations with respect to his mother and the arrangements he contrived for her death are reported at some length by Tacitus, Suetonius, and Dio Cassius.[3] For the purposes of the present study, however, it suffices to cite Plutarch's cameo characterization of Nero. In his succinct description of Nero, Plutarch focuses on that which was most salient about him—that he instigated the murder of his mother.[4]

And Claudius, having adopted Agrippina's son, gave him the name of Nero Germanicus. This Nero came to the throne in my time. He killed his mother, and by his folly and madness came near subverting the Roman empire. He was the fifth in descent from Antony. (*Antony* 87.4)

It has been stated above that the principal purpose for this section is to set forth the context that Paul faced as a prisoner in Nero's Rome. Accordingly, significant reports regarding Nero's debaucheries and his murderousness have now been presented. Seemingly Nero's brutality began to express itself without restraint in the years following his mother's murder. Nevertheless, significant expressions of this depravity can be traced virtually from the outset of his reign and these did not escape notice within the capital.[5]

When was Paul a prisoner in Rome? There is justification for considering this question once more in an effort to consider Paul's custody with reference to two events whose dates are established. The first of these events, the matricide of A.D. 59, has already been mentioned. The second event, the brutal measures of Nero in A.D. 64, must now receive attention. For according to Tacitus, Suetonius, and other sources, it was in that year that a mysterious fire devastated a considerable part of Rome; and, according to Tacitus in one of his most well-known passages, *Christians* were subsequently put to death with outrageous barbarism as Nero sought to divert away from himself popular suspicion about the origins of the fire.

Can it be supposed that Paul arrived in Rome as a prisoner sometime within the interval bounded by Nero's murder of his mother in 59 and Nero's execution of numbers of Roman Christians in 64? The mere posing of such a question almost immediately serves to generate an entire series of related facets and images pertaining to prisoner Paul in Nero's Rome. Before exploring some of the avenues that are opened by this question, it is well to cite Tacitus' report regarding Nero's persecution of Christians, an undertaking carried out with the same uninhibited callousness and brutality that have just been analyzed as characteristic of Nero:

> Nero substituted as culprits, and punished with the utmost refinements of cruelty, a class of men, loathed for their vices, whom the crowd styled Christians. Christus, the founder of the name, had undergone the death penalty in the reign of Tiberius, by sentence of the procurator Pontius Pilatus, and the pernicious superstition was checked for a moment, only to break out once more, not merely in Judaea, the home of the disease, but in the capital itself, where all things horrible or shameful in the world collect and find a vogue. First, then, the confessed members of the sect were arrested; next, on their disclosures, vast numbers were convicted, not so much on the count of arson as for hatred of the human race. And derision accompanied their end: they were covered with wild beasts' skins and torn to death by dogs; or they were fastened on crosses, and, when daylight failed were burned to serve as lamps by night. Nero had offered his Gardens for the spectacle, and gave an exhibition in his Circus, mixing with the crowd in the habit of a charioteer, or mounted on his car. Hence, in spite of a guilt which had earned the most exemplary punishment, there arose a sentiment of pity, due to the impression that they were being sacrificed not for the welfare of the state but to the ferocity of a single man. (*The Annals* 15.44)

In writing to the Philippians did Paul have any knowledge of events such as these? At least two scenarios can be delineated in response to this question. The less likely scenario is that Paul arrived in Rome in the midst of, or after, this persecution. If such were the case, then Paul, in writing to the Philippians, would have known that Nero had specifically proceeded against Paul's sisters and brothers in the faith in a brutal, ferocious manner. Under such a scenario, Paul's decrying of those who "live as enemies of the cross of Christ" in Phil 3:18b reflects this added dimension of meaning.

Alternatively, Paul may have arrived in Rome after Nero's matricide in 59 but prior to Nero's persecutions in 64. In this scenario Paul would have had a definite perspective regarding Nero's depraved conduct when he wrote Philippians but would not have been responding to the emperor's harsh measures specifically against Christians. Nevertheless, a superabundance of recitals pertaining to the cruelty and murderousness of Nero would have become available to Paul once he was in Rome, and these reports alone would be sufficient for influencing his perspective regarding allegiance to the emperor.

2. Paul's Earlier Repudiation of Murder and Licentiousness

That Paul enunciated an approach to sexuality that was plainly at variance with the wantonness of Nero and his associates seems indisputable. Evidence of the disciplined character of Paul's approach is to be found in 1 Thessalonians, 1 and 2 Corinthians, Galatians, and Romans, that is, in virtually all of Paul's undisputed letters prior to Philippians.[6]

For the purposes of the present study there is no better quarry from which to mine key features of Paul's sexual ethic than from his letter to the Christians of Nero's capital. Previously, in chapter three of this study, Paul's concern to provide support for a Christian sexual ethic that was profoundly challenged by the sexual attitudes and practices of pagan Rome was identified as one of his purposes in writing. It is now appropriate to elaborate on the treatment provided in chapter three taking account of two passages from Romans that were not previously considered.

The first passage, in which Paul provides an extended critique of licentious conduct and a comprehensive listing of other forms of immorality, occurs at the beginning of the letter. As will now be seen, Paul is convinced that the purposes of God's created order provide

the standard for right human conduct, and he is also convinced that
these purposes have been violated egregiously:

> For the wrath of God is revealed from heaven against all ungodliness
> and wickedness of men who by their wickedness suppress the truth.
> For what can be known about God is plain to them because God has
> shown it to them. Ever since the creation of the world his invisible
> nature, namely, his eternal power and deity, has been clearly perceived
> in the things that have been made. So they are without excuse; for
> although they knew God they did not honor him as God or give
> thanks to him, but they became futile in their thinking and their sense-
> less minds were darkened. Claiming to be wise, they became fools, and
> exchanged the glory of the immortal God for images resembling mor-
> tal man or birds or animals or reptiles.
>
> Therefore God gave them up in the lusts of their hearts to impurity,
> to the dishonoring of their bodies among themselves, because they
> exchanged the truth about God for a lie and worshipped and served
> the creature rather than the Creator, who is blessed for ever! Amen.
>
> For this reason God gave them up to dishonorable passions. Their
> women exchanged natural relations for unnatural, and the men like-
> wise gave up natural relations with women and were consumed with
> passion for one another, men committing shameless acts with men and
> receiving in their own persons the due penalty for their error.
>
> And since they did not see fit to acknowledge God, God gave them
> up to a base mind and to improper conduct. They were filled with all
> manner of wickedness, evil, covetousness, malice. Full of envy, mur-
> der, strife, deceit, malignity, they are gossips, slanderers, haters of
> God, insolent, haughty, boastful, inventors of evil, disobedient to par-
> ents, foolish, faithless, heartless, ruthless. Though they know God's
> decree that those who do such things deserve to die, they not only do
> them but approve those who practice them. (Rom 1:18-32)

A close analysis of this passage reveals that Paul's presentation
regarding the created order and human violations of this order is
made with extreme care.[7] Given the principal concerns of the present
study it is not necessary to consider the various detailed aspects of his
argument. Rather basic observations stressing the applicability of
this passage to the situation of the Roman Christians are sufficient in
the present context.

It has been debated whether the present passage includes Jews as
well as Gentiles within its frame of reference. Certainly the attitudes

and practices of Gentiles are definitely circumscribed by Paul's words even if Jewish practice is also included within his overview. Also Gentiles presently living, as well as those of earlier eras, are criticized for engaging in practices that are inimical to God's created order. And thus does God's "wrath" extend to those who *presently* give themselves over to sinful and idolatrous practices.

How would the members of the Christian community at Rome have responded to this part of the letter when they read it or heard it proclaimed? If this letter reached them during the initial years of Nero's reign, its teaching would have been fresh in their mind as Nero's personal sexual depravity began to manifest itself. Not that such practices were unheard of in Rome prior to Nero!

At this juncture it is useful to reflect again on the status of Paul's letter between the time it was written and the time when Paul arrived in Rome as a prisoner. Did it circulate among the members of the community or was it retained in one place? Would copies have been made in order to facilitate a wider distribution. And (such a development, adverted to in chapter three, should not be ruled out), could this letter ever have fallen into the hands of the imperial authorities?

It is useful to conjecture briefly regarding the potential impact of this letter on the authorities in Rome. As indicated in chapter three above, any Roman official, Nero included, who became familiar with the contents of Rom 13:1-7 could only have commended Paul! But what of the teaching contained in 1:18-32? To what degree would such a line of teaching have engendered uneasiness and hostility on the part of Nero and the other prominent Romans who readily and frequently engaged in debauchery? In this regard it should be noted that Paul explicitly names *murder* when he lists the forms of conduct that are inimical to God's intentions and God's created order.

Significantly, this is the only instance in any of his undisputed letters in which Paul expressly condemns murder. Is Paul convinced that murderous conduct is an evil that the Christians at Rome need to be expressly warned against? Or is it simply that he includes murder for the sake of completeness given the fact that he is setting forth a comprehensive catalogue of immoral conduct that is to be rejected? Nero accomplished the murder of his mother in the year 59. Presuming that Paul's letter was already in the hands of his Roman readers by that date, Nero's matricide seemingly would not explain the listing of murder in Paul's catalogue. Nevertheless, the murder of Claudius, bringing Nero to power, had taken place five years earlier. Also prior to the poisoning of Claudius, murder was not an unknown phenomenon in Rome!

Seemingly the least that may be said is that Paul's teaching against murder and against libidinous behavior represented, *in principle,* a powerful critique of the brutal and depraved practices that Nero came to exemplify. Presumably composed before Nero's aberrations came to be publicly manifested, Paul's articulate decrying of such reprehensible conduct retained its validity for all of Nero's years.

Given the forcefulness and comprehensiveness of Paul's teaching against sexual misconduct and violent behavior in this passage, it is intriguing to find Paul returning to the same subject, albeit more briefly, in chapter thirteen. Paul seemingly considered counsel to avoid profligate behavior and all forms of behavior associated with orgies as one of his definite objectives in Romans.

In this latter passage, perhaps because it focuses on the conduct appropriate for committed Christians, there is a change in the rationale that Paul presents. Formerly his appeal was to God's order in creation. Now his appeal is integrally related to the premise that Christ's return is not distant. (The eschatological thrust of these verses has already been noted in chapter three.) Nevertheless, Paul's conclusions regarding the types of conduct to be rejected agree fundamentally with the conclusions that he presented at the beginning of the letter:

> Besides this you know what hour it is, how it is full time now for you to wake from sleep. For salvation is nearer to us now than when we first believed; the night is far gone, the day is at hand. Let us then cast off the works of darkness and put on the armor of light; let us conduct ourselves as in the day, not in reveling and drunkenness, not in debauchery and licentiousness, not in quarreling and jealousy. But put on the Lord Jesus Christ and make no provision for the flesh, to gratify its desires. (Rom 13:11-14)

3. Nero's Obsession with Titles and Acclaim

The present section of this study returns to the writings of Dio Cassius, Suetonius, and Tacitus in order to establish Nero's near megalomaniacal desire for titles, prizes, and other forms of popular acclaim. In addition to the reports provided by these historians, reference will be made to inscriptions and other archaeological findings which indicate that "lord" and "savior," two titles of extraordinary value for Paul, were regularly accorded to Nero.

For the purposes of the present study, it is not necessary that the reports cited from Dio Cassius, Suetonius, and Tacitus be accurate in every particular. In particular, several of Dio Cassius' stories pertaining to Nero's fixation on his own acclaim are bizarre, nearly to the point of being ludicrous. Yet even if the following reports, and others comparable to them, are discounted a certain percentage to allow for exaggeration, the picture that emerges is still that of dangerous obsession.

As his reign progressed, and particularly after the murder of his mother, Nero became more and more concentrated on his unsurpassed sovereignty and the acclaim that he considered due him. Along with his imperial prerogatives, he increasingly desired to have his artistic talents in music and acting and his abilities in wrestling and chariot driving celebrated universally. And thus, while there is room for dispute regarding the degree to which Nero violated conventions in seeking to fulfill his own desires for affirmation and adulation, that he did overstep the traditional norms in these areas can hardly be disputed.

As an orienting statement regarding Nero's behavior in these matters, Suetonius' summary paragraph near the end of his treatment of Nero's life is useful. Did Nero *seriously* contemplate renaming the month of April in his own honor? If so, that would be but one example of the unconventional behavioral patterns that Suetonius attributes to him:

> He had a longing for immortality and undying fame, though it was ill-regulated. With this in view he took their former appellations from many things and numerous places and gave them new ones from his own name. He also called the month of April Neroneus and was minded to name Rome Neropolis. (*Lives of the Caesars: Nero* 55)

In delineating Nero's obsessive concern with popularity and honors, Dio Cassius describes a number of the devices that Nero employed to *insure* that he would be well acclaimed. Dio locates the episodes that will now be considered in the year 67 in connection with Nero's tour of Greece. Inasmuch as the uprisings against him brought about Nero's suicide in 68, the tour of Greece was, in retrospect, one of Nero's final projects. Nevertheless, it may be argued that such self-aggrandizing behavior was not unknown for Nero in his earlier years as emperor.

Can there be exaggeration in Dio's descriptions of how Nero contrived to gain the first-place awards in the prestigious Olympian and Pythian games while on his tour? Clearly, there may be. As will be seen in the text and notes below, however, Dio describes numerous occasions on which Nero's obsessions in these matters manifested themselves. And what Dio describes in some detail is not unknown to the other ancient historians who have written of Nero. In the following excerpt, Dio emphasizes Nero's desire not only for the victories but also for the titles of acclaim that his victories would bring:

> All this behavior, nevertheless, was witnessed, endured, and approved, not only by the crowd in general, but also by the soldiers. They acclaimed him Pythian Victor, Olympian Victor, Victor in the Grand Tour, Universal Victor, besides all the usual expressions, and of course joined to these names the titles belonging to his imperial office, so that every one of them had "Caesar" and "Augustus" as a tag. (*Roman History, Epitome of Book* 62.10)

According to Dio Cassius, Nero's obsession also extended to the very wording of the proclamations with which his victories in these contests were announced. Again, caution should be exercised in attributing a high degree of accuracy to an author who wrote about these episodes well over a century later. Significantly, Dio Cassius expressly portrays Nero autonomously bestowing his crown upon the Roman people (there is no mention of the Roman senate), and upon all in the world he ruled. In his own editorial comment Dio Cassius then critiques inappropriate aggrandizing behavior by someone who already "possesses" a world:

> The proclamation always ran: "Nero Caesar wins this contest and crowns the Roman people and the inhabited world that is his own." Thus, though possessing a world, according to his own statement, he nevertheless went on playing the lyre, making proclamations, and acting tragedies. (*Roman History, Epitome of Book* 62.14.4)

The foregoing episodes all related to Nero's conduct in Greece. Yet, as Dio Cassius' account continues, it is clear that Nero's triumphant return to Rome in 68 was orchestrated in the same vein. That several of the previously mentioned accolades now fill the Roman air is not surprising given the fact that Nero previously standardized his official victory proclamations. Nero's fall was at hand. Ironically, right to the very end, his desire for acclaim is portrayed as insatiable:

> The city was all decked with garlands, was ablaze with lights and reeking with incense, and the whole population, the senators themselves most of all, kept shouting in chorus: "Hail, Olympian Victor! Hail, Pythian Victor! Augustus! Augustus! Hail to Nero, our Hercules! Hail to Nero, our Apollo! The only Victor of the Grand Tour, the only one from the beginning of time! Augustus! Augustus! O, Divine Voice, Blessed are they that hear thee." (*Roman History, Epitome of Book* 62.20.5)

Nero's previously described murderousness cannot be prescinded from in considering these almost farcical reports about his obsession with honors and prerogatives.[8] For the same person who murdered without regard for any conventional standards is also the same person who sought prized titles without any regard for conventional means.

According to still another report by Dio Cassius, Nero, once having acquired a title, did not stop short of ordering the murder of persons who threatened his own absolute possession of a prized title. Helius was Nero's surrogate in Rome during the just described campaign for victories and titles in Greece. Acting in accord with what were presumably Nero's wishes, Helius ordered the execution of Sulpius Camerinus on the following grounds:

> In Rome during this same period Helius committed many terrible deeds. Among other things he put to death one of the foremost men, Sulpicius Camerinus, together with his son, the complaint against them being that they would not give up their title of Pythicus, received from some of their ancestors, but showed irreverence toward Nero's Pythian victories by their use of this same title. (*Roman History, Epitome of Book* 62.18.2)

Two reports by Tacitus provide further testimony that Nero's fanatical concern with prerogatives also extended to the titles he wanted *uniquely* held by the members of his own administrative staff. As Tacitus recounts the matter, Nero sought to discredit Torquatus Silanus whom he regarded as a threat. At the heart of the case that Nero contrived against Torquatus was the charge that this senator allowed his staff members to hold titles parallel to those held by Nero's own aides. Tacitus reports that Nero then subsequently proceeded against Torquatus' nephew on the same grounds, grounds that were totally implausible in the latter's case. The excerpts that follow contain the substance of Tacitus' reports as regards each of these cases:

> For in those very days, Torquatus Silanus was driven to die. . . . The accusers had orders to charge him with a prodigal munificence which left him no hope but in revolution, and to insist, further, that he had officials among his freemen whom he styled his Masters of Letters, Petitions, and Accounts—titles and rehearsals of the business of empire. (*The Annals* 15.35)

> He then attacked Silanus himself in the same strain as his uncle Torquatus, alleging that he was already apportioning the responsibilities of empire, and appointing freemen to the charge of "accounts, documents, and correspondence": an indictment at once frivolous and false; for the prevalent alarms had made Silanus vigilant, and his uncle's doom had terrified him into special caution. (*The Annals* 16.8)

Up until this point in the discussion, nothing has been said regarding Nero's appreciation for efforts in different parts of the Roman world to ascribe a quasi-divine or divine status to the persons of the Roman emperors. Certainly a comprehensive investigation of the various facets pertaining to this "ruler cult" and its relationship to the complex Greco-Roman system of gods and goddesses lies beyond the scope of this study.

Nevertheless, it is of considerable importance to establish that Nero was the eager recipient of several of the major titles that were used within this imperial cult. As will now be seen, Nero was addressed and reverenced as "lord" and "god" and acclaimed as "savior" and "world rescuer." These terms, in this study used of Nero with lower-case spelling, obviously held great significance for Christians at Rome and at Philippi and clearly have foundational importance for Paul when he confesses Jesus Lord and Savior.

Dio Cassius again proves an invaluable source in testifying to Nero's embrace of the terms "lord" and "god" and his willingness to receive servile prostration as though he were somehow more than human. Dio's reports on these practices both concern the Parthian leader Tiridates. As a part of a compromise for Armenia that was achieved as a result of the military successes of the Roman general Corbulo, Tiridates consented to travel to Rome to be officially recognized as ruler of Armenia by Nero.

Visibly pleased with these developments, Nero hurried to Naples to welcome Tiridates and his retinue to the Italian mainland. According to Dio, Tiridates, upon meeting Nero, obsequiously knelt on the ground, crossed his arms, and petitioned Nero as *despotēn* ("lord").[9]

This obeisance at Naples was only the prelude, however, to a far more elaborate ceremony in Rome. Before reporting the Parthian king's self-abasing words, Dio Cassius clearly explains that Tiridates was so concentrated on being crowned ruler of Armenia that he cared little how subservient he rendered himself. The event was orchestrated to exalt Nero to the highest degree. Tiridates' speech was the astounding culmination of the entire proceedings, and, by means of it, Nero was assigned to the heights of the gods, or at least to the level of the god Mithras:

> *Lord,*[10] I am the descendant of Araces, brother of the kings Gologae-sus and Pacorus, and thy slave. And I have come to thee, my god, to worship thee as I do Mithras. The destiny thou spinnest for me shall be mine; for thou are my Fortune and my Fate. (*Roman History, Epitome of Book* 62.5.2)

Given the purposes of the present study it is not necessary to establish that Nero considered himself to have divine standing or that he relentlessly sought to have the titles of divinity bestowed on him. What suffices here is to establish that Nero desired to be at the summit of human acclaim and that he was concerned to have a pantheon of titles indicating exalted standing ascribed to him and, in many cases, exclusively to him.

Did Nero consider himself comparable to the traditional Roman gods? Indeed, what did Nero really think and believe about the power of such gods? Given the paucity of the surviving data, no definitive answer can be supplied to questions such as these. What can be established from ancient inscriptions, papyri, and ostraca is that Nero esteemed such divinity-resonating titles as "lord" and "savior" and was pleased to have himself designated and acclaimed in such terms.

One of the most startling accolades ever bestowed on Nero is the divinizing reference to him as "the good god" (*ho agathos theos*), included in an inscription recovered from the Mediterranean island of Cos.[11] Was this the only such inscription of its kind or were there others like it that have not survived?

In contrast, numerous references to Nero as "the lord" have survived and serve to establish the use of this particular title from Egypt to Greece.[12] In addition to the use of *ho kyrios* absolutely (equivalent to "the lord"), this title is also found accompanied by various adjectival phrases and in combination with Nero's own name. In one reference, Nero is auspiciously referred to as "the lord of the whole world" (*ho tou pantos kosmou kyrios Nerōn*).[13] In a second reference, *kyrios* becomes virtually a component part of the emperor's proper name resulting in the august expression: "Nero lord."[14]

With respect to the terms and formulas acclaiming Nero as a savior, the data surviving are approximately comparable to the data for his "lordly" standing except that the term "savior" (*sōtēr*) almost always seems to have been used with reference to a saving of the world. Nero is thus described in surviving evidence as "savior of the world" (*sōtēr tou kosmou*) and as "savior and benefactor of the world" (*tōi sōtēri kai euergetēi tēs oikoumenēs*).[15] Further, certain phylae in Egypt were designated *sosikosmios*, that is, "belonging to the world-savior" or "world-rescuer."[16]

In light of the available evidence, it may be concluded that in the eastern parts of the empire there was an established cult acclaiming Nero as savior of the world and that Nero personally orchestrated some aspects of this cult. If Nero did particularly covet veneration as savior of the world, two reports from Tacitus concerning this title become all the more interesting. For, according to Tacitus, Nero did allow Milchius, the freed slave of Scaevinus, to use this title.[17] Yet when the full context is known, such a concession is not at all astonishing. For Milchius had betrayed his master's participation in the assassination conspiracy led by Piso in the year 65 thereby preserving Nero's own life![18]

4. Paul's Perspective on "Lords and Gods"

In the analysis of Philippians that will be made in the chapter eleven, Paul's perspective on the claims for allegiance advanced by such a ruler as Nero will be considered in close detail. Within the present section, an examination of Paul's perspective regarding the role of "gods" and "lords" is conducted in very preliminary fashion. Indeed, only one passage will be considered, a passage from the part of 1 Corinthians in which Paul is principally treating pastoral questions concerning the suitability of meat sacrificed to idols for Christian consumption.

Paul's surviving letters to the Christians at Corinth were written prior to Romans and consequently well before Philippians. The passage now to be cited is thus chronologically prior to the somewhat comparable passages in Philippians that will be considered below. Paul's fundamental perspective that Jesus his Lord surpassed all other "lords" had thus already been articulated well before the time of his Roman custody.

Inasmuch as sacrifices at the pagan sanctuaries in Corinth provided the immediate occasion for Paul's reflections in 1 Corinthians, such "gods" and "lords" as Aesclepius (the god of healing) probably constituted Paul's primary frame of reference in the verses now to be considered. Still, what Paul states, and then repeats, about "lords" and "gods" would seemingly also have had relevance regarding the quasi-divine honors that were contemporaneously being accorded in the eastern provinces to Claudius and then, more emphatically, to Nero.

Again, uncertainty over the exact dates of Paul's various letters to the Corinthian Christians makes it difficult to know for certain which emperor ruled when Paul's words were composed.[19] There is, however, one aspect of Paul's teaching that brooks no uncertainty and requires no qualification. It is that there is one ultimate God from whom all things come and one ultimate Lord, who is Jesus Christ:

> For although there may be so-called gods in heaven or on earth—and indeed there are many "gods" and many "lords"—yet for us there is one God, the Father, from whom are all things and for whom we exist, and one Lord, Jesus Christ, through whom are all things and through whom we exist. (1 Cor 8:5-6)

Regarding the potential for these words to pose a counter for the claims and the self-aggrandizing behavior of one such as Nero, it should be recalled that, according to the analysis made in chapter three above, the perspective expressed in 1 Cor 8:5-6 did not prevent Paul from subsequently penning Rom 13:1-7. And therein lies a juxtaposition that is at once perplexing and challenging.

Taken at their face value, the words just cited seem to open the way for a critical assessment of a ruler like Nero who sought to arrogate suprahuman prerogatives and to claim unqualified allegiance. If Jesus Christ *alone* is Lord, then meat sacrificed to "lord" Aesclepius may be consumed. Presumably that was Paul's main focus in this passage. Yet, in principle, once Jesus' Lordship is declared absolutely, so are the claims of any imperial "lord" relativized. Paul did not seem to ponder this perspective, or even allude to it, in writing Rom 13:1-7. As will now be seen, however, he referenced it brilliantly in writing to the Philippians.

CHAPTER ELEVEN

The Perspective
of Philippians

ONLY FOUR CHAPTERS LONG, Paul's letter to the Philippians has traditionally been celebrated for its warmth and affection, for its encouragement, and for the depths of its reflection on Christ's self-emptying. These elements are indeed present and richly repay attention and analysis. Yet there are related vital elements and meanings present in the canonical letter that have traditionally not been as well recognized or appreciated. These pertain to the circumstances of Paul's imprisonment, the defense he makes regarding his chains, and the new perspectives he sets forth regarding allegiance to Jesus and the Roman order.

When attention is concentrated on these features, while maintaining a regard for the traditionally appreciated aspects of the letter, it emerges that Philippians is a truly preeminent letter.[1] Since the Philippian community to which Paul wrote was primarily composed of Roman citizens, his reflections and admonitions are all the more remarkable.[2] Given this extraordinary combination of circumstances—Paul in Roman chains and a Christian community composed of Roman citizens at Philippi—what were the principal reflections that Paul shared?

The sections that follow are each designed to shed light on this question. Initially, in section one an overview of Paul's various purposes in writing will be provided. Section two will then analyze Paul's manner of interpreting his own circumstances as a prisoner on behalf of the gospel. Section three will identify the key features of his appeal for faithfulness in the context of immorality. Finally, section four, the longest section of the chapter, will consider five passages in which Paul effectively encourages an uncompromised allegiance to Jesus, his exalted and sovereign Lord.

1. Overview of Paul's Purposes in Writing

Several different references within the text establish that Paul felt an enduring closeness with the Christian community at Philippi (1:7-8; 4:1). In particular, the step of the Philippians in sending one of their own, Epaphroditus, to support Paul during his imprisonment was a gesture that spoke volumes to Paul (2:30). Paul now judged it appropriate, especially given the life-threatening illness that Epaphroditus had experienced, to send Epaphroditus back to Philippi (2:25-29). In doing so, Paul took the opportunity to recall and express gratitude for his partnership with the Philippians, a partnership enduring from the time of his ministry in Thessalonica down to the present time (4:14-20).

Paul's desire to convey his gratitude to the Philippians was thus certainly one of his purposes in writing. There are also two other purposes to be noted, both pertaining primarily to the pastoral situation at Philippi. Paul intended to encourage two prominent women to overcome their dispute. He also intended to warn the entire community not to be misled by any who counseled that circumcision and the other practices of the Jewish law were obligatory for Gentile Christians.

Apart from Paul's mention of them in 4:2-3, nothing else is known of Euodia and Synteche from the Pauline letters that have survived. Yet, from 4:3, it is evident that Paul esteemed both of these women and well remembered their ministry "side by side with me." Presumably their disagreement had a public character to it or else Paul would not have addressed each woman by name. His hope seems to have been that, by publicly encouraging them and publicly invoking the assistance of another member of the community, their reconciliation would be more easily accomplished.

A third purpose motivating Paul to write was the challenge posed by nameless adversaries who advocated circumcision for the Gentile Christians at Philippi. As the following excerpt indicates, Paul responded to this challenge forcefully and brusquely:

> Look out for the dogs, look out for the evil-workers, look out for those who mutilate the flesh. For we are the true circumcision, who worship God in spirit, and glory in Christ Jesus, and put no confidence in the flesh. (Phil 3:2-3)

Given that Paul refers to these adversaries as "dogs" and "evil workers," and given that he charges them with "mutilating the flesh," it is evident that he desires to portray their challenge in highly unfavorable terms. Indeed, he seemingly tries to blast apart his adversaries' program by the very explosiveness of his words.[3]

Yet once it has been emphasized that Paul was understandably concerned to decry these adversaries and authoritatively expose their falsity, it must then be emphasized that this passage represents Paul's *only* response to this particular group of opponents within the present letter.[4]

Why is this consideration important? It is significant because, within many commentaries on Philippians, one finds the view expressed that Paul was engaged with these same adversaries and their mistaken views when he wrote 2:14-15 and 3:18-19. That such an interpretation is rejected in the present study is thus to be emphasized. In the present study, Paul's indicting words at 2:14-15 and in 3:18-19 are not directed against the advocates of the Jewish law and circumcision but rather against influential pagans whose sexual conduct is reprehensible. This interpretation will be elaborated in section three below, but it is important to preview it in this context.

In addition to the motivating factors that have just been identified, Paul was concerned to share his new perspectives regarding the challenges for Christian discipleship presented by the claims and conduct of the emperor and other principals of the Roman empire. Indeed, when several leading passages within Philippians are properly assessed, it emerges that his desire to impart a new perspective regarding Roman realities was actually a fundamental factor motivating Paul to write.

In the sections that follow, the perspectives regarding Roman rule that Paul shared with his readers will be analyzed in detail. Before proceeding to that analysis, however, it is well to note that several elements in Paul's situation as a prisoner may have impelled him to write to the Philippians without further delay. These elements may have also influenced the contents of the letter.

That his trial was drawing closer is indicated by Paul's decision not to send Timothy with Epaphroditus but rather to keep him at his side until Paul sees "how it will go with me" (2:23b). That his trial will be decisive is seen from Paul's silence about any appeal or recourse open to him once the verdict is given. Its decisive character is also seen from Paul's words preparing the Philippians well in advance for his death and interpreting the meaning of such an outcome if it should occur. In 1:21 Paul refers to his death as "gain" and in 2:17 as a "libation." In 1:23 he expresses his desire "to depart and be with Christ." These three references attest to Paul's awareness of a decisive verdict in the not distant future. This awareness may well have influenced Paul to compose a letter that would strengthen and console the Philippians in the event of his death.

Paul may conceivably also have been convinced that writing about the various factors pertaining to his case would assist him in formulating the presentation he hoped to make at the time of his trial.[5] Inasmuch as Paul's trial will be held in Rome and since the charges against him are capital in nature, Nero or another high imperial official would presumably serve as the supreme judge of Paul's case.[6] Accordingly, Paul may have been motivated to write to the Philippians as a means of ordering the presentation he hoped to make before Nero.[7]

The presumed constraints on any writings by a prisoner awaiting such a trial are also appropriately considered at this juncture. Would Paul have been able to send a letter past his Roman guards and their superiors without censorship? This question has previously been raised with respect to Paul's letter to Philemon but deserves to be posed again in the present context.

It will be demonstrated below in sections two, three, and four that Paul adopts a critical stance toward various practices and claims of the authorities at Rome. The claims and practices critiqued within the letter are indeed those associated with Nero. Yet, as noted in chapter nine, the name of Nero never appears in the text. Nor, apart from reference to "the whole praetorian guard" at 1:13 and the closing reference to "those of Caesar's household" (4:22), are there any explicit references to the imperial apparatus. Did Paul compose in such a fashion because he knew that his guards would never allow any letter to pass that directly criticized the emperor or overtly questioned loyalty to the Roman government?

It is interesting to conjecture about Epaphroditus' prerogatives as a Roman citizen from the colony of Philippi. Did Paul's letter pass uncensored because Epaphroditus, who possibly possessed citizenship, carried it past Paul's guards? Or can it have been the case that Paul's immediate censors were themselves not reflective enough to grasp the thrust of Paul's message regarding the Philippians' absolute allegiance to Jesus and the implications of heavenly citizenship?

2. Paul's Explanation Regarding His Imprisonment

This and the following sections will indicate that Paul had a significant number of reflections to share with the Philippian Christians concerning their mutual experiences of Roman patterns, power, and practices. That the Philippians possessed the awareness necessary for grasping Paul's nuanced message in these areas emerges from the previously mentioned fact that the populace of Philippi consisted principally of Roman citizens.

Given their intimate familiarity with the Roman ethos, it can be presumed that the Christians at Philippi did not require extended background explanations regarding the juridical aspects of Paul's situation. Easily apprehending Roman law and Roman procedures, they would have had little difficulty in grasping certain aspects of Paul's imprisonment once they became aware of it.

What constituted criminal activity? What constituted seditious activity? The Philippian Christians must be presumed generally knowledgeable about such matters. So also were they conversant with the practice of keeping a prisoner in chains prior to the actual trial and sentencing of a capital case. The Roman procedures under which such a prisoner might receive visitors and the support of friends were also presumably procedures that the Philippians knew well. Finally, perhaps more than any of Paul's friends and associates, the Christians at Philippi would certainly be aware of the judicial steps that the authorities at Rome had open to them in resolving Paul's case.

These and comparable points of "Roman" information would have been particularly salient when the news that Paul had become a prisoner first reached Philippi. That this news had already reached them before Paul sent his letter is evident from the fact that his Philippian friends had already sent gifts to Paul and from the estimable step they had taken in sending Epaphroditus to minister to Paul. Both of these steps indicate that the response of the Philippian Christians to Paul, the prisoner, was fundamentally positive. In contrast to the response given by a minority of the Christians at Rome,[8] the Christians at Philippi were not so scandalized or embarrassed by the news of Paul's chains that they rejected him as an authoritative spokesperson for Christ's gospel.

Still, Paul's friends at Philippi were presumably desirous of knowing more about Paul's situation and especially about how he was coping with various aspects of confinement. When would his case be heard? What were his prospects for acquittal and release? And, in the meantime, what were his circumstances and how was his spirit?

Almost every part of Philippians testifies in some way regarding Paul's circumstances. Within chapter one, however, Paul does focus on several key aspects in order to signal immediately that he is persevering in Christ's service without diminution. After greeting his readers with joy and gratitude and after reaffirming his partnership with them (1:3-5), Paul proceeds in 1:7 to the subject of his chains (*tois desmois mou*) and to the subject of "the defense and confirmation of the gospel" (*en tē apologia kai bebaiōsei tou euangeliou*). Seemingly, he uses these expressions in their root juridical meanings, thereby indicating his continued sharing with the Philippians whether as a prisoner in chains or as a defendant upholding the gospel before an imperial tribunal.[9] Clearly Paul rests secure in knowing that the Philippians, far from being ashamed of him, actually share with him—all in the context for Christ's grace.

Whatever the nuances of Paul's meaning here, it is unmistakable that Paul himself is not ashamed of his chains![10] He has received them not as a result of any fall from grace, but rather because of his sharing in grace. Further, his imprisonment has actually served to carry the gospel *forward*. This is the essence of Paul's bold affirmation just a few verses later: "I want you to know, brethren, that what has happened to me has really served to *advance* the gospel" (Phil 1:12; emphasis added).

Paul's use of the adverb *mallon* ("really") probably indicates his awareness that at least some of his readers would not have been expecting such a positive development.[11] As the analysis presented above in chapter nine has established, Paul explains this advance in terms of three developments. In the present context it is appropriate to list these developments again.

First, it has become known "throughout the whole praetorian guard and to all the rest" that Paul's chains are for Christ (1:13). Second, because of Paul's chains, most of the Christians at Rome have been made more confident and emboldened to speak the word of God without fear (1:14). Third, a minority of the Roman Christians has begun preaching Christ with new vigor even though they do so out of rivalry, seeking to diminish Paul (1:15, 17-18).

Before concluding the present section, one additional passage illuminating Paul's circumstances requires attention. This passage, positioned at the end of chapter one, is highly exhortative in character. Paul's principal objective is to urge his Philippian friends to stand firm in their own commitments to the gospel.[12] Yet as he proceeds with his encouragement, he mentions that the Philippians are "engaged in the same conflict which you saw and now hear to be mine" (1:30). What precisely is Paul's meaning at this juncture? It is desirable to cite this clause as it appears within the larger context of Paul's exhortation:

> Only let your manner of life be worthy of the gospel of Christ, so that whether I come and see you or am absent, I may hear of you that you stand firm in one spirit, with one mind striving side by side for the faith of the gospel, and not frightened in anything by your opponents. This is a clear omen to them of their destruction, but of your salvation, and that from God. For it has been granted to you that for the sake of Christ you should not only believe in him but also suffer for his sake, *engaged in the same conflict which you saw and now hear to be mine.* (Phil 1:27-30; emphasis added)

What "conflict" or "struggle" (Greek, *agōna*) is Paul referring to here? Does Paul refer more narrowly to the conflict that he experiences as he struggles with his chains and the other realities of his imprisonment? Or is it possible that Paul is referring more generally to the ongoing struggle to be faithful to the gospel that he and the Philippians both know so well from experience.

While Paul's meaning cannot be determined with complete certainty, it is probable that the commonality between himself and the Philippians is that both are suffering at the hands of the Roman authorities in their respective locations.

The analysis giving rise to this conclusion is as follows. From the letter as a whole it is clear that the struggle and suffering that Paul now experiences result from measures imposed by the Roman authorities at Rome. Yet at 1:30 Paul's words indicate that the Philippians are engaged in *the same* struggle and suffering that are Paul's. In what way is it the same? It is the same because these measures are being initiated in both cities by authorities vested with power in the imperial system.[13] The Roman authorities at Philippi are thus the "opponents" of the Philippian Christians that Paul mentions at 1:28. Indeed, only the Roman authorities hold enough power to cause suffering for the Philippian Christian community as a whole.[14]

3. Fidelity in the Context of Immorality

The focus of the present section is on two passages in which Paul contrasts the high moral calling that he and the Philippian Christians have with the immorality prevailing in the Roman world around them. In the first of these passages, 2:14-15, Paul accentuates the innocence and blamelessness that Christians are called to maintain while situated in an ethos of licentiousness. In the second passage, 3:17-19, his accent falls more on the destruction that will ultimately befall those who are enemies of the cross of Christ and glory in the shame of their immorality.

As noted in section one above, numerous commentators on Philippians espouse the view that Paul was decrying the approach of those who advocated circumcision and the full observance of the Jewish law when he authored these two passages. Such a line of interpretation, however, overlooks the significance of the Roman context in which the Philippian Christians are living, and it also fails to take adequate account of Paul's own situation in the heart of Nero's Rome.

Bearing in mind that one of Paul's key phrases in 2:14-15, his reference to "a crooked and perverse generation," also appears in Deut 32:5, let Paul's words now be considered in their entirety:

> Do all things without grumbling or question, that you may be blameless and innocent, children of God without blemish in the midst of a crooked and perverse generation, among whom you shine as lights in the world. . . . (Phil 2:14-15)

Given that Moses is criticizing the Israelites for their rebellious attitude toward God in Deut 32:5, it is not difficult to see how commentators might conclude that, somehow, Paul is decrying efforts to promote the observance of the Jewish law by those who are "a crooked and perverse generation." This line of reasoning receives additional support from Paul's words in 3:2-3, where it is apparent that a controversy over the advisability of circumcision is taking place at Philippi.[15]

Nevertheless when attention is properly given to the fact that, in Paul's statement, the Philippian Christian presently live *in the midst* (*meson*) of a depraved generation, it emerges that Paul's warning must pertain to the surrounding Roman context. For, in point of fact, the Roman system is indeed the only hostile "generation" that can be understood to surround the Philippians.

Paul's use of the adverb *meson* is thus decisive for his meaning here. In this passage he is not warning against the influence of false-minded missionaries who have arrived at Philippi. Nor is he warning regarding some within the Philippian Christian community who may be advocating circumcision. Rather his meaning is that the Roman ethos of licentiousness which surrounds the Philippian Christians is itself highly hostile to the sexual morality envisioned by the Christian gospel.

Geneas ("generation") is also highly significant to Paul's meaning in this passage. This word essentially indicates that Paul's negative judgments regarding the prevailing sexual practices are at a "cultural" or even "systemic" level. In effect, Paul is now articulating a negative assessment of the social climate and context in which the Philippian Christians are living.[16] In addition to urging them to keep their life as a community above reproach in every way,[17] Paul is concomitantly warning his audience that they live within a "generation" whose approach to sexuality is categorically twisted and depraved.

The Philippian Christians are thus to remain apart from and uncontaminated by the patterns of profligate and dissolute behavior that reign in both imperial Rome and provincial Philippi. Positively, they are to provide an unimpeachable witness through the consistent integrity of their own lives. By doing so, the Philippian Christians will be "holding fast to the word of life, so that in the day of Christ I may be proud that I did not run in vain or labor in vain." These are Paul's concluding words of encouragement in 2:16 before his transition in 2:17 to a reflection that also has an "imperial" frame of reference, that is, his own prospects for death and life when he faces the Roman tribunal.

When Paul again takes up the subject of sexual immorality in 3:18–4:1, his focus, as previously noted, is more on the destruction toward which those who are enemies of the cross of Christ are headed. This passage is now appropriately cited in full even though its latter verses will not be treated until the beginning of section four:

> Brethren, join in imitating me, and mark those who so live as you have an example in us. For many, of whom I have often told you and now tell you even with tears, live as enemies of the cross of Christ. Their end is destruction, their god is the belly, and they glory in their shame, with minds set on earthly things. But our commonwealth is in heaven, and from it we await a Savior, the Lord Jesus Christ, who will change our lowly body to be like his glorious body, by the power which enables him even to subject all things to himself. Therefore, my brethren, whom I love and hope for, my joy and crown, stand firm thus in the Lord, my beloved. (Phil 3:17-4:1)

It should be noted that a principal line of interpretation regarding this passage is to hold that Paul's objective is to counter the appeals of those who advocate circumcision.[18] Arguing against this interpretation is Paul's affirmation that he and his Philippian readers have their commonwealth in heaven; the implication is that they thus have a point of reference that the adversaries just referred to do not have. If these adversaries are actually Christians, such a statement would be inappropriate. But if the adversaries are actually obdurate and arrogant pagans, then Paul's words are fully plausible.

Elsewhere in this letter, Paul encourages the Philippians to regard the example of other Christians and, preeminently in 2:5-11, the example of Christ himself. Nevertheless, in the present passage, Paul calls attention to his own example. He does not want his Philippian friends to be influenced by the scandalous behavior of others, behavior that is all the more a temptation because it is widespread, practiced by many. Rather, let the Philippians "join in imitating me" and in emulating the conduct of others who live in Paul's manner.[19]

Recalling that he has previously warned them regarding the immoral conduct of others, Paul now warns the Philippians "even with tears." Why has this matter now become so intense and so grievous for Paul?

At this juncture an explanation that focuses on Paul's venue in Rome suggests itself. That Paul's time in Rome has made him painfully familiar with the egregiously lawless behavior of Nero and his accomplices is the fundamental insight in which this interpretation is grounded. Previously Paul had counseled the Philippians to avoid all forms of sexual immorality, but now he has become aware of how Nero and his confederates casually and flagrantly engage in the most degrading forms of sexual conduct.

Such behavior is lamentably widespread, and the fact that no one can order the cessation of this behavior may also be the grounds for Paul's tears. The lives of many are being abused and disfigured. And those who perpetrate these abuses do so with impunity because they hold supreme power. Paul thus gives vent to his frustration that there is no human tribunal before which Nero and his accomplices can be summoned. This situation is indeed a reason for tears.

At least three specific forms of behavior are decried within these verses. It should again be stressed that Paul is controverting with great intensity here. He may be driven to denounce those who perpetrate such immorality in the strongest possible terms lest the Philippian Christians be intimidated or seduced by the fact that such conduct is being conspicuously engaged in by those in the highest echelons of Roman power.

Paul begins with a forceful denunciation of those whose behavior he is reproving stating that they are actually living as "enemies of the cross of Christ." Such strong invective is almost unparalleled within Paul's letters. Its rationale may lie in Paul's judgment that this arrogant self-indulgence is diametrically at odds with the spirit of self-sacrifice with which Jesus embraced his crucifixion.[20]

Paul's second denunciation is also extremely incendiary. He denounces his adversaries for making their *kolia* their god! What is his meaning in making this charge? *Kolia* may be translated "belly" as in the RSV version given above. However this word may also be used as a euphemism for the male sex organ and, given the context of Nero's Rome, that is probably Paul's meaning in this passage.[21]

Paul is not merely decrying his adversaries for the fact that they have been practicing gluttony, letting their stomachs or their appetites be their gods. His denunciation here is extremely sharp. And it is difficult to imagine that the abuse or misuse of food would constitute sufficient ground for such an explosive rebuke. Paul is in fact concerned with his opponents' unrestrained lascivious conduct, and he attacks their excess with his own rhetorical excess.

In effect, when he states that they make their sex organs their gods, he portrays them in worship before their own sex organs! Their conduct has been so depraved and so dissolute that Paul is motivated to state coarsely that they have reified their own sex organs and are now in worship before them. (Recall the reports of Nero's debauchery and licentiousness presented in chapter ten.)

The third indictment that Paul makes is in the same vein as the first two with respect to vividness and forcefulness. Paul writes that these enemies of Christ's cross "glory in their shame." Their arrogance is such that they publicly "glory" in what is truly shameful[22] and usually clandestine. Paul is seemingly motivated to castigate this effrontery lest the publicity that is afforded somehow make what is blatantly shameful seem officially "approved."

In reality, according to the standards of God, those who engage in such immoral conduct are headed for destruction. That is Paul's fundamental proclamation in this passage. Whatever their high status, whatever the legitimacy they have achieved for their dissolute and depraved practices, these practitioners are truly headed for destruction. The Philippian Christians should not be deluded, for any reason, into thinking otherwise. Those who live as enemies of the cross of Christ, those who make idols of their sexual organs, those who glory in their shame—these all will be brought to their ruin by reason of the power that enables Jesus to exercise his sovereignty over all things.[23]

4. Unqualified Allegiance to Jesus

The sovereign power of Jesus risen! The unqualified allegiance that is due Jesus as Lord! Such sentiments as these are powerfully expressed within Paul's letter to the Philippians, and the time has now come to accord them focused attention and appreciation. Paul has manifested his allegiance to Christ many times previously in many diverse circumstances. Now, in four brilliantly phrased passages, he subtly, yet intensely and profoundly, considers the implications of Jesus' sovereignty from his situation in imperial Rome. Paul now writes with reference to what previously befell Jesus and now looms near for Paul, that is, Roman execution.

A. *The Interpretation of Phil 3:20–4:1*

The first passage now to be considered is actually constituted by the final verses of the passage assessed at the end of the preceding section. These verses indicate clearly that Christians conceive reality in far different terms and thus reject the outlook and practices of those who demean the human body and live with unbridled self-indulgence as enemies of the cross of Christ:

> But our commonwealth is in heaven, and from it we await a Savior, the Lord Jesus Christ, who will change our lowly body to be like his glorious body, by the power which enables him even to subject all things to himself. Therefore, my brethren, whom I love and long for, my joy and crown, stand firm thus in the Lord, my beloved. (Phil 3:20-4:1)

It is to be noted that these verses contain not merely one or two terms and references that are rich in meaning for the present study but as many as seven. Further, several of the key terms in the present passage also appear in one or more of the other passages to be considered in this section. Each of these other passages is also laden with other terms and references that are significant. The net result is that Philippians contains at almost every turn claims, affirmations, and encouragements that (a) uphold the sovereignty of Jesus and (b) relativize the standing of Roman officials and benefits, including the benefit of Roman citizenship.

This topic of citizenship is actually the logical starting point for the analysis of this passage. *Politeuma*, usually translated "citizenship," "commonwealth," or "colony,"[24] appears in verse 3:30. It is a term whose root meaning references the political and civic sphere, and Paul consciously employs it in writing to an audience comprised primarily of Roman citizens. Significantly, he also uses the verb form *politeuesthe* earlier in 1:27.[25] These two occurrences represent the only instances of such usage within Paul's undisputed letters.[26]

In so utilizing *politeuma*, what affirmation does Paul set before his Philippian readers? He affirms that their true commonwealth, their true citizenship, is *in heaven*!

It is not difficult to see that, whether considered from the standpoint of the Philippians Christians or viewed from the standpoint of

Nero and the Roman authorities, this affirmation is also implicitly a challenge. In effect, in setting forth such a pronouncement, Paul is actually asserting a standard beyond the standards of the empire and a status more ultimate than the status of Roman citizenship. Further, as Paul continues, it becomes clear that the higher realities of heaven do exercise and should exercise an influence on the expectations and conduct of Christians in this world.

Although these Christians live in an empire in which Nero audaciously claims such titles as "lord" and "savior," they confidently affirm that Jesus alone is truly *Savior* and truly *Lord* (3:20b). Again Paul's particular vocabulary in Philippians is to be noted. Although the cognate "salvation" appears relatively frequently in the Pauline writings, including Phil 1:28 and 2:12, this is the only time that the term "Savior" appears in his undisputed letters.[27] Significantly, this Savior will intervene in the earthly realms for a purpose: "to change our lowly body to be like his glorious body" (3:21a). Indeed Jesus has the "power" (*energeian*) to do so (3:21b).

Writing from a setting in which practices that degrade the human body are rampant, Paul appropriately stresses the truth that Jesus, who has definitive power, will surely come to transform the human body and human existence into a heavenly body and heavenly existence. Having articulated this particular manifestation of Jesus' saving intervention, Paul then proceeds to elaborate the dimensions of Jesus' sovereignty in a way that is nearly astonishing given the perspective he previously expressed about the sovereignty of the Roman authorities in Rom 13:1-7.

In Rom 13:1 Paul wrote, "Let every person *be subject* to the governing authorities." In Rom 13:5 he wrote, "Therefore one must *be subject*, not only to avoid God's wrath but also for the sake of conscience." The use of *hypotassō* in these earlier passages, represents the relevant point of comparison for Paul's use of this same verb form in Phil 3:20b where he boldly emphasizes Christ's power, "which enables him *to subject* all things to himself."

How remarkable the change in perspective that has occurred! Previously Paul endorsed subjection to the Roman authorities without saying a word to indicate that these authorities were subject to Christ. Now he sweepingly affirms the sovereignty of Christ, stating that Christ has the power to subject *ta panta* ("all things") to himself. The universalism expressed in 3:21c is indeed breathtaking. And it will be seen below that this claim regarding the subjection of all things to Christ occurs even more memorably in 2:9-11, one of the other Philippian passages still awaiting consideration.

The response that Paul urges in the wake of this delineation of Christ's sovereignty should now be noted. In words comparable to those used in 1:27, Paul urges his beloved Philippians to "stand firm in the Lord." In effect, he calls on his readers to persevere *with* and *in* Christ. Both dimensions of meaning are present. Along with Paul the Philippians are strengthened in their union *with* Christ. Because they are so strengthened, they are to stand fast *in* Christ, that is, in their commitment to the Lord.[28]

B. The Interpretation of Phil 1:27-30

Within 1:27-30, the passage now to be analyzed, four elements that have been treated in the preceding pages appear in a new context. It is significant that Paul's teachings concerning standing firm in reference to the salvation of Christians, regarding the destruction of their adversaries, and relating to worthy civic living all appear in the following verses (*politeuesthe* in 1:27a is appropriately translated as "civic living"):[29]

> Only let your civic living be worthy of the gospel of Christ, so that whether I come and see you or am absent, I may hear of you that you stand firm in one spirit, with one mind striving side by side for the faith of the gospel, and not frightened in anything by your opponents. This is a clear omen to you of their destruction, but of your salvation, and that from God. For it has been granted to you that for the sake of Christ you should not only believe in him but also suffer for his sake, engaged in the same conflict which you saw and now hear to be mine. (Phil 1:27-30)

Inasmuch as vv. 29-30 have received treatment in section one of this chapter, the focus here is appropriately on Paul's counsels in vv. 27 and 28. In v. 27a, Paul urges his hearers to manifest a public conduct, a civic living, that is *worthy* of the gospel of Christ. This gospel is for Paul at once his greatest treasure and his highest standard. He himself strives to live in such a way that his allegiance to

Christ's truth is evident to all. And that is his encouragement to his beloved Philippians.

In v. 27b Paul also seems to ask the Philippians to join in strengthening one another for public witness on behalf of the gospel. Together in spirit[30] and in mind, and striving "side by side" they are to remain committed and resolute in their witness. In effect, this "standing firm" is vital for the cause of the gospel.

In v. 28 Paul then draws his readers' attention to two future developments that God will achieve. The first is the coming "destruction" (apōleias) of their opponents. (As previously noted Paul mentions this outcome again in 3:19 using the same Greek word.) The second is the coming event of his readers' "salvation" (sōtērias), a situation of beneficence to which they will be brought in the future.[31] Who is the authority, the power, who will bring them to this desired state? This salvation will be achieved by God.[32]

Recalling the claims of Nero to bestow salvation and his pleasure at being acclaimed as "savior," Paul's skill in introducing Christian claims regarding salvation is all the more to be appreciated in this letter. Paul states that God is the author of salvation at 1:28b, and he acclaims Jesus as Savior in 3:20. There is, of course, no mention of Nero's capacity in this arena of salvation. But for those standing firm in the gospel of Christ, how could there be any substantive reference to "salvation" from Nero?

C. The Interpretation of Phil 2:6-11

It is now appropriate to treat Phil 2:6-11, a passage that is justly esteemed by many as the zenith of Philippians. These exceedingly rich verses have been extensively analyzed and interpreted, but there are two fundamental insights regarding them that have been undervalued if not overlooked completely.[33] Recalling again that Paul is writing to those who are Roman citizens and that he is a chained Roman prisoner, it is desirable to state the following two perspectives at the outset:

1. Phil 2:6-11 is fundamentally about Jesus' exalted status and about the allegiance and deference that is due to him as sovereign Lord.
2. Jesus' path to exaltation and sovereignty involved a downward movement of humility and abasement that reached its nadir when the Roman authorities put him to death by crucifixion.

Within the present study, the emphasis that verses 2:9-11 place on submission of all beings to Jesus as Lord is vital for the argument that Paul's teachings in Philippians supersede the counsel he presented in Rom 13:1-7. These verses will receive treatment in due course, but, at the outset, the overall character of this passage must be considered, including the structural pivot that occurs when Paul refers to Jesus' crucifixion in 2:8.

Essentially there are three alternatives as regards the authorship of 2:6-11, verses with a noticeable hymnlike quality to them. These verses might originally have been composed as a hymn to Christ by an author now unknown. Or Paul himself might have composed these verses previously, perhaps for liturgical use. Third, these verses might not have preexisted but rather could have been beautifully crafted by Paul at the time of the letter as he sought ways to delineate the sovereignty of Christ for his friends at Philippi.

There are substantive grounds for concluding that Paul himself authored these verses.[34] Yet even if it be concluded that Paul utilized the verses of a preexisting Christian hymn to express his own thoughts, what is significant is the fact that *Paul's own perspective is communicated by these verses*. Paul may well have authored every phrase within these five verses, including the phrase "even death on a cross," which is positioned prominently at the end of verse 2:8. But even if he incorporated concepts authored by another Christian, Paul knew the meaning he himself sought to communicate. In other words, the finished form, the final text of the letter, is what expresses Paul's own meaning regardless of the compositional path in arriving at this final formulation.

In the same vein, given the focus of the present study, it is not necessary to resolve the long-standing dispute regarding the exact nuances of Paul's meaning in v. 2:5. It is sufficient to observe that Paul is unmistakably directing his readers' attention to the figure of Christ Jesus. As disciples of Jesus they are fundamentally oriented to all that Jesus has accomplished and all that the Father has accomplished in Jesus.[35] Paul is now especially concerned to have them dwell on Jesus' unsurpassed sovereignty, both initially and finally. In effect Paul is setting before his Philippian readers a powerfully summoning delineation of the "status path" of Jesus their Lord. Jesus' status is central to the first verses of this passage, and it is the central feature of the last three verses, which celebrate the Father's intervention to confer formally upon him a status and a sovereignty that are cosmic in nature.

The first verses of the passage, in which Jesus' self-emptying attitude to his preexistent divine status is reverently delineated are as follows:

> Have this mind among yourselves, which is yours in Christ Jesus, who, though he was in the form of God, did not count equality with God a thing to be grasped, but emptied himself, taking the form of a servant, being born in human likeness. And being found in human form he humbled himself and became obedient unto death, even death on a cross. (Phil 2:5-8; author's translation)

What precisely does it mean that Jesus was "in the form of God"? What precisely does it mean that Jesus "did not count equality with God a thing to be grasped"? And what is the exact meaning of the statement that Jesus was born "in human likeness"? The limitations imposed by the character of the present study prevent a full discussion of these and other important concepts introduced by Paul in this passage. What must be focused on is that Paul here portrays Jesus consistently initiating steps that lessen his status. Jesus empties himself in taking the human form, the form of a *doulos*.[36] And he empties himself in becoming obedient unto death. Finally he empties himself by submitting to the most humiliating manner of death, death by crucifixion.

Even death on a cross. This memorable phrase ends the first part of Paul's reflection on the "downward path" that Jesus entered on. Especially in the context of the present study, it is a phrase that well repays attention and reflection. Crucifixion, hanging on a tree, was a shameful, accursed form of death according to Jewish tradition. From a Roman perspective, such an execution was brutal and demeaning, reserved for those whose status and conduct merited public degradation. Paul thus memorably documents Jesus' embrace of an abject status when he emphasizes that Jesus voluntarily accepted crucifixion as his manner of dying.

While it was scandalous to Jews and Romans alike, crucifixion was a form of execution that, during this period, could only be enacted by the Roman authorities. This feature should not be overlooked. Within the boundaries of the Roman empire, no other political entity, no other officials save those with imperial authorization, could legally crucify. This integral relationship between crucifixion and Roman power was certainly well known to Paul's audience in Philippi. Thus, in emphasizing that Jesus suffered death by crucifixion, Paul is inevitably drawing attention to the fact that Jesus was put to death by the Roman authorities. To reiterate and expand this point: Jesus died by the degrading form of execution that the Roman authorities enacted against low-status individuals and various insurgents as a consequence of their alleged violation of Roman rule.[37]

Throughout these verses Paul is obviously concerned to illuminate the humility and faithfulness of Jesus his Lord. But may there not also be another factor motivating Paul at this juncture? Is it not possible that, in pondering the humbleness and faithfulness of Jesus in suffering death under the Roman authorities, Paul was granted the insight that Jesus might now be calling Paul himself to undergo a comparable death at the hands of a new generation of Roman authorities?

Paul's death, if it occurs as the outcome of his present imprisonment, will indeed be at the hands of the Roman authorities! And should it occur, it will represent the nadir of Paul's own status path. This being the case, is it not plausible to suppose that, in writing about Jesus' self-giving in the face of mistreatment and execution, Paul is also cognizant of his own call to unswerving faithfulness in the face of comparable Roman mistreatment? It will be seen below that Paul's words in 3:10 provide support for an affirmative answer to this question.

As already noted, this reference to Jesus' crucifixion marks the end of the first part of this passage. In the second part of the passage, with its emphasis on upward movement, the one initiating this movement is God the Father. Paul now strongly emphasizes that it is God the Father who has exalted Jesus to a sovereignty that is actually cosmic in its scope:

Therefore God has highly exalted him and bestowed on him the name which is above every name, that at the name of Jesus every knee should bow, in heaven and on earth and under the earth, and every tongue confess that Jesus Christ is Lord, to the glory of God the Father. (Phil 2:9-11)

That Paul was admonishing and instructing his readers regarding a conflict over sovereignty when he included these verses in his letter is a significant thesis of the present study. Frequently commentators on Philippians have suggested that Paul included 2:9-11 because he wanted to emphasize to his readers that their own humble self-giving would ultimately be confirmed by the Father.[38] Such an interpretation is affirmed within the present analysis. Nevertheless, the present study also affirms that Paul was concerned here to draw contrasts between the sovereignty of Jesus and that of Nero and his confederates.

Paul's initial powerful affirmation in 2:9-11 is that God the Father intervened to exalt Jesus from the depths of humiliation. Paul then projects the concept of "a name which is above every name" in order to illuminate the high status and sovereignty that Jesus now enjoys. Two remarkable consequences resulting from the fact that Jesus now possesses an unsurpassed name are then identified.

When they are analyzed in this fashion, these verses are thus seen to contain a powerful series of affirmations about Jesus' exalted position. Further each affirmation in this sequence implicitly challenges various claims and prerogatives that have been asserted by Nero.

A principal insight to be grasped relative to the Father's exaltation of Jesus is that God's initiative totally invalidates the Roman verdict against Jesus and fully overcomes the effects of Roman crucifixion. As emphasized above, Jesus' abject humiliation resulted from the power of the Roman authorities to decree a degrading and demeaning crucifixion. Precisely the validity of this Roman decree against Jesus and precisely the Roman power to end life through crucifixion are now overturned in the exaltation of Jesus.

The Roman verdict against Jesus was decisive within the limits of the world ruled by Rome. But in the cosmic, eternal world ordered by God, the Roman verdict has now been fully dissolved. Jesus was indeed crucified by the power of the Roman authorities. Yet Roman power is now shown to be a circumscribed power, a power fully subject to the uncircumscribed power of the Father.

What can be said regarding the name that God bestowed on Jesus in exalting him? Very probably Paul is referring here to that name Lord.[39] Yet even if Paul meant the name Jesus, or even if he did not have a particular name in mind, the fundamental point that he asserts is not in doubt. Paul is affirming that Jesus now has been given a name that places him above every other person or entity in sovereignty and status. The presence of the adjective pas ("every") is highly significant here. Jesus' name is indeed above *every* other name.

In terms of sovereignty this means that Jesus' power surpasses that of any other person or entity, including those with the power for ordering crucifixion. And Jesus now enjoys a status that surpasses the status of even the most extravagantly acclaimed human rulers, Nero and other Roman rulers of various ranks included.

Phil 2:9 thus effectively presents the key affirmation of the entire passage, the affirmation that the Father has exalted Jesus and bestowed unsurpassed sovereignty and status on him. Conceivably, Paul could have stopped at this point without proceeding to develop this train of thought further. Yet he continued with two additional verses that brilliantly elaborate and concretize the meaning of Jesus' sovereignty. Paul wanted to reflect precisely and emphatically regarding all who were now subject to Jesus. Further, he wanted his readers to be schooled as to the most appropriate way of confessing Jesus' sovereignty.[40]

Consider the comprehensive range of Paul's words in v. 10 when he identifies all who are now called to defer to Jesus in a movement of submission and worship. Three groups are expressly enumerated: those "in heaven," those "on earth," and those "under the earth." Strikingly, in indicating that intelligent beings in all three of these sectors shall confess Jesus, Paul implicitly indicates that *no one* is excluded from rendering acclaim to Jesus.

It should be noted that Paul employs "the bending of every knee" as an exceptionally vivid image. This image may well reflect Paul's familiarity with a significant verse from the book of Isaiah, in which the meaning of reverent submission to God is expressed.[41] Also, by reason of his use of the qualifier *pas* ("every") in v. 10a, Paul insists that the sovereignty of Jesus is so surpassing that the bending of *every* knee is mandated.

And the emperor Nero? Is Nero somehow exempt from this deference to Jesus and this submissiveness before him? Could the Roman emperor be the single person throughout the entire created universe to be excused from this submission? Such rhetorical questions serve to underscore the point that, despite his power to end Paul's life in this world, Nero is not ultimately exempt from bending his knee before Jesus.

Nor can Nero be excused from the second form of worshipful

response that Paul now specifies. Jesus Christ is to be acclaimed as *Lord*. That is the verbal complement to the worshipful bow that is as mandatory for every creature. Every human being—there can be no exemption for Nero—is called to participate in this reverent acclaim. For Jesus now holds the status of *Lord*, a wondrous outcome that *must* be proclaimed "to the glory of God, the Father."[42]

As a means of concluding this treatment of Phil 2:9-11, it is useful to observe how creatively Paul has intertwined two concepts in order to advance a teaching on Jesus' sovereignty that is of unsurpassed importance. The repeated use of the modifier *pas* ("every" or "all") and the various occurrences of the word *onoma* ("name") serve to promote Paul's teaching in a rhetorically powerful way. The exalted Jesus has received a name that is above *every* other *name*. At the *name* of Jesus *every* knee must bend. And, at the *name* of Jesus, *every* tongue must speak a *name* that fundamentally expresses and reveres Jesus' exalted identity. Jesus Christ is to be acclaimed as *Lord* to the glory of God the Father.

D. The Interpretation of Phil 3:7-11

In 3:7-11, the final passage to be treated in this chapter, concepts already encountered echo and reverberate. As will soon be evident, the passage as a whole wondrously expresses Paul's full-hearted allegiance to Jesus. Indeed, his present experience of being in Christ is so surpassing that Paul counts everything that preceded as so much refuse.

Consider then the intense commitment to Christ that Paul now testifies to using language that is at times rhapsodic. Paul already deeply experiences the richness of being in Christ. Yet he writes as one who still strives to "gain" Christ, one who still strives to "know" him:

> But whatever gain I had, I counted as loss for the sake of Christ.
> Indeed I count everything as loss because of the surpassing worth of
> knowing Christ Jesus my Lord. For his sake I have suffered the loss of
> all things, and count them as refuse, in order that I may gain Christ
> and be found in him, not having a righteousness of my own, based on
> law, but that which is through faith in Christ, the righteousness from
> God that depends on faith; that I may know him and the power of his

resurrection, and may share his sufferings, becoming like him in his death, that if possible I may attain the resurrection from the dead. (Phil 3:7-11)

In the analysis that follows, emphasis will be placed on two motifs that possess major significance for the present study. Elements pertaining to the motif of Paul's allegiance to Jesus permeate this passage and will be considered first. Subsequently an analysis will be made of the way in which the motif of death and resurrection is also delineated in this passage.

Paul emphasizes "the surpassing worth of knowing Christ Jesus my Lord" (3:8a). He indicates that he gladly suffers the loss of all things in order to "gain Christ and be found in him" (3:8c-9a). And, ever more intently, he aspires to "know him and the power of his resurrection" (3:10a). Clearly Christ has become everything for Paul, surpassing and superseding everything else. Paul now gratefully strives to draw even closer to Christ.

The phrases just cited do indeed attest to the great loyalty and the deep allegiance that Paul feels toward Christ. With respect to the theme of personal allegiance, however, the phrase in which Paul refers to Christ Jesus as "*my* Lord" (3:8a) deserves particular attention. For, within all of Paul's letters, only in this single instance does he refer to Jesus with this personal intimate expression.[43] Further, the fact that he does manifest his highly personal commitment to Jesus here in Philippians augments the meaning of the sentiments that he has already expressed earlier in the letter.

Since Paul has already acclaimed Jesus as the Lord of the cosmos in Phil 2:9-11, when he now refers to Jesus as *his* Lord, he creates a kind of "magnetic field" for the domain of Jesus' sovereignty. Let Paul's readers at Philippi position Phil 3:8-11 alongside Phil 2:9-11 and consider the powerful, reciprocal currents of meaning that result when one passage is considered in the light of the other. Jesus has been exalted to universal sovereignty. Every being of the cosmos shall manifest allegiance to him through the acclamation of his name and the bending of the knee before him. Yet the Jesus who is the Lord of the entire universe is also known personally by his disciples and Paul can refer to him intimately as "*my* Lord."

The effect is the same when the two passages are read in reverse order, something that might occur in the various community gatherings at Philippi. Jesus, at once so intimately bonded with his disciples, is simultaneously the Lord of the entire universe with a dignity so exalted that manifestations of allegiance are called for from every being of the cosmos, even those most hostile. Regardless of the reading sequence, is it not evident that Paul has provided for his readers a powerful meditation on the various meanings of Jesus' identity as "Lord"?

It is also remarkable that both of these dimensions of Jesus' "Lordship" appear in a letter written in Roman chains and in the only letter in which the great majority of the Christians Paul is addressing are also Roman citizens! Paul's Philippian readers know well of the allegiance that is demanded by Nero and those at the upper echelons of the empire. Nevertheless, writing from the capital of Nero's empire and writing as a prisoner in Roman chains, Paul still boldly proclaims to the Philippians that Christ Jesus is both the Lord of the universe and "my Lord."

To facilitate analysis at this point, it is well to focus on the two concluding verses of the passage presently being considered. Paul's words in these verses are as follows:

> that I may know him and the power of his resurrection and may share his sufferings becoming like him in his death, that if possible I may attain the resurrection from the dead. (Phil 3:10-11)

What is the trajectory that Paul projects for himself in these two verses? He envisions himself proceeding forward in terms of the allegiance to Jesus he has already professed. But what does he anticipate for the future? Essentially Paul reckons with the possibility that he could be found worthy to complete the same status path that Jesus his Lord has already completed.

The nature of the trajectory that Paul now contemplates for himself is comparable to that which he has already described for Jesus in Phil 2:6-11. Paul there praised Jesus' downward path in humility to the point of accepting death by crucifixion. He then celebrated the wonders of Christ's glory in being given a name above every other name.

Paul is not certain that the trajectory of Jesus will be his own. Previously it has been emphasized that Paul does not know what the outcome of his imprisonment will be and scarcely knows which outcome he prefers. Certainly, whatever the time and manner by which he dies, Paul does not want to suggest that life in the resurrection will somehow be achieved by *his* power. Life with Christ in the resurrection is the goal for which Paul strives faithfully. But only the "power" (*dynamin*) of Jesus' own resurrection is capable of bringing him to that ultimate goal.[44]

In light of these observations regarding the various facets of Paul's meaning within this passage, let attention now be focused on the following words (3:10b): "becoming like him in his death" (*symmorphizomenos tō thanatō autou*). What precisely is Paul's meaning in this phrase? And what motivated him to include this particular concept in his letter to the Christians at Philippi?

Paul's ultimate desire is to be with Christ in the life of the resurrection. Yet death *in some form* is the necessary prelude to this fuller union with Paul's Lord. The insight that Paul now broaches is that he may well be called on to suffer death *in the form of Jesus*! On just a moment's reflection, it can be grasped that such an insight would have had a benumbing effect on Paul when it first occurred to him.

As a disciple of Jesus, ever faithful over thousands of miles of missionary endeavor, had it occurred to Paul that his life and ministry might end almost exactly in the manner in which Jesus' own earthly life had ended? As the final episode on Paul's long journey such an outcome would be truly astonishing. During the years that Paul founded and nurtured Christian community after Christian community in the eastern provinces, who from among his converts would have ever thought that such a form of death would be Paul's? Who would have thought that, decades after Jesus' death, Paul would die in nearly the precise manner that Jesus had died?

Certainly Paul's writings testify to his conviction that faithful Christian discipleship inevitably involved a dying to self. Certainly Paul's letters stress that he is willing to embrace suffering for Christ's sake and to spend himself to the point of death for the sake of his Lord. Further, on prior occasions, when Paul pondered the sufferings he had already endured, he reflected that he was approximating to some degree Jesus' own sufferings and death.[45] Yet the full meaning now conveyed by the words "becoming like him in his death" carries forward these earlier dimensions of meaning and enhances them with a new dimension.[46] This new dimension of meaning involves the almost unnerving juxtaposition of Jesus' death by capital sentence at the hands of the Roman authorities and Paul's possible death by capital sentence at the hands of the Roman authorities.

Let the analysis made previously in chapter six now be recalled. At that time it was suggested that Paul came to terms with his status as a chained prisoner gradually and gained new perspectives about his chains as his time wearing them lengthened. It can now be conjectured that Paul required a certain amount of time to come to terms with his initial insight regarding the close parallels between the circumstances of Jesus' death and his own.[47] Nevertheless, as his own circumstances evolved and the possibilities for such an outcome became more evident, Paul was eventually able to formulate this insight for his beloved friends at Philippi.

The question now to be asked is whether Paul, by including this reference to "becoming like him in his death," consciously intended to "acclimate" the Philippian Christians to the additional scandal that would arise if Paul, like Jesus, also were to die by Roman execution.

In his letters to the Christians of Corinth and Galatia, Paul explicitly asserts that Christ's death by crucifixion is held to be scandalous by Gentiles and Jews alike.[48] Clearly Paul does know the implications of Roman crucifixion in a world ruled by Rome! Yet now the Christian communities founded by Paul are on the verge of being asked to respond to a second major scandalous death, the death of Paul himself by formal decree of the Roman authorities. If Paul's imprisonment and the chains with which he was bound could be, for some, the occasion for scandal, how much more so would an imperial death sentence and beheading by Roman soldiers?

Upon Paul's death, those Christians surviving him would become witnesses to Paul's own Roman execution at the same time that they continued to confess Jesus crucified.[49]

Paul's execution, should it occur, would also undoubtedly have serious implications for the Philippians' sense of their own future discipleship. Already deeply cognizant of Jesus' crucifixion and learning now that Paul faced a comparable execution, it is plausible to assume that at least some of Paul's readers would begin to wonder whether their own faithfulness would ultimately lead them to the same fate suffered by Jesus and Paul?[50] If this letter was to be Paul's last opportunity for writing to his beloved Philippians, then it was incumbent on him to treat these matters writing very carefully, at times even obliquely.[51]

Finally Paul may also have wanted the Philippians to begin reflecting about his possible path toward death as a means of encouraging them toward a new critical perspective regarding the realities of Roman rule. In effect, the line of reflection that Paul intended to engender may have been as follows: (1) Jesus was executed by the governor of Judea. (2) After much deliberation, the highest authorities at Rome now were prepared to execute Paul. (3) What allegiance shall the Philippian Christians have to the policies and decrees of the Roman authorities?

Once again it should be underscored that the recipients of this letter hold Roman citizenship and are well familiar with the principles and the operating procedures proper to the empire. Accordingly, the death of Paul by Roman decree could well provide a significant impetus for such persons to reassess all things Roman. First, Jesus, their sovereign Lord, and now Paul, their cherished founder and friend!—what was to be thought of the ruling authorities who enacted death sentences on two such as these?

CHAPTER TWELVE

Situating Paul's Perspective in Philippians

THE PRINCIPAL TASK of this final chapter is to recapitulate Paul's perspective in Philippians and to situate his approach within the context of three other approaches to Roman rule. To accomplish these tasks, the chapter is structured into four sections with sections one and four presenting the principal conclusions of this study. Section one reviews and consolidates the findings made in chapter eleven regarding Paul's outlook on the Roman order in writing to the Christians at Philippi. Section four then compares the approach of Paul in Philippians to the three approaches previously described in chapter two, the approach of Cerialis according to Tacitus, that of Judas the Gaulanite according to Josephus, and that of Jesus according to Luke.

While not central to the argument of this study, sections two and three nevertheless present significant material that is complementary to sections one and four. It should be noted from the very outset that these sections are both distinctly conjectural in character. Each of them represents an attempt to enter into a different aspect of Paul's consciousness. Section two hypothesizes regarding the factors influencing the dramatic change in Paul's perspective that occurred between Romans and Philippians. Section three revisits Rom 13:1-7, prognosticating as to the modifications Paul *would have* introduced into that text given the new viewpoints expressed in Philippians.

1. A Summary of Paul's Changed Perspective on the Roman Order

It should be observed at the outset that, in writing to his beloved community at Philippi, Paul does not systematically address the topic of the Roman social order. Considerations regarding censorship and the security of his correspondence are relevant here. In addition, it is not certain that Paul had formulated for himself a systematic critique of the various facets of Roman rule. Nevertheless, the text of Philippians unmistakably manifests a range of criticisms, subtle indictments, denunciations, and warnings about various aspects of imperial rule, the net effect of which is to establish that Paul has distanced himself dramatically from the approach he advocated at the time of Rom 13:1-7. For purposes of a concise exposition, the relevant passages in Philippians will now be considered under three headings: (a) Paul's critique of the prevailing Roman ethos; (b) Paul's relativizing of Roman citizenship; (c) Paul's affirmations concerning Jesus' unsurpassed sovereignty.

A. Paul's Critique of the Prevailing Roman Ethos

By way of a summary of the findings of chapter eleven, it can be stated that Paul vividly critiques the Roman ethos at two separate points in his letter. Three other passages are also relevant because they allude to the role of the Roman authorities in the death of Jesus, to their role in Paul's custody, and to their role in the persecution that the Philippian Christians themselves have experienced.

To appreciate properly Paul's first criticism of the Roman ethos, it should be emphasized once more that the Christians at Philippi lived in highly Romanized circumstances. As much as any city outside of Italy, Philippi partook in the ethos of the empire. It was a city of Roman citizens, a decisive percentage of whom are Roman veterans. Yet, in his assessment of their context at 2:15b Paul states that the Philippian Christians are situated "in the midst of a crooked and perverse generation."

Further, when he returns to this theme in chapter three, Paul's criticism is more trenchant and sustained. In this second passage he states:

> For many, of whom I have often told you and now tell you even with
> tears, live as enemies of the cross of Christ. Their end is destruction,
> their god is the belly, and they glory in their shame with minds set on
> earthly things. (Phil 3:18-19)

As discussed previously, Neronian sexual depravity may well be
the focus of Paul's critique in this passage. Certainly the wanton
behavior that he decries is not restricted to gluttony. Paul's critique
against those who embrace such a life is intensified by his supple-
mental indictment of them for glorying in their shame. In effect, they
have lost their moral compass to such a degree that reprehensible
behavior is paraded by them as "glorious."

Are those disparaged by Paul's epithet "enemies of the cross of
Christ," so charged because their profligate behavior is an affront to
the standard of Jesus crucified and risen? This may be so. But it is
conceivable that, while decrying Nero and his ilk for their scandalous
sexual excesses, Paul is also reprobating the barbarous measures that
Nero has already begun to enact against the Christians of Rome.

Any brutalizing treatment of virtuous Christians by utterly
unprincipled Roman officials would be particularly heinous for Paul
to contemplate. Whatever its exact nature, this situation is so painful
to Paul that it brings tears to his eyes when he ponders it. And he
states forcefully the judgment that awaits those who are responsible:
"Their end is *destruction*" (3:19a; *emphasis added*).

The possibility that those who are named "enemies of the cross of
Christ" in 3:19 may actually be persecutors of Christians provides a
conceptual link to three other passages within Philippians in which
Paul indirectly refers to the role of the Roman authorities in meting
out persecution and death to Jesus and his followers. In the first of
these passages Paul is counseling his Philippian friends to stand firm
in the face of persecution. In the latter two passages Paul is adverting
to the role of the Roman authorities in Jesus' death and in Paul's own
death should it come by their decree.

As previously indicated, Paul's words in Phil 1:27-30 have been
viewed by many scholars as referring to a conflict with advocates of
circumcision and the Jewish law. Yet, in light of the predominance of
Roman power at Philippi, Paul's reference to suffering for Christ's
sake at 1:29b very probably refers to persecution by the Roman
authorities. This interpretation is buttressed by Paul's statement at
1:30 that the Philippians are engaged in the same struggle that he,

Paul, is now engaged in. In effect, then the Christians at Philippi and Paul in Rome are both facing affliction from the Roman authorities. Only Roman officials possess the power for acting decisively in both locations, in Philippi as well as Rome.

And yet the power of these Roman authorities is hardly decisive! Whether based at Philippi or based at Rome, their hold on power is only transitory. Using the same word that he uses to prophesy their demise in 3:19a, Paul here juxtaposes two outcomes. The outcome of those who stand firm with Jesus will be salvation. The persecutors in contrast will end in *destruction*: "This is a clear omen to them of their destruction but of your salvation, and that from God" (Phil 1:28b).

As observed in chapter eleven, Paul's hymnlike words in Phil 2:6-11 possess extreme significance in the present study. Other aspects of this passage will be considered below, but at this juncture attention is now appropriately given to a single phrase, "even death on a cross" (2:8b). By means of this phrase, Paul portrays the nadir of Jesus' downward path in status. From equality with God, downward to human form, downward to death, even to death on a cross: such was the path of self-emptying adhered to by Jesus.

Crucifixion was an extremely degrading form of death for anyone to suffer. Crucifixion was almost impossible to fathom for one who possesses equality with God. Surely these were central considerations with Paul as he meditated on the meaning of the path that Jesus had followed.

But crucifixion was the form of execution reserved to the imperial forces. Crucifixion was decreed for Jesus by the Roman authorities. Were these reflections about crucifixion not also within Paul's horizon as he endured Roman custody and Roman chains and considered the nature of Roman power from his location in the imperial capital?

The interpretation that Paul does have the peculiarly Roman aspects of Jesus' death in view at the time of Philippians is strongly buttressed by the reflections he shares later in the letter:

> that I may know him and the power of his resurrection, and may share his sufferings, becoming like him in his death, that if possible I may attain the resurrection from the death. (Phil 3:10-11)

How is it possible that Paul may share Jesus' suffering and become like Jesus in his death? It should be recalled that elsewhere in the letter Paul does consider the possibility that his own case may conclude with a verdict of death. If such a verdict should occur, then through crucifixion or whatever decreed form of execution, Paul would be dying in circumstances comparable to those experienced by Jesus.

In both cases a Roman verdict would have been the formal cause of death. In both cases Roman soldiers would have carried out the verdict. In both cases an innocent person would have suffered a definitive abuse of Roman power. In both cases death would have proved the official Roman response to Christian ministry. Reflection on these as well as on other parallels may well have led Paul to express the words, "becoming like him in his death. . . ."

B. Paul's Relativizing of Roman Citizenship

Paul's significant words in Phil 3:18-19 have just been treated in the preceding subsection, and his words in 3:21 forecasting Jesus's intervention with power will be considered below. Philippians 3:20 thus occurs as a part of a larger passage in which contrasts are being drawn between the destiny of those who live as enemies of the cross of Christ and the power and destiny that Christ's faithful disciples have. Nevertheless, because it contains a specific teaching on the important topic of heavenly citizenship, it is useful to consider this verse separately. Paul expresses his perspective in the following words: "But our citizenship (*politeuma*) is in heaven and from it we await a Savior, the Lord Jesus Christ" (Phil 3:20; author's translation).

Before considering the implications of heavenly citizenship, it is well to recall the status of Philippi as a favored Roman colony, populated with Roman veterans. Philippi was indeed "a city of citizens" with its inhabitants possessing rights and privileges comparable to those enjoyed by citizens in Rome and Italy proper. Roman citizenship was highly coveted, and those living at Philippi participated in this high status. Their ancestors before them and they themselves had contributed to the expansion and the defense of the Roman empire. The citizenship they now enjoyed represented the highest status that those who ruled the empire could bestow. In its turn, this citizenship intensified the Philippians' bonds with those who ruled the empire from Rome.

In order to underscore the reverberating character of Paul's declamation, it is useful to supply italics and an exclamation point in the

English translation. Paul's words then read as follows: "But *our* citizenship is *in heaven*!" When this profession is viewed against the background of citizenship within the Roman empire, there are at least two important dimensions of meaning to consider.

First, Paul's emphasis on the heavenly citizenship that the Philippian Christians possess tends to diminish the importance of the Roman citizenship that they have heretofore treasured. From the perspective of those living in an *earthly* empire, Roman citizenship may well be esteemed as a supreme benefit. Yet clearly the realities of the realm of heaven far surpass the realities of life on earth. Citizenship *in heaven*, belonging *in heaven*, standing *in heaven* is thus more to be treasured than any form of citizenship within the limitations of the earthly realm.

Second, an emphasis on heavenly citizenship is also of great consequence because it implicitly sets in place critical standards for assessing earthly conduct. Any individual focused on citizenship in heaven and the life of heaven will necessarily be concerned with the criteria for that realm and the criteria for that life. What are the qualities, what is the belief, what is the conduct here on earth that credentials a person to enjoy the fullness of citizenship in heaven? Further, is it conceivable that there could be a disparity between what is required for the enjoyment of earthly citizenship and that which is presumed for the higher citizenship of the heavenly realm?

Paul's own situation as a chained prisoner awaiting trial on charges related to *maiestas* testifies to the impact that heavenly citizenship may have in terms of the prevailing standards of the Roman empire. Paul's words thus emphasize to his Christian friends and supporters at Philippi that there is a priority of testifying on behalf of their heavenly citizenship despite any cost to their earthly benefits. Regardless of their earthly circumstances, their heavenly citizenship thus exercises a pervasive influence on the lives of Christians. This is so even in instances in which they may hold Roman citizenship.

C. Passages in Which Paul Insists on Jesus' Unsurpassed Sovereignty

Paul's Christian readers at Philippi would have grasped his critical perspectives on the Roman order in the passages surveyed in the two preceding subsections. But it can be conjectured that these somewhat subtle features of Paul's letter might have been passed over by any Roman officials charged to censor Paul's correspondence. Can the same assessment be given regarding the passages now to be considered? Would Roman censorship have been lax enough to enable Paul's claims regarding Jesus' sovereign power to pass through the channels of censorship?

The considerations regarding *maiestas* presented in chapters five and ten are particularly relevant here. In Nero's Rome, all language recognizing Nero's status, power, and claims is of paramount importance. Yet in writing to the Philippians, Paul is steadily insistent on Jesus' unsurpassed power, status, and sovereignty. If Paul's letter was subject to Roman censorship, is it conceivable that his passages touching on these areas were assessed without any reaction? To draw attention to the politically controversial character of the Christology that Paul expresses in Philippians, let a sharper question be posed: If they had been detected or intercepted, could passages from Paul's letter have been used to sustain the charge of *maiestas* against him in a trial before Nero?

As Phil 3:20 continues, Paul states that, from heaven, Christians await "a *Savior*, the *Lord* Jesus Christ." Given the predilections of Nero (as well as emperors who preceded and succeeded him) for these two titles, Paul's use of them would be highly significant, even if he had not proceeded to speak regarding Jesus' comprehensive power. Yet Paul did indeed proceed to speak exultantly regarding the sovereign power of Jesus:

> and from it (heaven) we await a *Savior*, the *Lord* Jesus Christ who will change our lowly body to be like his glorious body, by the *power* which enables him *to subject all things to himself*. (Phil 3:21; emphasis added)

What persons or beings have sovereign existence outside the domain of Jesus' power? According to Paul in this passage, there is no entity that is not subject to Jesus. Does "all things" include Roman emperors such as Nero? Does it include the various manifestations of Roman power? Does it include the greatest institutional accomplishments of Rome as well as Rome's greatest cruelties and depravities? Paul's paean acclaims Jesus' power as a power that knows no limits. In this perspective, every natural power, every human power, every political power is ultimately subject to Jesus.

While the concepts expressed in 2:9-10 occur first chronologically, they logically complete and complement the reflections regarding Jesus' sovereignty that Paul expresses in 3:20-21. For, if it is true that every form of power is ultimately subject to Jesus, then what response to Jesus is incumbent on those so subject? Philippians 2:9-10 may be taken as the answer to this question. God's purpose in exalting Jesus and giving him a name above all others is:

> that at the name of Jesus every knee should bow, in heaven, on earth, and under the earth, and every tongue confess that Jesus Christ is Lord, to the glory of God the Father. (Phil 2:10)

To bring home the nature of the radical claim that Paul is here advancing on Jesus' behalf, it is only necessary to substitute the emperor's name for the word "every" (*pan, pasa*) at the two places where this adjective occurs within this clause. The following reading emerges: "that at the name of Jesus, *Nero's* knee should bow ... and *Nero's* tongue confess that Jesus Christ is Lord. ..."

Can such a substitution be justified as a concretizing that is faithful to Paul's fundamental meaning? The answer to this question hinges on how all encompassing a frame of reference Paul intended his words to have. Presumably, Paul did not desire to have the Roman emperors exempted from the requirement. For, as just noted, he images *every* knee bowing and *every* tongue confessing.

Recalling again that Paul wrote as a supervised, chained prisoner in the heart of Nero's Rome, it is inconceivable that he could have mentioned Nero by name in formulating such a passage. It thus seems warranted to conclude that, within the highly restricted circumstances in which he wrote, Paul imaginatively affirmed the fundamental truth that Nero himself is subject to the sovereignty of Jesus.

As a means of coalescing the various facets of Paul's efforts to proclaim Jesus's sovereignty, let the image of Paul standing before the imperial tribunal again be adduced. As previously suggested, Paul's letter could have been introduced as evidence of *maiestas* if it had been intercepted. Let it now be considered that the sentiments he expressed in writing to the Philippians were first of all present within

Paul's heart. Regardless of whether his letter became known to the Roman authorities, it is fully plausible to suppose that *the sentiments of Paul's heart* would have become known to these authorities as his trial proceeded.

Let it be supposed that Paul would be asked by Nero or by other high officials to explain more clearly the nature of Jesus' sovereignty and Paul's allegiance to Jesus. Would Paul not have brought upon himself a verdict of *maiestas* and a sentence of death by expressing impassioned sentiments comparable to those expressed in Phil 2:9-11 and 3:20-21?

If such a scenario unfolded, what would Paul's response have been to his impending execution? Surely Paul would have responded with words resembling those expressed in Phil 3:8-11, where he remains so insistent that Jesus is *his* Lord. The ideas contained in this latter passage are one more indication of how central the issue of Jesus' sovereignty is to Philippians:

> Indeed I count everything as loss because of the surpassing worth of knowing Christ Jesus *my* Lord. For his sake I have suffered the loss of all things, and count them as refuse, in order that I may gain Christ . . . that I may know him and the power of his resurrection, and may share his sufferings, becoming like him in his death. . . . (Phil 3:8-10; emphasis added)

2. Factors Influencing the Shift in Paul's Outlook

To enter into the mind of Paul is at once the objective and the challenge of the present section. Paul's perspective on the Roman order had manifestly shifted by the time he came to write to the Christians at Philippi. By the time of Philippians Paul had become far more critical of the patterns prevailing within the empire and far less endorsing of the Roman authorities. What factors influenced Paul to depart so radically from his perspective at the time of Rom 13:1-7?

From all that has been said earlier in this study, it is clear that Paul's extended confinement in chains profoundly affected the course of his ministry and profoundly affected his own self-image. Presumably this experience of chained confinement also impelled him to a reassessment of the Roman authorities and the allegiance that was

owed them. At least three other factors can also be plausibly conjectured as influences on Paul in making this new assessment: Paul's
new reflections regarding two Roman executions, his increased
familiarity with the depravity and licentiousness of Nero's Rome,
and his personal encounters with imperial propaganda aggressively
stressing Nero's exalted status and sovereignty. Each of these four
influences will now be considered.

A. Paul's Extended Confinement in Chains

As exposited in chapter eight, a significant period of time intervened
between Paul's letter to the Romans and his letter to Philemon. During that interval Paul came to wear Roman chains and he endured
these chains for a period of time sufficient for him to instruct Onesimus and become his spiritual father. Further, he endured these
chains long enough for his own self-image to become that of "*a prisoner* for Christ Jesus" (Phlm 1).

Between the writing of Philemon and the writing of Philippians,
another significant period of time elapsed. Several significant developments occurred within this interval, some of them perhaps concomitantly. First, a change has occurred in the support group around
Paul (five of Paul's associates mentioned as present with him at the
time of Philemon are not numbered among his supporters in Philippians). Second, the explanation of Paul's imprisonment has been dif-
fused in such a way that "it has become known throughout the
whole praetorian guard and to all the rest that my imprisonment is
for Christ" (Phil 1:13). Third, Paul has had success in emboldening
many of the Roman Christians to speak the word of God fearlessly.
Fourth, he has also suffered affliction from a minority of the city's
Christians who proclaimed Christ out of envy and rivalry.

By the time of Philippians Paul had thus had ample opportunity to
consider the various implications of what had transpired. Indeed, the
passage of time had brought him forward from an initial period
when he perhaps regarded his chains as a temporary phenomenon, a
brief miscarriage of justice, that would be quickly rectified.

Rectified by whom? The answer to this question is straightfor-
ward. Any rectification of Paul's situation would have to come from
the very authorities who had consigned him to chains and then kept

him in this condition. In effect, any rectification in Paul's situation would have to come from the Roman authorities.

Why was he not being expeditiously released from these chains? From one perspective, in his mission on behalf of Jesus, Paul was utterly blameless as to the decrees of Rome. Why then did the Roman authorities persist in keeping him in chained confinement as they would if Paul were a criminal? Were these Roman authorities not derelict and uncaring in the measures they had enacted against him and in their continuance of his custody? Presumably, overlapping thoughts such as these began to recur with increasing frequency as Paul's time in chains wore on.

As he pondered such questions, Paul's own earlier words regarding these Roman authorities very probably began to assume startlingly new and disconcerting meaning. For such were Paul's words prior to his confinement: "For rulers are not a terror to good conduct, but to bad. Would you have no fear of him who is in authority? Then do what is good and you will receive his approval" (Rom 13:3). Did not such words echo within Paul's consciousness in a disturbing and distressing way as he considered his own blameless conduct and the chains that the Roman authorities were continuing to mandate against him?

B. His Meditations Regarding Two Roman Executions

What did Paul know regarding the circumstances of Jesus' death? Did Paul know the approach that Pilate had followed in interrogating Jesus and the nature of the testimony that Jesus himself had given? What did Paul know regarding the attitude and behavior of the Roman soldiers who supervised and carried out Jesus' crucifixion? Such questions open the way to a potentially fruitful avenue of inquiry. For the more it can be assumed that Paul possessed detailed information regarding Jesus' trial before Pontius Pilate and detailed information regarding his execution, the more it can be assumed that Paul had the incentive to combine meditations about Jesus' death with reflections about his own proximity to death.

It is conceivable that the indisputable *fact* of Jesus' crucifixion may have been Paul's nearly exclusive focus during the initial stages of his own discipleship. Subsequently, however, as his own custody wore on, Paul can easily be imagined pondering the various Roman actors involved in Jesus' case and the violation of justice that Jesus' crucifixion represented.

Had Pilate erred through misunderstanding? Or had Pilate been vulnerable to concern for his own career, vulnerable to such a degree that Jesus' adversaries were able to manipulate him against his better judgment? Had Pilate simply reached the conclusion that Jesus' crucifixion was the alternative to the outbreak of an embarrassing riot? These questions and others related to them serve to indicate the lines of reflection Paul might have pursued in assessing the various factors and circumstances that had resulted in Jesus' crucifixion.

Now Paul found himself, like Jesus, under the jurisdiction of Roman officials. These Roman authorities had relegated him to chains and had kept him in custody over a significant interval of time. As he wrote to the Philippians, Paul knew well that his own execution might be decreed by these authorities. And on what grounds? For, by Paul's reckoning, his own execution by Roman soldiers would echo the transgression of justice that had occurred in Jesus' case.

A Roman governor sovereignly decreed the crucifixion of Jesus, and Roman soldiers had carried out this decree. A high imperial judge, very probably Nero himself, could now issue a verdict of death in Paul's case. And with dispatch Roman soldiers would then carry out Paul's execution. How friendly the reigning Roman authorities are to Jesus, Paul's Lord, and to Paul!

It can plausibly be conjectured that reflections such as these would have presented themselves to Paul as his confinement wore on. Dwelling as he did in *Roman* chains, the violation of truth and justice activated by Jesus' *Roman* crucifixion now presented itself as ever more compelling to Paul. Finally, after prolonged reflections of this type, it would only be a short step to the superseding of Paul's earlier counsel that submission and deference should be the leading elements in a Christian response to these reigning *Roman* authorities.

C. New Familiarity with Nero's Depravity

As discussed in chapter nine, Paul critiqued various forms of sexual misconduct in writing to the Christians of Rome. Since he had not yet visited Rome, on what basis did he make this criticism? Conceiv-

ably Paul may have received specific reports regarding sexual depravity in the imperial capital. He may also have been reflecting his own
general concerns during his apostolic journeys in the eastern
provinces regarding dissolute sexual behavior.

As a prisoner in Rome for a significant interval of time, information regarding the depraved excesses fostered by Nero presumably
had been brought to Paul's attention through various channels. Here
it should be recalled that Paul had contacts opening to "the whole
praetorian guard and to all the rest" (1:13b). Further, he was in communication with various Christians in the city (1:14). Most significantly he was in contact with a number of Christians who served in
the "household" of Caesar (4:22).

Given Paul's previously expressed criticism regarding sexual licentiousness, given Nero's role as a leading practitioner and orchestra-
tor of notoriously depraved and exploitative sexual conduct, and
given Paul's presumed new awareness of Nero's character and activity, what specific conclusions now present themselves? The first conclusion pertains to the correct interpretation of Phil 3:18-19 and has
already been presented in chapter eleven and referred to in section
one above. In effect, Paul is decrying Nero's egregious behavior when
he writes, "Their end is destruction, their god is the sexual organ,
and they glory in their shame. . . ." Further, the intensity behind his
words, "[I] now tell you even with tears," is an intensity arising from
his anger and frustration that such conduct is being propagated at
the highest echelons of Roman authority.

The second conclusion pertains to the present discussion of the
factors that impelled Paul to set aside his previously expressed counsel that the Christians of Rome should cooperate unreservedly with
the imperial authorities. The conclusion now expressly conjectured is
that Paul's disgust over Nero's lasciviousness urged him to reconsider
the lines he had originally penned in Rom 13:1-7. Faced with the
wantonness of Nero and his collaborators at Rome, so the present
argument, Paul would have been extremely reluctant to urge a high
degree of Christian subjection to authorities such as these.

D. *Paul's Encounter with the Assertions of Nero's Sovereignty*

Just as his custody in Rome presumably brought the depravity of
Nero's capital decisively to Paul's attention, so too would custody in

Rome have expedited his awareness regarding Nero's claims to sovereignty and the emperor's bizarre efforts to enforce these claims by brandishing the charge of *maiestas*. Paul may have encountered Nero's claims to be "savior" and "lord" prior to his arrival in Rome as a prisoner. Yet during his Roman confinement, guarded by members of the praetorian guard (1:3) and in contact with Christians who were themselves members of Caesar's staff (4:22), he did not lack ample opportunity for becoming painfully aware of Nero's deluded pretensions and aspirations.

The term "clash of allegiance" can be utilized to characterize the situation in which Paul now found himself. From all those under his sway, including Paul, Nero demanded subservience and compliance. But it was to Jesus that Paul had turned with all of his being, and it was to Jesus' intended purposes that Paul was unalterably committed.

Given his own abiding allegiance to Jesus and faced with Nero's demands for deference and subservience, what course was Paul to follow? The text of Philippians indicates that Paul's response at this juncture was to testify steadfastly and creatively to the overarching sovereignty of Jesus. Notwithstanding the claims of Nero to lordship, Paul confesses Jesus as Lord (1:21-23; 3:12). Notwithstanding the claims of Nero to earthly rule, Paul affirms that Jesus is truly sovereign not only over the earth but over the entire cosmos (2:9-11). Further, it is Jesus alone who has the power to subject all things to himself (3:20-21).

Granted that Philippians decisively and unalterably resolves the clash of allegiance in favor of Jesus, what implications follow for the admonitions that Paul earlier set forth in Rom 13:1-7? As with the factors discussed in the preceding sections, Paul's new conviction that Jesus should aggressively be proclaimed as Lord, Nero's maniacal claims notwithstanding, simultaneously urges a general revision of Rom 13:1-7. This general reformulation would presumably involve the specific deletion of any and all phrases that countenanced divine authorization for rulers such as Nero.

Now, well aware of the emperor's delusions and pretensions regarding sovereignty, Paul could no longer have desired that Christians in Rome and throughout the empire consider that Nero was "God's servant for your good" (Rom 13:4c). Nor could Paul, with first-hand experience of Nero and his cohorts, have any longer continued to postulate, "For there is no authority except from God, and those that exist have been instituted by God . . ." (Rom 13:1b).

3. Conjecturing Paul's Modifications in Romans 13:1-7

It is now appropriate to revisit the text of Rom 13:1-7. Given the analysis made in the preceding sections of this chapter, it can be supposed that Paul would have modified the text of Rom 13:1-7 had he been given such an opportunity. That Paul was actually in custody at a location in Rome is a matter of great significance for this effort to imagine him revising Rom 13:1-7. For it was precisely to the Christians at Rome that these words had been originally written. Indeed, at this juncture members of the Christian community of Rome can be envisioned communicating with Paul about parts of the letter he had earlier sent to them.

If asked by these Christians to state his present outlook regarding the Roman authorities, Paul might well have responded that his basic perspective should now be sought within the paragraphs of his letter to the Philippians. Yet if pressed to comment on Rom 13:1-7, how would Paul have responded? Would he have endorsed any of the precepts and counsels he had previously expressed? And, if so, with what modifications?

Given the perspectives and the admonitions he expressed in Philippians, it can be surmised that Paul would have modified Rom 13:1-7 extensively, possibly, by taking the following steps: First the exhortation in 13:1a to "be subject" would be radically transformed in its orientation so as to focus on the sovereignty of Jesus. Second, Rom 13:1b-5, which previously delineated a divine sanction for the Roman authorities and their rule, would now be eliminated entirely. Third, in addressing the topic of taxation in 13:6, Paul would probably forsake his previous mode of address and adopt wording encouraging careful *deliberation* about taxes.

Romans 13:1a and 13:6 can thus be refashioned to present a "Philippian" perspective on the topics of allegiance to the Roman authorities and the payment of their taxes. As a means of giving concrete expression to the shift that has occurred in Paul's perspective, a revised version of Rom 13:1a will now be juxtaposed with Paul's original text. Brief comments will then be appended in order to explicate more precisely the change in Paul's outlook. This same procedure of juxtaposing a revised version with Paul's original text will then be followed for Rom 13:6.

Consider then the following two perspectives regarding the topic of allegiance:

1. Let every person be subject to the governing authorities (Paul's original wording in Rom 13:1a).
2. Let every person, including the governing authorities, be subject to the Lord Jesus (Paul's conjectured wording at the time of Philippians).

As is evident from a brief consideration of these two versions, the issue of Jesus' sovereignty and the implications of his sovereignty are now issues of axial importance. For whatever reason, when he authored Rom 13:1-7, Paul was not expressly concerned to emphasize Jesus' sovereignty. By the time of Philippians, this is the central issue around which everything else turns. If Jesus has truly been given a name above all other names, are not the Roman authorities themselves to be subject to Jesus? And being subject to him, are they not obligated to lead their own civic lives responsibly in his name? From the perspective of passages like Phil 2:6-11 and 1:27, such questions as these can only be answered in the affirmative. As a consequence, the entire question of suitable Christian conduct in the civic realm is reopened.

Further, once it is grasped that the governing authorities, as well as Jesus' disciples, are subject to Jesus, the nearly metaphysical propositions that Paul originally set forth in Romans 13:2-5 become anomalous. These verses are thus simply deleted. Indeed any attempt to visualize Paul as a chained prisoner continuing to enunciate such tenets overwhelms the imagination.

As indicated above, Paul's "Philippian" outlook on the payment of Roman taxes can be identified by utilizing subjunctive mood verb forms in the two places within Romans 13:6 where Paul used indicative forms. The two contrasting perspectives then appear as follows:

1. For the same reason you also pay taxes, for the authorities are ministers of God attending to this very thing (Paul's original wording in Rom 13:6).
2. . . . you *may* pay taxes, for the authorities *can be* ministers of God attending to this very thing (Paul's conjectured wording at the time of Philippians).

It should be observed that the Philippian perspective now conjectured for Paul does not locate him as completely in opposition to Roman taxes nor does it portray him as completely supporting these taxes. Rather, following from his teaching in Philippians regarding the priority of citizenship in heaven (3:20), Paul now counsels that the question of paying Roman taxes is to be assessed against the criteria of the heavenly commonwealth.

In effect, no unqualified, universal answer can be given regarding tax obligations. The authorities *can be* ministers of God, depending on their conduct. And if they are functioning in a laudable manner, their administration may be supported through the payment of just taxes. Yet conversely, if the authorities are not governing in such a way as to be considered ministers of God, then presumably there is no Christian obligation to cooperate with the taxes they impose.

To move from Romans 13:6-7 to a Philippians-grounded perspective on the subject of taxes is thus to travel a considerable distance. Finally, it should be remembered also that in Rom 13:1-7 the governance of the Roman authorities is viewed with great benignity. This is not the case with Philippians, where reference is made to "a crooked and perverse generation" (2:15) and where the term "enemies of the cross of Christ" (3:18) is employed.

4. Paul in Philippians and the
Contrasting Approaches to Roman Rule

It is now appropriate to draw this study to a close. Paul's journey from Romans to Philippians has unfolded in such a way that his own perspective regarding the Roman authorities and their rule has shifted dramatically. This concluding section will locate Paul alongside the approaches of Tacitus' Cerialis, Josephus' Judas the Gaulanite, and Luke's Jesus as a further means of identifying and illuminating the dramatic shift that has occurred in Paul's own outlook.

A. Paul in Philippians and the Approach of Cerialis

At the end of chapter two it could be stated without hesitation that, when Paul wrote to the Christians at Rome, his approach regarding taxation and regarding the Roman authorities was congruent with the approach of Tacitus' Cerialis.

Granted that a favorable response for Rom 13:1-7 can be projected for Tacitus' general, what reaction would Cerialis have had to the perspective that Paul subsequently adopted in Philippians? Clearly this response would have been far less favorable. Paul's strong emphasis on uncompromised allegiance to Jesus as Lord and Savior, his emphasis on the heavenly citizenship to which Christians were called, and his characterization of the Roman society surrounding the Philippians as "a crooked and perverse generation"—all would have elicited a negative reaction from Cerialis.

It should be emphasized that nothing in Philippians counseled Paul's Christian readers to replace Roman rule with some other form of government. And nothing in Philippians suggested that Christians should immediately reject the payment of Roman taxes. Philippians, in sum, is not a document written by someone aggressively pursuing the demise of Roman rule in the territories of Greece or Gaul or anywhere else.

Nevertheless, despite its lack of any sentiments explicitly urging revolution, Philippians represented a considerable distance from the accommodation vouchsafed to the Roman authorities in Rom 13:1-7. And in particular this letter's explicit affirmation of the Roman-crucified Jesus as Lord and Savior could also only have been startling and disconcerting for someone of Cerialis' outlook.

B. Paul in Philippians and the Approach of Judas the Gaulanite

Up until this point in the analysis, the response of Josephus' Judas the Gaulanite to Paul's counsel in Rom 13:1-7 has not been projected. Yet, it is not difficult to conclude that Judas and those of like persuasion could only have responded to Rom 13:1-7 with disdain. Judas tenaciously espoused the violent overthrow of Roman rule and advocated resistance to Roman taxes as one component in this struggle. In contrast, the Paul of Romans 13 counseled full compliance with all Roman taxes and buttressed the legitimacy of the reigning Roman authorities on theological grounds.

Had he become familiar with the Paul of Philippians, it can be conjectured that Judas would no longer had disdained him as a de facto collaborator with the Roman regime. Nevertheless, as just noted, Philippians certainly does not advocate the violent overthrow of Roman rule and thus would be assessed as deficient by Judas. Given Paul's reference to himself in Roman chains and given Paul's admonition that the prevailing Roman society stood forth as "a crooked and perverse generation," Judas might question whether Paul would offer at least some degree of support to Judas' insurrection against Roman rule. From Philippians' perspective the answer to this hypo-

thetical question is negative. Yet Judas could be confirmed in the
basic insight that Paul was now resistant to the Roman authorities in
a way that he had not previously been.

C. Paul in Philippians and Luke's Jesus

Until this point, the perspective of Paul in Rom 13:1-7 and the perspective of Jesus within the Gospel of Luke have not been juxtaposed. What is now to be said regarding Paul's approach in Romans
13 and the "evaluative" approach of Luke's Jesus?

As previously noted, Rom 13:1-7 does not envision the possibility
of a conflict or clash between God's sovereignty and the sovereignty
claimed by the Roman authorities. Nor does Romans 13 provide any
mandate for Christians to evaluate the practices of the Roman
authorities before determining whether the payment of Roman taxes
is warranted. For these reasons there is a significant lack of compatibility between the perspective of Romans 13 and the perspective of
Jesus as presented in Luke's Gospel.

If Rom 13:1-7 thus stands profoundly in tension with the evaluative approach of Luke's Jesus, what degree of compatibility exists
between the perspective of Paul in Philippians and the perspective of
Jesus in Luke? It can now be concluded that, as a chained Roman
prisoner, Paul articulated an outlook on the Roman order that is
strikingly compatible with the nuanced evaluative approach adhered
to by Jesus within Luke's Gospel.

The first major point of similarity to be noted is that Luke's Jesus
and Paul in chains both testify to someone whose sovereignty far
exceeds that of the Roman emperor or that of any other human
authority. In Jesus' case, it is God's sovereignty that is consistently
imaged and upheld. In Paul's case, it is the cosmic sovereignty of
Jesus himself that is testified to and reverenced. In Philippians' memorable depiction, it is at Jesus' name that every knee shall bend.

Second, Jesus in Luke and Paul in Philippians both maintain a critical perspective regarding certain patterns and features of the Roman
social order. For example, in Jesus' case, there is a critique of "the
kings of the Gentiles," who dominate others while embracing the
honorific "benefactor." In Paul's case there is a critical reference to
"a crooked and perverse generation" and an indictment of those who
live as "enemies of the cross of Christ."

Third, Luke's Jesus and Paul in Rome both propose a standard by which the patterns and practice of the empire or any social institution are to be assessed. In Jesus' case "the things of God" constitute the standard against which "the things of Caesar" are to be evaluated. In Paul's case the authenticating standard is that of "citizenship in heaven." For Paul, even Roman citizenship, the highest offering of the Roman empire, is relativized by the realities that pertain to the life of heaven.

Nevertheless, while both proposed a standard for evaluating the Roman order, Luke's Jesus did not explicitly propose an institutional alternative to Roman rule and neither did Paul in Philippians. Further, neither advocated violent efforts to overthrow Roman rule.

These last points bear amplification. To speak in terms of only two other institutional models, neither Jesus nor Paul argued on behalf of democracy on the Athenian model or theocracy on the Zealot model as a preferred alternative to the imperial model of Roman rule. Further, explicitly according to Luke's Jesus and implicitly according to Paul in Philippians, violent revolutionary uprising did not constitute a suitable means for advancing the reign of God.

Given these last considerations, multiple ironies abide in the outcome of Jesus crucified by the Roman governor for Judea and in the outcome of Paul facing a death sentence from the Roman emperor in the imperial capital. Pilate judged Jesus not dangerous to Roman rule, yet executed him as a Zealot. But was Pilate actually correct to conclude that Jesus posed no danger? And was Paul "dangerous" in any sense to Nero? *Given Nero's approach to personal and social reality*, Paul could indeed be regarded as posing a threat to the *maiestas* of Nero.

At the close of Philippians, significantly influenced by the experience of his chains and also by his increased familiarity with Nero's exorbitant claims and outrageous conduct, Paul stood at the center of the empire prepared to testify to Jesus his Lord with wholehearted conviction. With everything considered, Paul was no enemy of Rome, as was Judas the Gaulanite. Nor was he now, if ever he had been, friendly to the empire on the order of a Cerialis.

Rather, from his first Christian steps within the eastern provinces of the empire, Paul was, by reason of extraordinary grace, Christ's wondrously faithful apostle. Now, close to the end of his grace-guided journey, Paul found that he was his Lord's chosen ambassador to the capital, a most credentialed and trustworthy ambassador, precisely in his chains.

St. Peter and St. Paul Baptizing Their Warders
Altar Sculpture at the Mamertine Prison in Rome
Used with permission

Paul as a Chained
Prisoner in Acts

As is widely recognized, Luke, in authoring the Acts of the Apostles, has given extended attention to the ministry that Paul undertook after his astonishing conversion by Jesus. Consistent with the methodological considerations delineated in chapter one of this study, no reference has been made to Luke's reports about Paul up until this point. As an appendix to the preceding investigation of Paul's letters, however, the principal lines in Luke's portrait of Paul as a chained Roman prisoner are now appropriately considered. In the first section below, a brief overview of the dynamic that drove Paul's case will be presented. Sections two and three will then analyze Paul's specific circumstances as a prisoner at Caesarea and in Rome. In section four consideration will then be given to the various references that Luke makes to chains in portraying Paul in Acts.

1. The Dynamic of Paul's Case

According to Acts, how did Paul become a Roman prisoner in Jerusalem? And how was it that, four years later, he was still to be found in Roman chains, now in Rome itself? These questions serve to establish the parameters of the present summary of the later stages of Paul's journey in Acts. Since the answers now provided for these and related questions are based on the analysis previously made in R. Cassidy, *Society and Politics in the Acts of the Apostles,* that work should be consulted for a more detailed presentation.

According to Acts 16:19-40, denunciations after an exorcism by Paul at Philippi resulted in a public whipping for Paul and Silas and, with their feet confined in stocks, severe overnight incarceration in the inner jail. The Roman magistrates at Philippi were responsible for decreeing these punishments, and a jailer in their employ, subsequently a Christian convert, was made responsible for Paul's custody.

Paul also experienced other conflicts in which various Roman officials played a role. Conflict occurred at Thessalonica, where the politarchs demanded bail money from Paul's host (17:1-9), at Corinth where an anti-semitic Roman governor deigned not to proceed against Paul (18:12-17), and at Ephesus where the city manager pacified a riotous assembly that had been seeking Paul's death (19:23-41). Although not a stranger to controversy at any stage of his ministry, Paul did not experience prolonged Roman custody, replete with chains, until his final visit to Jerusalem.

In Jerusalem and Caesarea, the key figures in terms of Paul's binding with chains are a Roman tribune and two Roman governors. The particulars of Paul's case, as Luke presents them, are fairly complex. Nevertheless, from his portrayal of Antonius Felix and Porcius Festus, the two governors who oversee Paul's case, it emerges that no favorable view of the Roman imperial system is being communicated by Luke. Both of these Roman judges are portrayed as all too willing to collude with Paul's accusers and his enemies.

Claudius Lysias, the Roman tribune, initially intervenes when a violent riot breaks out in the Jerusalem temple (21:31-32). Paul is clearly innocent of the charge that he has profaned the temple by bringing Gentiles within the precincts restricted to Jews. Nevertheless, Paul's enemies on the Sanhedrin willfully manipulate this false charge once it has been raised by certain Jews from Asia. At first, considering Paul to be the instigator of the riot, Lysias arrests him and orders him bound with two chains. When Paul's subsequent address to the Jerusalem crowd re-ignites the riot, Lysias resolves to interrogate Paul by means of scourging. It is at this point that Paul brings his standing as a Roman citizen to light confounding Lysias and the soldiers under his command (22:25-30).

Within Acts, Paul's Roman citizenship is a factor in three different situations. After having been beaten and imprisoned overnight at Philippi, Paul discloses his citizenship to the Roman jailer in order to receive "conciliation" from the Roman magistrates. Then at

Jerusalem, he discloses it to Roman military officers to avoid the scourging prohibited for citizens. Finally, at his hearing before Festus, Paul will exercise the Roman citizen's right of appeal to circumvent Festus' machinations by having his case brought directly before the emperor.

Nevertheless, despite the fact that he invokes his citizenship in these three instances, Paul's basic approach toward his Roman citizenship is characterized by reserve and restraint. Paul never displays his citizenship before Christian and Jewish groups. And even in his dealings with Roman officials, his appeals to his citizenship are made virtually as a last resort and in response to specific violations of his rights. In the passage now under consideration, Lysias' astonishment upon learning that Paul is a citizen is understandable, given the manner in which Paul had identified himself in response to Lysias' initial question (21:39).

While Paul's reference to his citizenship has the immediate consequence of sparing him from a severe whipping, it does not result in his release. The next morning, still seeking to decipher whether Paul was guilty of the crimes alleged against him, Lysias temporarily removed Paul's chains and brought him to a hearing before the Sanhedrin. After a riot again ensued, Lysias sent his soldiers to extract Paul from the competing factions, and Paul was brought back to the barracks, still a prisoner (23:10). The next day, having been informed by Paul's nephew of a plot against Paul's life, Lysias ordered that Paul be brought, under heavy guard, to Antonius Felix's headquarters in Caesarea (23:19-24).

Felix's initial response was to command that Paul be guarded in Herod's praetorium (23:35b). Paul's accusers arrived five days later to state their case against him, bringing two well-rehearsed charges: (a) that Paul was an agitator engendering uprisings throughout the Roman provinces, and (b) that Paul had tried to violate the precincts of the Jerusalem temple (24:2-6). Both of these charges were capital in character. But after Paul's spirited response, Felix decided to defer his decision until he could gain more information from Lysias (24:22).

Initially portraying him as careful and evenhanded, Luke ultimately depicts Felix as derelict and venal. Felix keeps Paul in custody over a two-year period, conversing with him during the interval, yet hoping the while that he would receive a bribe from him. Luke's final report portrays Felix even more reprehensibly. Even though he had reached the end of his own term as governor, Felix still kept Paul imprisoned because he wished to extend a "favor" to Paul's enemies (24:27).

Luke's portrayal of Porcius Festus, the incoming governor, is somewhat comparable to his portrayal of Felix. At the outset he depicts Festus taking steps indicative of carefulness and evenhandedness. Initially rejecting the request of Paul's enemies that he be sent to Jerusalem (so that he may be assassinated along the way), Festus stipulates that they must proffer their charges formally in Caesarea (25:4-5). After they arrive and do so in an unconvincing way, Paul replies straightforwardly that he has not offended against the temple or against Caesar in any way (25:8).

Then, however, Luke portrays Festus tilting egregiously toward Paul's enemies, proposing, after all, that Paul's trial be shifted to Jerusalem (25:9). Outraged over this blatant breach of fair procedure, Paul forcefully chastises Festus for advancing such a proposal, emphatically refuses to countenance it, and appeals to have his case heard personally by Caesar (25:10-11).

Luke next portrays Festus embarking on a series of adroit maneuvers in order to insure that his own handling of Paul's case will not be faulted by his superiors in Rome. Herod Agrippa is brought into the proceedings, and Festus communicates to the king a slanted account of what has transpired (25:14-21). Ostensibly, he desires to have Agrippa's assistance in formulating the charges that should properly accompany Paul when he is sent, as a chained prisoner, to Rome.

While the narrative in Acts supposes that Festus eventually did submit charges, the "violations" he formulated cannot be determined from Luke's report. In the setting of a solemn assembly that included Agrippa, Bernice, and the leading military and civilian residents of Caesarea, Festus indicates publicly that Paul has done nothing deserving death. (In assessing Festus' pronouncement, it must be born in mind that Paul had already made his peremptory appeal.) At the conclusion of Paul's subsequent eloquent defense, Herod Agrippa's own assessment confirms the view that Festus has just proposed. There is no valid capital charge against Paul and he could have been set free. Now, however, his appeal to Caesar is in effect (26:31-32).

Paul's continuance in chains should be focused upon at this point. At Jerusalem, he was originally placed in bonds by Lysias. Presumably these Roman chains continued to bind him during the two years of his custody at Caesarea (see the analysis of section four below). In Luke's understanding, Paul may also have been chained while in the custody of the centurion Julius during a perilous sea voyage to Rome. After Paul's arrival in Rome, Luke again explicitly portrays him bound with a chain and conveys that Paul continued in his chains for two additional years. It will be explained below that this chain is a defining feature of Paul's "portrait" as Luke brings his narrative to a close.

2. Paul's Circumstances
as a Prisoner in Caesarea

Given the phenomenon of his extended custody at Caesarea and his extended custody in Rome, it is useful to analyze the particulars of Paul's circumstances in both of these locations. To expedite this process, the framework of headings and subheadings used within chapter four will now be used to shed light on Paul's prison circumstances in Acts.

A. Category of Custody

As mentioned above, Lysias the Roman tribune originally arrested Paul in Jerusalem. He subsequently transported Paul to Caesarea utilizing a large complement of soldiers to do so. Upon Paul's arrival, Antonius Felix commanded that he be guarded in Herod's praetorium until his accusers should arrive. An elaborate complex built by Herod the Great, this praetorium featured halls and rooms suitable for many functions and probably possessed its own jail facilities. Whether Paul was initially restricted to a jail cell or allowed to move more freely cannot be determined from Luke's brief reference. Whatever the area of his confinement, though, that he was restricted in his movements by chains is a factor that must not be overlooked.

It was noted above that, after the rioting in Jerusalem, Lysias ordered Paul bound "with two chains" (*halysesi dysi*). In the light of the other instances in which Luke uses this word (Luke 8:29; Acts

12:6-7), it can be inferred that Luke understands Paul to be fettered to a soldier on either side of him just as Peter was in Acts 12. If Paul was thus fettered in the Roman barracks in Jerusalem, was he chained in similar fashion in the Roman praetorium in Caesarea? Arguably, Luke does understand Paul's chains to bind him to his guards. He is at least bound with chains in some fashion.

After hearing the charges of Paul's accusers and Paul's own spirited reply, Felix decided to postpone his own decision, ostensibly electing to wait until Lysias could be summoned to provide further information about Paul's case (24:1-22). In the meantime Paul would be kept in custody according to the following terms:

> Then he gave orders to the centurion that he should be kept in custody but should have some liberty, and that none of his friends should be prevented from attending to his needs. (Acts 24:23)

Two aspects of the arrangements that Felix specified deserve to be treated here. First, brief attention should be given to the question of the technical form of custody under which Paul was held. Second, consideration should be given to the role that is expressly authorized for Paul's friends and supporters.

Does the wording of this report suggest that Luke viewed Felix now mitigating a relatively severe custody that Paul had been relegated to during the five days prior to the hearing? Or is it Luke's sense that Lysias was now simply formalizing the arrangements that he had enacted at the time of Paul's arrival in Caesarea? Given the relatively concise character of Luke's presentation here, no definite answer can be supplied for this specific question. Nevertheless, Luke's reports do establish that, for approximately two years, Paul was (a) confined in Herod's praetorium, (b) supervised by a centurion under orders from Felix, (c) almost certainly kept in chains, and (d) allowed to be assisted by friends and associates. In effect, then, Luke portrays Paul being held under the form of Roman custody known as *custodia militaris* ("military custody").

B. The Assistance of Friends

What friends, associates, and family members does Luke envision ministering to Paul when he reports Felix's pronouncement that

Paul's friends were not to be prevented from rendering assistance? In Luke's mind, what specific forms of assistance could Paul's associates extend to him?

Within Acts, Caesarea is a city with which Paul is well familiar. Indeed, his visit to Caesarea just prior to his arrest in Jerusalem reveals his good relations with various disciples there including Philip the evangelist and his four unmarried, spirit-filled daughters (21:8-9). Agabus, a prophet from the surrounding environs, was also a visitor to Caesarea at this time and prophesied publicly that Paul should not go up to Jerusalem (21:10-12). When Paul insisted that he was willing to be chained and even to die in Jerusalem, however, some of the disciples from Caesarea traveled up to Jerusalem in solidarity with him, bringing him to the lodging where he would stay (21:13-16).

Besides mentioning the disciples who actually resided in Caesarea and its environs, Luke indicates that Paul was sometimes accompanied by select Christians (these Christians are described as *synekdemous*, literally, "companions in travel"). Aristarchus is so designated at Ephesus (19:29); Aristarchus and Trophimus are later among the group traveling with Paul in Macedonia (20:4). Trophimus is portrayed with Paul in Jerusalem (21:29), and, at the time of Paul's remission to Rome, Aristarchus is portrayed embarking on the same ship that will carry Paul (27:2).

It should be noted that one consequence of the famous "we-passages" of Acts is to position Luke, the narrator of Acts, within the circle of Paul's supporters at Caesarea. From 21:1 forward, the narrator accompanies Paul on his journey to Caesarea and Jerusalem, and at 27:1-2 the narrator departs for Rome on the same ship with Julius the centurion, Paul, and Aristarchus.

Luke's narrative also leaves open the possibility for envisioning that various relatives and friends traveled from Jerusalem in order to assist Paul. Here it should be recalled that the son of his sister informed Paul about the ambush being planned and then played a key role in persuading Claudius Lysias about the gravity of the situation (23:16-22). To be sure, no explicit mention is made of this nephew visiting Paul in Caesarea during Paul's two years of custody there. Nevertheless, Luke has clearly portrayed this nephew as supportive of Paul and has located him at an accessible distance from his uncle.

Similarly, Luke portrays Paul's last interactions with the various members of the Christian community in Jerusalem in such positive terms that members of this group can also be conjectured to be present within the group assisting Paul. Luke reports that the members of the Jerusalem Church received Paul and his companions "gladly" (*asmenōs*) when they arrived from Caesarea (21:17). The following day's interactions with James and the elders are also portrayed in positive terms. In particular, the tension arising from reports that Paul has advocated abolishing the observance of the Jewish law is dealt with harmoniously: Paul readily complies with James' request that he undertake a particular temple ritual, a step designed to reassure his critics (21:18-26).

C. Factors Affecting Survival

What were the material conditions of the custody that Paul experienced at Caesarea? What were the arrangements regarding food? What clothing did Paul wear while in custody? What were the conditions under which he slept? What was Paul's situation in the praetorium in terms of light, ventilation, access to water, and other factors pertaining to a prisoner's personal hygiene and overall health? Luke's report that Paul's friends attended to his needs images a significant connectedness and indicates a basic level of support. Yet, apart from this fundamental statement, Luke prescinds almost completely from any description of the circumstances under which Paul was confined.

Did Paul have financial resources available to him that could be used to alleviate the confinement he faced? One of Luke's reports concerning Felix is intriguing with respect to such a possibility. At 24:24-26 Luke indicates that Felix held a conversation with Paul in which the prisoner challenged the governor concerning right conduct. Nevertheless, Felix continued to send for Paul and converse with him because "he hoped that money would be given him by Paul."

In portraying Felix's ignoble purpose, is Luke also tangentially providing his readers with a perspective regarding Paul's financial resources? Does Luke intend to suggest that Paul, through his friends, possessed resources in enough abundance to warrant Felix's desire for a bribe? Given that his principal concern is with Felix's greed and with his corruption, it is difficult to determine whether

Luke himself considered Felix's efforts nonsensical. Once again, Paul's precise material circumstances in Caesarea remain beyond the horizon of Luke's broad-stroke reports.

D. Other Prisoners, Informers, Censorship

Were there other prisoners confined with Paul at Caesarea? In Caesarea, was Herod's praetorium the only place of confinement for all who became subject to the governor's judgment? In 27:2 Luke notes that other prisoners were being transported to Rome along with Paul under the care of the centurion Julius. Whether these prisoners had previously been confined with Paul in the Caesarean praetorium is not indicated.

Nor does Luke's narrative provide any indication that Paul was ever subjected to surveillance and manipulation by informers and spies during the two years of his confinement. If Luke understands Paul to be constantly chained to one of the soldiers guarding him, then the question of informers and spies is moot. The presence of a soldier, literate in Greek, immediately at hand, would also affect Paul's situation with respect to censorship.

While censorship pertains especially to the contents of any written communication, it may also be understood in a broader sense as pertaining to the searching and surveillance of those who visited Paul. Regarding the censorship of letters, it is a noteworthy feature of the Acts narrative that Luke nowhere portrays Paul engaging in written communication. Inasmuch as he makes no mention of Paul writing from such locations as Ephesus or Corinth it is perhaps not so surprising that Paul does not send or receive letters during his custody at Caesarea.

E. Paul's Endeavors While in Custody

It has just been observed that Luke does not portray Paul engaging in correspondence during his two years in Herod's praetorium. What then were Paul's activities during this interval? What endeavors did he undertake? What forms of ministry did he engage in? Once again, it is not Luke's intention to describe Paul's circumstances at Caesarea in precise detail.

Does Luke depict Paul undertaking legal initiatives or preparing a defense in order to gain release from custody? Putting the question in this way serves to sharpen appreciation for the nuances contained within the narrative of Acts. Fundamentally, the answer to this question must be sought in Luke's reports concerning the series of encounters, formal and informal, that transpired between Felix and Paul during the period of Paul's custody.

Luke indicates that Paul presented a vigorous defense before Felix when he rebutted the charges of the chief priest Ananias and other adversaries (24:10-21). Had Paul consciously prepared this defense during the initial days of his custody or were his words an outpouring of sentiments of innocence coupled with the explanation that everything he had done was fundamentally in response to the resurrection of Jesus? On the one hand, this speech seems to reflect impassioned spontaneity. On the other hand, Paul shrewdly also draws attention to two areas of weakness in the case that has been presented by his opponents. Yet such shrewdness, in and of itself, does not establish that Paul has formally prepared his defense.

In the aftermath of this speech Paul's conversations with Felix take place. In 24:26 it is stated that these conversations were held "often" (*pyknoteron*). It has been noted above that Felix hoped to receive a bribe from Paul. But what concerns did Paul bring to these conversations? Luke states that, in their first conversation, Paul argued "about justice and self-control, and future judgment" (24:25a). Does Luke intend to suggest that Paul continued exclusively with these topics during his subsequent conversations with Felix? or can Paul also be envisioned protesting his ongoing confinement? Here it should be reflected that Paul's legal situation, as described by Luke, is a situation of disequilibrium. It is a situation that calls out for juridical adjustment.

One additional development supports the interpretation that, in Luke's own understanding, Paul pondered and weighed his legal alternatives during the time of his custody at Caesarea. This development consists in the bold response that Paul gives to Festus when Paul demands that his case be transferred to the emperor's jurisdiction. Paul's indignant reply to Festus in 25:11 seems at first reading to be spontaneous and unpremeditated. Yet, in recalling Paul's frequent meetings with Felix (24:26) and in considering Paul's evident resentment of his chains (26:29), are Luke's readers not led to conclude that Paul already had such an appeal under consideration?

Given the degree of conjecture involved in the preceding considerations, it seems advisable to return to the terra firma of Luke's report in 24:23 in bringing this section to a close. What endeavors did Paul the prisoner undertake at Caesarea? Seemingly Luke desires to convey that Paul's principal endeavors flow from his position as a central figure for the group of disciples who are drawn to him and who attend to his needs.

Despite his new and startling circumstances, Paul's *friends* are not ashamed of him. They are not deterred by his chains; neither are they intimidated by his guards. Rather, they gather about Paul and constitute a worthy community of disciples. Revering Paul, they assist him; and at the same time they themselves are nourished. And thus does Paul's principal endeavor as a Roman prisoner at Caesarea begin to emerge: while bearing witness faithfully, he participates in the life of a small Christian community. In a real sense, despite being a prisoner, he calls forth that life.

3. Paul's Circumstances as a Prisoner in Rome

As previously mentioned, Paul, as well as a number of other prisoners, was transported to Rome under the supervision of a centurion of the Augustan cohort named Julius (27:1). Both Aristarchus and the narrator of Acts are portrayed accompanying Paul on his journey; and, in addition, Paul is able to receive assistance from other friends at Sidon (27:3). A key feature of the custody that Paul experienced at Caesarea—the assistance of friends—is thus portrayed as continuing to be in effect for the voyage to Rome.

A. Category of Custody

Luke does not describe the procedures that Julius followed in handing Paul over to the authorities in Rome, but various reports within the narrative indicate that Paul continued to be held under a form of military custody. Key parameters of this custody emerge from Luke's report that a soldier guarded Paul (27:16b), and from his portrayal of Paul as bound with a chain (28:20). It is also significant that Paul was able to welcome and discuss with all who came to him (28:17, 23, 30-31).

The location and circumstances of Paul's quarters in Rome cannot be determined from Luke's account. Luke's wording, however, suggests that Paul himself assumes a role in arranging for and/or paying for these quarters. Significantly, Paul's confinement in Rome under these arrangements endures for two years (28:30a) and is still in effect as Acts closes.

B. *The Assistance of Friends*

During the two years that he was a prisoner in Rome, from whom did Paul receive support and assistance? This question is more difficult to answer for Rome than for Caesarea.

It is to be noted at the outset that, other than the narrator (Luke), no one from Paul's larger circle of friends and associates is explicitly situated at his side in Rome. Aristarchus, as noted above, had embarked with Paul and Luke on the ship bound for Rome. By special grace, the lives of all on board the ship were preserved (27:22-25), and Aristarchus can thus be imagined safely ashore with the others at Malta and continuing with Paul for the remainder of the journey to Rome. Nevertheless, the last time that Aristarchus is mentioned by name is in 27:2, and it is not clear whether he is at Paul's side once Paul is in the capital.

Luke indicates the existence of a Christian community in Rome prior to Paul's arrival, but is it his understanding that these Christians rendered assistance to Paul? In an effort to shed light on this question, it is useful to give careful attention to Luke's report regarding Paul's encounter with Christians from Rome while he was still approximately forty miles from the city. It should be kept in mind that Paul is a prisoner under Julius' supervision, very probably bound with chains, when the following meeting occurs:

> And so we came to Rome. And the brethren there, when they heard of us, came as far as the Forum of Appius and Three Taverns to meet us. And seeing them Paul thanked God and took courage. (Acts 28:14b-15)

When it is considered *without* reference to other episodes in Acts in which Paul receives welcome, the present scene can be interpreted as having distinctly positive overtones. First, that the Roman Christians have traveled a considerable distance to meet Paul is clearly one positive feature. Second, Paul so appreciates the arrival of these Christians that he takes strength and returns thanks to God. Third, if the term *apantesis*, "meeting," has here the connotation of official welcome, then Luke may be indicating that the Roman Christians continued with Paul and his Roman guards, assisting him on this last stage of his journey.

If Luke here uses *apantesis* without implying hospitality (*apantesan* is used at 17:12 of Luke's Gospel without the connotation of hospitality), then the image of the Roman Christians cordially escorting Paul forward may not be justified. This note of caution having been struck, it is now appropriate to consider the present scene against the background of other scenes in Acts in which Paul is accorded extremely positive welcome.

When Paul arrived in Jerusalem prior to his arrest, Luke stated that (21:17b) "the brethren received us gladly." Later, at the port of Sidon on the voyage to Rome, Paul was given leave "to go to his friends and be cared for" (27:3b). After shipwreck Paul's party came to Malta where there were two instances of hospitality from Gentiles. In 28:2 Luke states, "And the natives showed us unusual kindness, for they kindled a fire and welcomed us all because it has begun to rain and was cold." He then reports the hospitality of Publius (28:7b), "who received us and entertained us hospitably for three days." Finally, Luke indicates the following regarding the hospitality tendered by the Christians at Puteoli (28:14): "There we found brethren, and were invited to stay with them for seven days." In comparison with these five preceding scenes, Luke's scene depicting Paul the prisoner meeting with the Roman Christians at the Forum of Appius may portray a lesser degree of *hospitality* being accorded to Paul.

If, as Luke's narrative proceeds, the reader were to find other scenes of the Roman Christians gathering around Paul and extending their support to him, then the conclusion would easily follow that Luke was actually signaling the beginning of hospitality and benevolence with his description of the events that occurred at the Forum of Appius. Yet strikingly, as he portrays Paul's situation for the next two years, Luke makes no further explicit reference to contact between Paul and the Christians already resident in Rome.

In effect, then, the supposition that the Roman Christians played a significant role in assisting Paul during his confinement rests solely on the encounter that Luke describes taking place at the Forum of Appius. Once Paul is in custody in Rome, Luke portrays two significant meetings between Paul and the representatives of the Roman Jewish community. But, as noted, he does not describe any comparable meetings with representatives of the Christian community.

Luke's closing report about Paul's inclusivity in welcoming *all* who came to him (28:30a) is certainly open to the interpretation that the Christians of Rome were numbered among his visitors. Yet there is no explicit mention of Paul himself being ministered to or assisted. In Luke's portrayal it is Paul who is engaged in welcoming and teaching.

Did Luke understand the meeting at the Forum of Appius as having inaugurated support for Paul that continued undiminished for the next two years? Such may indeed have been his understanding. Yet, if Luke did understand the Roman Christians to have assisted Paul in a significant way, he has not presented this aspect of Paul's situation in high relief.

C. Other Prisoners, Informers, Censorship

Once in Rome Paul's custody was arranged in such a way (note that Luke is silent regarding the identity of the Roman officials who decreed these arrangements) that he remained "by himself with the soldier that guarded him" (28:16b). Considerations regarding other prisoners and informers are thus not germane. In contrast, the topic of censorship does need attention, especially in light of Luke's reports that Paul met with the leaders of the Jewish community (28:17-28) and welcomed all who came to his quarters (28:30).

At the time of his arrest in Jerusalem, Paul addressed Claudius Lysias in Greek (21:37). Subsequently, Lysias permitted Paul to address the assembled crowd in Hebrew, a language he himself apparently did not comprehend well (22:2, 24b). These considerations regarding Hebrew and Greek, as well as considerations regarding Latin, lie in the background of Luke's portrayal of Paul, his visitors, and his soldier guards in Rome.

According to Luke's presentation, Paul's conversations with the

Jewish leaders at Rome are comprehensive and challenging. Their second meeting, in fact, extended from morning to evening (28:23b). Where does Luke understand the soldier(s) guarding Paul to be located during these conversations? Was Paul's guard patrolling outside the room in which these discussions were held? Was he present within the room, perhaps chained to Paul, but unable to comprehend anything spoken in Hebrew? Questions such as these point to the difficulty involved in trying to interpret Luke's presentation of the surroundings in which these conversations were held.

If the degree to which Paul's guards censored his conversations cannot be determined, the related effort to determine any role for these guards in censoring Paul's written communication is also fruitless. Here the governing consideration is that Luke never shows Paul authoring or receiving letters during his two years of imprisonment in Rome. On this point Luke's portrayal of Paul in Rome is comparable to his portrait of him in Caesarea. For in the preceding section the "absence" of written communications has already been noted for Paul's two years as a prisoner in Caesarea.

D. Paul's Endeavors While in Custody in Rome

As just discussed, Luke portrays Paul's efforts to evangelize the members of Rome's Jewish community as one of Paul's key undertakings as a prisoner. Yet, while prominently featured by Luke, these particular meetings with the Jewish leaders occupied only two days of the two years in which Paul was kept in custody. What then were prisoner Paul's other endeavors during this interval?

It is principally within the confines of Luke's remarkable closing sentence that the answer to this question must be sought. An extended analysis of this comprehensive final sentence has previously been made in *Society and Politics in the Acts of the Apostles*. The results of that analysis will now be utilized with new attention given to the topic of Paul's juridical testimony. Luke's closing sentence is as follows:

> And he lived there two whole years at his own expense, and welcomed all who came to him, preaching the kingdom of God and teaching about the Lord Jesus Christ with all boldness, unhindered. (Acts 28:30-31; author's translation)

In this description three interwoven strands of Paul's ministry as a prisoner are presented. First, Paul has a ministry of hospitality; significantly he is said to welcome *all* who come to him. Second and third, he has a ministry of preaching and a ministry of teaching. This preaching and teaching are focused on two subjects that are especially auspicious in a Roman location: "the *kingdom* of God" and "the *Lord* Jesus Christ." To be noted is that these aspects of Paul's ministry in Rome are fully in continuity with his previous ministry on Jesus' behalf. Paul has served Jesus in this manner throughout the eastern provinces. He now continues to do so in Rome itself.

In identifying these features of Paul's activities as a prisoner, Luke here says nothing regarding any concern of Paul regarding the preparation of his defense. Are there references elsewhere in the narrative to suggest that Luke at least tacitly understood Paul engaging in such activity while a prisoner in Rome? Such a question sharpens the reader's appreciation for what Luke does and does not include within his account.

In following this line of inquiry, three considerations should be kept in mind. The first consideration is that Acts propels Paul toward Caesar's tribunal according to a divine mandate. On the level of juridical process, Acts makes clear that Paul had appealed to Caesar and was told by Festus that he would indeed be sent to Caesar (25:11-12). On a more exalted level Acts also indicates that Paul's testimony before Caesar was actually a specific element within God's overarching plan. In Jerusalem the risen Jesus himself appeared to Paul encouraging him and indicating that he "*must*" (*dei*) testify in Rome (23:11). And subsequently, in the midst of a life-threatening storm, Paul received a salvific word from an angel that he "*must*" (*dei*) testify before Caesar (27:24). Nor does this element in Paul's mission drop from sight once he is in Rome: Paul straightforwardly explains to the representatives of the Jewish community that it is because of his appeal to Caesar that he has been brought to Rome (28:19).

A key aspect of Paul's mission in Rome is thus to testify before Caesar's tribunal. Yet, as noted, Luke's summarizing final sentence makes no mention of Paul undertaking to prepare a defense.

It is precisely at this point that a second aspect of Luke's full narrative needs to be considered. This aspect pertains to the two passages in the Gospel where Luke portrays Jesus alerting his disciples to expect persecution and denunciation before authorities and tribunals of various kinds. Significantly both times that he enunciates this prophecy, Jesus counsels that no testimony need be prepared. This is the thrust of his words at 12:11-12. It is also the thrust of his words in the passage from Luke 21 that will now be cited:

> But before all this they will lay their hands on you and persecute you, delivering you up to the synagogues and prisons, and you will be brought before kings and governors for my name's sake. This will be a time for you to bear testimony. Settle it therefore in your minds, *not to meditate beforehand how to answer;* for I will give you a mouth and wisdom, which none of your adversaries will be able to withstand or contradict. (Luke 21:12-15; emphasis added)

Nowhere in Acts does Luke ever explicitly indicate that Paul was aware of this dominical imperative. Yet, significantly, the *lack* of any Lukan report that Paul prepared testimony for Caesar actually functions to place Paul in conformity with Jesus' instructions. Paul, remarkably in conformity with Jesus in the other areas of his life and ministry, is thus portrayed in conformity with his Lord's counsel in this area as well.

The third consideration pertaining to the topic of Paul's defense emerges as an extension of the quality of faithfulness to Jesus that has just been noted. For, it is Luke's intimation in his closing sentence that Paul *will continue* in this faithfulness. He has been propelled to Rome with a mandate to testify loyally to his Lord before Caesar's tribunal. When the time for this testimony comes, Paul, without having prepared what to say, will nevertheless testify with all boldness and with utter faithfulness.

In effect, then, Luke's Paul does not *need* to prepare a defense in order to render the faithful witness to which he is called. Just as he has testified faithfully in a variety of circumstances and before other tribunals as well, so will he testify faithfully before Caesar's tribunal at God's appointed time.

4. Paul Chaining and Chained in Acts

The preceding sections have presented analyses of Paul's circumstances as a prisoner at Caesarea and as a prisoner in Rome. While

Paul's chains were emphasized as a feature of his imprisonment in both settings, Luke's overall presentation regarding Paul and his chains is so rich that it is now fitting to consider his reports on this topic in a sustained fashion. One function of this presentation will be to buttress the assertion made above that Paul is hardly free from his chains during the last four years depicted in Acts.

Throughout the remainder of this section Luke's reports will be analyzed under the following five headings: (a) Paul as persecuting with chains; (b) revelations and prophecies concerning Paul's suffering and chains; (c) Paul's experience of sustained chaining; (d) Paul's attitude toward his chains at Caesarea; (e) Paul's attitude toward his chains at Rome. This very schematization suggests that *chains* constitute a significant feature of Luke's presentation of Paul within Acts. Still it must be cautioned that such a feature must be appreciated within the context of Luke's interweaving of multiple images of Paul. This caution is particularly relevant with respect to the interpretation of Luke's final scene in Rome where multiple facets of meaning are evidently present.

One further observation pertains to the translations for the various forms of the verb *deō* or the noun *desmos* as these terms occur in the passages now to be treated. Consistent with the analysis made in chapter six above, the verb forms of *deō* will be rendered by "chain," "chaining," or "chained"; and *desmos* in its plural form will be rendered by "chains." Apart from these modifications, and apart from minor modifications for the sake of inclusivity, the RSV translations will be followed.

With respect to the topic of Paul as a persecutor utilizing chains, there are two passages that require attention. At Acts 9:2 Luke reports that, after Paul had employed murderous threats against various Christians in Jerusalem, he then proceeded to Damascus to search out any disciples there. Paul's objective, Luke relates, was to bring "*in chains* to Jerusalem" any disciples that he found.

In his own narrative of these events in his speech before the Sanhedrin, Paul describes his activity in even more forceful terms. Particularly to be noted is that Paul refers to "chaining" and "delivery to prison" as distinct, although related, activities. It will be seen below that Paul himself experiences precisely such a fate in Jerusalem when he is both chained and delivered to prison. This section of Paul's speech is as follows:

> I persecuted the Way to the death, *chaining* and delivering to prison both men and women . . . and I journeyed to Damascus to take those also who were there and bring them *in chains* to Jerusalem to be punished. (Acts 22:4-5; emphasis added)

That Paul's conversion is narrated in three settings (9:1-19; 22:3-21; 26:9-18) is a testimony to the surpassing importance Luke attaches to it. Clearly the consequences of this initial encounter between the risen Jesus and Paul echo and re-echo in the later chapters of Acts. Paul, who has heretofore sought to destroy the Christian movement, now becomes its leading proponent; Paul, who heretofore inflicted much suffering on Jesus' disciples, now will endure much suffering in Jesus' name.

When the risen Jesus instructs Ananias to minister to blind Paul, several aspects of Paul's future mission are indicated. Paul will carry Jesus' name to both Gentiles and Jews. He will also give testimony before kings. Each of these concepts possesses great significance within Acts. In this context, however, the aspect of Paul's future suffering in focus. For this reason in the passage now cited, Jesus' prophecy regarding Paul's suffering is underscored:

> But the Lord said to him, "Go, for he is a chosen instrument of mine to carry my name before the Gentiles and kings and the people of Israel; *for I will show him how much he must (dei) suffer for the sake of my name."* (Acts 9:15-16; emphasis added)

As the narrative of Acts unfolds, Paul does indeed experience multiple forms of suffering for Jesus' name. Significantly, being bound with chains is twice prophesied as Paul's journey unfolds.

The first prophecy regarding suffering and chains occurs in Paul's farewell to the Ephesian elders at Miletus. Paul has already suffered confinement in stocks in Philippi in a prison where other prisoners were bound with chains (16:24-26). Now, however, he relates a revelation from the Holy Spirit that chains and affliction await him in Jerusalem. Paul's intimation that this revelation has been imparted to him "in every city" intensifies the sense that truly ominous developments will occur in Jerusalem. Paul's own words follow. Note that he contrasts his future chaining with his present experience of being "bound" in the Spirit:

And now, behold, I am going to Jerusalem, bound in the Spirit, not knowing what shall befall me there; except that the Holy Spirit testifies to me in every city that *chains* and afflictions await me. (Acts 20:22-23; emphasis added)

Departing from Miletus, Paul and his friends proceeded down the coast to Caesarea, where a comparable prophecy is given by Agabus, a prophet from Judea. In this second episode, Agabus does more than *speak* prophetically regarding the chaining that Paul will experience in Jerusalem. As an accompanying *symbolic action*, Agabus took Paul's girdle and bound his own hands and feet. As he did so he spoke the following words of the Holy Spirit:

So shall the Jews at Jerusalem *chain* the man who owns this girdle and deliver him into the hands of the Gentiles. (Acts 21:11a; emphasis added)

Agabus' prophecy should be regarded as delineating the causative role to be played by Paul's Jewish adversaries in Jerusalem. They themselves will not place Paul in chains, but they will cause Paul to be placed in chains by the Roman authority. Paul's response to Agabus' prophecy and the concern it engendered among his friends should also be noted. When *deō* is again translated to reflect its root meaning, Paul's response is "What are you doing, weeping and breaking my heart? For I am ready not only *to be chained* but even to die at Jerusalem for the name of the Lord Jesus" (21:13).

As discussed in section two above, soon after Paul arrived in Jerusalem, his opponents incited a riot in and around the temple. To quell the riot, Claudius Lysias arrested Paul "and ordered him *to be chained* with *two chains*" (21:33b) and brought back to the Roman barracks. When Paul subsequently brought his Roman citizenship to light, the gravity of having placed Paul in chains caused the Roman soldiers to recoil (22:29a). Luke then reports the following regarding Lysias: "and the tribune also was afraid, for he realized that Paul was a Roman citizen and that he *had chained* him" (22:29b).

The next day Lysias temporarily unbinds Paul in order to facilitate Paul's appearance before the sanhedrin (22:30). But after that session turned riotous, Lysias' soldiers extracted Paul from the mêlée and brought him back to the barracks (23:10). Subsequently, to avert the assassination attempt, Lysias sent Paul to Caesarea by horse, heavily guarded (22:23-24). In his self-exonerating letter to Felix, Lysias asserted that Paul has really done "nothing deserving death or *chains*" (23:29b). As previously discussed, however, Felix's initial response was to keep Paul in custody within Herod's praetorium. Paul continued to be confined there for two years.

Within Luke's narrative, the phrase just cited, "nothing deserving death or chains," takes on additional significance when almost identical words are used by Festus and Agrippa at 26:31b in jointly commenting on the juridical nature of Paul's situation. Expressing a regard for the seriousness of keeping Paul in chains (let alone executing him) these Roman officials opine that Paul has done "nothing to deserve death or chains." That Paul's actual chains are being discussed here is clear from the context. Paul has just dramatically closed his spirited defense by imploring all present to become like unto himself "except for these chains" (26:29b).

Except for these chains. These memorable words at the conclusion of Paul's speech are italicized with a view to capturing something of their electrifying impact as the conclusion for an already remarkable speech. Functioning to evangelize his audience even as it functions to exonerate him of the charges against him, Paul's speech (26:1-29) is truly stunning in its unexpected ending. For several reasons related to the meaning of Paul's chains, this speech and its ending merit further attention.

That Festus breaks into Paul's discourse to remonstrate that Paul's great learning is driving him mad (26:24) is one aspect of the narrative that testifies to the intensity of Paul's words. That Paul responds with a direct, personal appeal to King Agrippa to embrace Christian faith is yet a second indication of the intensity that Luke attributes to Paul in this scene (26:26-29a). Paul's incandescent conclusion then reveals that the prisoner delivering this compelling discourse has just done so while standing in chains.

On one level Luke's readers can only be startled at the clash between the soaring quality of Paul's words and the restricting baseness of his chains. Why is Paul shackled with chains for such an occasion? Pondering such a question, Luke's reflective readers can only reach the insight that Luke understands Paul to have been constantly in chains. It is not simply for this occasion that Paul is fettered. Rather, in Luke's view, these chains have been a characteristic element of Paul's vesture for the past two years at Caesarea.

At a second level, not unrelated to the first, Paul's closing words also disclose his own attitude toward the chains he wears: Paul resents these chains and desires to be released from them. Paul wants his hearers to become disciples of Jesus just as he is, *except for these chains*. In Acts, Paul embraces his commission from the risen Jesus with every fiber of his being. Nevertheless, in this passage, he rues the chains that bind him, chains that have presumably bound him for two years.

The final episode in which Paul's chains are explicitly mentioned in Acts occurs after Paul has reached Rome, has been placed under a soldier's guard, and has invited the Jewish leaders of Rome to his quarters. While the sketch of his case that Paul sets before this Jewish delegation has been analyzed in *Society and Politics in the Acts of the Apostles*, no explicit attention was given there to Paul's concluding reference to his chain. Paul's explanation regarding this chain is now appropriately considered:

> For this reason therefore I have asked to see you and speak with you, since it is because of the hope of Israel *that I am bound with this chain*. (Acts 28:20; emphasis added)

From the perspective of the present study, the levels of meaning present within this passage run roughly parallel to the two levels of meaning that have been identified with respect to Paul's reference to his chains at Caesarea. Let attention first be given to what this verse indicates regarding chains as a part of Paul's normal vesture while in custody. Attention will then be given to what this verse discloses regarding Paul's *attitude* toward his chains.

Just as the final words of Paul's speech at Caesarea communicated Luke's view that Paul's chains were a characteristic feature of his custody under Felix and Festus, Paul's words to the Jewish leaders in Rome similarly serve to express Luke's view that chaining was a characteristic feature of Paul's custody in Rome. The conclusion that Paul continued to be chained in Rome also emerges from reflections regarding the assuredness and facility with which Paul comments regarding his chain. The sense of Luke's portrayal is that Paul's chain is a phenomenon with which Paul is now well familiar. His chain is not a temporary security measure specifically enacted for the visit by this particular group. Rather, it is a constant feature of his existence as a prisoner. Indeed, Paul has now borne his chains for such a long period that he is able to provide a persuasive interpretation of his experience.

Before proceeding to consider the nature of the interpretation that Paul presents, it is well to note that Paul's chains never disorient him. Was Paul cowed because he was brought to the Caesarean assembly in chains? Given the articulate, poised, and bold manner in which Luke portrays him carrying forward that day, a negative answer must be given to this question. Similarly, in the scene that Luke portrays in Rome, Paul reflects neither shame nor discomposure but rather forthrightness and boldness. It is Paul, after all, who has taken the initiative in inviting the Jewish leaders to his quarters knowing full well that, chained and guarded, he will receive them. Further, in Luke's depiction, Paul does not avoid the topic of his chain but rather raises the matter directly himself.

Granted that Paul is not ashamed or disoriented when he meets with the Jewish delegation, what interpretation of his chain does he set forth for them? Fundamentally, Paul cites Jesus as the explanation for what has happened to him. Specifically, it is because of Jesus that Paul is now in custody in Rome and bound with this chain.

In Luke's rendering of this scene, Paul presents his explanation in a way that stresses his common ground with the members of his audience. He uses the conceptually rich term "the hope of Israel" to affirm his own Jewish aspirations. (In his appearance before the Jerusalem Sanhedrin at 23:6, Paul followed a similar approach, stating that it was concerning "the hope and the resurrection of the dead" that he was being judged.) For Paul, Jesus fulfilled "the hope of Israel." And it is because of Jesus that Paul is chained.

In what sense is it *because* of Jesus? At least two dimensions of meaning seem present in Paul's assertion here. The first dimension has to do with Paul's faithfulness to Jesus his Lord. Since the time of his extraordinary conversion, Paul's every endeavor has been undertaken out of his desire to be radically faithful to Jesus. It is thus because of his faithfulness to Jesus that Paul has become a chained prisoner.

The second related dimension of causality has reference to the larger plan of Jesus and Paul's role within this plan. Paul is in his present circumstances *because* of this plan. It is no accident that Paul is in Rome. It is no accident that he is in custody. And it is no accident that he is in chains. Rather, all of these developments have taken place because they serve Jesus' purposes.

To summarize, Paul is a chained prisoner because of Jesus' plan for him and because of Paul's own faithfulness to Jesus. This explanation is tied to a truth that is even more fundamental, a reality about which Paul seeks to persuade his audience: Jesus is indeed the hope of Israel, the hoped-for Messiah.

Bearing in mind these considerations regarding Paul's associations with chains throughout the narrative of Acts, the image of Paul that Luke imparts to his readers at the very end of Acts is now fittingly considered. It has already been observed that Luke closes his narrative by bequeathing to his readers a truly inspiring image of Paul. In the present context, it should be emphasized that Paul remains bound with a prisoner's chain as Luke brings his long narrative to its completion.

Luke consciously focuses on Paul and Paul's faithfulness to Jesus in the closing verses of his work. And for Luke's attentive readers, the chain with which Paul is bound glistens unforgettably as Luke's spotlight plays upon this extraordinary disciple of Jesus now positioned at center stage in Rome.

From being a persecutor casting Christians into chains, Paul has now become Jesus' faithful witness in chains, a startling turn of events indeed. Yet, within Acts, Paul is only too willing to accept all that Jesus unfolds for him. And, as Acts closes, he continues to testify to Jesus his Lord with all boldness, his allegiance uncompromised and undiminished, imprisonment and chains notwithstanding.

Notes

Chapter One

1. Recent full-length studies that respect Paul's complexity and instructively treat his various facets are M. Hengel, *The Pre-Christian Paul* (Philadelphia: Trinity Press International, 1991), S. Légasse, *Paul apôtre* (Paris: Cerf/Fides, 1991), J. Murphy-O'Connor, *Paul: A Critical Life* (Oxford: Clarendon, 1996), and J. Gnilka, *Paulus von Tarsus: Apostel und Zeuge* (Freiburg: Herder, 1996).

2. See, for example, E. P. Sanders, *Paul and Palestinian Judaism* (Philadelphia: Fortress, 1977).

3. See, for example, the essays in T. Engberg-Pedersen, ed., *Paul in His Hellenistic Context* (London: Routledge, 1994), particularly D. Aune, "Human Nature and Ethics in Hellenistic Philosophical Tradition and Paul: Some Issues and Problems," 291–312.

4. See chapter three below for a discussion of the textual and thematic factors that argue for 13:1-7 as integral to the letter to the Romans.

5. R. Brown (*An Introduction to the New Testament* [New York: Doubleday, 1997] 496–98) concisely surveys the arguments and the Pauline scholars who favor, respectively, one unified letter, two original letters, or three original letters. Additional considerations in support of Philippians as a unified letter will be presented in chapters nine and eleven below.

6. R. Collins (*Letters That Paul Did Not Write* [Wilmington, DE: Glazier, 1988] 245) judges that the majority of exegetes have concluded that Colossians, Ephesians, and 2 Timothy (as well as 1 Timothy, Titus, and 2 Thessalonians) were not written by Paul. Pseudepigraphy will be discussed in some detail in chapters seven and eight below.

7. In 1990, addressing again the subject of the proper methodology for constructing Paul's chronology, John Knox reaffirmed the principles he previously articulated in articles in the 1930s and in his book *Some Chapters in the Life of Paul* (New York: Abingdon, 1950; rev. ed., Macon, GA: Mercer University Press, 1987). In Knox's methodology, data from Acts about Paul may be used only after material from Paul's own letters have been used to construct an out-

line of Paul's career as an apostle. And even then the material taken from Acts can never have the certainty and authority possessed by the material from Paul's letters. See J. Knox, "On the Pauline Chronology: Buck-Taylor-Hurd Revisited," in *The Conversation Continues,* ed. R. Fortna and B. Gaventa (Nashville: Abingdon, 1990) 258–74.

This skepticism regarding the value of material contained in Acts is hardly restricted to Knox and the other scholars referred to in his article. (See R. Riesner, *Paul's Early Period* (Grand Rapids: Eerdmans, 1998) 10–28, for a survey and criticism of various authors who are skeptical of Acts in their efforts to reconstruct Paul's chronology.) Further, among scholars who concentrate on Acts without any specific desire to construct Paul's chronology, a considerable number express serious reservations regarding Luke's general reliability.

In light of this prevailing situation, it has seemed advisable to ground the principal arguments of this study without making reference to Acts. Accordingly Paul's Roman citizenship, well testified to in Acts (see R. Cassidy, *Society and Politics in the Acts of the Apostles* [Maryknoll, NY: Orbis, 1987] 100–103), has not been appealed to in the present study. Similarly, Luke's reports pertaining to Paul's imprisonment in Caesarea and in Rome have not been integrated into the principal argument of this study. Nevertheless on the premise that these various Lukan reports do contribute important perspectives regarding Paul's trajectory as a Roman prisoner, they will be analyzed and presented in an appendix.

Chapter Two

1. After noting that Paul's use of *presbytēs* in Phlm 9 indicates someone between fifty to fifty-six years of age, J. Fitzmyer (*Paul and His Theology* [Englewood Cliffs, NJ: Prentice-Hall, 1987] 9) explains that this datum implies Paul's birth in the first decade A.D. In contrast, arguing that Paul's conversion experience occurred in A.D. 33 and that Paul was in his late thirties at that time, J. Murphy-O'Connor (*Paul,* 7–8) posits circa 6 B.C. as the date of Paul's birth. Very cautiously citing Eusebius, Fitzmyer (p. 21) mentions A.D. 67 as a possible date for Paul's death in Rome. Allowing for an abortive trip to Spain, followed by visits to Greece and Asia Minor to visit his churches, Murphy-O'Connor (p. 31) also places Paul's death in Rome in the year 67.

2. R. Martin, "Tacitus," *The Oxford Classical Dictionary* (3d ed.; New York: Oxford University Press, 1996; hereafter = *OCD*) 1469b.

3. The full citation is Cornelius Tacitus *The Histories* 4.74, trans. C. Moore (Cambridge, MA: Harvard University Press, 1956).

4. This capsule sketch of Josephus adapts that given in R. Cassidy, *Jesus, Politics and Society: A Study of Luke's Gospel* (Maryknoll, NY: Orbis, 1978) 178–80 and 198–99.

5. The citations for these two passages are Flavius Josephus *The Jewish War* 2.8.1, trans. H. Thackeray (Cambridge, MA: Harvard University Press, 1956), and Flavius Josephus *Jewish Antiquities* 18.1.1, trans. L. Feldman (Cambridge, MA: Harvard University Press, 1965).

6. 1 Thess 5:3 can be taken as evidence for Paul's recognition of Roman claims on behalf of "peace and security" (*eirēnē kai asphaleia*). Nevertheless, without disputing the existence of a measure of peace and order, Paul clearly emphasizes that no existing arrangements can safeguard the future of those unprepared for the sudden coming of "the day of the Lord."

7. See S. Wallace, *Taxation in Egypt from Augustus to Diocletian* (Princeton, NJ: Princeton University Press, 1938). See also R. Cassidy, "Matthew 17:24–27—A Word on Civil Taxes," *Catholic Biblical Quarterly* 41 (1979) 571–80.

8. See Fitzmyer, *Paul and His Theology*, 32–34, for a concise analysis of Paul's knowledge concerning the different facets of Jesus. Fitzmyer holds that Paul's familiarity with Jesus' ministry was probably minimal with Paul's primary focus falling on the decisive events of Jesus' death and resurrection. Fitzmyer writes (p. 33): "Paul, not having been an eyewitness, emphasizes the salvific effects of the passion, death, and resurrection of Christ, which for him transcend the data of this historical ministry of Jesus. His interest lies in these climactic events of Jesus' career rather than in the minutiae of Jesus' manner of life, his ministry, his personality, or even his message."

Chapter Three

1. See P. Lampe, *Die stadtrömischen Christen in den ersten beiden Jahrhunderten* (2d ed.; Tübingen: Mohr, 1989) 124–35, for an in-depth analysis of the twenty-six Christian names in Romans 16 and the conclusion that this chapter was dictated "in einem Atmen" with the preceding fifteen chapters of the letter. Lampe summarizes his findings regarding the social background of these Christians and his findings regarding the House congregations of Rome in "The Roman Christians of Romans 16," in *The Romans Debate*, ed. K. Donfried (Peabody, MA: Hendrickson, 1991) 216–30. After an extensive discussion of the textual and literary factors that bear on the questions of the unity and integrity, J. Fitzmyer (*Romans* [New York: Doubleday, 1993] 64) adopts the view (a departure from his previous position) that Romans is a unified letter of sixteen chapters.

2. Much has been written regarding the situation of the first Christians at Rome. R. Brown initially presented a concise overview of what could be known and conjectured regarding this community in R. Brown and J. Meier, *Antioch and Rome* (New York: Paulist, 1983) 92–127. Brown's subsequent "Further Reflections on the Origins of the Church of Rome," in *Conversation*, ed. Fortna and Gaventa, 98–115, amplified his earlier analysis in the light of Lampe's findings regarding the social realia of Christians at Rome and in response to the comments of twenty-five scholars who reviewed Brown's initial work. See also R. Penna, "Jewish-Christian Structures of the Roman Church in the First Century," in *Paul the Apostle* (Collegeville, MN: Liturgical Press, 1996) 1:48–59.

3. In light of his different degrees of familiarity with the twenty–six Christians named in chapter 16 of his letter, Paul was presumably somewhat conver-

sant with the broad lines of the pastoral situation at Rome. For example, at the time when Paul wrote, the Roman church was a mixed community with Christians from a Gentile background outnumbering those from a Jewish background (Fitzmyer, *Romans*, 33). Paul certainly knew such basics regarding the situation of his readership at Rome. Still, as Fitzmyer also points out (p. 33), Paul penned Romans "with a certain ignorance" of the exact situation of his audience. See below for a discussion of how much Paul actually knew regarding the political and tax conditions prevailing in Rome.

4. Given the character of his presentation on several crucial topics (relations between Gentile and Jewish Christians, justification, his travel plans, and so on) Paul might well have envisioned the possibility that a copy of this letter could be sent to Jerusalem, where he was headed, and to Ephesus for use by the churches of Asia. A strong proponent of the view that Romans was intended for a broader audience than the Christians at Rome is T. Manson. In "St. Paul's Letter to the Romans—and Others" (in *Romans Debate*, ed. Donfried, 3–15), Manson argues that Romans 16 was a cover note for the copy of the letter (Romans 1–15) that Paul sent to Ephesus. He summarizes his argument that the contents of Romans 1–15 would have high value at Ephesus and elsewhere in the following terms (p. 15): "Looked at in this way Romans ceases to be just a letter of self-introduction from Paul to the Roman church, and becomes a manifesto setting forth his deepest convictions on central issues, a manifesto calling for the widest publicity, which the Apostle did his best—not without success— to give it."

5. Paul's purposes in Romans are indeed multiple. For a discussion of Paul's doctrinal themes, see A. Wedderburn, *The Reasons for Romans* (Edinburgh: Clark, 1988) 108–39. See also Fitzmyer, *Romans*, 71–80.

6. See R. Karris, "Romans 14:1—15:3 and the Occasion of Romans" (in *Romans Debate*, ed. Donfried, 65–84), for a strong defense of the connection between Paul's doctrine in Romans 1–11 and his paraenesis in Romans 12–15.

In "Obligation: Paul's Foundation for Ethics," *Trinity Seminary Review* 19 (1997) 91–112, W. Taylor argues that Paul's exhortations in 12:1–15:3 flow from the exposition that he has given in the earlier chapters regarding the mercies of God. In Taylor's analysis (p. 105), Paul's use of "therefore" (*oun*) in 12:1 signals that what follows in terms of obligation is the logical consequence of what has preceded in terms of grace.

7. See Karris, "Romans 14:1—15:3," 71–81. See also T. Manson, "St. Paul's Letter," 15.

8. In "Romans XIII.1-7: An Interpolation," *New Testament Studies* 11 (1964-65) 365–74, J. Kallas argues that these verses were inserted into Paul's letter years later when the perceived failure of the world to end forced the church to the conclusion that accommodation should be made with the secular authorities (p. 371). According to Kallas (p. 374), Romans 13:1-7 is an interpolation. J. O'Neill (*Paul's Letter to the Romans* [London: Penguin, 1975]) also concludes that Romans 13:1-7 is an interpolation. On p. 108, O'Neill theorizes that this passage is actually made up of injunctions that were collected by a Stoic teacher and given a Stoic philosophic grounding in the first verse. M. Dibelius

also holds deep reservations about this passage. In vol. 2 of *Botschaft und Geschichte* (Tübingen: Mohr, 1956) 183, his own view seems to be that Paul authored these verses but is not fully responsible for them (!): "Dann ist also Paulus fur die Formulierung von Rom 13 nicht in vollem Mass verantwortlich." According to Dibelius, Paul seemingly appropriated Hellenistic-Jewish sources uncritically.

9. See J. Dunn, "Romans 13.1-7—A Charter for Political Quietism?," *Ex Auditu* 2 (1986) 60–63. See also V. Furnish, *The Moral Teaching of Paul* (2d ed.; Nashville: Abingdon, 1985) 122–24.

10. For example, Fitzmyer, *Romans*, 70, and Murphy-O'Connor, *Paul*, 328–31.

11. Paul's reference to his collection efforts in Macedonia and Achaia in Romans 15:26 suggests a location in Greece. Under the interpretation that Romans 16 is an integral part of the letter, several references point to Corinth/Cenchreae. In 16:1 Paul commends Phoebe, who will presumably carry his letter to Rome; he indicates that Phoebe is a minister of the church of Cenchreae, Corinth's port. In 16:23a, Paul mentions that he is hosted by one Gaius, probably the same person whose baptism is noted in 1 Cor 1:14. In 16:23b Paul sends greetings from Erastus, whom he identifies as a city treasurer. An extant Latin inscription from first-century Corinth identifies an Erastus as having held such an administrative position.

12. That Romans is preceded by 1 Thessalonians and 1–2 Corinthians is widely accepted. Arguing against the common opinion that Galatians also pre-ceded Romans, J. Knox ("Pauline Chronology," 263–64) would locate Gala-tians after Romans partially because the collection mentioned in 1–2 Corinthians and Romans is not mentioned in Galatians.

Knox also theorizes that Galatians was written while Paul was in prison, not-ing that, in Galatians, Paul never proposes to visit Galatia in order to deal with the issues about which he is so angry. To at least threaten to visit was Paul's approach in dealing with the problems at Corinth, and Knox argues that Paul's custody was why the apostle ends his letter on a note of frustration without proposing such a visit.

Recognizing that nowhere within Galatians is there any reference to impris-onment, Knox nevertheless attaches considerable importance to the vivid words and images with which Paul concludes, quoting the sentiments of Gal 6:17, "Henceforth, let no one trouble me, for I bear in my body the marks of Jesus." This verse is frequently interpreted with reference to 2 Cor 4:10, where Paul describes himself "carrying in the body the death of Jesus." Knox himself cites Gal 6:17 without giving an exegesis of it. Seemingly, his argument would be strengthened if it could be shown that "the marks of Jesus" on his body actu-ally references Paul's chains.

13. These points regarding the significance of *sustained* imprisonment will be developed more fully in chapter six below.

14. Josephus (*Jewish Antiquities* 18.3.5) explains that Tiberius acted after he was given a report about the activities of four Jewish schemers who bilked an influential Roman matron. According to Josephus, Tiberius expelled the entire

Jewish community from Rome, with four thousand of these Jews being conscripted for military service in Sardinia. Suetonius (*The Lives of the Caesars: Tiberius*, trans. J. Rolfe [Cambridge, MA: Harvard University Press, 1960] 36) reports this expulsion with less detail but still notes that Jews of military age were ordered to serve in provinces that were at a distance from Rome.

15. Suetonius (*The Lives of the Caesars: Claudius* 25) reports that Claudius expelled the Jews because they "constantly made disturbances at the instigation of Chrestus" (*Judaeos impulsore Chresto assidue tumultuantis Roma expulit*). Dio Cassius (*Roman History*, trans. E. Cary [Cambridge, MA: Harvard University Press, 1914], 60.6.6) reports an initiative by Claudius against the Jews of Rome in the year A.D. 41. In Dio's report Claudius ordered the Jews not to hold any public meetings. According to Penna ("Jewish-Christian Structures," 35), these reports both refer to the same event and Penna would place it at A.D. 41 as opposed to A.D. 49. Penna (p. 36) also holds that, while the name, *Chrestus*, could designate a Jewish troublemaker, it is more likely a reference to Jesus Christ. In this reading, controversy over Jesus within the Jewish community led to Claudius' response, a response that presumably resulted in Jewish Christians being expelled along with Jews.

16. Tacitus (*The Annals*, trans. J. Jackson [Cambridge, MA: Harvard University Press, 1956] 13.50–51) portrays unrest regarding taxation and Nero pondering what course of action to take. After considering the alternative of abolishing all indirect taxes (such a step would have meant that the direct taxes would have increased in all of the provinces), Nero decided instead to institute various reforms. He published an edict that required the public posting of all tax regulations and instituted closer controls over the practices of the official tax collectors.

Without mentioning that any protests had taken place, Suetonius (*The Lives of the Caesars: Nero* 10) comments briefly that Nero took steps to modify the types of taxation that were more oppressive. These two passages from Tacitus and Suetonius have been highlighted by J. Friedrich, W. Pöhlmann, and P. Stuhlmacher in "Zur historischen Situation und Intention von Röm 13, 1-7," *Zeitschrift für Theologie und Kirche* 73 (1976) 131–66.

17. As an illustration of the uncertainties that perdure with respect to Paul's knowledge of the pastoral situation at Rome, it should be recognized that Paul would have had familiarity with both types of taxes as a result of his extensive travels within the provinces. Thus he might not have been influenced by reports of tax-related unrest in Rome when he counseled payment of both categories of taxes. That Paul advocates the payment of *both* forms of taxes is a point to be emphasized. As will be seen below, Paul leaves few, if any, loopholes in penning these verses.

18. In *The Epistle to the Romans* (Edinburgh: Clark, 1975), C. Cranfield indicates that A.D. 54–59 is the time band within which scholarly opinions concerning the date for Romans converge. Cranfield states (p. 12): "That it was written during the period of winter and early Spring in one of the years between late A.D. 54 and early A.D. 59 is certain, but within those limits the opinions of scholars vary." Cranfield himself (p. 16) favors either late 55/early 56 or late 56/early 57. Fitzmyer (*Romans*, 87) favors the winter of 57/58 but cites with

approval Cranfield's comment that Romans must have been authored sometime within the 54–59 interval.

19. How significant is it that Romans was not written until a generation after the death of Gaius/Caligula who ruled from A.D. 37 to 41? Gaius' demented attempt to acclaim himself as quasi divine by ordering that a giant statue of himself be placed within the sanctuary of the Jerusalem temple was presumably an episode with which Paul was familiar. See Philo *The Embassy to Gaius*, trans. F. Colson (Cambridge, MA: Harvard University Press, 1962) 29–43. Also Josephus *Jewish Antiquities* 18.8.2-9 and *Jewish War* 2.10.1-5.

20. F. Lepper ("Some Reflections on the 'Quinquennium Neronis,'" *Journal of Roman Studies* 47 [1957] 95–103) analyzes the various difficulties involved in interpreting the report by Aurelius Victor, in the late fourth century A.D., that the emperor Trajan had often characterized the (initial) five years of Nero's regime in favorable terms. Referring to the *Quinquennium Neronis* in "Romans 13," in *Jesus and the Politics of His Day* (Cambridge: Cambridge University Press, 1984) 365–83, E. Bammel (p. 381) is specifically concerned to refute the view that Paul's approach in Romans 13 can be explained by making reference to any favorable impression created by Nero's first years.

21. Paul's authorship of Romans within the first years of Nero's rule also means that powerful correspondences and reverse correspondences exist with Philippians. It will be demonstrated below that Paul authored Philippians later in Nero's reign. While Paul wrote Romans to the members of the Christian community *at Rome*, it was *from Rome* that he authored Philippians. Paul authored Romans as someone who had traveled, and was continuing to travel, widely in Nero's eastern provinces. When he authored Philippians his location was Nero's capital, and his status was that of a prisoner in chains.

22. A. Strobel ("Zum Verstandnis von Rm 13, *Zeitschrift für die neutestamentliche Wissenschaft* 47 [1956] 67–93) understands "the governing authorities" as having an extremely broad frame of reference. In Strobel's view (p. 79), Paul encompasses "die zahllosen obrigkeitlichen Ämter des umfangreichen Staatsapparates des Weltreiches."

Given the concrete references to earthly political realities that are sprinkled throughout this passage, and especially in light of the fact that the payment of taxes is central to 13:6-7, it seems unlikely that *exousiais hyperechousais* actually refers to angelic powers that stand behind the Roman authorities and act through them. Such a view has been advocated recently by O. Cullmann, *The State in the New Testament* (London: SCM, 1957), 95–114, and C. Morrison, *The Powers That Be* (Naperville, IL: Allenson, 1960). See Fitzmyer, *Romans*, 666, for an analysis of the vocabulary of political administration within this passage. See J. Dunn, *Romans* (Dallas: Word, 1988) 760, for the argument that any call by Paul for submission to angelic powers would actually run counter to one of the main thrusts of Paul's accepted theology.

23. The integrated logic of Paul's presentation in these seven verses should be appreciated. Two recent analyses that exposit the logic of Paul's approach are R. Stein, "The Argument of Romans 13:1-7," *Novum Testamentum* 31 (1989) 325–43, and J. Botha, *Subject to Whose Authority* (Atlanta: Scholars Press, 1994) esp. 49–55. Stein (p. 343) concludes that the logic of Paul's argument is

advanced by means of a chiasmic summary in 13:5, a poetic parallelism in 13:7, and an inclusio of imperatives introducing and concluding the passage. Botha (p. 55) states the following: "From this analysis of the relationships between the clusters, it becomes clear that the most marked element in the passage is the statement in colon 1: 'every soul should obey the governing authorities.' All the other elements are subsidiary to it, elaborating it in several ways. The call for obedience to the authorities, therefore, serves to give coherence to the passage."

24. Dunn (*Romans*, 760) notes that this phrasing makes Paul's counsel all-embracing "though here naturally the Christian audience is primarily in view."

25. Fitzmyer, *Romans*, 665. So also Dunn, *Romans*, 761. Drawing on the work of Louw and Nida, Botha (*Subject to Whose Authority*, 46) proposes that the lexical sense of *hypotassō* in 13:1 is "to submit to the orders or directives of someone." Looking ahead to the interpretation of Philippians, it should be noted that *hypotassō* is precisely the verb that Paul employs in Phil 3:21.

26. Dunn (*Romans*, 761) would argue that Paul derives such premises from Jewish wisdom tradition. See the following section of this chapter for reflections regarding the fundamental accommodation of Paul's statement here and the ultimate conclusion that his reasons for adopting such an approach cannot be determined.

27. Fitzmyer, *Romans*, 669. Stein ("The Argument of Romans 13:1-7," 339–40) holds that Paul introduces no new motivating factor in using this term. Rather Paul is directing attention to the fact that "conscience" is what enables his readers to know that the Roman authorities enjoy divine sanction.

28. K. Wengst (*Pax Romana and the Peace of Jesus Christ* [Minneapolis: Fortress, 1987] 82) argues that Romans 13:11-14 puts Romans 13:1-7 and the passages around it into an eschatological perspective. Wengst correctly notes that Romans 13:1-7 still supplies a counsel of virtually unqualified loyalty to the Roman emperor (p. 84). He accordingly recommends that this passage should be read in conjunction with 1 Thess 5:1-11 and other texts such as Phil 3:20. In Wengst's interpretation, the Roman authorities are characterized negatively in 1 Thess 5:3ff. when their "peace and security" claims are shown to be inconsequential at the coming of the day of the Lord.

N. Elliott (*Liberating Paul* [Maryknoll, NY: Orbis, 1994] 223) similarly argues that Paul's words in Romans 13:11-14 contextualize 13:1-7 and indicate that the present disposition, in which God keeps the authorities in power, is viewed by Paul as temporary until the day of judgment.

In contrast to these interpretations, E. Bammel ("Romans 13," 381) suggests that a *lessening* of eschatological influences may have actually prepared the way for Paul to write as acquiescently as he did in Romans 13:1-7. On the whole Bammel is highly critical of Paul's approach in this passage, arguing that Romans 13 is written as a kind of alibi to the Roman officials, a proof of Paul's innocence and the beginning of Christian apologetic (p. 375). Bammel's own response (pp. 380–81), similar to the approach of scholars such as Wengst and Elliott, is to underscore the contrast between 1 Thessalonians 5 (along with 2 Thess 2:6ff.) and Romans 13, placing greater emphasis on the former.

Chapter Four

1. For useful background information pertaining to Justinian's sixth-century achievement, see the preface by A. Watson in *The Digest of Justinian* (Philadelphia: University of Pennsylvania, 1985) 1:xi–xiii. *The Digest* itself is a compilation of the opinions of leading Roman jurists primarily within the interval extending from the first century B.C. to the first third of the third century A.D.

2. The three categories of custody described in the text are those identified by the Roman jurist Ulpian in *The Digest* 48.3.1. Ulpian's principal works were written between A.D. 213 and 223; he is cited extensively in Justinian's compilation.

3. Under the heading of "punishments," *The Digest* also includes Ulpian's description of two other types of severe custody, that is, condemnation to the mines and condemnation to the *opus metalli*. Ulpian's comments regarding the weight of the prisoners' chains should be noted in reference to the question of the weight of the chains with which Paul himself was bound. At 48.19.8, Ulpian formulates the following distinction: "The only difference between those condemned to the mines and those to the *opus metalli* lies in their chains, that those condemned to the mines are weighed down with heavier chains and those to the *opus metalli* with lighter. . . ."

One additional distinction pertaining to the severity of custody is also to be noted. Within the passage just referred to, Ulpian also reflects that condemnation to the lime quarries or to the sulphur mines is more severe than condemnation to the ordinary mines.

4. C. Oldfather, *Diodorus of Sicily* (Cambridge, MA: Harvard University Press, 1933)1:x–xi.

5. P. Derow, "Perseus," *OCD*, 1144.

6. See *Philostratus: The Life of Apollonius of Tyana*, trans. F. Conybeare (Cambridge, MA: Harvard University Press, 1948) 1:vii.

7. In his study *Im Kerker vor und nach Christus* (Freiburg: Mohr, 1895) 56–67, F. Krauss identifies ancient references to four prisons within the precincts of Rome: the *Carcer Tullianum*, the *Carcer Lautumiarum*, the *Carcer Centumviralis*, and the *Carcer Mamertinus*.

Whether Philostratus could have had accurate information that one or more of these prisons featured confinement with chains in contrast with those prisons in which chains were not employed is an open question. It is to be noted that Philostratus portrays Apollonius discussing with other prisoners and officials in the manner of a philosopher discoursing with disciples and interlocutors. These discourses could plausibly be imagined in open air settings where philosophers more customarily gathered. For further considerations regarding Philostratus' reliability, see chapter five and its endnotes.

8. *Philostratus: Life of Apollonius* 7.22.

9. Ibid. 7.26.

10. Ibid. 7.27.

11. Ibid. 7.29.

12. Ibid. 7.34.

13. Ibid. 7.36.

14. A useful summary of Herod Agrippa's early career is provided by A. Barrett in *Caligula: the Corruption of Power* (New Haven: Yale University Press, 1989) 34–37.

15. Josephus uses verb forms with the *desm* root when he describes the placing and removing of Agrippa's manacles and he uses *desmote* to indicate Agrippa's status as prisoner. See chapter six below for an analysis of Paul's use of words with this root in writing to Philemon.

16. T. Mommsen (*Römisches Strafrecht* [Graz: Akademische Druck, 1955] 317) observes that, since military custody might not necessarily involve the restraint of the prisoner with chains, some forms of military custody were not significantly distinguished in severity from some forms of free custody. As disclosed above, Agrippa himself was kept in chains while under military custody. In Mommsen's analysis, however, such chaining was not obligatory.

17. The *Epistles* of Seneca that are cited below appear in *Seneca: Ad Lucilium Epistulae Morales*, trans. R. Gummere (Cambridge, MA: Harvard University Press, 1953).

18. These phrases are cited from "Ignatius: To the Romans, 5.1," trans. G. Walsh in *The Fathers of the Church*, vol. 1 (New York: Christian Heritage, 1947).

19. A schematization of the types of chains and stocks used for prisoners with a brief discussion of the relationship between custody in general and chaining in particular is given in Mommsen, *Römisches Strafrecht*, 300–301 and notes.

20. The two passages from *Toxaris or Friendship* that are cited in this chapter as well as the passage from *The Passing of Peregrinus* are from *Lucian*, vol. 5, trans. A. Harmon (Cambridge, MA: Harvard University Press, 1955).

21. A useful reconstruction of the life of Peregrinus, including an interpretation of the circumstances under which he was imprisoned by the Roman legate for Syria, is given by G. Bagnani in "Peregrinus Proteus and the Christians," *Historia* 4 (1955) 107–12.

22. Suetonius *The Lives of the Caesars: Vitellius* 7.3. In *The Annals* 6.5.8, Tacitus indicates that Publius became despondent because Tiberius repeatedly caused his trial to be postponed.

23. *The Digest* 48.3.14.

24. Ibid. 48.3.12.

Chapter Five

1. A survey of the positions adopted by recent writers on the question of Philostratus' reliability concerning Apollonius and Nero and Apollonius and Domitian will be presented in n. 10 below.

2. The analysis presented in this section follows the main lines of J. Balsdon, "*Maiestas*," *OCD* (2d ed., 640–41), who adopts "treason" as the preferred

English rendering of *maiestas*. See also R. Bauman, *The Crimen Maiestatis in the Roman Republic and the Augustan Principate* (Johannesburg: Witwatersrand University Press, 1967) 88–90, and the revision of Balsdon's article by A. Lintott in the *"Maiestas," OCD* (3d ed., 913–14).

3. Domitian, himself later to be assassinated, is reported by Suetonius (*The Lives of the Caesars: Domitian* 21) to have complained that no one believed an emperor's statements regarding a conspiracy against him until the conspiracy had succeeded and he was dead.

4. Tacitus' reports concerning Tiberius and *maiestas* are given in *The Annals* 1.72-73.

5. The custom of serving hot water with spice along with wine is also referred to by Dio Cassius in *Roman History* 57.14 and 60.6. In a footnote to *Roman History* 57.14, E. Cary explicates how this hot water was used.

6. Tacitus *The Annals* 12.42.

7. Suetonius *The Lives of the Caesars: Vitellius* 3.1.

8. For a discussion of the diverse accounts of Tacitus, Suetonius, and Dio Cassius regarding the circumstances of Claudius' poisoning, see B. Levick, *Claudius* (New Haven: Yale University Press, 1990) 76–77.

9. In his reports for A.D. 62, Tacitus describes Nero's involvement in the proceedings against the praetor Antistius who had allegedly composed and delivered verses satirizing Nero. Nero also used *maiestas* as a grounds for expelling (relegating) Fabricius Veiento from Italy. According to Tacitus, Veiento's offense involved libelous comments against the senate and corruption in the sale of imperial *munera*. See *The Annals* 14.48–49.

10. The contemporary discussion concerning the trustworthiness of Philostratus' presentation of Apollonius ranges across a wide spectrum. In "Apollonius of Tyana: Fact and Fiction," *Journal of Religious History* 5 (1969) 189–99, B. Harris classes *The Life of Apollonius* in the genre of a "travel-romance" (p. 195) and argues that Philostratus and his patroness, Julia Domna, promoted Apollonius as "a worthy symbol of a new syncretism" (p. 199). Harris himself offers a reconstruction of the historical Apollonius and is negative on the specific point of Apollonius' interactions with Nero and Domitian (p. 198): "There seems no reason to deny that he was ever in Rome, but his challenges to Nero and Domitian are apocryphal. . . ."

Offering a developed assessment of Philostratus' use of sources, E. Bowie ("Apollonius of Tyana: Tradition and Reality," *Aufstieg und Niedergang der Römische Welt* 2.16.2 [1978] 1652–99) presents a forceful negative assessment of Apollonius' interactions with emperors. After stating that the historical Apollonius probably intervened publicly in the affairs of cities, Bowie then states (p. 1690): "Meddling in the affairs of the emperors is another matter. The ignorance of Apollonius in any of the other Latin Greek writers touching on first century emperors combines with the ready availability of explanations for Philostratus' contrasted association of his hero with Nero and Domitian, Vespasian, Titus and Nerva to make that association patently fictitious. The same applies to other prominent figures in the Italian political arena—the consul Telesinus, Tigellinus, and Casperius Aelianus."

In his introduction to *The Life of Apollonius* (Harmondsworth: Penguin, 1970), G. Bowersock alludes to the lack of agreement among contemporary scholars regarding Philostratus' historical reliability, observes that some references regarding Apollonius' activities do have plausibility, and argues for a case-by-case assessment (p. 16): "The astute reader of Philostratus' work will have, however uncomfortably, to hover at times between total belief and total unbelief. Each item has to be tested on its own merits."

In *Politiek, Paideia, & Pythagorisme* (Groningen: Styx, 1993), J. Flintermann offers a perspective similar to Bowersock's, stating (p. 313) that *The Life of Apollonius* is essentially a *vie romancée* that incorporates some pre-Philostratean traditions regarding the hero's contact with monarchs. On p. 318, Flintermann notes that the portrayal of Apollonius as a fearless opponent of tyrants corresponds with an ideal dating from the classical period. He also notes that the evidence for Apollonius' hostility toward Domitian is considerably stronger than any evidence establishing the sage's hostility toward Nero.

More positively disposed on the question of the historicity of Apollonius' encounters with the emperors is G. Anderson in *Sage, Saint, and Sophist* (New York: Routledge, 1994). On pp. 160–61, Anderson offers the following assessment, one diametrically opposed to those offered by Bowie and Harris: "The involvement Philostratus assigns to this Apollonius of Tyana entails a strong association with Roman emperors and their retinue from Nero to Nerva. Not all of the material can be allowed to stand in precisely the form in which Philostratus presents it, though at least a proportion of his slips may stem from attempts to harmonise treacherously incompatible sources. For the reign of Nero, Philostratus presents in effect a syncrisis between two encounters of Apollonius: with Telesinus, one of the consuls for A.D. 66, favorable to the sage; and with the hostile praetorian prefect Tigellinus." A similar comment regarding Apollonius' encounter with Nero's Telesinus appears on p. 123.

To complete this survey of scholarly assessments regarding Philostratus' reliability, the favorable assessment of S. Jackson should be noted. In "Apollonius and the Emperors," *Hermathena* 137 (1984) 25–32, Jackson concentrates his attention on Philostratus' reports pertaining to Apollonius' interactions with various emperors and leading imperial officials. On p. 31 Jackson concludes that, in light of the reports about the emperors and imperial events that are available from other ancient writers, what Philostratus portrays regarding Apollonius' involvements with these emperors and events is highly credible.

11. In his introduction to *Philostratus: Life of Apollonius*, F. Conybeare notes (p. v) that most of what is known regarding Philostratus is derived from the author's own writings. After his education at Athens, Philostratus came to Rome and, during the reign of the emperor Septimus Severus (A.D. 193–211), became a member of the salon of Julia Domna, the emperor's wife. In this position he enjoyed access to the imperial archives and he received traditions regarding Nero. Thus, whatever the reliability of Philostratus' sources regarding Apollonius, he presumably had access to "semi-official" sources pertaining to Nero.

12. In chapter ten below it will be demonstrated that Nero was fanatically and dangerously self-exalting. Against the backdrop of these other reports,

Philostratus' portrayal of Nero as obsessively, even ridiculously, concerned with his prerogatives as a singer and composer becomes more credible.

13. Again, it is to be emphasized that this study's principal concern is with the credibility of Philostratus' portrayal of Nero and Domitian, two tyrannical emperors who were preoccupied with their *maiestas*. Although Paul's trial took place before Nero, Philostratus' reports regarding the attitude and conduct of an emperor with many similar dispositions (Domitian) can provide categories and images that possess a degree of relevance for Paul's conjectured appearance before Nero's tribunal. Philostratus portrays Domitian being profoundly challenged by a prisoner whose "reality" was grounded in a set of references foreign to the emperor. With qualifications, such a dynamic can be envisioned for Paul's interactions with Nero.

14. Philostratus *Life of Apollonius* 7.20.

15. Ibid. It is to be noted that the accusations against Apollonius range along a wide spectrum from the substantively treasonous to the merely petty.

16. Ibid. 7.29.

17. Ibid. 7.30.

18. Ibid. See 7.32-33 for additional features in Domitian's interrogation of Apollonius.

19. Ibid. 7.34.

20. Ibid. 7.36.

21. The events referred to in this paragraph are narrated in Philostratus *Apollonius* 7.38-41.

Chapter Six

1. Indicative of the tendency by numerous Pauline scholars to prescind from investigating the Roman context for Paul are two English works that bear the same title: G. Caird, *Paul's Letters from Prison* (Oxford: Oxford University Press, 1976), and J. Houlden, *Paul's Letters from Prison* (Baltimore: Penguin, 1970). Both works convey very little sense that an appreciation for Roman patterns is important for the fundamental meaning of Philemon, Philippians, and the other prison letters.

Houlden, in fact, *minimizes* the significance for Paul of the Roman authorities' decision to confine him in chains. On pp. 23–24, regarding the four letters that he will analyze, Houlden states, "In any case, the fact that they were, supposedly at least, written in prison is not among the more significant features of any of them." Later, commenting on the venue for Philippians (p. 58), he states, "*In getting himself put in prison*, and in Rome above all, he has acted the Trojan horse, entering into the very heart of the Gentile world to which Christ had dispatched him as apostle" (emphasis added).

In editing a collection of essays under the title *Paul and Empire* (Harrisburg, PA: Trinity Press International, 1997), R. Horsely is commendably sensitive to the imperative of situating Paul against the backdrop of Roman rule. Horsley correctly discerns that Paul's approach has the potential for colliding with the patterns of domination and allegiance promoted under the empire, and Horsley's own introductions to the various sections of the book contain numerous valuable insights.

Nevertheless, this volume offers no analysis regarding Paul's experiences and writings as a Roman prisoner and thus neglects the most fruitful locus from which to analyze the clash between Paul's allegiance and the allegiance promoted by the imperial authorities. Absent any treatment of Paul's prison writings, Horsley's documentation for a counter-imperial stance by Paul rests significantly on two analyses of Paul's letter to the Romans (D. Georgi, "God Turned Upside Down" and N. Elliott, "Romans 13:1-7 in the Context of Imperial Propaganda"). As indicated in chapter three above, Romans is scarcely able to provide support for the view that Paul challenged the imperial authorities.

2. Whether the Greek is rendered in active voice (pointing to the aorist first person singular), R. Mellick (*Philippians, Colossians, Philemon* [Nashville: Broadman, 1991] 361) emphasizes that the literal meaning is "I begat in my bonds") or the passive ("whose father I have become"—RSV), it is clear that a *process* of formation has been completed. Clearly the primary intention of this process was to enable Onesimus to become a committed disciple of Jesus. How many meetings did he have with Paul to this end? Keeping in mind Paul's chains, it is worth conjecturing whether Onesimus was eventually baptized by Paul himself.

A further dimension concerns the fact that Onesimus now stands ready to return to Philemon. What amount of counsel from Paul was required in order to bring Onesimus to the point where he could return, in faith, to the master from whom he had departed? This second dimension also provides support for the view that Onesimus and Paul were in contact over an extended period of time.

3. Developing the suggestion advanced by Houlden (*Paul's Letters*, 226), C. Wansink (*Chained in Christ* [Sheffield: Sheffield Academic Press, 1996] 175–99) argues that Onesimus had not departed from Philemon's household as an estranged or runaway slave. Rather Philemon had actually sent Onesimus (in a manner corresponding to the way in which the Philippian Christians sent Epaphroditus) as a messenger and minister to Paul.

While the text of the letter does not indicate Onesimus' exact status vis-à-vis Philemon (see the exposition of *amicus domini* in n. 22 below), the force of Paul's rhetoric in vv. 15-19 is to persuade Philemon to take a step about which he has, *in Paul's estimation*, significant reservations. If Philemon had generously sent Onesimus to Paul in the first place, such careful extended pleading for Onesimus' continued service would not be necessary. More generally, the failure of Houlden and Wansink to reckon with the significance of Paul's extended imprisonment and the impact of his chains on his self-understanding is a neglect that skews the interpretation of the dynamics that are operating within the situation of Paul, Onesimus, and Philemon. As expressed in n. 1, the neglect of the impact of Paul's chains is widespread within commentaries on Philemon and the other prison letters.

4. There are two segments of time that should be distinguished here. The first is the interval between the time of Paul's last visit to Philemon's household and

the time when he was placed in chains; it is not possible to determine the length of this first interval. Second, once Paul was imprisoned, how much time elapsed before he wrote to Philemon? As noted previously, this second interval was, at the minimum, long enough for Paul to "beget" Onesimus in the faith.

5. The text of Philemon does not evidence any apprehension that Philemon and his household might be ashamed of Paul because of his confinement and his chains. Nevertheless, it is useful to advert to the response of being ashamed as one possible response for Philemon and his associates to make. In 2 Tim 1:8, Timothy, Paul's most beloved associate, is counseled in the following way: "Do not be ashamed of testifying to our Lord, nor of me his prisoner. . . ." Other references relevant for this topic occur at Rom 1:16 and Phil 1:20. Cf. also Mark 8:38 par. Luke 9:26 and 1 Pet 4:16.

6. It should be recognized that Paul's condition is materially a negative one in that he is bound with chains against his will. Two observations by F. Staudinger are relevant here: (a) "The root *desm-* has the basic meaning 'bind.'" (b) "All terms associated with the word group *desm-* have a negative and disdainful connotation." See his entry *"desmos," The Exegetical Dictionary of the New Testament* (Grand Rapids: Eerdmans, 1990) 1:289.

Paul is thus boldly proclaiming by his choice of opening words that he is in a materially negative situation. The critical explanation, however, is that he is in this situation because of his faithful witness to Christ Jesus. This consideration makes all the difference in the world to Paul himself—and to Philemon.

7. J. Gnilka (*Der Philemonbrief* [Freiburg: Herder, 1982] 43) concludes after surveying various ancient schematizations of the stages of human life, including that by Hippocrates, that Paul is here identifying himself as someone between fifty-five and sixty years old. So also Fitzmyer, *Paul and His Theology*, 9.

8. Ibid. Gnilka observes that Paul invokes the "authority" of age here and then intensifies his claim to be heard respectfully by invoking his standing as a prisoner for Christ; Gnilka additionally notes that the authority Paul claims here is not the authority of office.

9. As discussed in n. 3 above, it is highly unlikely that Philemon sent Onesimus to Paul. Accordingly, Philemon may have been surprised at several points of information contained in the letter: (a) that Paul is now a prisoner in chains; (b) that Onesimus is now at Paul's side; (c) that, under Paul's tutelage, Onesimus has now become a Christian.

10. F. Staudinger ("*desmos,*" 289) indicates that as a derivative of its fundamental meaning, *desmos* can be translated as "imprisonment." If such a translation is adopted, it should be noted that the imprisonment envisioned is one in which the prisoner is kept in chains. Staudinger cites Mark 6:14-29, Acts 12:3-6, and 21:33 as New Testament references indicating that the New Testament writings understand imprisonment with reference to chains.

11. Paul's latitude in making the decision to send Onesimus back to Philemon should be underscored. Although he is in chains, Paul still possesses a significant ability to act decisively. It is his decision to send Onesimus (clearly Onesimus is not in Roman custody!) and to do so precisely at this time.

12. J. Lightfoot (*St. Paul's Epistles to the Colossians and to Philemon* [New

York: MacMillan, 1879] 341) comments that Paul's appeal has a note of authority inasmuch as he bases it upon the chains "with which Christ had invested him." Lightfoot perceives echoes of such a perspective in the writings of Ignatius of Antioch, for example, *To the Trallians*, 12: "my chains exhort you which I wear for the sake of Jesus Christ. . . ." Gnilka (*Philemonbrief*, 48) comments that Paul here references his chains with a certain honor: "Die Fesseln, sonst für den Träger Zeichen der Schande, werden dem Zeugen des Evangeliums zum Ruhm."

13. Although no definite explanation can be given for it, the *timing* of Paul's decision deserves consideration. Since Paul anticipates being released in the not very distant future and since at that time he intends to visit Philemon (v. 22), why does he send Onesimus back to Philemon *now* instead of keeping him at his (Paul's) side for a short while until they could presumably travel together back to Philemon's location? Clearly this decision might be due to one or more factors. One conjecture is that Paul was not fully certain about his own release and wanted to provide for Onesimus regardless of anything that might subsequently happen in Paul's juridical situation.

14. Although there is some uncertainty regarding the exact meaning with which Paul uses *synaichmalōtos*, it seems evident that he is not indicating that Epaphras actually shares in Paul's chains. First, Paul himself was not literally an *aichmalōtos*, that is, he was not literally a "prisoner of war." Second, if he had wanted to indicate that Epaphras too was chains, the word, *syndesmos* was available to him (*syndesmos* is so used in Hebrews 13:3).

It is to be noted that this same honorific is bestowed upon Andronicus and Junias in Rom 16:7. Aristarchus also receives this designation in Col 4:10. This latter reference is intriguing because Epaphras is mentioned very laudably in Col 4:12 but is not designated *synaichmalōtos*. In contrast, Aristarchus is named as one of Paul's "co-workers" (*synergoi*) in Phlm 24.

In discussing the various alternatives, Lightfoot (*St Paul's Epistles*, 236) mentioned the hypothesis that a *synaichmalōtos* was someone who shared Paul's confinement by living with him. Could Epaphras have voluntarily lived with Paul in Paul's place of confinement without being himself bound with chains? Seemingly the custody that Paul was under could have permitted such assistance. Or, as mentioned in the text above, Epaphras may have found some other means of sharing significantly in Paul's circumstances even if he were not permitted to live in Paul's quarters.

15. It is also possible that Onesimus himself had served Paul as an amanuensis. Paul's statement in v. 19, "I, Paul write this with my own hand, I will repay it . . . ," emphasizes Paul's personal commitment to be responsible for anything Onesimus might owe to Philemon. The chained Paul may thus be visualized physically writing this promissory note in a highly dramatic fashion. That Paul wrote v. 19 with his own hand does not preclude him from having written the entire twenty-five verses of this short letter, and many scholars consider it likely that he did so. For example, J. Fitzmyer ("Philemon," in *The New Jerome Biblical Commentary* [Englewood Cliffs, NJ: Prentice-Hall, 1990] 870) favors such an interpretation.

In the end, the phenomenon of Paul's chains, combined with his access to a circle of co-workers make it more likely that the remainder of the letter, apart from this verse, was dictated. Presumably chained much or all of the time, Paul would have found it congenial to continue his usual practice of dictating to a secretary (cf. Gal 6:11; Rom 16:22; 1 Cor 16:21). A point of interest is that Col 4:18 similarly portrays Paul taking the writing instrument with his own hand at the end of the letter in order to write a particularly dramatic sentence.

16. See A. Deissmann, *St. Paul: A Study in Social and Religious History* (London: Hodder and Stoughton, 1912) 212–14, for an appreciation of Paul's facility in applying expressive titles that were full of personal feeling to so many of those associated with him over the course of his ministry.

17. Once again, the fact that the Roman empire is the shared context for Paul and for Philemon and his household should be underscored. Paul's explanation of his situation thus concentrates on fundamental points and does not bother with details that Philemon and his circle would be familiar with because of their knowledge of Roman procedures. The two fundamental points that Paul stresses are that he is now in chains and that these chains are because of his faithfulness to Christ Jesus. It is to be noted that Paul never explains precisely *how* he came to be in chains.

18. Timothy is also the co-sender of Philippians. In what precise way does Timothy join Paul in sending these two letters, both authored while Paul was in chains? Gnilka (*Philemonbrief,* 15) proposes that Timothy stayed near the place of Paul's confinement and was able to discuss the contents of the letter when he visited Paul. Gnilka also points out that Timothy and Philemon himself are both referred to as "brother" within the letter and Apphia is referred to as "sister." It is thus significant that in v. 16 Paul asks Philemon now to receive Onesimus as "a beloved brother." (For additional considerations, see n. 21 below.)

19. As discussed above, Epaphras, designated *synaichmalōtos,* may have shared in Paul's prison conditions in an especially noteworthy manner. Mark, Aristarchus, Demas, and Luke, characterized as *synergoi* in v. 24, are presumably present at the site of Paul's custody, supporting him in a significant way. It should be noted that, in the very first verse of the letter, Philemon himself is characterized as *synergos.*

20. It is well appreciated that the name *Onesimus* has the meaning of "useful." (Such a name might easily be given to a slave.) In v. 11 Paul has actually constructed a wordplay on the meaning of this name, indicating that Onesimus, formerly not "useful" to Philemon, is now "useful" to both Philemon *and* Paul. How had Onesimus already rendered service to Paul? In what specific ways could Onesimus have continued to serve Paul if Paul had elected to keep him at his side? These questions remain unanswered although it is clear that, having begotten him in Christian faith, Paul retains a deep affection for his spiritual child.

21. Central to the interpretation that Paul is seeking Onesimus' full emancipation are vv. 16 and 17. In v. 16 Philemon is being urged to welcome Onesimus as a beloved brother "both in the flesh and in the Lord" (*kai en sarki kai en kyriō*). Especially given that this phrase occurs only here, the precise meaning is difficult to determine.

Yet if "in the flesh" is understood to mean "according to human standards," then Paul is calling on Philemon to relate to Onesimus as a free person as well as a person with whom he shares warmly in Christian faith. This interpretation is strengthened by Paul's exhortation in v. 17 that Philemon receive Onesimus "as you would receive me." Philemon receives Paul both as a free person and as a brother in the Lord and so shall he henceforth receive Onesimus.

See N. Petersen, *Rediscovering Paul: Philemon and the Sociology of Paul's Narrative World* (Philadelphia: Fortress, 1985) 95–97, for the trenchant observation that the words "both in the flesh and in the Lord" refer to two social domains, that of the world and that of the church and the conclusion that Paul is asking Philemon to bring the legal aspect of his worldly relationship with Onesimus into conformity with the realities of their new relationship in Christ. See S. Bartchy, "Philemon, Epistle To," in *The Anchor Bible Dictionary* (New York: Doubleday, 1992) 5:305–10, for an analysis of the letter's "story," in which a decision by Philemon to make Onesimus his freedperson soon (rather than at the time of Philemon's death) would best respond to Paul's urging for a new social reality to be created between Philemon and Onesimus.

22. In his brief article "Keine 'Sklavenfluct' des Onesimus," *Zeitschrift für die neutestamentliche Wissenschaft* 76 (1985) 135–37, P. Lampe analyzes material from Proculus and other Roman jurists and writers in arguing that Onesimus was not a runaway slave but actually came to Paul's side with the idea that Paul could serve as an *amicus domini* ("a friend of the master"). In his own extended treatment, B. Rapske ("The Prisoner Paul in the Eyes of Onesimus," *New Testament Studies* 31 [1991] 187–203) discusses five hypotheses regarding how Onesimus and Paul came to be together in a place of imprisonment and then presents a developed argument on behalf of a sixth hypothesis, namely, the *amicus domini* hypothesis presented by Lampe.

Rapske's argument (pp. 201–2) that Paul would be an ideal person to serve in the *amicus domini* capacity is well made, and it may well be the case that Onesimus consciously traveled to Paul's side for that purpose even with the knowledge that Paul was in chains. Nevertheless, that Onesimus was actually a *fugitivus* is still a tenable position, and the circumstances and motives that brought him to Paul's side remain, in the end, beyond view.

What is certain is that Onesimus became a Christian under Paul's tutelage. (Did he have a disposition to such a step from his prior experiences in the household of Philemon? Had he been present when Paul previously visited there?) And Paul seems to intercede for him in a way that is beyond the boundaries of the cases of *amicus domini* cited by Rapske and Lampe—such is the interpretation just presented in n. 21.

Rapske sees quite correctly (p. 203) that a remarkable pervasive feature of this letter is that (regardless of whether he sees himself as a kind of *amicus domini* or not) Paul consistently draws on his own status as a chained prisoner in addressing his request to Philemon. See S. Bartchy, "Philemon," 309, for a listing of six other rhetorical arguments that Paul brings to bear in seeking to persuade Philemon.

23. Gnilka (*Philemonbrief*, 90) correctly observes that a favorable outcome

seems near at hand; nevertheless, the necessary judicial decision has not occurred. Gnilka, along with many others, including J. Knox, considers that Paul was being held in Ephesus and that upon his release his plans changed and he did not travel to Philemon's location but probably to Macedonia. In the perspective of the present study, it is more probable to hold that Paul's legal situation worsened and that he continued in an ever-lengthening custody during which he then wrote Philippians.

Regarding the hypothesis that Paul wrote to Philemon from Ephesus (W. Michaelis, *Die Gefangenschaft des Paulus in Ephesus* [Gütersloh: Bertelsmann, 1925] is a noted proponent of this view), two observations should be made at this juncture. First, the paucity of data for establishing this hypothesis is to be noted. In 2 Cor 6:5 and again at 2 Cor 11:23, Paul alludes to the fact that he has suffered a number of "imprisonments" (*phylakais*) without specifically referencing the place(s) or durations of these imprisonments. Also in 1 Cor 15:32, in a reference that does not explicitly indicate any imprisonment, Paul writes that he "fought with beasts at Ephesus" (*ethēriomachēsa en ephesō*). In summary, the Corinthian correspondence indicates that Paul experienced controversy at Ephesus, and it is possible that he could have experienced one or more brief episodes of imprisonment at that location. On the basis of the available data, however, it is not certain whether Paul was ever actually imprisoned at Ephesus.

Second, in the analysis of this study, any imprisonment that Paul might have experienced in Ephesus occurred before the time of the *extended* imprisonment that is reflected in Philemon. In the perspective of this study (see n. 24 below), the Corinthian correspondence antedated Paul's letter to Philemon, and, therefore, the imprisonments referred to in 2 Cor 6:5 and 11:23 occurred prior to the extended imprisonment that was Paul's situation at the time of Philemon.

24. Paul's references to this collection occur in 1 Cor 16:1-4; 2 Cor 8:1-4, 9:1-14; Rom 15:25-28. J. Knox ("On the Pauline Chronology: Buck-Taylor-Hurd Revisited" [in *Conversation*, ed. Fortna and Gaventa]) emphasizes the importance of the collection in determining the chronology of Paul's letters and for this reason rightly separates Philemon from the time of the Corinthian correspondence and the letter to the Romans. Knox, however, accomplishes this temporal demarcation by placing Philemon *before* these other letters on the supposition that Paul wrote Philemon while serving "a *brief* (emphasis added) prison term not very far from Colossae and his other churches in the Lycus valley, more probably than not in Ephesus" (p. 265). From the perspective of the present study, Knox overlooks the significance of Paul's references to his chains and misses the crucial insight that the imprisonment reflected in Philemon is not brief.

Chapter Seven

1. Referencing the survey of R. Collins (*Letters That Paul Did Not Write*, 71), R. Brown (*An Introduction to the New Testament*, 610) indicates, regard-

ing Colossians, that about sixty percent of critical scholarship denies Paul's authorship of this letter. Regarding Ephesians, Brown's assessment (p. 629) is that seventy to eighty percent of critical scholarship rejects Paul's authorship. Brown's estimation regarding the authorship of 2 Timothy, the letter to be analyzed in chapter eight below, is also appropriately cited here. By Brown's reckoning (p. 673), only ten to twenty percent of critical scholarship presently favors the view that Paul authored 2 Timothy.

2. As the analysis of this chapter unfolds, it will become clear that the Paul of Colossians and Ephesians has had a significant interval of time in which to reflect on the meaning of his chains. In both letters Paul emerges as a prisoner who has reflectively pondered the implications of his chains.

3. As argued previously, Paul did not experience *sustained* Roman imprisonment prior to the time when he authored his letter to the Christians at Rome.

4. In this context, the reference to a letter to the Christians at Laodicea in Col 4:16 should be noted. This letter has not survived, but conceptually it would be considered a letter from the period of Paul's sustained imprisonment. See R. Martin, *Colossians and Philemon* (Grand Rapids: Eerdmans, 1981) 137–39, for a discussion of various theories concerning this letter, including the hypothesis that canonical Ephesians is actually this Laodicean letter.

5. See, for example, the analysis by F. F. Bruce, *The Epistles to the Colossians to Philemon and to the Ephesians* (Grand Rapids: Eerdmans, 1984). Regarding Colossians, see pp. 28–33. Regarding Ephesians, see pp. 229–40. See also Martin, *Colossians and Philemon,* 32–40. It will be noted below that Martin is quite sensitive to the reality of Paul's chains.

6. In arguing that Colossians is deutero-Pauline, E. Lohse (*Colossians and Philemon* [Philadelphia: Fortress, 1971]) provides an excursus on "The Imprisonment of Paul" (pp. 165–76). The analysis presented within this excursus, however, concentrates almost exclusively on the question of *where* Paul was imprisoned. Lohse argues that Ephesus is the place at which Paul was imprisoned when he wrote Philemon and that Paul wrote this letter prior to the Corinthian correspondence.

According to Lohse, however, the theology of Colossians is such that it must have been written after the major Pauline letters and thus could not have been written from Ephesus *at the time of Philemon*. From where was Colossians written? According to Lohse (p. 167 n. 24), Colossians was probably written from Ephesus, but much later and not by Paul. On p. 181 he amplifies that authorship was by a member of "a Pauline school tradition" based in Ephesus.

Granting Lohse's implied view that Colossians does not reflect a *real* imprisonment, Lohse is still open to criticism for his neglect of Paul's chains in his assessment of the *Paulusbild* of Colossians. Lohse neglects the force of Paul's rhetorical appeals, based upon these chains, within the letter.

With respect to Ephesians it should be noted briefly that scholars who affirm deutero-Pauline authorship for Ephesians frequently do not take pains to discuss the putative location of Paul's imprisonment. Presumably one reason for this lies in the fact that Ephesians is not linked with Philemon (a letter written from a definite prison site) in the way that Colossians is.

In the estimation of C. L. Mitton (*Ephesians* [Grand Rapids: Eerdmans, 1981]), a later author who knew Paul's authentic letters well (and who also knew Colossians well) composed Ephesians around the year 90 from a location that cannot be determined. Perhaps on the assumption that the prisoner references in Ephesians have little to do with any real historical imprisonment suffered by Paul, Mitton generally does not investigate the topic of imprisonment. Proceeding in such a fashion, he is vulnerable to the criticisms made against Lohse's approach, namely, that he neglects to treat adequately Paul's chains as a part of Ephesians' *Paulusbild* and that he neglects the force of Paul's rhetorical appeals, based upon these chains, within the letter.

7. To my knowledge, the political implications of imaging Paul as a chained prisoner has not been considered by scholars who adopt the position that Colossians, Ephesians, and 2 Timothy were written by Christians a generation or more after Paul's death.

One frequently encounters the assertion that the deutero-Pauline images of Paul emphasize his sufferings, but this generalization fails to attend to the concreteness of his suffering as a chained *Roman* prisoner. Thus Lohse (*Colossians and Philemon*, 167) writes, "Paul had written the letters to Philemon and Philippians in prison. In post-Pauline times this situation was generalized and the Apostle was represented as constantly suffering." For a similar view, see Martinus de Boer, "Images of Paul in the Post-Apostolic Period," *Catholic Biblical Quarterly* 42 (1980) 359–80, esp. 366–70.

In essence, by treating the *Paulusbild* of these letters with reference to only a general suffering, such scholarship overlooks the fact that the real *Paulusbild* is actually far more controversial. The perspective of the present study is that later Christian authors would be unlikely to assume such a politically charged persona in order to advance doctrinal and pastoral objectives.

For many who posit deutero-Pauline authorship in the 70s and 80s, an unreflected upon assumption is that such authorship occurred in a political vacuum. Yet such is hardly the case. As Christianity extended its mission during these decades it did so precisely under the conditions of the Flavian emperors. Accordingly, for later authors to adopt Paul's persona as a chained Roman prisoner would be highly controversial for the audience of these letters, both Christian and Roman.

8. In the following sections of this study, when Paul is referred to as the letter writer, it is to be understood that the question remains open as to whether it is Paul himself or another Christian who writes under Paul's name. These references to "Paul" are for the purpose of avoiding clumsiness in the presentation of the analysis being made.

9. The interpretation of Col 1:24 as an entire verse is complex, and commentators from Lightfoot to Gnilka have considered the nuances present in the Greek in considerable detail. The issue now explicitly focused on is whether the words "in my sufferings" and "in my own flesh," have particular reference to the sufferings that Paul is experiencing as a prisoner in chains. In other words, the issue is about the *kinds* of suffering by which Paul "completes" what needs to be completed in Christ's sufferings.

J. Gnilka (*Der Kolosserbrief* [Freiburg: Herder, 1980] 98) writes that the term "flesh" here connotes the entire person under the aspect of capacity for suffering. Bruce (*Epistles*, 83) speaks in terms of Paul absorbing a quota of affliction in his own "flesh." Granting the validity of these and similar assessments by other interpreters, the question still remains regarding the kind of suffering that is being referred to. Does Paul actually have in mind the particular suffering that he now experiences as a prisoner in chains? An affirmative answer is tentatively given to this question based upon the fact that later in the letter (4:3, 18) these forms of suffering are explicitly in view.

10. This particular question is moot if Colossians is judged to be deutero-Pauline. Nevertheless, the subsequent analysis—to the effect that Paul is depicted as being in chains for a noble purpose—still retains its force.

11. So also Martin, *Colossians and Philemon*, 126: "Paul writes as a prisoner (4:18) under close surveillance and restricted in so far as an active ministry of public preaching is concerned. He is 'bound' in chains (as his Greek verb *dedemai* makes clear in the light of 4:18: 'remember my chains', Gr. *tōn desmōn*) and is not simply 'in prison.'"

In *Colossians* (Minneapolis: Augsburg, 1985), J. Reumann considers whether the door Paul wishes to have opened for him through prayer is actually the door of his prison (p. 159). Reumann answers negatively noting that Paul's references in 1 Cor 16:9 and 2 Cor 2:12 denote the "door" of missionary opportunity. Nevertheless, Paul does wish to be free from his chains and through the door of his prison as a *precondition* for the resumption of his previous wideranging missionary activity.

12. Ibid., p. 127: "His present captivity is a limiting factor, which he longs to see removed."

13. See chapter six, section one, and n. 14.

14. Bruce (*Epistles*, 186–87) expresses this idea in proposing the following as an alternative translation for 4:18b: "Remember that the hand that writes this is a chained hand."

15. For an appreciation of the impact of this verse in stressing and encouraging faithfulness to Paul's gospel, see Gnilka, *Kolosserbrief*, 248. The complementary view of Martin (*Colossians and Philemon*, 141) is that Paul, by referencing his chains in this way, summons his readers to respect the authority that is his as a prisoner for the gospel's sake.

16. Bruce (*Epistles*, 187) writes that his desire to receive the Colossians' prayers is Paul's essential reason for closing the letter in this way. In the perspective of this study, there are actually multiple grounds on which Paul decided to close with this startling reference to his chains. Along with other dimensions of meaning, the idea that these words also express Paul's outcry and protest against his chains is a particular aspect not to be overlooked.

17. The concern of Ephesians with the mission to the Gentiles will be noted below in the exegesis of 3:1. A. Patzia (*Colossians, Philemon, Ephesians* [San Francisco: Harper and Row, 1984] 184) notes that Ephesians' emphasis on Paul's mission to the Gentiles is a feature distinguishing it from Colossians.

18. The absence of references to local issues, the fact that the words *en Ephesō* do not appear in 1:1 in the earliest manuscripts, and the probability that

the superscription "to the Ephesians" was not attached to the letter are factors that have led many scholars to conclude that this letter was intended as a general epistle that would instruct various Christian communities (with the Ephesian Christians included).

Nevertheless, there are grounds for holding that the letter had the territories of the province of Asia as a principal destination. This letter is closely linked with the letter to Colossae in terms of content even to the point of identical clauses and sentences. Further, Tychicus, identified as the bearer of this letter in 6:21, is also portrayed as a bearer of Colossians in 4:7. Given these affinities with Colossians and the specific mention of Ephesus in the later manuscripts, Christians in the region around Ephesus (the province of Asia) would seem to constitute a key segment of the letter's audience.

It will be noted below that, since Asia was a significant province within the Roman network, persons residing there would have been familiar with the prevailing Roman practices regarding ambassadors. For a concise discussion of the leading theories about destination, see F. Stagg, "Ephesians," in *Mercer Commentary on the Bible* (Macon, GA: Mercer University Press, 1995) 1217.

19. Ibid. Stagg himself favors Paul's authorship of Ephesians but allows for the possibility that the letter could have come from "some cogent, unknown writer with amazing insight into Paul's mind and experience." It will be indicated below that the *Paulusbild* of Ephesians remarkably integrates the experiences and perspectives of someone who is chained for the gospel.

20. J. Gnilka (*Der Epheserbrief* [Freiburg: Herder, 1977] 162) comments: "Der erste Satz ist ein Torso! Es fehlt him das Prädikat."

21. As delineated in the outlines of the letter presented by various commentators, the first two chapters of Ephesians celebrate God's wondrous accomplishment in reconciling Gentiles and Jews into one people through the saving cross of Christ. In particular, 2:11-22 describe and celebrate the incorporation of the Gentiles.

At least two references within these auspicious verses are deserving of further attention. The first is the image of the breaking down of "the dividing wall of hostility" in 2:14. (This image is considered to be at the heart of Ephesians by Stagg among others.) The second is the statement in 2:19 that the Gentiles are now "fellow citizens" (*sympolitai*) and members of the household of God. It is to be noted that this concept of a heavenly citizenship is a governing image. It will be shown in chapter eleven below that this same image, heavenly citizenship, is central to the presentation that Paul makes in Philippians.

For a comprehensive study analyzing the *pax Christi* referenced in Ephesians against the framework of Roman imperial rule, see E. Faust, *Pax Christi et Pax Caesaris* (Göttingen: Vandenhoeck und Ruprecht, 1993). Without moving far beyond the limits of the present study, it is possible to note the thrust of Faust's summary statement on p. 482: "Die Ekklesia unter ihrem Haupt Christus ersheint als universale, soziale Gegengrösse zum Imperium Romanum unter seinem kaiserlichen Haupt."

22. It will be noted below that in 3:13 Paul indicates that his suffering is "for you" (*hyper hymōn*). The Gentile readership of Ephesians is thus engaged in two major ways. First, the letter as a whole emphasizes their belonging and

bondedness in the body of Christ. (Gnilka [*Epheserbrief*, 161] draws attention to the three instances of belonging language in 3:6.) Second, Paul's personal (sacrificial) relationship with them through his sufferings as a chained prisoner is also set forth.

23. W. Taylor (*Ephesians* [Minneapolis: Augsburg, 1985] 54) correctly emphasizes this meaning for *desmios*.

24. For this reason, Patzia (*Colossians, Philemon, Ephesians*, 187) supports the Good News Bible's translation of this verse as opposed to the RSV's rendering: "*a* prisoner."

25. The forcefulness of this wording should not be passed by casually—as can be the case when commentators move quickly to consider the ways by which Paul's prisoner status is explained in the next two phrases of the verse. The *Paulusbild* of Ephesians 3:1 is thus formidable on two counts: (a) Paul is decisively portrayed as *the* bound prisoner; and (b) two explanations are presented for why he is a prisoner: "for Christ Jesus" and "on behalf of you Gentiles."

26. That Eph 3:13 recalls the serious situation of Paul in 3:1 is emphasized by R. Schnackenburg, *Ephesians* (Edinburgh: Clark, 1992) 142. The apostle's sufferings are endured for the sake of the letter's recipients, to assist them in reaching their goal, which is glory with God.

27. That a distinct change in thought comes at 4:1 is emphasized by R. Martin, *Ephesians, Colossians, and Philemon* (Atlanta: John Knox, 1991) among others. Martin observes (p. 46) that Ephesians can be considered as a diptych with a theological side from 1:3–3:21 and a side relating to the church's life in the world from 4:1–6:20. In Martin's schematization, 4:1-16 functions as a hinge connecting the two panels of the diptych.

28. If Paul or another author of Ephesians had omitted all reference to imprisonment in 4:1, the words remaining, *parakalō oun hymas*, would be exactly the same words that Paul uses in effecting a transition at Rom 12:1. Paul's wording in 2 Cor 10:1a is also relevant here. In that instance Paul used his own name, the first personal pronoun and the reflexive pronoun to emphasize the appeal that he was making: *autos de egō Paulos parakalō hymas*. The dramatic impact achieved by this wording is not far short of the dramatic impact achieved in Eph 3:1 and 4:1.

29. In 3:1 Paul is characterized as *ho desmios tou Christou Iēsou*; here in 4:1 as *ho desmios en kyriō*. In the estimation of Mitton (*Ephesians*, 137) and Schnackenburg (*Ephesians*, 162 n. 6), the meaning in both places is comparable. It is out of Paul's faithfulness to Christ that his imprisonment has occurred.

30. The similarity between the phrasing in 3:1 and 4:1 is commonly noted by commentators on Ephesians. In the estimation of Gnilka (*Epheserbrief*, 196), both phrasings are the work of a deutero-Pauline author, with the version at 4:1 evidencing a more formulaic character.

31. Taylor (*Ephesians*, 61) comments to the effect that the deutero-Pauline author is invoking the authority that Paul has as a prisoner. Rhetorically, this appeal to prisoner status, by Paul or else by a follower, clearly adds a particular weight to Paul's ethical exhortations. As noted above, scholars who adopt the position of deutero-Pauline authorship should elaborate the circumstances in

which a follower of Paul, located within the empire and writing for an audience within the empire, decided to appropriate the controversial persona of a *Roman* prisoner.

32. See n. 40 below for an explication of the range of meanings connoted by *en halysei*. In the RSV excerpt cited here, the plural form "in chains" has been selected by the translators whereas the Greek indicates but a single chain.

33. A. Deissmann (*Light from the Ancient East* [Grand Rapids: Baker, 1965] 374) states: "we know that *presbeuō*, 'I am an ambassador,' and the corresponding substantive *presbeutēs*, 'ambassador,' were the proper terms in the Greek East for the Emperor's Legate." Similarly, G. Bornkamm, "*presbeuō*," *Theological Dictionary of the New Testament* (Grand Rapids: Eerdmans, 1964) 6:681.

34. On the topic of embassies to Rome and the importance of securing an ambassador with comportment, diction, and a choice of words that would be in accordance with the canons of Greco-Roman culture, see F. Millar, *The Emperor in the Roman World* (Ithaca, NY: Cornell University Press, 1977) 385.

35. The presentation made in the following paragraphs regarding the duties and prerogatives of an ambassador reflects the analysis of A. von Premerstein's extended entry, "Legatus," in *Paulys Real-Encyclopädie der Classischen Altertumswissenschaft* (Stuttgart: Metzlersche, 1925) ser. 1, vol. 12, cols. 1133–49.

36. Millar (*Emperor*, 325–26) analyzes the range of activities that Pliny fulfilled as legate under Trajan. Millar comments that Pliny's powers were so extensive that he was hardly to be distinguished from an imperial governor.

37. See "*presbeuō*," in J. Moulton and G. Milligan, *The Vocabulary of the Greek Testament* (London: Hodder and Stoughton, 1930).

38. In his article "Ambassador," in *The International Standard Bible Encyclopedia* (Grand Rapids: Eerdmans, 1979) 1:109–10, D. Pratt comments as follows regarding service as Christ's ambassador: "The bible contains no finer characterization of the exalted and spiritual nature of the minister's vocation as the representative of Jesus Christ, the King of kings and the Savior of the world."

39. As discussed above, there are grounds for holding that Ephesians is intended for Christian communities in Asia, including that at Ephesus. Whether by Paul or by a deutero-Pauline author, whether to the churches of Asia or churches elsewhere, and regardless of the date of composition, the author's use of "ambassador" would have had resonance with the letter's readership. For throughout the empire, the role of a legatus would have been well recognized.

40. Paul is here imaged as bound with a single chain. (*En halysei* is singular, as Gnilka [*Epheserbrief*, 318] rightly insists.) It is difficult, however, to specify the precise way in which this chain binds him. In *St. Paul's Epistle to the Philippians* (London: Macmillan, 1913) 8–9, J. Lightfoot commendably surveys the New Testament references to chains and advances the view that *halysis* refers to hand fetters (*manicae*) as distinguished from *pedai* (*pedicae*), which refer to foot chains. Lightfoot refers to Josephus' account of Agrippa being handcuffed to his guard and suggests that *halysis* can be taken in Eph 6:20 as indicating the handcuff or "coupling-chain" by which Paul was attached to his guard.

Nevertheless, in contrast with the situation of Agrippa in Josephus' narrative, Ephesians does not portray any guard(s) at Paul's side. And thus the exact manner in which Ephesians images Paul's chain remains uncertain. Possibly the author of Ephesians does intend to suggest the image of Paul handcuffed to a guard with a coupling chain. But possibly the author understands Paul's hands bound with a chain that is attached to some object. Further it should not be ruled out that, for the author of Ephesians, *halysis* refers simply to any chain and not necessarily to a hand chain. In this case, *halysis* would have a meaning closer to that of *ta desma*.

Other occurrences of *halysis* in the New Testament show that this word can refer specifically to a chain(s) for the hand. Luke 8:29a, the verse describing the chain binding the Gerasene demoniac, is particularly significant since *halysesin* occurs with *pedais* and probably should be translated "handchains" if *pedais* is translated "footchains." *Ta Desma* as a general term encompassing both of these forms of chains also occurs in this verse. Alternatively *halysis* is used in the general sense of "a chain" in Rev 20:1, where the angel coming to bind Satan carries with him *halysin megalēn*, "a great chain."

It will be noted below in the appendix treating the Acts of the Apostles that Peter in Acts 12:6-7 is bound with two chains, *dedemonos halysesin dysin*. Peter is presumably handchained to the soldiers on either side of him because, at the angel's commands, "the chains fell off his *hands*" (*kai exepesan autou hai halyseis ektōn cheirōn*). Paul himself seems to experience a similar method of chaining in Acts 21:33 when the tribune orders him "to be bound with two chains" (*dethēnai halysesi dysi*).

When Paul makes reference to his chains in Acts 26:29, the genitive plural of *desmos* is used, and the RSV translation is "except for these chains." In the final reference in Acts 28:20, *halysis* in the singular is used as Paul states that it is because of the hope of Israel that "I am bound with this chain" (*tēn halysin mou ouk epaischynthē*).

41. See H. Schlier, "*parrēsia, parrēsiazomai*," *Theological Dictionary of the New Testament* (Grand Rapids: Eerdmans, 1964) 5:871–86. See also S. Marrow, *Speaking the Word Fearlessly* (New York: Paulist, 1982) 65–67. The background meanings of *parrēsia* are also discussed in R. Cassidy, *Society and Politics in the Acts of the Apostles* (Maryknoll, NY: Orbis, 1987) 45–46 and 133–35.

For an interpretation that *parrēsia* pertains to a mode of speech that befits a free human being, see R. Wild, "The Warrior and the Prisoner," *Catholic Biblical Quarterly* 46 (1984) 284–98, esp. 290–94. Wild's interpretation that the author of Ephesians portrays Paul as free within his bonds and that prayers are asked so that Paul will proclaim the divine mystery with the freedom proper to him spiritualizes the concrete political meaning that is attached to the image of "an ambassador in a chain." Wild cogently discusses the struggle against "principalities and powers" that Eph 6:10-17 references and provides valuable insights regarding the closing prisoner image of Ephesians. He prescinds entirely, however, from any investigation of the meaning of "ambassador." For this and other reasons, Roman rule and Roman imprisonment as key elements in the context for Ephesians are overlooked.

42. The words "as I ought to speak" (*hos dei me lalēsai*) appear in identical

fashion in Col 4:4b. Regarding the broad similarity between Col 4:2-4 and Eph 6:18-20, Mitton (*Ephesians*, 229) comments: "The writer of Ephesians clearly has Col. 4:2-4 freshly in his mind at this point, but the way he reproduces the thought suggests that he does so from memory rather than by copying from the other letter verbatim."

Chapter Eight

1. See M. Prior, *Paul the Letter-Writer and the Second Letter to Timothy* (Sheffield: Sheffield Academic Press, 1989) 37–45, for a discussion of the often neglected phenomenon of co-authorship by Timothy and others within the Pauline corpus. Prior points out that within this corpus only Romans, Ephesians, and the Pastorals are authored (or said to be authored) *solely* by Paul.

2. Would a pseudepigrapher feign an address to Timothy and intimately mention other individuals as a part of a strategy for establishing authenticity? In an excursus, H. Conzelmann (*The Pastoral Epistles* [Philadelphia: Fortress, 1972] 127–28) discusses the relatively abundant information about Timothy and other persons that is given in 2 Timothy and concludes that the pseudepigrapher has included such detailed information in order to buttress the impression that the letter actually originated with Paul.

In *The Function of Personal Example in the Socratic and Pastoral Epistles* (Rome: Biblical Institute Press, 1986) 235, B. Fiore reaches a similar conclusion, holding that this "art" of including detailed information was taught in schools of rhetoric within the ancient world.

3. Recognizing the differences between Paul's undisputed letters and the Pastorals, Prior (*Paul the Letter-Writer*, 57–59) explains these differences on the basis of three considerations. First, there is no co-authorship indicated for the Pastorals. Second (in Prior's judgment), Paul did not use a secretary in writing the Pastorals. Third, the Pastorals are addressed to individuals and are thus in the category of private correspondence.

Prior is also persuaded that the contents of 2 Timothy bring it closer to Paul's undisputed letters than is the case for 1 Timothy and Titus. He notes (p. 168) that 2 Timothy lacks the emphasis on church structure that is found in 1 Timothy and Titus; 2 Timothy's emphasis upon Paul's sufferings also distinguishes it from 1 Timothy and Titus.

4. This passage will be the focus of analysis in section four below.

5. A scenario based on Paul's authorship and a scenario based on deutero-Pauline authorship must both be considered. To hold that Philemon was written by Paul himself *after* 2 Timothy would require that Paul later became astonishingly relaxed about the perilous and frustrating circumstances that he details in 2 Timothy. Such a sequence would also require the supposition that Demas had somehow returned to Paul's side.

It is indeed surprising that the high drama of desertion and a first trial are not alluded to in Philemon if Paul had in fact already experienced these phe-

nomena. And regarding Demas, could Paul have written so benignly in Philemon that Demas was among the co-workers sending greetings (Phlm 23-24) if
earlier "Demas, in love with this present world" had deserted him and gone to
Thessalonica (2 Tim 4:10)?

If 2 Timothy is pseudepigraphical and if the pseudepigrapher knew the text
of Philemon, the foregoing considerations continue to have validity. The letter
with the desertion of Demas must "logically" be positioned *after* the letter in
which Demas is presented benignly as a faithful co-worker.

6. A more extended analysis of the significance of Demas' departure will be
given in section six below.

7. As G. Fee observes (*1 and 2 Timothy, Titus* [San Francisco: Harper &
Row, 1984] 178), two dimensions of meaning relative to humiliation appear to
coalesce in 2 Tim 1:8 and 1:12. Regarding undeserved humiliation, it is desirable not to be discouraged (for the humiliated person will ultimately receive
divine vindication). It is also desirable to stand with the person suffering undeserved humiliation. In this context, "do not be ashamed" means "do not turn
away out of embarrassment."

See H. Kee, "The Linguistic Background of 'Shame' in the New Testament,"
in *On Language, Culture, and Religion: In Honor of Eugene A. Nida* (The
Hague: Mouton, 1974) 133–47, for an analysis of the complex range of meanings that *aischynō* and its related forms can have within the New Testament
writings.

8. In this verse the second meaning that Fee (*1 and 2 Timothy*) adduces for
"do not be ashamed" seems to predominate. Timothy is encouraged to stand
with two persons who have experienced humiliation: the crucified Jesus and the
chained Paul. Fee comments (p. 178): "There is a stigma to being associated
with a crucified Messiah (thus a state criminal) and his (political) prisoner. Yet
it is 'undeserved' humiliation from which there will be vindication 'on that Day'
(see v. 12)."

It should also be noted that, when "Lord" (*kyrion*) in 1:8a is taken as a reference to Jesus, the meaning of "me his prisoner" (*eme ton desmion autou*) in
1:8b is not far from the meaning of similar phrases in Phlm 1 and 9 and in Eph
3:1 and 4:1.

9. The significance of this use of *epiphaneias* and *sōtēros* within the context
of the imperial ruler cult will be elaborated in section six below.

10. There are presumably three dimensions of meaning coalesced in Paul's
declarations here: (a) he is not embarrassed by what has befallen him; (b) he is
in no way turning from his allegiance to Christ crucified; and (c) he trusts in his
own vindication from the humiliation he presently endures. The latter two
dimensions can be readily noted in the remaining clauses of 1:12.

11. A. Hultgren (*I–II Timothy, Titus* [Minneapolis: Augsburg, 1984] 116)
notes that this statement gives rise to further questions. After considering
whether Paul could have been disowned by Christians in Asia, Hultgren judges
it more probable that certain Asian Christians *who had been in Rome* retired to
Asia, thereby deserting Paul. Hultgren notes a possible connection with 4:16
where it is stated: "At my first defense, no one took my part; all deserted me."

12. Inasmuch as the present chapter on 2 Timothy (as well as the preceding

chapter on Colossians and Ephesians) leaves open the possibility of deutero-Pauline authorship, the reconstruction of the situation in Asia is made in terms of the logic of the text of the letter. Several references within the letter seem to suggest that Timothy is located somewhere within the province of Asia although probably not at Ephesus. 2 Tim 1:16 may imply that Onesiphorus is from Asia, and in 4:19 Timothy is instructed to greet the household of Onesiphorus. The wording in 4:12, where it is indicated that Paul sent Tychicus to Ephesus, suggests that Timothy himself is not at Ephesus. Wherever Timothy is located it seemingly would not be a great detour for him to stop at Troas (4:13) in order to pick up Paul's cloak.

13. G. Knight (*The Pastoral Epistles* [Grand Rapids: Eerdmans, 1992] 384) observes that Onesiphorus' simple presence to Paul would have "refreshed" him. *Anepsyxen* may also imply that food brought by Onesiphorus refreshed him. It should be noted that the conditions of Paul's custody were such as to allow for this support by Onesiphorus.

14. See T. Lea, *The New American Commentary: 1, 2 Timothy* (Nashville: Broadman, 1992) 198, for a concise discussion of the views of commentators who are pro and con on the topic of Onesiphorus' death.

15. See especially 2 Tim 2:14-19; 3:8-9.

16. Along with the entreaty that Timothy come quickly to Rome, Prior (*Paul the Letter-Writer,* 51–64) considers these instructions regarding Timothy's faithfulness and his formation to be a principal purpose of the letter.

17. Prior (*Paul the Letter-Writer,* 91–112) surveys the scholarly discussion on this question and notes that 2 Tim 4:6-8 is a crucial text. Prior's own interpretation of 4:6-8, which is not accepted with the present study, leads him to conclude that Paul is actually confident about the future and is indeed preparing an apostolic team for further missionary activity.

18. Murphy-O'Connor (*Paul,* 359–60) observes that Onesiphorus first faced the problem of ascertaining just where Paul was among the one million plus inhabitants of Rome and then faced the problem of reaching him in a city that had no street names and no house numbers. As an illustration of Onesimus' dilemma, Murphy-O'Connor cites a passage from Terence's *The Brothers,* in which Demea experiences incredible frustration in gaining viable directions to his destination in Athens, a city much smaller in population than Rome.

19. Regarding the nuances of *hēdē* and *spendomai*, Knight (*Pastoral Epistles,* 458–59) writes: "He does not mean that his death will take place immediately, since he can ask Timothy to come to be with him (vv. 9, 21) and bring him some items (v. 13). But he does indicate its certainty and that it is near."

20. J. Kelly (*A Commentary on the Pastoral Epistles* [New York: Harper and Row, 1963] 207) draws attention to the various dimensions of meaning that Paul brings forward in using *spendomai* and *analyseōs* in speaking about his death. Kelly suggests that *spendomai* draws from the Jewish liturgical custom of pouring out and suggests that *analyseōs* evokes the picture of a ship weighing anchor or a soldier or traveler striking camp. Along with other commentators, Kelly notes that the image of Paul pouring himself out as an offering occurs in Phil 2:17, where *spendomai* is used. Further, the concept of Paul's "departure" also appears in Phil 1:23 where the cognate verb *analysai* is used.

21. The conjecture that Timothy would have possessed knowledge of Paul's acquittal if Paul had actually been formally tried and acquitted can be put forward if Paul is the author of this letter. If deutero-Pauline authorship is posited, it becomes difficult to determine whether a preliminary hearing or a formal trial is being imaged here.

22. Fee (*1 and 2 Timothy*, 245) believes that the Roman juridical practice of *prima actio*, a preliminary hearing before the emperor or a magistrate, is being referenced here. The actual trial would then follow although there might be a considerable interval of time between the preliminary hearing and the formal trial. Fee's interpretation on this point comports well with the sense of the letter (a) that Paul has an interval of time before him and desires to have Timothy with him and (b) that Paul definitely has the outcome of his condemnation and death in view.

23. As referenced in n. 11 above, A. Hultgren alludes to yet another possibility when he argues that Christians from Asia who were present in Rome failed to come to Paul's assistance.

24. The letter's comment regarding Luke in 4:11 weighs against this interpretation. Luke's supportive presence is highlighted; in contrast to Demas and others he is imaged as steadfastly at Paul's side. Would Luke have been depicted in this way if he had profoundly disappointed Paul at the time of Paul's first "defense"?

25. See M. Zerwick and M. Grosvenor, *A Grammatical Analysis of the Greek New Testament* (Rome: Pontifical Biblical Institute, 1988) 645.

26. For a discussion of the possible juridical meanings, see Knight, *Pastoral Epistles*, 469.

27. *Egkataleipō* is also used in 4:10, where Paul laments that Demas "deserted" him. Thus in 2 Timothy Paul twice references desertion, and in 1:15, as previously discussed, he speaks of his experience of having others "turn away" from him.

28. As observed by various commentators, the meaning of Paul's words here are similar to the meaning of Jesus' words according to Luke 23:34.

29. Again, conjectures and influences of this type are plausible if Paul is the author of the letter. If deutero-Pauline authorship is assumed, the writer is still obviously concerned to portray Paul experiencing desertion but may not be concerned with presenting this as the act of someone who was previously Paul's co-minister.

30. See section six below for an extended reflection on the meaning that Christ's "appearing" has for Paul in 2 Timothy.

31. 2 Timothy testifies to a very strong bondedness between Paul and Timothy (indicated by such passages as 1:25; 2:1; 3:14-15). Paul does not appear to doubt that Timothy will respond wholeheartedly to his request.

32. On the assumption that Paul himself authored this request, various commentators have conjectured about the contents of the books/parchments that he desires to have Timothy bring. Suggestions include writings from the Old Testament, Paul's personal documents, or blank sheets of writing paper. Hultgren (*I–II Timothy*, 143) advances the idea that Paul might conceivably be referring to copies of letters that he had previously written.

33. As Fee (*1 and 2 Timothy*, 198) notes, the relationship between Paul's suffering and salvation is not clear here. Nevertheless the relationship is definitely affirmed, and it is thus vitally important that Paul endure his suffering faithfully. It will be explicated below that this use of *sōtērias* had implications in reference to the imperial ruler cult. Knight (*Pastoral Epistles*, 400) emphasizes that the *salvation* brought by Jesus in the present has the decisive future attribute of "eternal glory."

34. Rom 1:5 and Gal 3:8 are among the New Testament texts in which a group that is representative of the Gentile peoples is referred to as "all the Gentiles."

35. From among these possibilities, Fee (*1 and 2 Timothy*, 246) thinks that Paul may mean deliverance from death. Fee's argument is on the grounds that there appear to be echoes of Psalm 22 within this passage on desertion, rescue, and deliverance from the lion's mouth. It should be noted that Fee considers these words to have been penned by Paul after he experienced the proximity of death. If this passage is deutero-Pauline, the author seemingly wanted to emphasize that Paul experienced a very precarious situation while under the custody of the imperial authorities at Rome.

36. Knight (*Pastoral Epistles*, 472) is among the commentators who discern the similarity between these words and those in Matt 6:13 in a petition of the Lord's prayer. Knight notes that the eschatological direction of this passage makes it evident that Paul is not excluding any evil that might be done to him, but is excluding the power of evil to destroy him finally.

37. Deissmann (*Light*, 344) cites this text from *Sylloge Inscriptionum Graecarum*. For a discussion of these two terms and other terms from 2 Timothy that have significance in the imperial ruler cult, see W. Bossuet, *Kyrios Christos* (Nashville: Abingdon, 1970) 310–12. See also the excursus on these two terms in Conzelmann, *Pastoral Epistles*, 100–104.

For an extended treatment of the various Egyptian acclamations of Augustus (and some discussion of subsequent emperors, including Nero) as "savior," see W. Otto, "Augustus Soter," *Hermes* 45 (1910) 448–60.

Two of the entries pertaining to Nero as savior are collected in E. M. Smallwood, *Documents Illustrating the Principates of Gaius, Claudius and Nero* (Cambridge: Cambridge University Press, 1967). The first (no. 419) is an inscription from Egypt in A.D. 60 or 61. As translated by D. Braund (*Augustus to Nero: A Sourcebook on Roman History 31BC—AD68* [London: Croom Helm, 1985] 254), the initial address is as follows: "To Nero Claudius Caesar Augustus Germanicus, imperator, the saviour and benefactor of the world. . . ." The second entry (no. 142), an inscription from Cyprus in 60 or 61, is broadly similar to the Egyptian inscription, and specifically acclaims Nero as "savior."

38. The challenge to the imperial ruler cult posed by 2 Timothy should not be overlooked. If this letter is written by Paul, it represents a significant shift away from the perspective of Rom 13:1-7. If 2 Timothy is deutero-Pauline, the writer delineates a *Paulusbild* whose features are highly controversial with the context of Roman rule.

It should be emphasized that the writer of 2 Timothy is presenting a far more politically charged *Paulusbild* than is commonly appreciated. Thus, for example, Conzelmann (*Pastoral Epistles,* 128) puts forward the following statements regarding 2 Timothy's imaging of Paul: "Its purpose is to portray Paul as the model of patient endurance in suffering, and thereby of the Christian life in general . . ."; and "This purpose is also served by the picture of the abandoned prisoner and the description of his exemplary attitude. . . ."

From the perspective of the present study, such descriptions are neglectful of the concrete circumstances of Paul in 2 Timothy where Paul is a Roman prisoner in chains reflecting about Roman judgment from the perspective of Jesus' ultimate vindication of him.

39. This depiction of Jesus as judge of the living and of the dead in 4:1 complements the description of him at 1:10 as the one who abolished death and brought life and immortality to light. Having himself passed from death to life, Jesus now sovereignly judges both the living and the dead.

40. As observed by Knight (*Pastoral Epistles,* 461), *ho kritēs dikaios* indicates that Jesus, the supreme judge, is absolutely "righteous" and "just." For this reason he is qualified to give the crown of righteousness.

Knight does not take into consideration the implied contrast between Jesus as sovereign judge and Paul's Roman judges. Will the Roman authorities give a just verdict in Paul's case? The implied meaning of 2 Timothy is that they will not do so. Yet Paul looks beyond any Roman judgment. He looks beyond any negative Roman verdict to the judgment that will be given by a sovereign judge whose righteousness is unsurpassed.

41. The implications of Paul's repeated references within 2 Timothy to Jesus as "the Lord" should not be overlooked in assessing the letter's challenge to the developing imperial ruler cult. For reflections regarding the upsurge in the use of *ho kyrios* for the emperor during Nero's reign, see R. Cassidy, *John's Gospel in New Perspective* (Maryknoll, NY: Orbis, 1992) 13–14 and notes. In this closing section of 2 Timothy, besides 4:8, there are three other references to Jesus as the Lord who possesses full sovereignty for judgment and vindication (see 4:14, 17, 18).

42. See Knight, *Pastoral Epistles,* 461, for a discussion of the range of meanings possible for *stephanos tēs dikaiosynēs.* Knight favors the view that this genitive is appositional and should be translated: "the crown, namely, righteousness."

43. This closing reference provides encouragement for Timothy personally, as well as for other Christians, to long for Christ's return. Kelly (*Pastoral Epistles,* 210) suggests that the outlook expressed here bears resemblance to the perspective regarding heavenly citizenship that is expressed at Phil 3:20.

Chapter Nine

1. The analyses made in this chapter and in chapter eleven are premised on the judgment that canonical Philippians is a unified entity and not a composite of letter fragments. (See chapter eleven n. 1 for a discussion of various relevant factors.) In addition, the present study maintains that Paul's critical perspective

regarding the Roman authorities is present in virtually every part of canonical Philippians.

2. See *The Letter of St. Clement of Rome to the Corinthians*, trans. and intro. F. Glimm, in *The Apostolic Fathers* (New York: Christian Heritage, 1947). The vague, abstract references to Paul's endurance and martyrdom occur in chapter five of this letter. For the Greek text, see K. Lake, *The Apostolic Fathers*, vol. 1 (Cambridge, MA: Harvard University Press, 1912).

3. For a summary treatment of the tradition concerning Paul's martyrdom in Rome, see F. Bruce, "St. Paul in Rome: 5. Concluding Observations," *Bulletin of the John Rylands Library* 50 (1967–68) 262–79; see esp. 270–77.

4. A classic study attempting to reconstruct Marcion's career and teaching is A. von Harnack, *Marcion* (Durham, NC: Labyrinth Press, 1990). It is von Harnack's conclusion (p. 15) that Marcion was not born until A.D. 85 or somewhat after. If Marcion did author the prologues to Paul's letters that are attributed to him, he presumably did not do so earlier than the second decade of the second century A.D.

5. J. Knox includes an English translation of this prologue on p. 171 in an appendix to his *Marcion and the New Testament* (Chicago: University of Chicago Press, 1942). Knox follows the version of the Latin text given by von Harnack. The English translation utilized is that given by F. Burkitt in *The Gospel History and Its Transmission* (Edinburgh: T&T Clark, 1906).

6. For the reasons given earlier, Paul's Greek words *tous desmous mou* are now translated as "these chains of mine."

7. See the analysis of *praetorium* and *praitōrion* provided by F. Bruce, *Philippians* (San Francisco: Harper and Row, 1983) xxii.

8. In a shift from his 1967 position favoring Ephesus as the site for Philippians (see "St. Paul in Rome: 5. Concluding Observations," 262), Bruce (*Philippians*, xxiii–xxvi) now argues on behalf of a venue in Rome. In part this shift is to be explained by Bruce's judgment that Ephesus, located within the *senatorial* province of Asia, never had the headquarters of its proconsuls designated as a *praetorium*. Bruce rejects the appeal to Latin inscriptions indicating that a *praetorianus*, a member of the praetorian guard, discharged official duties in the vicinity of Ephesus. On p. xxii, Bruce emphasizes that this soldier was actually a *former* member of the praetorian guard who subsequently discharged police duties as a *stationarius* on a Roman road in the province of Asia.

As discussed in chapter six n. 23, no imprisonment (and certainly no *extended* imprisonment) for Paul at Ephesus can be established on the basis of the writings of the New Testament. On the basis of 1 Cor 15:32 ("I fought with beasts at Ephesus"), it can be said that Paul engaged in an intensely sharp controversy there. A severe, menacing conflict, however, is not the same as an extended imprisonment. Further, Paul's recollections in 1 Cor 6:5 and 2 Cor 11:23 that he had previously suffered "imprisonments" are far from establishing that these imprisonments were at Ephesus or that they were protracted in duration. What are seemingly referenced in these passages are brief, ad hoc periods of confinement that did not involve formal judicial proceedings.

In seeking to understand why the Ephesian hypothesis has enjoyed noteworthy support when its basis in the text of Philippians and in the text of the other New Testament writings is so frail, the connection between a relatively early *chronological* location for the letter and the desirability of the Ephesian hypothesis should be noted. Scholars who decide to locate Philippians near the middle of Paul's literary output are virtually constrained to posit an Ephesian venue.

Philippians is obviously a letter from prison surroundings. And thus some location must be found that has facilities for Roman imprisonment and still fits into the schema of Paul's movements and writings prior to his journey to Jerusalem. In effect, then, if scholars wish to interpret Philippians as an earlier letter (rather than a final or near final letter), Ephesus "must" be chosen.

9. On this point, P. O'Brien (*The Epistle to the Philippians* [Grand Rapids: Eerdmans, 1991] 92) states: "Further, since the second part of the phrase (*kai tois loipois pasin*) clearly refers to individuals, then the first part must designate the same." Similarly, B. Reicke, "Caesarea, Rome and the Captivity Epistles," in *Apostolic History and the Gospel* (Grand Rapids: Eerdmans, Paternoster, 1970) 283.

10. The praetorian guard was a large permanent force of guards protecting the person of the emperor and the members of the imperial family. Augustus broadened the *cohors praetoria* of republican times into a force of nine cohorts. These guards were under the supervision of two praetorian prefects although Augustus retained personal command. Under Tiberius, at the instigation of the notorious prefect Aelius Seianus, the praetorians, instead of being dispersed in various locations around Rome, were centralized in one permanent camp in the eastern suburbs of the city. From that location the guards frequently became embroiled in the intrigues and controversies of the succeeding emperors, including Nero, especially at junctures of uncertain transition. See J. Campbell, "Praetorians," in *OCD* (3d ed., 1241).

11. The Philippian Christians know the place of Paul's custody because they have already sent one of their members, Epaphroditus, to minister to Paul (2:25). The implications of Epaphroditus' mission will be considered in chapter eleven below.

12. J. Lightfoot provides a classic treatment of the various possible meanings for this reference in *Saint Paul's Epistle to the Philippians* (Grand Rapids: Zondervan, 1961) 99–104. After presenting his analysis that *tō praitōriō* refers to the praetorian guard as opposed to a praetorian camp or administrative location, Lightfoot also reflects that this particular phrase also sheds light on Paul's juridical situation (p. 102): since he is being guarded by members of the praetorian corps, Paul is an imperial prisoner under the supervision of the prefect of the praetorian guard.

13. Bruce (*Philippians,* 17) notes that Paul does not claim converts from among the praetorian guards. Yet, in Bruce's words, Paul is still satisfied that "the gospel had become a topic of conversation in the capital, at the heart of the empire." It will be explicated in the pages below that this emerging spokesperson role for prisoner Paul was actually engendering a divided response from the Christians who were living at Rome prior to Paul's arrival.

14. Bruce (*Philippians,* xxiii) dismisses the possibility that Paul would have expressed such satisfaction if his witness was only being given at Caesarea: "But Caesarea was a political backwater. If it was there that Paul was imprisoned when he wrote to the Philippians, certainly everybody in Herod's praetorium would know that he was there and why he was there, but would there be anything very remarkable about that?"

15. See P. Weaver, *Familia Caesaris: A Social Study of the Emperor's Freemen and Slaves* (Cambridge: Cambridge University Press, 1972), for a comprehensive study of those who constituted the *familia* of an emperor and the various gradations of office and service within this network. See also A. Jones, "The Roman Civil Service (Clerical and Sub-Clerical Grades)," in *Studies in Roman Government and Law* (New York: Barnes and Noble, 1968) 152–213.

16. The argument of this paragraph, emphasizing the great concentration of imperial household members in Rome, is essentially that made by Bruce (*Philippians,* xxiv). Lightfoot (*Philippians,* 19) considers it probable that there were already numbers of the imperial household who had embraced the Christian faith prior to their contact with Paul. Further, within his valuable excursus "Caesar's Household" (pp. 171–78), Lightfoot proposes that, in sending greetings to various Roman Christians at the end of his letter to the Romans, Paul addressed many who were already members of the imperial household.

17. It may also be argued that it is "especially" (*malista*) significant that the Christians at Philippi receive greetings from members of the household of Caesar at Rome because of the strong ties that Philippi, as a Roman colony, had with Rome. In this perspective, the Philippian Christians (many of whom are citizens) could conceivably already have had contact with some of the Roman Christians who were members of Caesar's staff. Lightfoot (*Philippians,* 19) comments that Paul seems to reference this group "as a body both prominent enough to deserve a special salutation and so well known to his correspondents that no explanation was needed."

18. It is to be underscored that Paul envisions his death by decree of the Roman authorities as *a very distinct possibility.* Although he certainly makes no percentage calculation regarding the likelihood of the two alternatives, the parallelism in Paul's phrasing throughout this section of the letter contributes to the reader's sense that, in Paul's mind, both alternatives are equally likely. C. Talbert ("Philippians," in *Mercer Commentary on the Bible* [Macon, GA: Mercer University Press, 1995] 1229) notes that Paul provides two reasons for accepting either outcome. If death, Christ will be honored and Paul will be with Christ. If life, there will be additional fruitful labor of Paul and glory for Christ.

19. J. Gnilka (*Der Philipperbrief* [Freiburg: Herder, 1976] 154–55) underscores the careful, nuanced fashion in which Paul *again* (1:20ff., as previously discussed) refers to the possibility that he will experience a martyr's death. Regarding the liturgical reference to a libation being poured out, Gnilka leans to the interpretation that Greek rituals may have given the frame of reference for this image although he does not rule out a Jewish ceremonial frame of reference.

20. It cannot be established beyond doubt that Paul's case will be judged by

the emperor, and for this reason the phrase "the authorities at Rome" is sometimes used in the text of this chapter. Nevertheless, for two reasons, it is probable that the emperor (as discussed below—Nero) will give the ultimate verdict in Paul's case.

The first reason has already been alluded to in n. 12 above. As Lightfoot has observed, since Paul is being guarded by the praetorian guard, it follows that he is an *imperial* prisoner. Thus, according to the chain of command, the emperor is the official with ultimate jurisdiction over Paul's imprisonment. Since he already has jurisdiction over the conditions of Paul's custody, will the emperor not also have ultimate jurisdiction over Paul's sentence?

The second reason regards the emperor's established role (from Tiberius onward) in cases involving capital sentences. Here the analysis of A. Jones (*The Criminal Courts of the Roman Republic and Principate* [Totowa, NJ: Rowman and Littlefield, 1972]) is highly pertinent. On pp. 95–96, Jones' assessment is the following: "Tiberius, finding that Clutorius Priscus had been condemned by the senate for *maiestas* and straight away executed in his absence, procured a *senatus consultum* whereby condemnations in the senate should not be registered and executed until ten days had elapsed. Later it would seem that all capital sentences were submitted to the emperor for his confirmation: we find Nero at the beginning of his reign declaring that he wished he could not write, when he was urged to subscribe 'in the usual way' to the punishment of a man who had been condemned to death."

In a supporting note Jones references the report supplied by Suetonius in *Lives of the Caesars: Nero* 10.2. Suetonius indicates that, at the beginning of his reign, Nero found his role in confirming death sentences onerous. Suetonius' Latin reads: "*Et cum de supplicio cuiusdam capite damnati ut ex more subscriberet admoneretur: 'Quam vellum,' inquit, 'nescire litteras.'*"

21. See O'Brien, *Philippians*, 100–107, for a comprehensive survey of the previously proposed interpretations of this passage.

22. Talbert (*Philippians*, 1229) states that the *motives* of these opponents are what is questionable; Paul finds their *message* acceptable.

23. The translation proposed by M. Silva (*Philippians* [Chicago: Moody Press, 1988] 72) is: "supposing that they will add pressure to my chains." Silva contends that Paul consciously employs a wordplay regarding his own chains in lamenting his opponents' motives.

24. A full analysis on the point that Paul was in chains for a significant period of time prior to writing to Philemon has been presented in chapter six above. Several aspects of this analysis are briefly noted here.

25. In chapter six's analysis of Philemon, no attempt was made to determine the location from which that letter was written. In light of the criticism made against the hypothesis that Ephesus was ever a site for an *extended* imprisonment, it can now be stated that the two principal candidates for the location of Philemon are Rome and Caesarea. (Here the reports of Acts concerning extended imprisonment at Caesarea are to be noted.)

For the reasons just given, Philippians was written after Philemon and was written from Rome. If Philemon was written from Rome, significant time elapsed and Paul's associates departed before Paul came to author Philippians. If Philemon was written from Caesarea, Paul's associates at that earlier time were not subsequently with him in Rome.

26. In the chronology he supplies at the conclusion of *Paul: Apostle to the Gentiles* (Philadelphia: Fortress, 1984), G. Luedemann offers no projections for Paul's life beyond the spring of A.D. 52 (or 55) when, according to Luedemann, Paul undertook the journey to Jerusalem to deliver the collection. Luedemann's reticence to give attention to Acts' reports regarding Caesarean and Roman imprisonment (it is to be noted that other scholars beside Luedemann conclude their presentations of Paul's life with his journey to Jerusalem) is pointedly criticized by Riesner (*Paul's Early Period*, 227), who comments that, in effect, Luedemann suggests Paul's "disappearance from the history of early Christianity after his journey to Jerusalem."

27. For example, F. Bruce (*Paul: Apostle of the Heart Set Free* [Grand Rapids, Eerdmans, 1977] 475) calculates that Paul arrived in Rome in February of A.D. 60. R. Jewett (*A Chronology of Paul's Life* [Philadelphia: Fortress, 1979] 102) places his arrival in early March of 60. Fitzmyer (*Paul*, 20) reconstructs that Paul arrived in the capital in the spring of 61. Légasse (*Paul*, 237) favors April of the same year. Murphy-O'Connor (*Paul*, 31) posits the spring of A.D. 62.

Chapter Ten

1. According to S. Jackson "Apollonius and the Emperors," 29–30, Dio Cassius carried out only limited independent research but diligently studied the writings of earlier historians.

2. The description of Agrippina and Nero presented in these paragraphs follows from the analysis of M. Griffin, *Nero: The End of a Dynasty* (New Haven: Yale University Press, 1984) 67–75.

3. Accounts of Agrippina's murder are given in Tacitus *The Annals* 14.3-8; Suetonius *Lives of the Caesars: Nero* 34; Dio Cassius *Roman History, Epitome of Book* 61.12-13.

4. Bearing in mind that hermeneutical caution must be exercised in assessing Philostratus' reports concerning Apollonius, the characterization of Nero's murderousness that is given by Apollonius still merits attention. Philostratus wrote approximately 150 years after Nero's death. The central image of Nero that Apollonius presents is that of a matricide: "In any case, though this monster is said to be a social beast and to inhabit the heart of cities, yet he is so much wilder and fiercer in his disposition than animals of the mountain and forest, that whereas you can sometimes tame and alter the character of lions and leopards by flattering them, this one is only roused to greater cruelty than before by those who stroke him, so that he rends and devours all alike. And again there is no animal anyhow of which you can say that it ever devours its own mother, but Nero is gorged with such quarry. It is true, perhaps, that the same crime was committed in the case of Orestes and Alcmaeon, but they had some excuse for

their deeds, in that the father of the one was murdered by his own wife, while the other's had been sold for a necklace; this man, however, has murdered the very mother to whom he owes his adoption by the aged emperor and his inheritance of the empire; for he shipwrecked and so slew her close to land in a vessel built for the express purpose of doing her to death" (*Life of Apollonius* 4.38).

5. See Griffin, *Nero*, 84, for the perspective (based upon her analysis of Tacitus) that Nero's initial five years should be considered only "a *relatively* innocent time."

6. Other examples of Paul's conservative sexual ethic are 1 Thess 4:3-8; 1 Cor 5:1-2, 6:15-20; 2 Cor 12:21; Gal 5:19-21.

7. See, for example, Fitzmyer, *Romans*, 269–90.

8. Another farcical example of Nero attempting to safeguard his prerogatives is reported by both Suetonius and Dio Cassius. According to both reports Nero had the procurator of Egypt recalled and then banished because he had the effrontery to bathe in the imperial bath that was being constructed and readied for a forthcoming visit by Nero. See Suetonius *Lives of the Caesars: Nero* 35.5 and Dio Cassius *Roman History, Epitome of Book* 62.18.

9. Dio Cassius *Roman History, Epitome of Book* 62.2.4.

10. The Greek word here translated "lord" is *despota*.

11. Deissmann, *Light*, 345.

12. Ibid., 353–54.

13. Ibid., 354.

14. Ibid.

15. Ibid., 364. See also the discussion and the references cited in chapter eight n. 36 above.

16. Deissmann, *Light*, 364.

17. Tacitus *The Annals* 15.71.

18. Tacitus *The Annals* 15.54ff.

19. Diversity in scholarly circles regarding the date of 1 Corinthians makes it difficult to locate this letter with certainty under the reign of Claudius or under that of Nero. For example, Luedemann (*Paul*, 263) projects composition either in A.D. 49 or 52, years which are both still under Claudius. Murphy-O'Connor (*Paul*, 280) projects composition in 54, the year in which Claudius and Nero both ruled. And Fitzmyer (*Theology*, 104) considers composition probable in 57, three years into Nero's reign.

Chapter Eleven

1. In the perspective of the present study, canonical Philippians was authored by Paul as a single letter. The apparent conclusion that some commentators detect in 3:1 has led to the hypothesis that canonical Philippians is actually an amalgam of two or more letter fragments. Yet L. Alexander has demonstrated that Paul's wording in 3:1 is actually consistent with what is now known about

the patterns of writing characteristic of Hellenistic letters ("Hellenistic Letter-Forms and the Structure of Philippians," originally published in *Journal for the Study of the New Testament* 37 [1989] and now collected in *The Pauline Writings* [Sheffield: Sheffield Academic Press, 1995] 232–46). Also, in Alexander's analysis, the positioning in 4:10-12 of Paul's thanks to the Philippians for their gift and the fact that Paul does not express formal gratitude also have their parallels in ancient "familiar" letter-writing.

For an analysis stressing the strong thematic links between chapter 2 and chapter 3 of the letter, see D. Garland, "The Composition and Unity of Philippians: Some Neglected Literary Factors," *Novum Testamentum* 27 (1985) 141–73, and W. Kurz, "Kenotic Imitation of Paul and of Christ in Philippians 2 and 3," in *Discipleship in the New Testament* (Philadelphia: Fortress, 1975) 103–26.

In the analysis made by G. Fee (*Paul's Letter to the Philippians* [Grand Rapids: Eerdmans, 1995] 12–14), Philippians should be regarded as "a hortatory letter of friendship." On pp. 21–22, Fee argues forcefully against the theory that a "letter B" is embedded within canonical Philippians. See also the brief excursus by H. Marshall, "Philippians—One Letter or Several Fragments?" in *The Epistle to the Philippians* (London: Epworth, 1991) xxxi–xxxii.

2. Within his chapter "The Cities of the Roman Empire," in *The Roman Economy* (Totowa, NJ: Rowman and Littlefield, 1974) 1–34, esp. 3 and 7, A. Jones describes the Roman imperial practice of "planting" colonies of Roman citizens. These colonies were constituted in whole or in part of discharged Roman veterans. In cases where the veterans were planted into already existing communities, Roman citizenship was granted to the natives as well; these peoples were, in effect, assimilated in status to the colonists. What this means for the Christians at Philippi is that as members of an official colony they themselves possessed Roman citizenship and were thereby presumably particularly oriented to the procedures and practices of the capital.

Aspects of the strong orientation of the Philippians to Rome are described by A. Lincoln (*Paradise Now and Not Yet* [Cambridge: Cambridge University Press, 1981] 100) in the following terms: "To commemorate his victory in the struggle for control of the empire in 42 B.C. on the plain of Philippi, Octavian had conferred the Roman form of constitutional government on the city. The official language became Latin, Roman coinage was adopted and the two chief magistrates of the city were now appointed in Rome and exempt from any interference by the provincial governor. In fact under the provision of the 'ius Italicum' Philippi was governed as if it was on Italian soil and its administration reflected that of Rome in almost every respect."

3. In the familiar verses that continue this passage, Paul decisively asserts that his own credentials in reference to the Jewish law are impeccable: "Though I myself have reason for confidence in the flesh also. If any other man thinks he has reason for confidence in the flesh, *I have more*" (3:4; emphasis added).

4. Similarly Fee, *Philippians*, 9. Fee also saliently points out: "There is no suggestion in the text that they (opponents who try to bring Gentile Christians under obligation to the Jewish law) are actually present in Philippi. This text is

a *warning* against them pure and simple; those who consider them *present in Philippi* either assume that or read it into the text."

5. In Phil 1:20, Paul states that he wishes to give honor to Christ *meta pasē parrēsia*. The RSV translates this phrase "with full courage," but a better rendering, one that accounts for the meaning of *parrēsia* as resolute speech before political authorities, would be "with all boldness." See chapter seven, section five above, and the references in n. 41, especially pp. 45–46 and 133–35 in R. Cassidy, *Society and Politics in the Acts of the Apostles.*

6. The factors that make it likely, but not certain, that Nero would serve as Paul's judge have been presented above in chapter nine, esp. n. 20.

7. That prisoners in the ancient world sometimes used the time before their trials to prepare their cases has been established in chapter four above. It is useful to speculate about Paul's attitude toward a trial before Nero if indeed he knew such a trial to be in the offing. This possibility should be kept in mind in considering the key statements and concepts of Philippians as these receive analysis in section four below. For example, if Paul presented them, what would Nero's response have been to the concepts contained in the following assertion: "But our *commonwealth* is in heaven, and from it we await a *Savior*, the *Lord* Jesus Christ, who will change our lowly body to be like his glorious body, by the *power* which enables him even *to subject all things to himself*?" (Phil 3:20-21; emphasis added).

8. The situation portrayed in Phil 1:15-17 has previously been analyzed in section one of chapter nine above.

9. The interpretation just made reflects the insights of J. Michael, *The Epistle of Paul to the Philippians* (London: Hodder and Stoughton, 1954) 16, and those of R. Martin, *Philippians* (Grand Rapids: Eerdmans, 1976) 66–67.

10. In 1:20 Paul expressly states: "it is my eager expectation and hope that I shall not be at all ashamed. . . . ." Here, in these opening references to his chains and to the trial that he is facing, Paul's sense of being free from shame is implicitly (yet still significantly) present. Speaking broadly, it can be said that Paul's refusal to be shamed is grounded in his conviction that the criterion of honorable conduct is not Roman public opinion, but rather the will of God. Further, Paul is convinced that Christ is both the exemplar and enabler of the honorable conduct to which he, Paul, aspires. From the standpoint of public opinion, humiliation, suffering, and shaming were the outcome of Jesus' arrest and Roman trial. Yet Paul knows that no such shaming occurred before the heavenly tribunal.

For an extremely useful treatment of "honor and shame in a theological key," see J. Elliott, "Disgraced Yet Graced. The Gospel according to 1 Peter," *Biblical Theology Bulletin* 25 (1995) 166–78, esp. 172. Other valuable background perspective is given in B. Malina, "Honor and Shame: Pivotal Values of the First-Century Mediterranean World," in *The New Testament World* (Atlanta, GA: John Knox, 1993) 28–62; H. Moxnes, "*BTB* Readers Guide: Honor and Shame," *Biblical Theological Bulletin* 23 (1993) 167–76; J. Pilch, "Death with Honor: The Mediterranean Style Death of Jesus in Mark," *Biblical Theology Bulletin* 25 (1995) 65–70.

11. See O'Brien, *Philippians,* 90.

12. For an analysis that concludes that Paul used military imagery at 1:27ff. when he urged his Philippian friends to "stand firm in one spirit, with one mind striving side by side for the faith of the gospel," see T. Geoffrion, *The Rhetorical Purpose and the Political and Military Character of Philippians* (Lewiston, NY: Mellen Biblical Press, 1993) esp. 54–65. See also E. Krentz, "Military Language and Metaphor in Philippians," in *Origins and Method* (Sheffield: Sheffield Academic Press, 1993) 105–27, esp. 120–24.

13. Fee (*Philippians,* 30–32) distinguishes between the *source* and the *reason* for the Philippians' suffering. For Fee, the pagan populace of Philippi should be considered the source of the suffering. Fee does not appear to rule out the role of the magistrates and the other Roman authorities at Philippia, but he does not explicitly consider their involvement. As to the reason for the suffering, Fee's plausible view is that Philippi was a center for the imperial cult, a cult in which Paul and the Christians of Philippi could not participate. Fee argues that, at the time when Paul wrote, *kyrios* ("lord") and *sōtēr* ("savior") were primary titles for acclaiming the emperor and probably were firmly established at Philippi. Yet for Christians only Jesus fully merited these titles. Thus Paul is concerned to emphasize in Philippians that these titles belong definitively to Jesus.

The argument that the imperial cult at Philippi presented a grave challenge to the Philippian Christians is also made by M. N. Keller, "Choosing What Is Best: Paul, Roman Society and Philippians" (Ph.D. diss., Lutheran School of Theology at Chicago, 1995).

With respect to the closing clause of this passage, "which you *saw* and now hear to be mine" (emphasis added), the following scenario may be envisioned. The struggle that Paul is presently engaged in with the authorities at Rome is not the first time that he has experienced such a conflict. Rather, some conflict involving the Roman authorities previously occurred at Philippi. (Note that the time and nature of this earlier conflict did not prevent Paul from writing Rom 13:1-7.) What Paul is now experiencing is thus a re-emergence (or renewal) of that earlier conflict.

14. A careful reading of this passage reveals that the power of the opponents at Philippi is sufficiently menacing that Paul feels compelled to counsel the Philippian Christians "not to be frightened in anything" (*mē ptyromenoi en mēdeni*). Seemingly, the power of these opponents (the Roman authorities) *to coerce* is what elicits this counsel from Paul. The situation at Philippi is thus more ominous than one in which the power of the opposing groups is to seduce or persuade.

15. J. F. Collange (*The Epistle of Saint Paul to the Philippians* [London: Epworth, 1979] 112) is representative of those commentators who would link this passage with 3:2ff.

16. Fee (*Philippians,* 245) points out that, although Paul's language is influenced by the Septuagint text that he is citing, his basic statement is "a fair reflection of his view of pagan society."

17. The initial part of Paul's counsel in 2:14 (his admonition to avoid "grumbling" and "disputing") appears to refer to any divisive conduct that may be

occurring within the Christian community. In the latter part of his counsel in 2:15, he indicates qualities ("blameless," "innocent," "without blemish") that would render the Philippian Christians "fit to be presented to God and to be representatives of God" (so G. Hawthorne, *Philippians* [Waco, TX: Word, 1983] 102). Is it also possible to detect a reference to upright conduct in sexual matters in Paul's use of these three terms?

18. While it is not possible here to discuss extensively the voluminous literature on this passage, the position of Silva (*Philippians*, 196–98) to the effect that these opponents are linked with those whom Paul decries in 3:2 for promoting the observance of the Jewish law is duly noted. See the extended discussion of this and other theories that is given in Fee, *Philippians*, 362–75. Fee's own position is that Paul is not referring to the same opponents as in 3:2; nor is he describing those who are members of the Philippian community. Rather these opponents are Christians from outside, actually "some itinerants, whose view of the faith is such that it allows them a great deal of undisciplined self-indulgence" (p. 375).

In effect, the approach of the present study is to reject the interpretation that Christians of any persuasion are indicated here: not Christians who espouse the Jewish law; not those who have Gnostic tendencies; not those who give way to self-indulgence. It will be argued in the text that various key phrases in this passage point to the conclusion that Paul is here indicting the licentious, arrogant Roman leaders at Rome and at Philippi.

19. O'Brien (*Philippians*, 444–50) discusses the possible nuances of Paul's meaning in 3:17 at length, arguing persuasively that Paul is actually pointing to himself as the primary example here; nevertheless there are others besides Paul (Timothy, Epaphroditus, the leadership of the Philippian community) to whom the Philippian Christians can look. To this it may be added that Paul's personal testimony against the dissolute sexual conduct exhibited by and sponsored by the Roman authorities is principally referred to here. The Philippian Christians can thus be instructed by Paul's witness against these practices and by his own example in proclaiming the standards of heavenly citizenship and the sovereignty of Jesus as true Savior.

20. In "Our *Politeuma* Is in Heaven: The Meaning of Philippians 3:17-21," in *Origins and Method* (Sheffield: Sheffield Academic Press, 1993) 92–104, W. Cotter states (p. 98): "In the Philippian context to be an enemy of Christ's cross would mean a person opposed to any sort of humiliation. In contrast to Christ and to Paul too, such persons would be working for the increase of their own public name and vying for positions of importance without regard for others. . . ." In a similar vein, Bruce (*Philippians*, 105) states: "those who deliberately indulge in sin and repudiate the will of God deny all that the cross stands for." Both of these interpretations have merit. In the perspective of the present study, however, Paul's criticism is not directed against Christians.

Rather it is the arrogant self-indulgent behavior of the Roman authorities that is the focus of his criticism. By the reason of their attitudes and their behavior, these authorities are indeed "enemies" of the cross of Christ. As will be noted below in the interpretation of Paul's words regarding the death of Jesus,

Paul has come to a sharpened appreciation for the role of the Roman authorities in the death of Jesus, and it is possible that his criticism of Roman authorities here as enemies of the cross of Christ is tied to Paul's sense of the role of their predecessors as *perpetrators* of the cross of Christ.

21. In "*koilia,*" *Theological Dictionary of the New Testament* 3:786, J. Behm notes that, in the Septuagint, *koilia* can refer to the male sex organ. As a part of his nuanced discussion of this passage, Marshall (*Philippians*, xxiv) adverts to the possibility that Paul may intend such meaning in this passage: "However, the Greek word *koilia* can refer to several physical organs and not simply to the stomach. It can be used euphemistically for the sexual organ, so that Paul may be saying that they regard their circumcision as an idol." C. Mearns ("The Identity of Paul's Opponents at Philippi," *New Testament Studies* 33 [1987] 194–204) takes the position that such is indeed Paul's meaning in 3:19. On p. 198, Mearns states: "In the phrase *hōn ho theos hē koilia, kai hē doxa en tē aischynē autōn*, both *koilia* and *aischynē* are euphemisms for the *circumcised* male organ" (emphasis added).

Mearns thus aligns himself with those scholars (perhaps including Marshall) who regard Paul as criticizing adversaries who are seeking to impose the requirements of the Jewish law regarding circumcision. From the perspective of the present study, Mearns is correct to interpret *koilia* as a reference to the male organ but incorrect to conclude that the issue is circumcision. Rather the issue is debauchery, and the opponents Paul is criticizing are Nero and his confederates in profligacy.

22. In "*aischynē,*" *The New International Dictionary of New Testament Theology* (Grand Rapids: Zondervan, 1978) 3:564, H. G. Link notes that Paul uses this word in a sexual sense in Phil 3:19.

23. Paul thus has a highly consistent line of criticism in Phil 3:18-21. Paul's adversaries are Nero and his ilk at Rome and those who emulate Nero at Philippi. Their arrogant sexual misconduct is decried, and Paul's ultimate appeal is to the standards of heaven and to Jesus as Savior. Jesus will bring ruin to these adversaries *for their demeaning of the human body* at the same time that he transforms the fragile bodies of those who are faithful "to be like his glorious body."

24. *Politeuma* occurs only here in the New Testament writings and has been the subject of intensive study. See, for example, W. Ruppel, "Politeuma: Bedeutungsgeschichte eines staatsrechtichen Terminus," *Philologos* 82 (1927) 268–312 and 433–54. See also J. Reumann, "Philippians 3:20-21—A Hymnic Fragment?" *New Testament Studies* 30 (1984) 593–609; J. Lambrecht, "Our Commonwealth Is in Heaven," *Louvain Studies* 10 (1984–85) 199–205.

Fee (*Philippians*, 378–80) analyzes the various possible translations for this term and favors the interpretation that the Philippians and Paul are here designated as "citizens" of a commonwealth in heaven. (Note the Greek word order, *hēmōn gar*, emphasizing *our* citizenship.) Fee correctly emphasizes the crucial point that possessing this citizenship in heaven affects the Philippians' conduct within the Roman colony that is their own city.

25. Paul's meaning in Phil 1:27 will be analyzed more fully below. In prelim-

inary fashion, it can be noted that, just as with *politeuma* in 3:20, Paul's use of *politeuesthe* in 1:27 has the dual allegiance of the Philippian Christians in view. The priority, of course, belongs to the standards of the heavenly commonwealth. As citizens of that commonwealth, the Philippian Christians and Paul are to reflect its standards here below. For amplification on this point, see K. Wengst, *Pax Romana*, 79, who states: "If the citizenship of Christians is in heaven, that makes them strangers on earth. Anyone who talks like this cannot attach any special value to Roman citizenship." See also Lincoln, *Paradise*, 100–101.

26. In other letters, when he encourages his readers regarding their manner of living, the verb Paul selects is usually *peripateō* (or *zaō*). Noun forms of *politeuomai* are used in Eph 2:12 and 2:19. In 2:12 the RSV translates *politeias tou Israel* as "the commonwealth of Israel." In 2:19 the RSV renders *sympolitai* as "fellow citizens."

27. See chapter eight above for the analysis of *sōtēr* ("savior") in 2 Timothy. In Eph 5:23, Christ is said to be the head of the Church and its "Savior."

28. O'Brien (*Philippians*, 477) points to these two dimensions of standing firm "in the Lord." Lightfoot (*Philippians*, 158) views Paul as making heavenly citizenship the basis of his appeal here: the Philippians are to stand fast "as becomes citizens of a heavenly kingdom."

29. See the discussion in n. 24 above.

30. It is possible that Paul is alluding to the Holy Spirit as a strengthening and unifying agent here. More probably *en eni pneumati* refers to a common human spirit. O'Brien (*Philippians*, 150) would render this phrase as "with one common purpose."

31. As observed by various commentators, including Talbert (*Philippians*, 1232), there is a definite eschatological emphasis as Paul here contrasts the coming *destruction* of their opponents with the coming *salvation* of the faithful Philippians. W. Cotter ("Our *Politeuma* Is in Heaven," 104) comments that Paul reminds the Philippians "of the greater honours awaiting them, for they have their citizenship in heaven, God's own *politeuma* where the *cursum honorum* includes only the names of the faithful."

32. Fee (*Philippians*, 170) comments: "As often in Paul, God is both the first and the last word. Everything is from God; the Philippians can rest assured here."

33. The secondary literature on this passage is immense. Fee (*Philippians*, 7) points out that it exceeds even the huge output of the articles treating the topic of Paul's "opponents" in Philippians. Fee himself (pp. 191–229) provides an extremely careful discussion of the nuances involved in virtually every phrase of this passage. Fee's emphasis on the narrative dimensions of this passage (pp. 193–94) is especially congenial to the present study's concern with "the status path of Christ."

34. Marshall (*Philippians*, 48) is representative of many commentators who hold this view. Marshall makes reference to various passages in Paul's Corinthian letters and emphasizes that Paul was certainly capable of writing in such a "poetic" style.

35. See O'Brien, *Philippians*, 253–62, for the appendix "The Meaning of V. 5 and the 'Hymn' (vv. 6-11) Within Their Context." Under both the "ethical" and kerygmatic" interpretations discussed by O'Brien, the figure of Jesus and his "status path" are of central consequence.

36. O'Brien (*Philippians*, 223–24) suggests that Paul's portrayal of Christ as *doulos* would have had overtones of meaning for those at Philippi in light of the slavery practices with which they were familiar.

37. As detailed in M. Hengel, *Crucifixion* (Philadelphia: Fortress, 1977), crucifixion as a form of punishment employed by various powers in the ancient world and the Romans themselves may have taken it over from the Carthaginians (p. 23). Nevertheless, under the empire and within its boundaries, crucifixion became the supreme Roman penalty, a form of execution representing the utmost in cruelty and public degradation (p. 87).

A point that is largely implicit throughout Hengel's work needs to be made explicit in the present context: in the world of Jesus and Paul, crucifixion was an exercise of *Roman* power. In other words, under Roman rule, *only* the Roman authorities themselves could order and inflict this type of execution.

E. Lohmeyer (*Kyrios Jesus* [Darmstadt: Wissenschaftliche Buchgesellschaft, 1961] 45–46) contends that Paul emphasized Jesus' humiliating death by crucifixion precisely because he (Paul) intended to stiffen the resolve of the Philippian Christians for the martyrs' deaths that some of them might have to undergo.

38. Hawthorne (*Philippians*, 90) sees Paul encouraging the Philippians to hold fast to the premise "that in the divine order of things self-humbling leads inevitably to exaltation."

39. In the estimation of Gnilka (*Philipperbrief*, 125), this name can *only* be the name of "Lord." Collange (*Philippians*, 105) states: "the name is that of *Kyrios-Yahweh*; and with it is therefore bestowed upon Jesus power over all things." See also Silva, *Philippians*, 129–30.

40. It is to be emphasized that Paul did indeed include vv. 10-11 within his letter. If Paul were citing a pre-existent hymn, he certainly was not bound to cite all of its verses. Ultimately, then, Paul wanted to set these words regarding Jesus' sovereignty before his readers.

41. Hawthorne (*Philippians*, 92) discusses the way in which the vocabulary and sentiment of Isa 45:23 are woven into the framework of Phil 2:10-11. Again, a point to be underscored is that Paul himself consciously presented the final text of his letter regardless of concepts that he may have derived from various sources. In effect, Paul desires here to present the strongest possible affirmation of Jesus' sovereignty.

42. Fee (*Philippians*, 222) is commendably close to describing the full implications of this acclamation at Philippi when he writes, "this declaration would probably not be lost on believers in a city whose inhabitants are Roman citizens and who are devotees of 'lords many' including 'lord Caesar.'" Fee's commentary is virtually alone among the widely used contemporary commentaries on Philippians in stating this point. See also his observations on pp. 31–32.

E. Lohmeyer (*Die Brief an die Philipper, an die Colosser und an Philemon*

[Göttingen: Vandenhoeck und Ruprecht, 1930] 98) emphasizes that Paul's words acclaim Jesus as "Lord of the *world*" and not merely as the Lord of believers. Nevertheless, because he has posited a Caesarean venue for this letter (p. 3), Lohmeyer does not relate Phil 2:10-11 to Paul's situation in Rome and does not expressly comment that Rome's emperor is here brought into subservience before the sovereignty of Jesus.

43. Hawthorne (*Philippians*, 137).

44. O'Brien (*Philippians*, 404) discusses the nuances of Paul's meaning in this phrase including the majority interpretation that the source of this power emanates from Christ's resurrection. O'Brien himself favors Fitzmyer's view that this power is fundamentally from God the Father; God has manifested this life-giving power in raising Christ from the dead.

45. Paul's reflection in 2 Cor 4:7-12 is pertinent here, esp. v. 10a: "always carrying in the body the death of Jesus. . . ."

46. It is to be noted that Paul's words in 3:10c, *symmorphizomenos tō thanatō autou*, encompass several dimensions of meaning. Bruce (*Philippians*, 91) perceptively alludes to three of these dimensions when he states: "To become like Christ in his death was for Paul partly self-identification with Christ crucified, partly a matter of daily experience, partly an anticipation of bodily death, which would more probably than not take the form of martyrdom for Christ's sake (which in the event it did)."

Within the present study, the dimension of meaning pertaining to Paul's own death is being emphasized and further insights concerning parallels with Jesus' death are being marshaled. To emphasize the parallel circumstances of Paul's death and Jesus', however, is not to overlook the other dimensions of meaning present in Paul's words. In his own careful analysis of the nuances of this complex passage, O'Brien (*Philippians*, 408–10) references Bruce's interpretation but appears not to engage with Bruce's third area of meaning regarding the concrete form of Paul's death, that is, martyrdom at the hands of the Roman authorities.

47. The list that follows is not comprehensive but suffices to indicate that Paul, upon reflection, could have perceived that there were remarkable parallels between his own circumstances and those that pertained to the death of Jesus. Caught up as he was within the framework of Roman power, Paul could now foresee how his own death might actually take place. The following parallels may thus have suggested themselves to him: (1) Paul, like Jesus before him, was being held as a Roman prisoner. (2) Paul, like Jesus, was charged with a capital offense. (3) Paul, like Jesus, would face a Roman judge who possessed the power to release or condemn him. (4) Paul, like Jesus, could have the experience of having his own testimony rejected. (5) If condemned, Paul, like Jesus, would be executed by Roman military personnel. (6) Paul, like Jesus, would have his execution carried out according to officially authorized Roman procedures. (7) For Paul, as for Jesus, the grounds for execution would probably be conduct hostile to the empire and/or its emperor.

48. In the Corinthian correspondence the *skandalon* of the cross is spoken of in 1 Cor 1:23. In the letter to the Galatians Paul uses this term in 5:11.

49. The consequence of Paul's Roman execution for the proclamation of the gospel at Philippi (and elsewhere) should be underscored. If Paul, who was presumably known by many at Philippi, were executed by the imperial authorities at Rome, how would news of this death be received by both the authorities and residents of Philippi, by Christians and non-Christians alike? Paul may thus have intended to alert his Christian readers to the possibility of his death in order to strengthen them for continuing the proclamation of the gospel. As noted in the paragraphs that follow in the text, he may also have intended to acclimate them for the possibility that some of them might face martyrdom.

50. Paul's words in Phil 1:30 ("engaged in the same conflict which you saw and now hear to be mine") and the analysis provided in section two of this chapter should be recalled at this juncture.

51. It is to be underscored that, within Philippians, Paul's condemnation and death are far from certain. Paul may in fact soon be reunited with his Philippian friends. Yet, *if* he is to be condemned, it is conceivable that this letter would be Paul's last written communication with the Philippian community. Under such circumstances, there is much that Paul wishes to share. Because several elements in his message are politically controversial, however, Paul sometimes expresses his concerns in implicit and oblique, albeit still powerful and memorable, terms. Philippians, after all, was written while Paul was a chained prisoner whose communications were presumably subject to some form of censorship.

Select Bibliography

The bibliography that follows lists works cited in the text as well as other selected works. For additional listings under the heading of "Ancient Sources" and "Studies Pertaining to Roman Rule," the bibliographies provided in R. Cassidy, *Jesus, Politics and Society,* and R. Cassidy, *John's Gospel in New Perspective,* should be consulted.

I. Ancient Sources

The Apostolic Fathers. Translated by K. Lake. Cambridge, MA: Harvard University Press, 1912.

Augustus to Nero: A Sourcebook on Roman History 31 BC—AD 68. Edited by D. Braund. London: Croom Helm, 1985.

The Coinage of Nero. Edited by E. Sydenham. London: Spink and Son, 1920.

The Digest of Justinian. 4 volumes. Latin text edited by T. Mommsen. Translated by A. Watson. Philadelphia: University of Pennsylvania Press, 1985.

Diodorus Siculus. *Diodorus of Sicily.* Translated by C. Oldfather. Cambridge, MA: Harvard University Press, 1933.

Dio Cassius. *Dio's Roman History.* Translated by E. Cary. Cambridge, MA: Harvard University Press, 1914.

Documents Illustrating the Principates of Gaius, Claudius and Nero. Collected by E. M. Smallwood. Cambridge: Cambridge University Press, 1967.

The Epistles of St. Clement of Rome and St. Ignatius of Antioch. Translated by J. Kleist. Westminster, MD: Newman, 1946.

The Fathers of the Church. *The Apostolic Fathers*. Translated by F. Glimm, J. Marique, and G. Walsh. New York: Christian Heritage, 1947.

Josephus. *The Jewish Antiquities*. Translated by H. Thackeray and others. Cambridge, MA: Harvard University Press, 1930.

———. *The Jewish War*. Translated by H. Thackeray. Cambridge, MA: Harvard University Press, 1928.

———. *The Life and Against Apion*. Translated by H. Thackeray and others. Cambridge, MA: Harvard University Press, 1926.

Lucian. Translated by A. Harmon. Cambridge, MA: Harvard University Press, 1936.

Philo. *The Embassy to Gaius*. Translated by F. Colson. Cambridge, MA: Harvard University Press, 1942.

Philostratus. *The Life of Apollonius of Tyana*. Translated by F. Conybeare. Cambridge, MA: Harvard University Press, 1912.

Pliny. *Letters*. Translated by W. Melmoth and W. Hutchinson. Cambridge, MA: Harvard University Press, 1915.

Plutarch. *Plutarch's Lives*. Translated by B. Perrin. Cambridge, MA: Harvard University Press, 1926.

———. *Plutarch's Moralia*. Translated by F. Babbitt. Cambridge, MA: Harvard University Press, 1927.

Seneca (the Elder). *Controversiae*. Translated by M. Winterbottom. Cambridge, MA: Harvard University Press, 1974.

Seneca (the Younger). *Ad Lucilium Epistulae Morales*. Translated by R. Gummere. Cambridge, MA: Harvard University Press, 1917.

Suetonius. *The Lives of the Caesars*. Translated by J. Rolfe. Cambridge, MA: Harvard University Press, 1913.

Tacitus. *The Annals*. Translated by J. Jackson. Cambridge, MA: Harvard University Press, 1931.

———. *The Histories*. Translated by C. Moore. Cambridge, MA: Harvard University Press, 1931.

II. Studies Pertaining to Roman Rule

Alexander, L., ed. *Images of Empire*. Sheffield: Sheffield Academic Press, 1991.

———. "The Relevance of Greco-Roman Literature and Culture to New Testament Study." In *Hearing the New Testament*, 109–26. Edited by J. Green. Grand Rapids: Eerdmans, 1995.

Anderson, G. *Sage. Saint and Sophist: Holy Men and Their Associates in the Early Roman Empire*. New York: Routledge, 1994.

Balsdon, J. "Maiestas." In *The Oxford Classical Dictionary*, 640–41. 2d ed. New York: Oxford University Press, 1970.

———. *Romans and Aliens*. Chapel Hill, NC: University of North Carolina Press, 1979.

Barnes, A. *Christianity at Rome in the Apostolic Age*. Westport, CT: Greenwood Press, 1971.

Barnes, T. "Legislation Against Christians," *Journal of Roman Studies* 50(1968): 32–50.

Barrett, A. *Caligula: The Corruption of Power*. New Haven: Yale University Press, 1990.

Bauman, R. *The Crimen Maiestatis in the Roman Republic and Augustan Principate*. Johannesburg: Witwatersrand University Press, 1967.

Bell, H. "The Economic Crisis in Egypt under Nero." *Journal of Roman Studies* 28(1938): 1–8.

Benko, S. "Pagan Criticism of Christianity during the First Two Centuries A.D." *Aufstieg und Niedergang der römischen Welt* 2.23.2 (1980): 1055–76.

Bilde, P. *Flavius Josephus between Jerusalem and Rome*. Sheffield: Sheffield Academic Press, 1988.

Bishop, J. *Nero: The Man and the Legend*. New York: Barnes, 1964.

den Boer, W., ed. *Le culte des souverains dans l'Empire roman*. Geneva: Fondation Hardt, 1973.

Bowersock, G. "Introduction." In *Life of Apollonius* by Philostratus, 9–22. Translated by C. Jones. Harmondsworth: Penguin, 1970.

———. *Martyrdom and Rome*. Cambridge: Cambridge University Press, 1995.

Bowie, E. "Apollonius of Tyana: Tradition and Reality." *Aufstieg und Niedergang der römischen Welt* 2.16.2 (1978): 1652–99.

Brown, R., and J. Meier. *Antioch and Rome*. New York: Paulist, 1982.

Bruce, F. F. "Christianity under Claudius." *Bulletin of the John Rylands Library* 44 (1962): 309–26.

Campbell, J. "Praetorians." In *The Oxford Classical Dictionary*, 1241. 3d ed. New York: Oxford University Press, 1996.

Cerfaux, L., and J. Tondriau. *Le culte des souverains*. Paris: Desclée, 1956.

Charlesworth, M. P. "Nero: Some Aspects." *Journal of Roman Studies* 40 (1950): 69–76.

Chilton, C. "The Roman Law of Treason under the Early Principate." *Journal of Roman Studies* 45 (1955): 73–81.

Deissmann, A. *Light from the Ancient East*. Translated by L. Strachan. Reprint, Grand Rapids: Baker, 1965.

Derow, P. "Perseus." In *The Oxford Classical Dictionary*, 1144. 3d ed. New York: Oxford University Press, 1996.

Duncan-Jones, R. *The Economy of the Roman Empire*. 2d ed. Cambridge: Cambridge University Press, 1982.

Fishwick, D. *The Imperial Cult in the Latin West*. 2 volumes. Leiden: Brill, 1991.

Flinterman, J. *Politiek. Paideia & Pythagorisme*. Groningen: Styx, 1993.

Garnsey, P. "The Criminal Jurisdiction of Governors." *Journal of Roman Studies* 58 (1968): 51–59.

———."The Lex Julia and Appeal under the Empire." *Journal of Roman Studies* 56 (1966): 167–89.

Grant, R. M. *After the New Testament*. Philadelphia: Fortress, 1967.

———. *Augustus to Constantine*. New York: Harper and Row, 1970.

———. *Greek Apologists of the Second Century*. Philadelphia: Westminster, 1988.

Griffin, M. *Nero: The End of a Dynasty*. New Haven: Yale University Press, 1984.

Griffiths, D. *The New Testament and the Roman State*. Swansea: John Penry Press, 1970.

Guterman, S. *Religious Toleration and Persecution in Ancient Rome*. London: Aiglon Press, 1951.

Hammond, M. "Imperial Elements in the Formula of the Roman Emperors during the First Two and a Half Centuries." *Memoirs of the American Academy in Rome* 25 (1957): 22–60.

Harris, B. "Apollonius of Tyana: Fact and Fiction." *Journal of Religious History* 5 (1969): 189–99.

Hopkins, K. *Conquerors and Slaves: Sociological Studies in Roman History*. Cambridge: Cambridge University Press, 1978.

Jackson, S. "Apollonius and the Emperors." *Hermathena* 137 (1984): 25–32.

Janssen, L. "'Superstitio' and the Persecution of the Christians." *Vigiliae Christianae* 33 (1979): 131–59.

Jones, A. H. *The Criminal Courts of the Roman Republic and Principate*. Totowa, NJ: Rowman and Littlefield, 1972.

———. "I Appeal unto Ceasar." In *Studies in Roman Government and Law*, 53–65. New York: Barnes and Noble, 1968.

———. "Imperial and Senatorial Jurisdiction in the Early Principate." In *Studies in Roman Government and Law*, 69–98. New York: Barnes and Noble, 1968.

———. "The Roman Civil Service (Clerical and Sub-Clerical Grades)." In *Studies in Roman Government and Law*, 153–75. New York: Barnes and Noble, 1968.

———. *The Roman Economy*. Edited by P. Brunt. Totowa, NJ: Rowman and Littlefield, 1974.

Jones, D. L. "Christianity and the Roman Imperial Cult." *Aufstieg und Niedergang der römischen Welt* 2.23.2 (1980): 1023–54.

Judge, E. *Rank and Status in the World of the Caesars and St. Paul*. ChristChurch, New Zealand: University of Canterbury Publications, 1982.

Keresztes, P. *Imperial Rome and the Christians*. 2 volumes. Lanham, MD: University Press of America, 1989.

Krauss, K. *Im Kerker vor und nach Christus*. Freiburg: J. C. B. Mohr, 1895.

Lepper, F. "Some Reflections on the Quinquennium Neronis." *Journal of Roman Studies* 47 (1957): 95–103.

Levick, B. *Claudius*. New Haven: Yale University Press, 1990.

Lintott, A., and J. Balsdon. "Maiestas." In *The Oxford Classical Dictionary*, 913–14. 3d ed. New York: Oxford University Press, 1996.

MacMullen, R. *Change in the Roman Empire*. Princeton: Princeton University Press, 1990.

Magie, D. *Roman Rule in Asia Minor*. 2 volumes. Princeton: Princeton University Press, 1950.

Martin, R. "Tacitus." In *The Oxford Classical Dictionary*, 1469. 3d ed. New York: Oxford University Press, 1996.

Millar, F. *The Emperor in the Roman World*. Ithaca: Cornell University Press, 1977.

———. "The Emperor, the Senate and the Provinces." *Journal of Roman Studies* 56 (1966): 155–66.

———. "The Imperial Cult and the Persecution." In *Le culte des souverains dans l'Empire roman*, 145–75. Edited by W. den Boer. Geneva: Fondation Hardt, 1973.

Momigliano, A. *On Pagans, Jews, and Christians*. Middletown, CT: Wesleyan University Press, 1987.

Mommsen, T. *Römisches Strafrecht*. Reprint, Graz: Akademische Druck und Verlagsanstalt, 1955.

Nock, A. "Soter and Euergetes." In *The Joy of Study*, 127–48. Edited by S. Johnson. New York: Macmillan, 1951.

———. *Essays on Religion and the Ancient World*. 2 volumes. Edited by Z. Stewart. Oxford: Clarendon, 1986.

Ogilvie, R. *The Romans and Their Gods*. New York: Norton, 1969.

Otto, W. "Augustus Soter." *Hermes* 45 (1910): 448–60.

Plescia, J. "On the Persecution of the Christians in the Roman Empire." *Latomus* 30 (1971): 120–32.

von Premerstein, A. "Legatus." In *Paulys Real-Encyclopädie der Classischen Altertumswissenschaft*, ser. 1, vol. 12, cols. 1133–49. Stuttgart: Metzlersche, 1925.

Price, S. "From Noble Funerals to Divine Cult: The Consecration of Emperors." In *Rituals of Royalty*, 56–105. Edited by D. Cannadine and S. Price. Cambridge: Cambridge University Press, 1987.

———. *Rituals and Power: The Roman Imperial Cult in Asia Minor*. Cambridge: Cambridge University Press, 1984.

Schowalter, D. *The Emperor and the Gods*. Minneapolis: Fortress, 1993.

Sherwin-White, A. "The Early Persecutions and Roman Law Again." *Journal of Theological Studies* 3 (1952–53): 199–213.

———. *Racial Prejudice in Imperial Rome*. Cambridge: Cambridge University Press, 1967.

———. *Roman Foreign Policy in the East*. London: Duckworth, 1984.

———. *Roman Law and Roman Society*. Reprint, Grand Rapids: Baker, 1978.

Shocat, Y. "The Change in the Roman Religion at the Time of the Emperor Trajan." *Latomus* 44 (1985): 317–36.

Stewart, R. "Judicial Procedure in New Testament Times." *Evangelical Quarterly* 47 (1975): 94–109.

Wallace, S. *Taxation in Egypt from Augustus to Diocletian*. Princeton: Princeton University Press, 1938.

Weaver, P. *Familia Caesaris: A Social Study of the Emperor's Freedmen and Slaves*. Cambridge: Cambridge University Press, 1972.

Wiedemann, T. *Adults and Children in the Roman Empire*. New Haven: Yale University Press, 1989.

III. Studies Pertaining to Paul's Life,
Theology, and Pastoral Practice

Aune, D. "Human Nature and Ethics in Hellenistic Philosophical Tradition and Paul: Some Issues and Problems." In *Paul in His Hellenistic Context*, 291–312. Edited by T. Engberg-Pedersen. Minneapolis: Fortress, 1995.

Barrett, C. K. *Paul: An Introduction to His Thought*. Louisville: Westminster/John Knox, 1994.

Bassler, J., ed. *Pauline Theology*. Volume 1: *Thessalonians, Philippians, Galatians, Philemon*. Minneapolis: Fortress, 1991.

Becker, J. *Paul: Apostle to the Gentiles*. Translated by O. Dean. Louisville: Westminster/John Knox, 1993.

Bornkamm, G. *Paul*. Translated by D. Stalker. New York: Harper and Row, 1969.

Bruce, F. F. *Paul: Apostle of the Heart Set Free*. Grand Rapids: Eerdmans, 1977.

———. *Paul and Jesus*. Grand Rapids: Baker, 1974.

Cotter, W. "Women's Authority Role in Paul's Churches: Countercultural or Conventional?" *Novum Testamentum* 4 (1994): 350–72.

Deissmann, A. *St. Paul: A Study in Social and Religious History*. London: Hodder and Stoughton, 1912.

Dodd, C. H. "The Mind of Paul." In *New Testament Studies*, 67–128. Manchester: Manchester University Press, 1967.

Engberg-Pedersen, T., ed. *Paul in His Hellenistic Context*. Minneapolis: Fortress, 1995.

Fitzmyer, J. *According to Paul: Studies in the Theology of the Apostle*. New York: Paulist, 1993.

———. *Paul and His Theology*. 2d ed. Englewood Cliffs, NJ: Prentice-Hall, 1987.

Fortna, R., and B. Gaventa. *The Conversation Continues: Studies in Paul and John in Honor of J. Louis Martyn*. Nashville: Abingdon, 1990.

Furnish, V. "Development in Paul's Thought." *Journal of American Academy of Religion* 38 (1970): 289–303.

———. *The Moral Teaching of Paul: Selected Issues*. Rev. ed. Nashville: Abingdon, 1985.

———. "On Putting Paul in His Place." *Journal of Biblical Literature* 113 (1994): 3–17.

————. *Theology and Ethics in Paul*. Nashville: Abingdon, 1968.

Gaventa, B. *First and Second Thessalonians*. Louisville: John Knox, 1998.

————. "The Maternity of Paul: An Exegetical Study of Galatians 4:19." In *The Conversation Continues*, 289–201. Edited by R. Fortna and B. Gaventa. Nashville: Abingdon, 1990.

————. "Our Mother Paul: Toward the Recovery of a Neglected Theme." *Princeton Seminary Bulletin* 17 (1996): 29–44.

Georgi, D. *Theocracy in Paul's Praxis and Theology*. Translated by D. Green. Minneapolis: Fortress, 1991.

Gnilka, J. *Paulus von Tarsus Apostel und Zeuge*. Freiburg: Herder, 1996.

Gunther, J. *Paul: Messenger and Exile*. Valley Forge, PA: Judson Press, 1972.

Hawthorne, G., R. Martin, and D. Reid, eds. *Dictionary of Paul and His Letters*. Downers Grove, IL: Inter-Varsity Press, 1993.

Hays, R. "Crucified with Christ: A Synthesis of the Theology of 1 and 2 Thessalonians, Philemon, Philippians, and Galatians." In *Pauline Theology*. Volume 1: *Thessalonians, Philippians, Galatians, Philemon*, 227–46. Edited by J. Bassler. Minneapolis: Fortress, 1991.

Hengel, M. *The Pre-Christian Paul*. Translated by J. Bowden. Philadelphia: Trinity Press International, 1991.

Horsley, R., ed. *Paul and Empire: Religion and Power in Roman Imperial Society*. Harrisburg, PA: Trinity Press International, 1997.

Jewett, R. *A Chronology of Paul's Life*. Philadelphia: Fortress, 1979.

Keck, L. *Paul and His Letters*. 2d ed. Philadelphia: Fortress, 1988.

Knox, J. "On the Pauline Chronology: Buck-Taylor-Hurd Revisited." In *The Conversation Continues*, 258–74. Edited by R. Fortna and B. Gaventa. Nashville: Abingdon, 1990.

————. *Some Chapters in the Life of Paul*. Rev. ed. Macon, GA: Mercer University Press, 1987.

Krodel, G., ed. *The Deutero-Pauline Letters: Ephesians, Colossians, 2 Thessalonians, 1–2 Timothy, Titus*. Minneapolis: Fortress, 1993.

Lambrecht, J. *Pauline Studies: Collected Essays*. Louvain: Louvain University Press, 1994.

Légasse, S. *Paul apôtre. Essai de biographie critique*. Paris: Cerf/Fides, 1991.

Longenecker, R. *The Ministry and Message of Paul*. Grand Rapids: Zondervan, 1970.

Luedemann, G. *Paul Apostle to the Gentiles: Studies in Chronology.* Translated by S. Jones. Philadelphia: Fortress, 1984.

Macoby, H. *Paul and Hellenism.* Philadelphia: Trinity Press International, 1991.

Malina, B., and J. Neyrey. *Portraits of Paul.* Louisville: Westminster John Knox, 1996.

Marrow, S. *Paul: His Letters and His Theology.* New York: Paulist, 1986.

Martin, R. A. *Studies in the Life and Ministry of the Early Paul and Related Issues.* Lewiston, NY: Mellen, 1993.

Martini, C. *The Testimony of St. Paul.* Translated by S. Leslie. New York: Crossroad, 1983.

Meeks, W. "The Social Context of Pauline Theology." *Interpretation* 36 (1982): 266–77.

Murphy-O'Connor, J. *Paul: A Critical Life.* Oxford: Clarendon, 1996.

———. *Paul the Letter-Writer: His World, His Options, His Skills.* Collegeville, MN: Liturgical Press, 1995.

Neyrey, J. *Paul in Other Words: A Cultural Reading of His Letters.* Louisville: Westminster John Knox, 1990.

O'Toole, R. "The Humane Saint Paul." *Review for Religious* 41 (1982) 80–90.

———. *Who Is a Christian? A Study in Pauline Ethics.* Collegeville, MN: Liturgical Press, 1990.

Penna, R. *Paul the Apostle: A Theological and Exegetical Study.* 2 volumes. Translated by T. Wahl. Collegeville, MN: Liturgical Press, 1996.

Perkins, P. *Ministering in the Pauline Churches.* New York: Paulist, 1982.

Plevnik, J. *Paul and the Parousia.* Peabody, MA: Hendrickson, 1997.

———. *What Are They Saying about Paul?* New York: Paulist, 1986.

Porter, S., and C. Evans, eds. *The Pauline Writings: A Sheffield Reader.* Sheffield: Sheffield Academic Press, 1995.

Ramsay, W. *St. Paul the Traveller and the Roman Citizen.* Reprint, Grand Rapids: Baker, 1962.

Riesner, R. *Paul's Early Period: Chronology, Mission Strategy, Theology.* Translated by D. Stott. Grand Rapids: Eerdmans, 1998.

Sampley, J. P. "From Text to Thought World: The Route to Paul's Ways." In *Pauline Theology.* Volume 1: *Thessalonians, Philippians, Galatians, Philemon,* 3–14. Edited by J. Bassler. Minneapolis: Fortress, 1991.

————. *Walking Between the Times: Paul's Moral Reasoning*. Minneapolis: Fortress, 1991.

Sanders, E. P. *Paul*. Oxford: Oxford University Press, 1991.

————. *Paul and Palestinian Judaism*. Philadelphia: Fortress, 1977.

Schultz, S. "Der frühe und der späte Paulus." *Theologische Zeitschrift* 41 (1985): 228–36.

Soards, M. *The Apostle Paul*. New York: Paulist, 1987.

Tambasco, A. *In the Days of Paul. The Social World and Teaching of the Apostle*. New York: Paulist, 1991.

————. *A Theology of Atonement and Paul's Vision of Christianity*. Collegeville, MN: Liturgical Press, 1991.

Taylor, W. "Obligation: Paul's Foundation for Ethics." *Trinity Seminary Review* 19 (1997): 91–112.

Tobin, T. *The Spirituality of Paul*. Wilmington, DE: Glazier, 1987.

Wallace, R., and W. Williams. *The Three Worlds of Paul of Tarsus*. New York: Routledge, 1998.

Witherington, B. *The Paul Quest*. Downers Grove, IL: Inter-Varsity, 1998.

Wright, N. T. *The Climax of the Covenant: Christ and the Law in Pauline Theology*. Minneapolis: Fortress, 1992.

————. "Paul's Gospel and Caesar's Empire." In *Paul and Politics*, 160–83. Edited by R. Horsley. Harrisburg, PA: Trinity Press International, 2000.

————. "Putting Paul Together Again: Towards a Synthesis of Pauline Theology (1 and 2 Thessalonians, Philippians, and Philemon)." In *Pauline Theology*. Volume 1: *Thessalonians, Philippians, Galatians, Philemon*, 183–211. Edited by J. Bassler. Minneapolis: Fortress, 1991.

————. *What Saint Paul Really Said*. Grand Rapids: Eerdmans, 1997.

IV. Studies Pertaining to Romans 13:1-7

Achtemeier, P. *Romans*. Atlanta: John Knox, 1985.

Bammel. E. "Ein Beitrag zur paulinischen Staatsanschauung." *Theologische Literaturzeitung* 11 (1960): 837–40.

————. "Romans 13." In *Jesus and the Politics of His Day*, 365–83. Edited by E. Bammel and C. Moule. Cambridge: Cambridge University Press, 1984.

Barrett, C. K. *The Epistle to the Romans*. New York: Harper and Row, 1957.

Bartsch, H. W. "The Historical Situation of Romans." *Encounter* 3 (1972): 329–39.

Barth. K. *The Epistle to the Romans*. Translated by E. Hoskyns. London: Oxford University Press, 1965.

Black, M. *Romans*. Grand Rapids: Eerdmans, 1973.

Borg, M. "A New Context for Romans XIII." *New Testament Studies* 19 (1972–73): 205–18.

Botha, J. *Subject to Whose Authority? Multiple Readings of Romans 13*. Atlanta, GA: Scholars Press, 1994.

Bruce, F. F. "Paul and 'The Powers That Be.'" *Bulletin of the John Rylands Library* 66 (1983–84): 78–96.

Campbell, W. "Why Did Paul Write Romans?" *The Expository Times* 85 (1973–74): 264–69.

Cranfield, C. *The Epistle to the Romans*. 2 volumes. Edinburgh: T&T Clark, 1975.

Dodd, C. *The Epistle to the Romans*. London: Hodder and Stoughton, 1932.

Donfried, K., ed. *The Romans Debate*. Revised and expanded edition. Peabody, MA: Hendrickson, 1991.

Dunn, D. G. *Romans*. 2 volumes. Dallas, TX: Word, 1988.

———. "Romans 13:1-7—A Charter for Political Quietism?" *Ex Auditu* 2 (1986): 55–68.

Dyck, H. "The Christian and the Authorities in Romans 13:1-7." *Direction* 14 (1985): 44–50.

Edwards, J. *Romans*. Peabody, MA: Hendrickson, 1992.

Elliott, N. *Liberating Paul*. Maryknoll, NY: Orbis, 1994.

———. *The Rhetoric of Romans*. Sheffield: Sheffield Academic Press, 1990.

Fitzmyer, J. *Romans*. 2 volumes. New York: Doubleday, 1993.

Friedrich, J., W. Pöhlmann, and P. Stuhlmacher. "Zur historischen Situation und Intention von Röm 13,1-7." *Zeitschrift für Theologie und Kirche* 73 (1976): 131–66.

Garrett, J. "The Dialectic of Romans 13:1-7 and Revelation 13: Part One." *Journal of Church and State* 18 (1976): 434–41.

Hultgren, A. *Paul's Gospel and Mission: The Outlook from His Letter to the Romans*. Philadelphia: Fortress, 1985.

————. "Reflections on Romans 13:1-7: Submission to Governing Authorities." *Dialog* 15 (1976): 263–69.

Hutchinson, S. "The Political Implications of Romans 13:1-7." *Biblical Theology* 21 (1971): 49–59.

Jeffries, J. *Conflict at Rome: Social Order and Hierarchy in Early Christianity*. Minneapolis: Fortress, 1991.

Kallas, J. "Romans XIII. 1-7: An Interpolation." *New Testament Studies* 11 (1964–64): 365–74.

Karris, R. "Romans 14:1–15:3 and the Occasion of Romans." In *The Romans Debate*, 65–84. Edited by K. Donfried. Peabody, MA: Hendrickson, 1991.

Käsemann, E. "Principles of the Interpretation of Romans 13." In *New Testament Questions of Today*, 196–216. Translated by W. Montague. Philadelphia: Fortress, 1969.

Kosnetter, J. "Röm 13,1-7: Zeitbedingte Vorsichtsmassregel oder Grundsatzliche Einstellung?" *Analecta Biblica* 17–18 (1963): 347–55.

Kuss, O. "Paulus uber die staatliche Gewalt." In *Auslegung und Verkundigung*, 1:246–59. Regensburg: Pustet, 1963.

Lampe, P. "The Romans Christians of Romans 16." In *The Romans Debate*, 216–30. Edited by K. Donfried. Peabody, MA: Hendrickson, 1991.

————. *Die stadtrömischen Christen in den erstern beiden Jahrhunderten*. Tübingen: J. C. B. Mohr, 1989.

Légasse, S. "Paul et César Romains 13,1-7 Essai de Synthèse." *Revue Biblique* 101 (1994): 516–32.

Manson, T. "St. Paul's Letter to the Romans—and Others." In *The Romans Debate*, 3–15. Edited by K. Donfried. Peabody, MA: Hendrickson, 1991.

Merklein, H. "Sinn und Zweck von Röm 13,1-7." In *Neues Testament und Ethik*, 238–70. Edited by H. Merklein. Freiburg: Herder, 1989.

Minear, P. *The Obedience of Faith: The Purposes of Paul in the Epistle to the Romans*. Naperville, IL: Allenson, 1971.

Morgenthaler, R. "Roma—Sedes Satanae. Röm. 13,1ff im Lichte von Luk. 4,5-8." *Theologische Zeitschrift* 12 (1956): 289–304.

Morrison, C. *The Powers That Be: Earthly Rulers and Demonic Powers in Romans 13,1-7*. Naperville, IL: Allenson, 1960.

O'Neill, J. *Paul's Letter to the Romans*. Harmondsworth: Penguin, 1975.

Pilch, J. *Galatians and Romans*. Collegeville, MN: Liturgical Press, 1983.

Stein, R. "The Argument of Romans 13:1-7." *Novum Testamentum* 31 (1989): 325–43.

Strobel, A. "Furcht, Wem Furcht Gebührt." *Zeitschrift für die Neutestamentliche Wissenschaft* 55 (1964): 58–62.

———. "Zum Verständnis von Rm 13." *Zeitschrift für die Neutestamentliche Wissenschaft* 47 (1956): 67–93.

van Unnik, W. "Lob und Strafe durch die Obrigkeit Hellenistisches zu Röm 13,3-4." In *Jesus und Paulus*, 334–43. Edited by E. Ellis and E. Grasser. Göttingen: Vandenhoeck und Ruprecht, 1978.

Walters, J. *Ethnic Issues in Paul's Letter to the Romans*. Valley Forge, PA: Trinity Press International, 1993.

Webster, A. "St. Paul's Political Advice to the Haughty Gentile Christians in Rome: An Exegesis of Romans 13:1-7." *St. Vladimir's Theological Quarterly* 25 (1981): 259–82.

Wedderburn, A. *The Reasons for Romans*. Edinburgh: T.&T. Clark, 1988.

Zsifkovits, V. *Der Staatsgedanke nach Paulus in Röm 13,1-7*. Vienna: Herder, 1964.

V. Letters in Chains Especially Philippians

Alexander, L. "Hellenistic Letter-Forms and the Structure of Philippians." In *The Pauline Writings*, 232–46. Edited by S. Porter and C. Evans. Sheffield: Sheffield Academic Press, 1995.

Bakirtzis, C. and Koester, H., eds. *Philippi at the Time of Paul and after His Death*. Harrisburg, PA: Trinity Press International, 1998.

Barth, K. *The Epistle to the Philippians*. Translated by J. Leitch. London: SCM, 1962.

Barth, M. *Ephesians*. 2 volumes. Garden City, NY: Doubleday, 1974.

Bartchy, S. "Philemon, Epistle to." *Anchor Bible Dictionary*, 5:305–10. Edited by D. Freedman. New York: Doubleday, 1992.

Beker, J. *Heirs of Paul*. Minneapolis: Fortress, 1991.

Bloomquist, L. G. *The Function of Suffering in Philippians*. Sheffield: Sheffield Academic Press, 1993.

deBoer, M. "Images of Paul in the Post-Apostolic Period." *Catholic Biblical Quarterly* 42 (1980): 359–80.

Bornhaüser, K. *Jesus Imperator Mundi (Phil 3:17-21 and 2:5-12)*. Gütersloh: Bertelsmann, 1938.

Böttger, P. "Die eschatologische Existenz der Christen." *Zeitschrift für die neutestamentliche Wissenschaft* 60 (1969): 244–63.

Brewer, R. "The Meaning of *Politeuesthe* in Philippians 1:27." *Journal of Biblical Literature* 73 (1954): 76–83.

Bruce, F. F. *Epistles to Colossians, Philemon, Ephesians.* Grand Rapids: Eerdmans, 1985.

———. *Philippians.* San Francisco: Harper and Row, 1985.

———. "St. Paul in Rome." *Bulletin of the John Rylands Library* 46 (1963–64): 326–45.

———. "St. Paul in Rome. 2. The Epistle to Philemon." *Bulletin of the John Rylands Library* 48 (1965–66): 81–97.

———. "St. Paul in Rome. 3. The Epistle to the Colossians." *Bulletin of the John Rylands Library* 48 (1965–66): 268–85.

———. "St. Paul in Rome. 4. The Epistle to the Ephesians." *Bulletin of the John Rylands Library* 49 (1966–67): 303–22.

———. "St. Paul in Rome. 5. Concluding Observations." *Bulletin of the John Rylands Library* 50 (1967–68): 262–79.

Byrne, B. "The Letter to the Philippians." In *The New Jerome Biblical Commentary,* 791–97. Edited by R. Brown, J. Fitzmyer, and R. Murphy. Englewood Cliffs, NJ: Prentice-Hall, 1990.

Caird, G. *Paul's Letters from Prison.* Oxford: Oxford University Press, 1976.

Collange, J.-F. *The Epistle of Saint Paul to the Philippians.* Translated by A. Heathcote. London: Epworth, 1979.

Collins, R. *Letters That Paul Did Not Write.* Wilmington, DE: Glazier, 1988.

Cotter, W. "Our *Politeuma* Is in Heaven: The Meaning of Philippians 3.17-21." In *Origins and Method,* 92–104. Edited by B. McLean. Sheffield: Sheffield Academic Press, 1993.

Craddock, F. *Philippians.* Atlanta: John Knox, 1985.

Dibelius, M., and H. Conzelmann. *A Commentary on the Pastoral Epistles.* Translated by P. Buttolph and A. Yarbro. Philadelphia: Fortress, 1972.

Donfried, K., and H. Marshall. *The Theology of the Shorter Pauline Letters.* Cambridge: Cambridge University Press, 1993.

Dunn, J. *The Epistles to the Colossians and to Philemon.* Grand Rapids: Eerdmans, 1996.

Fee, G. *Paul's Letter to the Philippians.* Grand Rapids: Eerdmans, 1995.

———. *1 and 2 Timothy, Titus.* San Francisco: Harper and Row, 1984.

Fiore, B. *The Function of Personal Example in the Socratic and Pastoral Epistles*. Rome: Biblical Institute Press, 1986.

Fitzmyer, J. "Philemon." In *The New Jerome Biblical Commentary*, 869–70. Edited by R. Brown, J. Fitzmyer, and R. Murphy. Englewood Cliffs, NJ: Prentice-Hall, 1990.

———. "To Know Him and the Power of His Resurrection: Phil. 3:10." In *Mélanges bibliques en hommage au R.P. Beda Rigaux*, 411–25. Edited by A. Descamps and A. deHalleux. Gembloux: Duculot, 1970.

Friedrich, G. "Der Brief eines Gefangenen: Bemerkungen zum Philipperbrief." In *Auf das Wort Kommt Es An*, 224–35. Edited by J. Friedrich. Göttingen: Vandenhoeck & Ruprecht, 1978.

Furnish, V. "The Place and Purpose of Philippians III." *New Testament Studies* 10 (1963–64): 80–88.

Garland, D. "The Composition and Unity of Philippians: Some Neglected Literary Factors." *Novum Testamentum* 27 (1985): 141–73.

———. "Philippians 1:1-26 The Defense and Confirmation of the Gospel." *Review and Expositor* 77 (1980): 327–36.

Geoffrion, T. *The Rhetorical Purpose and the Political and Military Character of Philippians*. Lewiston, NY: Mellen, 1993.

Gilchrist, J. "On What Charge Was St. Paul Brought to Rome?" *The Expository Times* 78 (1966–67): 264–66.

Gnilka, J. "Die antipaulinische Mission in Philippi." *Biblische Zeitschrift* n.s. 9 (1965): 258–76.

———. *Der Epheserbrief*. Freiburg: Herder, 1977.

———. *Der Kolosserbrief*. Freiburg: Herder, 1980.

———. *Der Philemonbrief*. Freiburg: Herder, 1982.

———. *Der Philipperbrief*. Freiburg: Herder, 1976.

Hanson, A. *The Pastoral Letters*. Cambridge: Cambridge University Press, 1966.

Harrington, D. *Paul's Prison Letters: On Paul's Letters to Philemon, the Philippians and the Colossians*. Hyde Park, NY: New City Press, 1997.

Hawthorne, G. "The Imitation of Christ: Discipleship in Philippians." In *Patterns of Discipleship in the New Testament*, 163–79. Edited by R. Longenecker. Grand Rapids: Eerdmans, 1966.

———. *Philippians*. Waco, TX: Word, 1983.

Horgan, M. P. "The Letter to the Colossians." In *The New Jerome Bib-*

lical Commentary, 876–82. Edited by R. Brown, J. Fitzmyer, and R. Murphy. Englewood Cliffs, NJ: Prentice-Hall, 1990.

Houlden, J. L. *Paul's Letters from Prison*. Philadelphia: Westminster, 1977.

Hugedé, N. *Saint Paul et Rome*. Paris: Les Belles Lettres, 1986.

Hultgren, A. *I-II Timothy, Titus*. Minneapolis: Augsburg, 1984.

Jewett, R. "Conflicting Movements in the Early Church as Reflected in Philippians." *Novum Testamentum* 12 (1970): 362–90.

Keller, M. N. "Choosing What is Best: Paul, Roman Society and Philippians." Ph.D. diss., Lutheran School of Theology at Chicago, 1995.

Kelly, J. N. *A Commentary on the Pastoral Epistles*. New York: Harper & Row, 1963.

Knight, *The Pastoral Epistles*. Grand Rapids, Eerdmans, 1992.

Knox, J. *Philemon Among the Letters of Paul*. London: Collins, 1960.

Kobelski, P. J. "The Letter to the Ephesians." In *The New Jerome Biblical Commentary*, 883–90. Edited by R. Brown, J. Fitzmyer, and R. Murphy. Englewood Cliffs, NJ: Prentice-Hall, 1990.

Koester, H. "The Purpose of the Polemic of a Pauline Fragment (Philippians III)." *New Testament Studies* 8 (1961–62): 317–32.

Krentz, E. "Military Language and Metaphors in Philippians." In *Origins and Method*, 105–27. Edited by B. McLean. Sheffield: Sheffield Academic Press, 1993.

Kurz, W. "Kenotic Imitation of Paul and of Christ in Philippians 2 and 3. In *Discipleship in the New Testament*, 103–26. Edited by F. Segovia. Philadelphia: Fortress, 1985.

Lampe, P. "Keine 'Sklavenflucht' des Onesimus." *Zeitschrift für die neutestamentliche Wissenschaft* 76 (1985): 135–37.

Lea, T., and H. Griffin. *1, 2 Timothy Titus*. Nashville: Broadman, 1992.

Levie, J. "Le Chretien Citoyen du Ciel (Phil 3,20)." *Analecta Biblica* 17–18 (1963): 81–88.

Lincoln, A. *Paradise Now and Not Yet*. Cambridge: Cambridge University Press, 1981.

———, and A. Wedderburn. *The Theology of the Later Pauline Letters*. Cambridge: Cambridge University Press, 1993.

Lightfoot, J. *Saint Paul's Epistles to the Colossians and to Philemon*. Reprint, Grand Rapids: Zondervan, 1961.

———. *St. Paul's Epistle to the Philippians*. Reprint, Grand Rapids: Zondervan, 1961.

Lohmeyer, E. *Die Briefe an die Philipper, an die Kolosser und an Philemon.* Reprint, Göttingen: Vandenhoeck & Ruprecht, 1964.

————. *Kyrios Jesus: Eine Untersuchung zu Phil.2,5-11.* Reprint, Darmstadt: Wissenschaftliche Buchgesellschaft, 1961.

Lohse, E. *A Commentary on the Epistles to the Colossians to Philemon.* Translated by W. Poehlmann and R. Karris. Philadelphia: Fortress, 1971.

Marshall, H. *The Epistle to the Philippians.* London: Epworth, 1992.

Martin, R. P. *Colossians and Philemon.* Grand Rapids: Eerdmans, 1973.

————. *Ephesians, Colossians, and Philemon.* Atlanta: John Knox, 1991.

————. *Philippians.* Grand Rapids: Eerdmans, 1976.

Mearns, C. "The Identity of Paul's Opponents at Philippi." *New Testament Studies* 33 (1987): 194–204.

Melick, R. *Philippians, Colossians, Ephesians.* Nashville: Broadman, 1991.

Michael, J. H. *The Epistle of Paul to the Philippians.* London: Hodder and Stoughton, 1928.

Michaelis, W. *Die Gefangenschaft des Paulus in Ephesus.* Gütersloh: Bertelsmann, 1925.

Miller, E. "*Politeuesthe* in Philippians 1:27: Some Philological and Thematic Observations." *Journal for the Study of the New Testament* 15 (1982): 86–96.

Mitton, C. L. *Ephesians.* Grand Rapids: Eerdmans, 1973.

Moule, C. F. *The Epistles of Paul the Apostle to the Colossians and to Philemon.* Cambridge: Cambridge University Press, 1958.

————. *Philippian Studies.* London: Pickering & Inglis, n.d.

Motyer, J. *The Richness of Christ: Studies in the Letter to the Philippians.* London: Inter-Varsity, 1966.

Müller, U. *Der Brief des Paulus an die Philipper.* Leipzig: Evangelische Verlagsanstalt, 1993.

O'Brien, P. *The Epistle to the Philippians.* Grand Rapids: Eerdmans, 1991.

Oberlinner, L. *Kommentar zum Zweiten Timotheusbrief.* Freiburg: Herder, 1995.

Patzia, A. *Colossians, Philemon, Ephesians.* San Francisco: Harper & Row, 1984.

Perkins, P. "Philippians: Theology for the Heavenly *Politeuma.*" In *Pauline Theology,* 1:89–104. Edited by J. Bassler. Minneapolis: Fortress, 1991.

Petersen, N. *Rediscovering Paul: Philemon and the Sociology of Paul's Narrative World*. Philadelphia: Fortress, 1985.

Pilhofer, P. *Philippi: Die erste christliche Gemeinde Europas*. Tübingen: Mohr, 1995.

Plummer, A. *A Commentary on St. Paul's Epistle to the Philippians*. London: Robert Scott, 1919.

Pobee, J. *Persecution and Martyrdom in the Theology of Paul*. Sheffield: Sheffield Academic Press, 1985.

Portefaix, L. *Sisters Rejoice*. Stockholm: Almqvist & Wiksell, 1988.

Pratt, D. "Ambassador." In *The International Standard Bible Encyclopedia*, 1:109–10. Grand Rapids: Eerdmans, 1979.

Prior, M. *Paul the Letter-Writer and the Second Letter to Timothy*. Sheffield: Sheffield Academic Press, 1989.

Rapske, B. M. "The Prisoner Paul in the Eyes of Onesimus." *New Testament Studies* 37 (1991): 187–203.

Reicke, B. "Caesarea, Rome, and the Captivity Epistles." In *Apostolic History and the Gospel*, 277–86. Edited by W. Gasque and R. P. Martin. Grand Rapids: Eerdmans, 1970.

Reumann, J. "Church Office in Paul, Especially in Philippians." In *Origins and Method*, 82–91. Edited by B. McLean. Sheffield: Sheffield Academic Press, 1993.

———. *Colossians*. Minneapolis: Augsburg, 1985.

———. "Contributions of the Philippian Community to Paul and to Earliest Christianity." *New Testament Studies* 39 (1993): 438–57.

———. "Philippians and the Culture of Friendship." *Trinity Seminary Review* 19 (1997): 69–83.

———. "Philippians 3.20-21—A Hymnic Fragment?" *New Testament Studies* 30 (1984): 593–609.

Rolla, A. "La Cittadinanza Greco-Romana e la Cittadinanza Celeste de Filippesi 3,20." *Analecta Biblica* 17–18 (1963): 75–80.

Ruppel, W. "Politeuma. Bedeutungsgeschichte eines staatsrechtlichen Terminus." *Philologus* 82 (1927): 268–312, 433–54.

Schnackenburg, R. *Ephesians*. Translated by H. Heron. Edinburgh: T&T Clark, 1991.

Silva, M. *Philippians*. Chicago: Moody Press, 1988.

Stagg, F. "Colossians." "Ephesians." In *Mercer Commentary on the Bible*, 1235–39 and 1217–25. Edited by W. Mills and R. Wilson. Macon, GA: Mercer University Press, 1995.

Stowers, S. "Friends and Enemies in the Politics of Heaven: Reading

Theology in Philippians." In *Pauline Theology*, 1:105–21. Edited by J. Bassler. Minneapolis: Fortress, 1991.

Talbert, C. "Philippians." In *Mercer Commentary on the Bible*, 1227–34. Edited by W. Mills and R. Wilson. Macon, GA: Mercer University Press, 1995.

———. The Problem of Pre-existence in Philippians 2:6-11." *Journal of Biblical Literature* 86 (1967): 141–53.

Taylor, W. *Ephesians*. Minneapolis: Augsburg, 1985.

Towner, P. *1-2 Timothy & Titus*. Downers Grove, IL: Inter-Varsity, 1994.

Wild, R. "The Warrior and the Prisoner: Some Reflections on Ephesians 6:10-20." *Catholic Biblical Quarterly* 46 (1984): 284–98.

Witherington, B. *Friendship and Finances in Philippi*. Valley Forge, PA: Trinity Press International, 1994.

Wright, N. T. *Colossians and Philemon*. Grand Rapids: Eerdmans, 1986.

———. "*Harpagmos* and the Meaning of Philippians 2:5-11" *Journal of Theological Studies* n.s. 37 (1986): 321–52.

VI. Works on Selected Topics

Aland, K. "Das Verhältnis von Kirche und Staat nach dem Neuen Testament und den Aussagen des 2. Jahrhunderts." In *Neutestamentliche Entwürfe*, 26–123. Edited by K. Aland. Munich: Kaiser, 1979.

Bagnani, G. "Peregrinus Proteus and the Christians." *Historia* 4 (1955): 107–12.

Brown, R. *An Introduction to the New Testament*. New York: Doubleday, 1996.

Bousset, W. *Kyrios Christos*. Translated by J. Steely. Nashville: Abingdon, 1970.

Cassidy, R. *Jesus, Politics, and Society: A Study of Luke's Gospel*. Maryknoll, NY: Orbis, 1978.

———. *John's Gospel in New Perspective: Christology and the Realities of Roman Power*. Maryknoll, NY: Orbis, 1992.

———. "Matthew 17:24-27—A Word on Civil Taxes." *Catholic Biblical Quarterly* 41 (1979): 571–80.

———. *Society and Politics in the Acts of the Apostles*. Maryknoll, NY: Orbis, 1987.

Cranfield, C. "The Christian's Political Responsibility According to the New Testament." *Scottish Journal of Theology* 15 (1962): 176–92.

Cullmann, O. *The State in the New Testament.* London: SCM, 1957.

Cuss, D. *Imperial Cult and Honorary Terms in the New Testament.* Fribourg: University Press, 1974.

Dibelius, M. "Rom und die Christen im ersten Jahrhundert." In M. Dibelius, *Botschaft und Geschichte,* 2:177–228. Tübingen: Mohr, 1956.

Duling, D. "Binding and Loosing: Matthew 16:19; Matthew 18:18; John 20:23." *Forum* 3 (1987): 3–31.

Elliott, J. H. "Disgraced Yet Graced. The Gospel according to Peter in the Key of Honor and Shame." *Biblical Theology Bulletin* 25 (1995): 166–78.

Exegetical Dictionary of the New Testament. 3 volumes. Edited by H. Balz and G. Schneider. Grand Rapids: Eerdmans, 1990.

Farmer, W., and R. Kereszty. *Peter and Paul in the Church of Rome.* New York: Paulist, 1990.

Gill, D., and C. Gempf. *The Book of Acts in Its Graeco-Roman Setting.* Grand Rapids: Eerdmans, 1994.

A Greek-English Lexicon. Compiled by H. Liddell and R. Scott. Revised and augmented by H. Jones. Oxford: Clarendon Press, 1968.

Greek-English Lexicon of the New Testament Based on Semantic Domains. 2 volumes. Edited by J. Louw and E. Nida. New York: United Bible Societies, 1988.

A Greek-English Lexicon of the New Testament and Other Early Christian Literature. Edited by W. Bauer. Translated and adapted by W. Arndt, W. Gingrich, and F. Danker. Chicago: University of Chicago Press, 1978.

Hengel, M. *Crucifixion.* Translated by J. Bowden. Philadelphia: Fortress, 1977.

von Harnack, A. *Marcion: The Gospel of the Alien God.* Translated by J. Steely and L. Bierma. Durham, NC: Labyrinth Press, 1990.

Hemer, C. *The Book of Acts in the Setting of Hellenistic History.* Edited by C. Gempf. Winona Lake, IN: Eisenbrauns, 1990.

The International Standard Bible Encyclopedia. 4 volumes. Edited by G. Bromily. Grand Rapids: Eerdmans, 1979.

Kee, H. "The Linguistic Background of 'Shame' in the New Testament." In *On Language, Culture and Religion,* 133–47. Edited by M. Black and W. Smalley. The Hague: Mouton, 1974.

Knox, J. *Marcion and the New Testament.* Reprint, New York: AMS Press, 1980.

Lentz, J. *Luke's Portrait of Paul*. Cambridge: Cambridge University Press, 1993.

Lohmeyer, E. *Christuskult and Kaiserkult*. Tübingen: Mohr, 1919.

Lohse, E. *Theological Ethics of the New Testament*. Translated by E. Boring. Minneapolis: Fortress, 1991.

Malina, B. "Honor and Shame: Pivotal Values of the First-Century Mediterranean World." In *The New Testament World*, 28–62. Edited by B. Malina. Revised edition. Atlanta: Westminster John Knox, 1993.

Marshall, H. "New Occasions Teach New Duties? 2. The Use of the New Testament in Christian Ethics." *The Expository Times* 105 (1994): 131–36.

Marrow, S. *Speaking the Word Fearlessly*. New York: Paulist, 1982.

Matera, F. *New Testament Ethics. The Legacies of Jesus and Paul*. Louisville: Westminster John Knox, 1996.

Moxnes, H. "*BTB* Readers Guide: Honor and Shame." *Biblical Theology Bulletin* 23 (1993): 167–76.

The New International Dictionary of New Testament Theology. Edited by L. Coenen, E. Beyreuther, and H. Bietenhard. Translated and edited by C. Brown. Grand Rapids: Zondervan, 1978.

The Oxford Classical Dictionary. 3d ed. Edited by S. Hornblower and A. Spawforth. Oxford: Oxford University Press, 1996 (2d ed. edited by N. Hammond and H. Scullard, 1970).

Paulys Real-Encyclopädie der Classisches Altertumswissenschaft. Edited by W. Kroll. Stuttgart: Metzlersche, 1925.

Petzke, G. *Die Traditionen über Apollonius von Tyana und Das Neue Testament*. Leiden: Brille, 1970.

Pilch, J. "Death with Honor: the Mediterranean Style of Death in Mark." *Biblical Theology Bulletin* 25 (1995): 65–70.

Quinn, J. "Seven Times He Wore Chains" (1 Clem 5.6)." *Journal of Biblical Literature* 97 (1978): 574–76.

Rapske, B. *The Book of Acts and Paul in Roman Custody*. Grand Rapids: Eerdmans, 1994.

———. "The Importance of Helpers to the Imprisoned Paul in the Book of Acts." *Tyndale Bulletin* 42 (1991): 3–30.

Schrage, W. *The Ethics of the New Testament*. Translated by D. Green. Philadelphia: Fortress, 1988.

Tajra, H. *The Trial of St. Paul*. Tübingen: Mohr, 1989.

Theological Dictionary of the New Testament. 9 volumes. Edited by G.

Kittel and G. Friedrich. Translated and edited by G. Bromily. Grand Rapids: Eerdmans, 1964–74.

The Vocabulary of the Greek Testament Illustrated from the Papyri and Other Non-Literary Sources. Edited by J. Moulton and G. Milligan. London: Hodder and Stoughton, 1930.

Wengst, K. *Pax Romana and the Peace of Jesus Christ.* Translated by J. Bowden. Philadelphia: Fortress, 1987.

Windisch, H. *Imperium und Evangelium im Neuen Testament.* Kiel: Lipsius & Tischer, 1931.

Winter, B. *Seek the Welfare of the City: Christians as Benefactors and Citizens.* Grand Rapids: Eerdmans, 1994.

Zerwick, M., and M. Grosvenor. *A Grammatical Analysis of the Greek New Testament.* 3d ed. Rome: Pontifical Biblical Institute, 1988.

Index of Ancient Sources

Index of Names
and Subjects

About the Author

Richard J. Cassidy is Professor of New Testament at Christ the King Seminary in East Aurora, New York. An authority on the political dimensions of the New Testament, Cassidy is also the author of *Jesus, Politics, and Society: A Study of Luke's Gospel; Society and Politics in the Acts of the Apostles; John's Gospel in New Perspective: Christology and the Realities of Roman Power;* and *Christians and Roman Rule in the New Testament: New Perspectives.*